C000104393

ISBN 978-1-332-03422-2
PIBN 10273062

1 MONTH OF
FREE
READING

at

www.ForgottenBooks.com

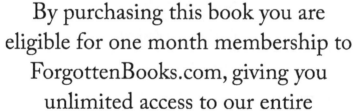

By purchasing this book you are eligible for one month membership to ForgottenBooks.com, giving you unlimited access to our entire collection of over 700,000 titles via our web site and mobile apps.

To claim your free month visit:

www.forgottenbooks.com/free273062

Similar Books Are Available from
www.forgottenbooks.com

THE

PUBLICATIONS

OF THE

𝕾𝖊𝖑𝖉𝖊𝖓 𝕾𝖔𝖈𝖎𝖊𝖙𝖞

περὶ παντὸς τὴν ἐλευθερίαν

VOLUME X

FOR THE YEAR 1896

𝔖𝔢𝔩𝔡𝔢𝔫 𝔖𝔬𝔠𝔦𝔢𝔱𝔶

FOUNDED 1887

TO ENCOURAGE THE STUDY AND ADVANCE THE KNOWLEDGE
OF THE HISTORY OF ENGLISH LAW.

————————••••————————

Patrons :
HER MAJESTY THE QUEEN.
HIS ROYAL HIGHNESS THE PRINCE OF WALES.
HIS ROYAL HIGHNESS THE DUKE OF YORK.
HIS EXCELLENCY THE HON. T. F. BAYARD.

President :
THE RIGHT HON. LORD HERSCHELL.

Vice=Presidents :
THE RIGHT HON. LORD JUSTICE LINDLEY.
THE HON. MR. JUSTICE ROMER.

Council :

THE HON. MR. JUSTICE BRUCE.	SIR F. POLLOCK, BART.
MR. A. M. CHANNELL, Q.C.	MR. W. C. RENSHAW, Q.C.
SIR H. W. ELPHINSTONE, BART.	MR. S. R. SCARGILL-BIRD.
MR. M. INGLE JOYCE.	THE HON. MR. JUSTICE STIRLING.
MR. B. G. LAKE.	MR. J. WESTLAKE, Q.C.
MR. H. C. MAXWELL LYTE, C.B.	HIS HONOUR JUDGE MEADOWS
MR. A. STUART MOORE.	WHITE.
MR. R. PENNINGTON.	THE HON. MR. JUSTICE WILLS.

Literary Director :
PROFESSOR F. W. MAITLAND (Downing College, Cambridge).

Auditors :
MR. J. W. CLARK.   MR. HUBERT HALL.

Honorary Secretary :
MR. B. FOSSETT LOCK (11 New Square, Lincoln's Inn, London).

Honorary Treasurer
MR. FRANCIS K. MUNTON (95A Queen Victoria Street, London).

Hon. Secretary and Treasurer for the United States :
MR. RICHARD W. HALE (10 Tremont Street, Boston, Mass.).

Select Cases in Chancery

𝔖𝔢𝔩𝔡𝔢𝔫 𝔖𝔬𝔠𝔦𝔢𝔱𝔶

SELECT CASES IN CHANCERY

A.D. 1364 TO 1471

Gt. Brit. Court of chancery.

EDITED

FOR THE SELDEN SOCIETY

BY

WILLIAM PALEY BAILDON

LONDON

BERNARD QUARITCH, 15 PICCADILLY

1896

PREFACE.

—◦◦◦—

My grateful thanks are due to many persons for much kind assistance. Sir Edward Fry has most kindly looked through my proofs and made valuable suggestions both for the introduction and the notes to the text. Mr. John A. C. Vincent has helped me with the original documents at the Record Office, many of which are in bad condition and very difficult to decipher. Mr. B. Fossett Lock has been most helpful in editorial matters; and lastly, Professor Maitland has been, as ever, most generous with that assistance that no one can give so well as he.

W. P. B.

Lincoln's Inn : *Dec.* 22, 1896.

CONTENTS

SELECT CASES IN CHANCERY

PART I

EARLY CHANCERY PETITIONS, BUNDLE III

PART II

SELECTED PETITIONS

INTRODUCTION.

1. The Contents of this Volume.

In the early part of the century the old Record Commission published in three volumes ' A Calendar of the Proceedings in Chancery in the Reign of Queen Elizabeth ; to which are prefixed examples of earlier proceedings in that Court, namely from the reign of Richard II to that of Queen Elizabeth, inclusive.' The first two volumes, published in 1827 and 1830 respectively, contain, by way of introduction, a large number of Chancery Proceedings during the period mentioned. None, however, had at that time been found for the reign of Henry IV, and but few for that of Henry V. We have no means of knowing what principle of selection was exercised by the editors of the Calendar, but many cases of very great interest and value are there printed. This was the first attempt to deal with the vast mass of Chancery Bills and Answers of an early date, and their value may be judged from the copious references given to them in the works of Spence and others. The bills printed in those two volumes were collected together, and are now known at the Public Record Office as Early Chancery Proceedings, Bundles 1 and 2.

It is proposed in the present volume to carry on the work that was thus begun. It has seemed to us, however, that in dealing with these records for the purpose of legal history, the principle of selection might be carried so far as to become positively misleading. To elucidate the history and growth of the Court of Chancery something more is required than a selection of cases, however carefully made, which may, after all, only illustrate a particular theory, or be influenced by the predisposed conclusions of the transcriber.

In order, therefore, to give a clear view of the whole scope of the proceedings in Chancery at its earlirst period, it has been decided to print the earliest bundle, Bundle 3, in its entirety, and to make up the volume with a smaller number of selected cases.

Part I. of this volume accordingly contains the whole of Bundle 3 (Bundles 1 and 2 having been already printed as stated above), and Part II. contains a selection of such petitions as seemed to the editor calculated to throw light on different points in the history of the Court. Particular attention has been paid to a number of petitions which contain nothing by which they can be dated, though many of them are undoubtedly of a very early period. This is Bundle 68 (until lately Bundle 112). One other bundle of dateless petitions remains for future investigation.

2. What is a Chancery Proceeding?

Before going further it will be well to define what is meant by the term 'Chancery Proceeding.' Petitions to the Chancellor in his capacity as a high officer of state are found at a very early period of our legal history, and many such are found among the 'Ancient Petitions,' as they are called, preserved at the Record Office. But clearly such petitions, although addressed to the Chancellor, are not in any sense 'proceedings.' There are four essentials to the Chancery Proceeding : (a) a petition addressed to the Chancellor or Keeper by a petitioner or plaintiff complainnig of (b) an alleged wrong done by some specified person or persons, and asking (c) that the person complained of may be sent for to answer the complaint, and (d) that a remedy may be provided.

a. *The Petition or Bill.*

The actual form of the petition or bill needs little comment. There is wonderfully little variation in these from the earliest known down to their abolition by the Judicature Act of 1873. They are almost invariably in French, down to the reign of Henry V, when English forms became customary. One Latin bill occurs in this volume, No. 9. As a general rule each bill is addressed at the top to the Chancellor or Keeper, mentioning him by name, or by the name of his see when he is a Bishop. By this means it is possible to date approximately many bills which it would otherwise be impossible to date. Still, a goodly number are addressed simply to the Chancellor without giving any name, and most of these cannot be dated (Nos. 123–134).

The bill, as I have said, is generally addressed to the Chancellor or the Keeper, but there are some interesting and instructive exceptions. It is occasionally addressed to the king. There are no examples in this volume, but several will be found in the Calendar already referred to. Thus, in vol. 1, p. xvi, in 1419 the king is asked to write to the Chancellor ' to do clepe the parties afor him and examine hem and make an end by twene hem of all that hangeth bitwene hem in ʒoure courtys.' The king accordingly writes to the Chancellor to that ' effect—' ye doo calle before yow bothe parties speciffied in the same supplicacion, and thair causes herd, that ye doo unto hem both righte and equite, and in especial that ye see that the porer partye suffre no wrong.'

In this volume, case 135 is a bill addressed to the Duke of Gloucester, the Protector, early in the reign of Henry VI, asking that the plaintiff may have of the Chancellor of England a writ that is called sub poena.

The most interesting variations from the usual form are those in which the Council is mentioned. No. 107, which can be dated about 1384, is addressed ' To the Chancellor of our most redoubted Lord the King, and to his most wise Council.' No. 19, which can be dated shortly after 1396, is addressed to the Chancellor, ' and to the other most wise Lords of the Council of our most redoubted Lord the King.' We shall see hereafter that the Council sat as judges in the Court of Chancery well into the fifteenth century ; it is perhaps a matter of surprise, therefore, that more petitions are not addressed to them.

b. *The alleged wrong.*

A petition to the Chancellor must allege some wrong done to the plaintiff if it is to be considered a Chancery Proceeding, and it must be a wrong of such a nature that the remedy thereof lies outside the administrative powers of the Chancellor. For it is obvious that many complaints could be remedied by the Chancellor of his own power and authority as a high official of state without calling for anything in the nature of legal proceedings or setting the machinery of the law in motion. At the same time it must be borne in mind that it is not easy by any means to draw a hard and fast line between the administrative and the judicial functions of the Chancellor in the fourteenth and early fifteenth centuries. Perhaps the safest plan is to say that when the Chancellor was asked to send for the defendant and to hear what he had to say, then the function was judicial, but not otherwise. Such a rule, however, must not be taken too strictly. For sometimes we find a petition asking for a general remedy without mentioning any writ, even though it may be perfectly clear from the terms of the bill that a proper investigation could not be made, and 'the full complement of justice' could not be given without the defendant's answer. Such a case must emphatically be considered as a Chancery Proceeding, and nos. 105 and 109 are therefore properly placed in this volume. We may reasonably suppose that such cases are early ones, and that the precise remedy was not clearly understood.

c. *The Writ.*

The third essential is the writ by which the defendant is brought before the Court. This is in by far the majority of cases the personal writ of sub poena. The same end might be secured by arrest, by venire facias, or by corpus cum causa. The sub poena was the ordinary writ; two early examples dated in 1388 and 1394 will be found in this volume, cases 7 and 11. Its history is obscure. John Waltham, who is credited with its invention (see *Rot. Parl.* iv. 84), was Master of the Rolls from 1381 to 1386, and a Master in Chancery during the same period. It is not known if he had previously been a Clerk in the Chancery (Foss). If the story is true, its inception must have been before his appointment to that office, as the writ was certainly known before 1381.[1] Palgrave[2] gives a writ of sub poena dated in 1364, and that issued upon a bill addressed to the King and Council. (*Rot. Pat.* 38 Edw. III, pt. 1, m. 15.)

The question is one of slight importance, for there was another and, I think, an earlier writ for compelling the defendant's appearance. This is generally known as the quibusdam certis de causis. The name is not a happy one, for the sub poena and the premunire also begin with the same words. Indeed, the form of these first two writs is

---

[1] See Spence, *Equitable Jurisdiction of the Court of Chancery*, 1846, i. 338, n. e.

[2] *An Essay upon the Original Authority of the King's Council*, 1834, p. 41.

almost identical save for the penalty; the one enjoins attendance under the penalty of a certain sum of money, the other ' sub periculo quod incumbit,' ' sub gravi indignatione,' or some similar expression. See cases 2, 8, 9, 14 and 35 for examples. Thus the ' ingenious author' (as Palgrave calls him) of the sub poena, whoever he may have been, simply substituted a definite pecuniary penalty for an indefinite threat of something terrible. For I think there can be little doubt that the indefinite writ, the quibusdam certis de causis, was the older writ of the two. As to the date when each writ first made its appearance, it is difficult to find any positive evidence.

d. *The remedy asked for.*

The fourth essential of a Chancery Proceeding is that the plaintiff prays for a remedy from the Chancellor. This is frequently in very general terms, especially in early cases. Sometimes the plaintiff evidently did not know what remedy to ask for, or whether he had any at all, but left it entirely to the Chancellor's superior wisdom and good graces. Thus in Case 58 the plaintiff asks for ' such a writ as to you shall seem reasonable in this case.'

3. The Tribunal.

In the early history of the Court of Chancery it is by no means easy to decide as to the tribunal before which the cases were heard. The petition, with the few exceptions that I have already noticed, was always to the Chancellor, but it by no means follows that the Chancellor adjudicated upon it. The regrettable scarcity of recorded judgments leaves the evidence on this point in a very unsatisfactory state. In this volume the earliest recorded judgment is in 1377 (Case 106), and there are only two others (Cases 95 and 109) before the reign of Henry VI. In the printed petitions (*Intro. Cal. Eliz.*) there are no judgments prior to that date. Of these the earliest (No. 106) is dated 1377; the Chancellor acting on his own responsibility dismissed the bill. In Case 109 (1407 to 1409) the Chancellor also dismissed a bill. In the 1408 case (No. 95), the judgment was by the Chancellor and Council, and in the judgments of the reign of Henry VI and Edward IV, we find decrees by the Chancellor and Council, or the Chancellor and the Justices, as well as by the Chancellor alone. As late as the middle of the century we find the Chancellor sitting with the Justices and giving a decree jointly with them (*Cal. Eliz.* ii. xxviii.) ; and the same occurs in this volume Cases 141 (1456) and 143 (1457). The only way to get at any idea of the distinction which existed between the Council and the Chancellor is to attempt some analysis and comparison of their respective jurisdictions.

a. *The Jurisdiction of the Council.*

It is not necessary here to go into the question of the extraordinary jurisdiction of the Council at any length. The subject has been well investigated by Palgrave[1] and others, and much information will also be found in Prof. Dicey's essay on the Privy Council.[2] We are not concerned here to inquire into the origin, growth, and decline of the Council as a court of law, but as to when and how the Court of Chancery became a separate tribunal from that of the Council. The judicial functions of the Council would seem to have been in aid of the common law, and not, as in the case of the Chancellor's jurisdiction, entirely outside it.

Thus, to quote Mr. Dicey, ' whenever, in fact, either from defect of legal authority to give judgment, or from want of the might necessary to carry their decisions into effect, the law courts were likely to prove inefficient, then the Council stepped in, by summoning before it defendants and accusers.'

Mr. Cooper (*Public Records*, i. 357) points out that ' most of these ancient petitions appear to have been presented in consequence of assaults and trespasses, and a variety of outrages, which were cognisable at common law, but for which the party complaining was unable to obtain redress, in consequence of the maintenance or protection afforded to his adversary by some powerful baron, or by the Sheriff, or some other officer of the county in which they occurred.' Thus we see that the primary duties of the Council were connected with the criminal law and cases of a quasi-criminal nature. It remains to be seen what part, if any, they took in those cases in which rules other than those of the common law were to be applied.

b. *The Jurisdiction of the Chancellor.*

Perhaps the most interesting question in the history of the Court of Chancery is this : at what period did the Chancellor become an exclusive judge, when did he first sit alone in judgment ? We have seen that he sat in company with other members of the Council ; when and how did he acquire the right to sit alone ?

That he had acquired this right as early as the reign of Richard II seems indisputable. Here is the evidence :

In 13 Richard II, 1389, the Commons petitioned in Parliament,

[1] *Op. cit.*   [2] *The Privy Council*, 1887.

' *qe al suite de partie ne al suggestion, null des lieges du Roy soit fait venir par brief Quibusdam certis de causis ne par null autre tiel brief, devant le Chanceller ou le Conseill le Roy de respondre d'ascune manere dont recoverer est done par la commune ley* ' (Rot. Parl. iii. 267) ; and again in 17 Richard II, 1393–4, the Commons alleged ' *qe par la ou plusours liges du Roialme, par nient vraies suggestions faitz si bien a Conseill nostre seignur le Roi come en la Chancellarie nostre Seignur le Roi, sont envoiez de comparer devant le dit Conseill ou en la Chancellarie, sur certeine peyne, a certein jour* ' (Rot. Parl. iii. 323) ; and again in 9 Henry V, 1421, complaint was made ' *qe diverses des lieges de nostre dit soveraigne seignur sont faitz venir devaunt son Conseil et son Chanceller par lettres de Priveez Seales et briefs sub pena,* ' and they pray ' *qe toutz tielx lettres et briefs ore pendantz devant le ditz Conseill ou le Chanceller* ' may be annulled, and that all persons so summoned ' *soient dimissez hors des Courtes suisdites* ' (Rot. Parl. iv. 156).

All these petitions seem to recognise some difference between the Council and the Chancellor, though what it was is not very clear.

This is strongly supported by several of the petitions here printed. Three of these mention the alternative, before the Chancellor *or* before the Council. Two of them are not dated, Nos. 79 and 130 ; the third, No. 101, is dated 1400.

The evidence for the reign of Edward III is not so satisfactory ; nevertheless, a tolerable case can be made out. In a statute passed in 1340, 14 Edw. III (cap. 5), for redressing delays of judgments in various courts, the preamble recites ' *pur ce qe moultz des meschiefs sont avenuz de ce qe en diverses places, aussibien en la Chauncellerie, en le Bank le Roi, le Commune Bank, et l'Escheqer, les Justices assignez, et autres Justices a oyer et terminer deputez, les jugementz si ount este delaiez.* '

Here the Chancery is mentioned among the law courts of the realm, though there is nothing to show that the Chancellor ever sat there without the Council.

The Chancellor is mentioned in various other statutes of this reign, but always in connection with the Council.

In 22 Edward III, 1349, occurs the famous proclamation in form of a letter to the Sheriffs of London (Close Roll, 22 Edw. III, p. 2, m. 2 d). The king writes, ' *volumus quod quilibet negocia tam communem legem regni nostri Anglie quam graciam nostram specialem concernencia penes nosmetipsos habens exnunc prosequenda, eadem negocia, videlicet, negocia ad communem legem penes venerabilem virum electum Cantuariensem confirmatum Cancellarium nostrum per ipsum expedienda, et alia negocia de gracia nostra concernenda penes eundem Cancellarium*

a

seu dilectum clericum nostrum Custodem sigilli nostri privati prosequan-
tur [sic]*, ita quod ipsi vel unus eorum peticiones negotiorum que per eos,*
nobis inconsultis, expediri non poterunt, una cum avisamentis suis inde,
ad nos transmittant vel transmittat, absque alia prosecucione penes nos
inde facienda, ut hiis inspectis ulterius prefato Cancellario seu Custodi
inde significemus velle nostrum.' The sheriffs are ordered to publicly
proclaim this notice.

It will be observed that matters ' of grace ' are here opposed to matters ' of common law,' which contrast certainly suggests that something
in the nature of equitable relief was in the king's mind. It will be
noted also that the Chancellor and the Lord Privy Seal, or one of
them, were to send to the king only such petitions as could not be
determined without so doing.

The Statute 36 Edw. III, st. 1, c. 9, provides relief in Chancery
to any one aggrieved by the statutes immediately preceding it, but as
the Chancellor is not mentioned, either alone or in conjunction with
the Council, it does not help us in this inquiry.

On this point I cannot do better than again quote Prof. Dicey's
essay :

' As the Law Courts had branched off from the " Curia Regis," so
the Chancery began to separate from the Council. The exact steps,
by which the process of separation was carried out, cannot be known.
But it may readily be supposed that the pressure of other business,
and a distaste for the niceties of legal discussion, made the Council
glad to first refer matters of law to the Chancellor, and next to leave
them entirely to his decision. Whatever the steps of the change, a
great alteration took place ; and before the death of Edward III the
Chancellor decided matters of equity on his own authority, and gave
assistance to those hindered by violence from obtaining aid through
the regular course of law. The date of his establishment as a Judge
of Equity is approximately marked by a proclamation of Edward III,
which referred matters of grace to the Chancellor's decision.[1] Though
from about this date the Chancellor exercised an independent jurisdiction, the Council's power suffered no diminution. Both the Council
and the Chancellor aided those whom the common law was unable to
protect. Both the Chancellor and the Council enforced obligations
binding in conscience though not in law. Attacks made on the power
of the Chancellor are attacks on the authority of the Council, and the
Council in Chancery can hardly be distinguished from the Chancellor's
own Court.'

[1] The proclamation already quoted, *ante,* p. xvii.

Palgrave, it is true, states (p. 25) that it is 'fully established that, until a comparatively recent period, the Chancellor never exercised any judicial functions, unless when directed by the Council, or acting by its authority.' That statement, though partially true, is, I think, on the whole contradicted by the weight of evidence. It seems clear that the Chancellor had and exercised judicial functions of his own as early as the reign of Richard II, if not of Edward III. Still the two courts had not, up to the middle of the fifteenth century, become entirely distinct. Dicey remarks (p. 35), 'There is little reason to suppose that in the fifteenth century persons brought before the Council and those summoned to the presence of the Chancellor came before an essentially different court.' He modifies this statement a little further on by saying that 'the Council's judicial authority had, to judge by the minutes of Henry VI's reign, been exerted chiefly in cases where from the might of the offenders the courts really were powerless to enforce justice.' If this be so, and it is fully borne out by the cases, then the cases involving principles of equity must have come before the Chancellor and not before the Council. Thus we are led to the interesting conclusion that the growth of the Chancellor's judicial functions and that of the principles of equity took place together, and side by side, and that the Chancellor as judge was created by equity rather than equity by the Chancellor.

The cases, and especially those in which a judgment is recorded, naturally throw much light on this part of the subject.

The Council is mentioned in thirteen of the present cases, in ten of them alone, and in three as an alternative to the Chancellor. Seven of these are cases of great violence or maintenance, two of aliens, and one under the Statutes of Provisors, the remaining three are cases of fraud, defaulting executors, and feoffees to uses respectively. Thus we see that ten out of these thirteen cases are legitimately within the jurisdiction of the Council as opposed to that of the Chancellor.

In the before referred to Calendar will be found a considerable number of cases in which the Council is mentioned. Stonehouse v. Stanshaw (i. xxix.), of the reign of Henry VI, is a purely equity matter, to set aside a bond and a conveyance made while the plaintiff was drunk, yet leave is asked to appoint attorneys to sue before the King and his Council.

In Soothill v. Harrington (i. 86) the defendants appeared before the King, the Chancellor, and others, lords of the Council; they were ordered by the Chancellor in the King's presence to produce two infants, the King's wards; this not having been done by the time appointed, the defendants were committed by the Chancellor, *per avisamentum Justiciariorum, Servientum ad legem, Attornati, et aliorum de Consilio dicti domini Regis in Camera Scaccarii.* Here clearly the Council sat in a judicial capacity, though apparently the orders were in the Chancellor's name only.

In 3 Edward IV, 1463, a bill of an equitable nature was dismissed ' by consideracion of this Court of the seid Chauncerie ' (i. lxvii.). This form is not uncommon ; its precise significance is, perhaps, doubtful.

In 13 Edward IV, 1474 (i. xc.), there is a decree by the Bishop of Durham, Chancellor, *ac per curiam Cancellarie predicte;* this was also an equitable matter.

In 14 Edward IV, 1474, is a decree by the Chancellor alone (i. xciv.) ; while in the same year judgment was given by the Chancellor *una cum avisamento et consilio dictorum Justiciariorum,* after deliberation had *cum Justiciariis et aliis de dicti domini Regis Consilio peritis ad hoc evocatis* (i. xcvii.). The first of these **was a** purely equity matter, and the second was concerned with certain fraudulent practices which were probably without remedy at common law.

In 16 Edward IV, 1476, a bill is dismissed by the Chancellor and the Court of Chancery ; a case of fraud (i. xcvii.).

In the same year a decree is recorded by the Chancellor and by authority of the same Court of Chancery ; also an equity case (i. xcix.). Another using the same words is in 1481 (i. cviii.) ; three in 1484 (i. cxiii. cxv. cxvii.), all equity matters. In Henry VII's reign there are decrees ' by the Chancellor and the Court of Chancery ' in 1492 (i. cxx.) and 1493 (i. cxxii.).

The expressions ' by the Chancellor and the Court of Chancery,' ' by the Chancellor and by the authority of the Court of Chancery,' perhaps mean no more than the Chancellor sitting in the Chancery in his judicial capacity.

Thus we see that towards the end of the fifteenth century purely equity matters generally came before the Chancellor alone, though this rule is not without exceptions.

The Statute 3 Henry VII, c. 1, was probably passed as much to make a final distinction between the Courts of the Chancellor and of the Council as to amend the Criminal law. By section 1 certain offences are handed over to the Council, and presumably thereby taken from the Chancellor. They are precisely those cases that we have seen belonged peculiarly to the Council from an early period : Maintenance, embracery, misdemeanors in sheriffs, taking of money by jurors, great riots and unlawful assemblies.

The Council, while parting with their equitable jurisdiction, thus retained the right to deal with cases of violence and the like; and in order, no doubt, to emphasise the difference, they adopted or received a distinctive name. Their court began to be known as 'The Lords of the Council sitting in the Star Chamber,' or more briefly, 'the Court of Star Chamber.' That Court, save as modified slightly by statute, continued to exercise this part of the Council's jurisdiction until its abolition in 1641, by Statute 16 Charles I, c. 10.

Some very interesting facts relating to the jurisdiction of the Chancellor and Council have been collected by Mr. L. O. Pike in the Introduction to the Year Books of 12 and 13 Edward III. Mr. Pike comes to the conclusion that 'as late as the reign of Henry V there was no distinction, such as was afterwards recognised, between the ordinary or common law and the extraordinary or equitable jurisdiction of the Court of Chancery ' (p. cx).

4. The Reasons for applying to the Chancellor.

The Court of Chancery became necessary because it was found that the Courts of Common Law were, from various causes, frequently unable to do justice to suitors. This might result from two classes of reasons: (1) from the inelasticity of its principles and practice; (2) from the peculiar situation of the parties in cases which could otherwise have been dealt with at common law.

The first of these classes constitutes what came at a later date to be called equitable matters—cases to be decided in Chancery on principles peculiar to itself, and will be dealt with later.

The second class was not concerned in any way with the doctrines of equity ; and, some time towards the end of the fifteenth century, the Court of Chancery ceased to deal with them altogether.[1] In the early days of that Court, however, such cases formed by far the principal bulk of the work of the Court. Such matters, as has already been pointed out, came within the jurisdiction of the Council. A reference to the first part of this volume will show how numerous such cases were, and how varied the detail, though the same principles underlay them all.

Most of these early cases allege some special reason why the Chancellor should interfere, and these allegations throw a useful light on the principles from time to time guiding and influencing the Court.

[1] The latest case in the Calendar is during the Chancellorship of Cardinal Wolsey (i. cxxviii.) ; but in that case the defendant was brother to two of the Chancellor's servants, which may have made a difference.

The reasons in what I may call the Council cases, that is, those for which in theory the common law provided a remedy, are mostly concerned with the power and violence of the defendant.

In case 5, we are told that the defendants will not be justified by the sheriff of the county against their will, nor will they at any time, unless the King betakes himself against them seriously.

In case 6, the plaintiffs, who are the constables of a Hundred, say that they dare not perform their office unless the defendants find sureties for the peace.

In case 10, the plaintiff states that no one dare bring suit against the defendant, as the common law demands, because of his great maintenance.

In other cases—21, 26, 29, &c.—the plaintiff simply states that he dares not sue at common law.

In case 24, the plaintiff would have sued at Lincoln in the King's Bench, but could not find any one who dared to act as her counsel, for fear of the defendant's malice.

In case 31, the plaintiff says piteously that he can never recover at common law because the defendant is so rich and so strong in friends in the country where he dwells.

In case 35, it is stated that no writs or orders of the King will be obeyed, and no jurors will dare to do their duty in those parts, if the defendants are not punished.

In case 36, the Chancellor is asked to interfere, so that the very good laws of the King and his noble realm may be honestly kept, virtues exalted, and crimes and oppressions of the people punished and chastised.

In case 41, the defendant has so many evildoers confederated with him, and is of such horrible maintenance, that the plaintiff cannot recover at common law.

In case 44, the defendants are so great in their country, in kinsmen, alliances, and friends.

In case 51, the defendant is so great a maintainer, extortioner, and conducer of inquests in his country, that no one dare contradict him.

In case 67, a case of forcible entry and ouster, the plaintiff merely says that there is no speedy remedy at common law.

In case 94, the plaintiff cannot sue at common law because he is employed in defence of the realm; while in case 98 the plaintiff asks for a special assize, because at the time of the assizes he is engaged with the Justices of Assize in other counties, and so cannot sue in Yorkshire.

In Cal. i. xix., the plaintiff cannot sue at common law because he is in prison.

In many cases the poverty of the plaintiff is urged as the sole reason why the Chancellor should interfere. See cases 37, 43, 80, 139, and Cal. i. xiii. ; ii. xii.

In this last case the plaintiffs say that they are ' so pouere that thay may not apparay wyth the said John in no sute ne tryall at the lawe.'

In Cal. i. xxxv., the Friars Minors of London say that they are ' pore men, gretely endetted, and loth to spende on plee.'

In Cal. i. xiv., the plaintiffs are poor, and one of them is so ill that they cannot sue at common law.

In case 73, the plaintiff says that the defendant absenteth himself and departeth from place to place so that she can have no recovery nor remedy against him at common law.

In case 110, the plaintiffs say that they can have no remedy at common law in the King's absence. This case is unfortunately not dated. Mr. Bayley, from whose MS. transcripts at the Record Office I have copied the bill, dates it as ' probably Henry V.' I have not been able to find the original, so cannot express any opinion. There was a Sir William Bardolf at that time. I confess I cannot understand the allegation ; so far as I know, the issuing of writs and the proceedings of the Common Law Courts were not affected by the King's absence.

In case 137 the plaintiff wishes to recover against the estate of one who died outlawed, and whose goods consequently were forfeited to the Crown, whereby the plaintiff was ' destitute of alle maner of remedie at the comune lawe.'

It will be seen from these illustrations that the rules laid down by the Council were not of a very rigid nature, and that there was some reason in the constant complaint of interference with the course of common law. On the other hand, it is not at all uncommon to find bills dismissed on the ground that the ordinary tribunals were able to deal with the matter, and if we had anything like a large percentage of recorded judgments, there is no doubt we should find that this was very frequently done.

In certain pleas which were supposed to concern the King, the allegation was of a different kind.

In case 12, the Mayor and citizens of Chichester state that the doings they complain of are ' to their great damage, and to the hindrance of the payment of the King's fee-farm rent.'

In case 15, the reason given is ' the contempt and prejudice done to the King,' with regard to the grant of some forfeited lands.

In case 17, it is ' in safeguard of the peace of the King, his crown, and dignity.' This case is one of violent assault on constables.

In case 32, the plaintiff says that certain outrages are openly done against the King, his crown, and his peace.

In case 48, the ouster of an incumbent, who was presented by Richard II., is said to be to the great prejudice, reproof, and damage of Henry IV. Case 92 is similar.

In case 81, the King's tenants complain of ejectment, and ask for a remedy for the King's profit as well as for that of the defendants.

In case 47, the plaintiff was grantee of the wardship of A, who was lord of the manor of B, which was held *in capite*. Defendant took possession of the manor, in contempt of the King and disinherison of the ward, as well as to the damage of the plaintiff.

In case 112, the plaintiffs allege that they have been unjustly deprived of the money paid for the ransom of certain prisoners, of which the King was entitled to a share.

In what may be termed the equity cases, the reason given for the Chancellor's interference is generally that the plaintiff has no remedy at common law. The stumbling-block might be either in principle or in procedure. Most of these matters will be more conveniently considered in the next sections, but one or two may be mentioned here.

In case 4, the defendants cannot have any remedy at common law because the tenements from which they have been ousted are within a franchise, and the lord of the franchise is implicated in the wrong-doing of the defendants.

1417–1422 ; Cal. ii. viii. The plaintiffs, the Provost and commonalty of P, complain of interruption in holding of their market. They cannot proceed at common law because the defendants are of the commonalty.

5. The Procedure.

The cases throw some interesting light on the practice of the Court. The first point is, of course, the bill. Before the reign of Henry V this is almost invariably in French ; English bills then became the rule and French ones soon died out. There is one Latin bill here printed, No. 9, where the plaintiff, being an alien, possibly drew up his own petition. One Latin answer occurs in the Calendar (ii. xii.). There is evidence occasionally of verbal petitions reduced into writing in Court, as was done with the answers. In Case 119 the bill states that the plaintiff is here in his proper person. The defendant in that case was a clerk of the Chancery, which makes it less unlikely that the complaint was a verbal one at first.

In cases 33 and 47 the bill states that the defendant is here present in Court, which argues an amount of prescience truly surprising, unless the bill had been written after the defendant's presence was known.

In another case, Cal. i. lxxxvii., the plaintiff having prayed for a corpus cum causa by a first bill, presents a second bill in which he says that he is here present in Court on a corpus cum causa.

The form of the bill varies wonderfully little from the earliest to the latest time, except in its final words. In the older bills the almost invariable expression is ' pur Dieu et en ouvre de charite ; ' the corresponding English form seems to have been ' for God and in way of charity,' though 'work,' which is nearer the French form, is occasionally found. The variations ' for God's sake,' ' at the reverence of God,' ' for love of God,' 'in the honour of God,' &c., are also met with. A bill early in Henry V's reign has 'at reverence of that worthy Prince ys sowle youre fader,' and ' at reverence of God and of that pereles Princes his moder' (Cal. i. xiii.). Another, to the same King, prays ' grace and sokoure for his love that deyde on the Rode Tree a Goode Fryday ' (Cal. i. xvi.).

The familiar expression ' and your petitioner shall ever pray, &c.,' in its various forms, came in about the middle of the fifteenth century. See Cal. i. xli. (1432–1443) ; xlv. (1450–1454) ; and cases 140 (1454), 142 (1456), 144, 145, 146 and 147, in this volume.

One case occurs, No. 133, where the plaintiff was sworn to his bill, but this appears to be an isolated instance ; no reason for it can be inferred from the tenor of the bill itself; indeed, for anything that appears to the contrary, the oath was a voluntary one.

The Plegii de prosequendo.—The petition of 17 Ric. II, 1393–4, already quoted [p. xvii], goes on to allege that '*les loialx liges du Roialme sont torcenousement travaillez et vexez, a grant damage de voz ditz liges et pluis anientissement de lour estat, sanz recoverir ent avoir de lour damages et coustages,*' and prays that the Chancellor might be given power to cause the plaintiffs to find sufficient pledges and surety to make amends to the defendant in case the suggestions should not prove to be true, and also to assess the costs and damages in such cases. The answer was : ' The King wills that the Chancellor . . . shall have power to ordain thereon, and to award damages according to his discretion.' A short Act of Parliament, 17 Ric. II, c. 6, was accordingly passed, to that effect.

' But it will be observed, as has indeed been long ago pointed out by Coke,[1] that the jurisdiction thus given only arose after proof of the untruth of the allegations, and, therefore, could be exercised only on or after the hearing of the cause. It cannot, therefore, be the foundation of the jurisdiction to award costs in all stages of the suit, and for the insufficiency as well as the untruth of the matters alleged.'[2]

It has been inferred from this statute that sureties for costs had been previously unknown.[3] Such, however, is not the fact. We find *plegii de prosequendo* or *plegges de pursuer* in 1385 (case 1), 1386 (case 2), and 1388 (cases 5 and 6), all prior to the petition of the Commons, showing that the practice was known before. The 'statutum,' referred to in several cases (12, 19, &c.; Cal. i. vii. xi. &c.), may not have been an Act of Parliament; it may have been an ordinance of the Council or Chancellor, though possibly the above-mentioned statute is meant. The first Act of Parliament which dealt with the subject generally was 15 Hen. VI, c. 4.

In very many cases sureties were not required, or, perhaps it will be safer to say, are not noted on the bill.

That the *plegii* in the short form (case 1, &c.) were the same as the *manucaptores* of the longer form (case 5, &c.) is shown by a note combining both forms of entry (Cal. i. xi.). The usual number of sureties was two, but occasionally three were required (Cal. i. xi.), while sometimes one was deemed sufficient (Cal. i. xxxix.).

Arrest of Defendant.—In not a few cases the plaintiff asks that the defendant might be arrested (Cal. i. xlviii., 1452-3). Cal. i. xi., *temp.* Richard II, the plaintiff asks for a venire facias.

Appearance of Defendant.—As a general rule, however, the defendant simply appeared in answer to the writ. The appearance was at first certainly a personal one, and not the mere entry that it afterwards became.

What happened when he refused or neglected to appear on the appointed day is not quite clear. He may have been arrested and brought up in custody, or the penalty named in the writ may have been exacted. This last proceeding seems almost too tame to have commended itself to the Chancellor or Council in the fourteenth or fifteenth century.[4]

There is no evidence on this point either in this volume or in the Calendar.

---

[1] 4 Inst. 83.
[2] Andrews *v.* Barnes, 39 Ch. Div. 139, judgment of Fry, L.J.
[3] Beames on Costs, 1; Seton, *Early Records in Equity*, 6.
[4] For the later practice, see Spence, i. 370.

The Answer.—For a long time the defendant's answer was not recorded in writ'ng. He appeared in answer to his sub poena, or was brought up in custody, as the case might be, and examined viva voce by the Chancellor. Judgment was thereupon delivered without further pleading, though possibly the plaintiff may have been examined when it was deemed necessary. This method of getting at the defendant's plea probably obtained in all the early cases, and accounts for the lamentable dearth of recorded answers.

The earliest notice of the defendant's answer is recorded in certain decrees; see cases 106 (1377), 109 (1401–1409), where the substance of the defendant's plea is prefixed to the judgment.

At a later date the defendant's answer, as obtained by his examination in Court, was put into writing, probably by one of the clerks of the Court, and filed with the bill. Examples will be found in cases 138 (1441), Cal. i. xxxvi. (1442), Cal. i. xliv. (*cir.* 1446). When, and why, the defendant first came to put in a written answer without examination in Court we have no means of knowing.

The earliest written answer in this volume is 1443–50, case 139; there is one in the Calendar, i. xlix., dated 1454–5. After this they are common.

The custom no doubt arose out of the practice of granting a commission by a writ of dedimus potestatem, to take the defendant's answer. This would be found a convenient course where the defendant lived at some distance, or was ill, or otherwise unable to appear personally. The earliest printed example of this writ seems to be in 1458 (Cal. i. li.).

The defendant was sworn to his answer, whether it was verbal or written. This practice continued both before the Council and the Chancellor after the complete separation of their respective jurisdictions. There is no evidence of the introduction of the defendant's oath at any time as a new thing, and we may perhaps assume that it dates from a very early period. The earliest case of such an oath in this volume is case 95, in 1408, but this late date is accounted for by the scarcity of recorded answers. There is one answer which does not mention the defendant's oath, case 138.

In many cases the prayer is simply to examine the defendant, leaving it to the Chancellor to act upon that examination.

This is most frequent in cases where a cross examination of the defendant is highly necessary to the plaintiff's case, as where the plaintiff complains of imprisonment on a false plea of debt (Cal. i. iv.). Where the defendants, feoffees to uses, were charged with having conveyed lands contrary to the terms of a will, they were examined, and the bill dismissed (Cal. i. xxi.).

And in the case of a bond given under duress while the plaintiff was in prison, the defendant was sworn and examined (Cal. i. xliv.). See also Cal. ii. xxviii.

The special commission of oyer et terminer was at one time the favourite device of the Council for carrying out its judicial functions. It was supposed that this process was reserved for such cases as could not be dealt with by the Courts of Common Law, and generally for cases where the defendant was a person of considerable power and influence in his own neighbourhood. These commissions were repeatedly petitioned against in Parliament, and various statutes were passed regulating and narrowing the powers of the Council in this respect (Palgrave, 31). Commissions of this kind gradually became less frequent, and Dicey states (p. 69) that they had been abandoned before Richard II ascended the throne. This statement is not quite accurate, for we have several examples in this volume. In cases 24, 25, 96, 97, and 98, such a commission was asked for but not granted. Case 96 is as late as 1412.

The commission of oyer et terminer gave place to the commission of inquiry and the writ of dedimus potestatem. The distinction between the two last was probably slight, more verbal than anything else. An example of the writ of inquiry will be found in No. 30 in this volume; the writ of dedimus potestatem in Cal. i. li. 69, 74, 85, &c. In case 142, in 1456, this latter writ is asked for because the defendant is so ill that he cannot travel.

Witnesses are mentioned in some early cases, and occasionally we find that a sub poena is asked against them to compel their appearance. See cases 95, 126; Cal. i. xix. li. lvi. lxxxiii., &c.

There is no doubt that at first they were examined viva voce in Court, just as the defendant was (case 95). The practice of taking evidence by written deposition came in probably about the same time as written answers, and no doubt for the same reasons. The early writs of dedimus potestatem frequently include the power to take depositions of witnesses as well as the defendant's answer. The earliest depositions in the Calendar are in 1458 (i. li.).

The early bills, though no doubt prepared by counsel, were not signed by them. The practice of signing bills began apparently in the reign of Edward VI.

Counsel were heard on behalf of the parties in 1456 (Case 141); the decree in that case mentions that counsel had been heard on both sides.

The question who were the judges of the Court has already been discussed (*ante*, p. xv). The decree itself in many cases seems not to have been recorded in any form ; at any rate, if it were so recorded, the record has been entirely lost. Judging from the subsequent practice of recording the decree on the back of the bill, and from the still later plan of having books and rolls in which to enter judgments, it seems almost certain that no record was made. For it is most unlikely that the Court would give up the convenient plan of having judgment rolls or books after they had once been started. Even when the plan of indorsing the decree on the bill had been introduced, in a great many cases it was not followed. The earliest indorsed decree is in case 106, dated 1377.

The decree rolls begin in 26 Henry VIII, 1534–5, the decree and order books in 36 Henry VIII, 1544–45.

This paucity of early judgments[1] is the more to be regretted, as we have, in their absence, no means of knowing with certainty when the various principles of equity were first recognised. In not a few of the cases printed here and in the Calendar so often referred to, the application to the Chancellor seems to have been very much in the nature of an experiment, and even a doubtful experiment. And, indeed, from the very nature of the tribunal, this must have frequently been the case. For instance, the first plaintiff to apply for relief against defaulting feoffees to uses must have felt considerable uncertainty as to the result, and the same necessarily applies to many other points in which equity ran counter to the common law. It would thus have been of the utmost value to have had preserved a continuous series of judgments. As it is, we can only say that, so far as we know, at such and such a time a plaintiff first applied for such and such relief, though, of course, in the majority of cases the fact of the application is evidence that this remedy was within his reach.

Subject, then, to these preliminary cautions, we may proceed to consider some of the principal doctrines of equity in more detail.

6. The Principles and Growth of Equity.

The general principles on which the Chancery was supposed to act in such matters as were not remediable at common law are variously expressed by the terms ' conscience,' ' good faith,' ' reason,' and so on,

[1] In this volume there are 147 cases, 9 final decrees, and 6 that may be called interlocutory. In vol i. of the Calendar are 136 cases, 19 decrees, and 3 interlocutory. In vol. ii. of the Calendar are 57 cases and 4 decrees. Total : 340 cases, 32 decrees, and 9 interlocutory orders. The percentage of final decrees to cases is about 9¼.

and more rarely 'equity.' One or more of these or some similar expressions occur in nearly all the early Chancery bills. The rarest of these, curiously enough, is the one that has survived and given its name to all cases of this class, equity. The word does not occur in this volume. It will be found in the writ from Henry V to the Chancellor in 1419 (Cal. i. 16, and *ante* p. xiii), where the Chancellor is directed to do both right and equity. Also in 7 Edw. IV, 1467-8, where the Keeper is directed to act according to equity and good conscience (Cal. i. 84).

The word 'conscience' is used frequently. In case 123, unfortunately not dated, the Chancery is called the 'Court of Conscience.' Such expressions as 'conscience and law' (case 138), 'the law of conscience' (case 143), 'law and conscience' (cases 121, 136), 'law and right' (case 8, &c.), 'law, right, and good conscience' (case 121), 'right and reason' (case 26, &c.), 'reason and good faith' (case 72), &c. &c., are common enough.

The subject-matter of this title has been so exhaustively treated by Spence, Story, and others, that it is quite unnecessary here to go into its general history at any length. Both Spence and Story had the advantage of seeing the cases printed in the introduction to the Calendar of Elizabeth, and made ample use of the rich store of material there found. It is, therefore, not proposed to do more than deal with the chronology of the subject, by calling attention to what appear at present to be the earliest cases on the specific relief referred to under the different heads noted. The cases in the Calendar are included both on account of the obvious advantage of bringing all the early printed cases together, and also because the absence of an index of subjects renders them somewhat difficult of access.

Accident —After 1398 ; case 39. The plaintiff was possessed of a corrody in a priory, the deeds relating to which were carried off by the prior, whereby the plaintiff is ruined. He asks for relief generally.

Account.—1385 ; case 1. The plaintiff asks for an account for the time when the defendant acted as his receiver. No reason is shown for applying to the Chancellor, except that the defendant is a clerk of the Chancery.

1474-84 ; Cal. ii. lxv. The plaintiff asks that the defendant may be compelled to render an account.

Administration.—No suits by or against administrators occur either in this volume or in the Calendar.

Boundaries.—A case to settle boundaries occurs in the reign of Elizabeth (Cal. i. cxlvii.) ; there are none in this volume.

Cancellation and Delivery of Instruments.—1337 ; case 134. See *Duress.*

1394 ; case 11. The plaintiff complains of the seizure and detention of his title deeds, but does not ask specifically for their delivery.

1396–1403 ; case 85. The Court is asked to ordain due remedy where A has made ' divers false writings sealed with his seal, without the knowledge of the persons under whose names the same writings are made, to the disinherison of many persons.' The cancellation of these fraudulent documents seems to be intended.

1396–1403 ; case 88. The defendant ' hath and detaineth ' certain muniments of title belonging to the plaintiffs' property. An order is asked for commanding him to deliver them up.

1337 ; case 134. See *Duress.*

1456 ; case 141. See *Mortgage.*

1460–1465 ; case 144. The Mayor and citizens of C complain that an ex-mayor declines to give up certain bonds made to a former Mayor on behalf of the city. General remedy asked for.

1432–1443 ; Cal. i. xxix. A bill to set aside a bond and a conveyance of lands sold by the plaintiff to the defendant, who had made him intoxicated, and otherwise taken advantage of his weakness of intellect, while absent from his wife and friends.

1432–1443 ; Cal. i. xxxi. The defendants forcibly took possession of the plaintiff's daughter, aged 11, and married her, whereby the plaintiff lost the profit of her marriage ; and also compelled the plaintiff by oppression to make a feoffment of all his lands to certain persons in trust for one of the defendants, who was to pay him an annuity, which he has neglected to do.

1452–1454 ; Cal. i. xlvii. The plaintiff, by duress of imprisonment, sealed a release of certain manors, &c., to A, who, in fear of death at the hands of Jack Cade, confessed the extortion, and charged his confessor to urge his wife to make restitution. General remedy asked against A's widow.

1465–1467 ; Cal. i. lxxvi. The plaintiff asks that the defendant may be ordered to bring into Court certain indentures and other documents signed under duress, there to be cancelled and annulled.

Charities.—After 1393 ; case 45. Lands to be sold ; proceeds to be given to Holy Church for masses for testator's soul. See *Trusts.*

1456–1460 ; Cal. i. lvi. The plaintiff's mother had placed 600 marks in the defendant's hands for the purpose of founding a chantry, which he had neglected to do. The defendant by his answer admits the receipt of the money, but states that it was the donor's wish in case the endowment of the chantry should not be completed within four years, not yet expired, that the money should be applied in a different way. He submits to the order of the Court.

1456–1460; Cal. i. lvii. Bill to compel defendant, who is a feoffee to uses, to enfeoff the plaintiff, who is master of a hospital ; the feoffor having desired to endow a priest in a newly built chapel of the hospital.

It is doubtful if any of these cases came before the Chancellor on account of their being concerned with charities.

Discovery.—1415–1417 ; case 112. The plaintiffs took certain prisoners at Agincourt, who were taken from them and ransomed by the defendant. Discovery of the names of the prisoners is asked for.

1424 1426 ; Cal. i. xix. The plaintiff complains of wrongful entry by the defendant ; he cannot sue at common law because of his imprisonment. He asks that both parties may show their evidences.

1432 1443 ; Cal. i. xxxix. The plaintiff complains that the defendant, his father's executor, refuses to deliver up to him, as heir, the principal goods of the deceased, according to the custom of Cornwall. He asks that the defendant may be examined as to what goods of the deceased have come into his possession, so that the plaintiff may be thereby enabled to bring an action at common law.

Dower.—1397 ; case 24. Although dower is mentioned in this case, it does not seem to have anything to do with the application to the Chancellor.

1432–1443 ; Cal. i. xxx. The plaintiff has been kept out of her dower for 22 years, and is too poor to sue at common law.

Duress.—1337 ; case 134.[1] The plaintiff was imprisoned in the defendant's house, and made to sign two bonds, upon which he was arrested and imprisoned in Newgate. He asks that the bonds may be cancelled.

1388 ; case 8. The plaintiff while in prison was 'constrained to account where he was not accountable,' and was also induced to sign a cognovit. *Prayer*—to do what law and right demand.

1393 ; case 10. The plaintiff complains that he was kept in the stocks by the defendant until he had found four pledges to abide by the defendant's award and judgment. No specific remedy is asked for.

1432–1443 ; Cal. i. xxxi. See *Cancellation.*

1443–1450 ; Cal. i. xliv. The plaintiff complains that by duress

[1] This case is referred to by Palgrave (p. 28). The Commission was issued 3 April, 11 Edw. III (ibid. p. 126).

of imprisonment he was compelled by the Mayor of London to deliver a bond to the Common Clerk of the City. He asks that the Clerk may be ordered to give it back to him.

Fraud.—1386; case 2. The defendant obtained a release from the plaintiff by pretending that he was going to pay him certain moneys; having got possession of the document, he refused to pay.

1399–1413; case 99. Lands were recovered from the plaintiff's feoffee to uses by means of a collusive action of formedon. General remedy asked for.

1417–1424; case 119. The plaintiff, intending to purchase a manor, retained the defendant as counsel. The defendant was a tenant of the manor under the vendor, doing certain services. He advised that he, the defendant, and others, should be enfeoffed jointly with the plaintiff, knowing that the rents and services due for the tenement held by him would be thereby extinguished. The plaintiff claims damages.

Temp. Ric. II; Cal. i. xi. The plaintiff was bound to E in the sum of 60*s.*; the defendant came with a forged power of attorney and acquittance, and the plaintiff paid him. Afterwards he had to pay E over again. General remedy asked for.

1426–1427; Cal. i. xx. The defendant has deprived one T. H. of five marks of annual rent by means of a forged charter.

1442–1443; Cal. i. xl. The defendant has purchased part of a cargo of salt taken at sea, with notice that it belonged to the plaintiff.

1476; Cal. i. xcvii. The plaintiff purchased from a third person an Exchequer tally for £100, made to the defendant; plaintiff went abroad; the defendant went to the Exchequer and swore that he had lost the tally, and, as there was no record of payment, a new tally was made, upon which he has obtained the money. The bill was dismissed.

Temp. Hen. VI; Cal. ii. xxxvii. The defendant was entrusted by the plaintiff's late husband to make his will; he fraudulently inserted his own name as executor, and has deprived the plaintiff of her goods and evidences. Prays to be restored.

Infants.—1417–1422; Cal. i. xv. See *Ward.*

1432–1443; Cal. i. xxxi. The defendants forcibly took possession of the plaintiff's daughter, aged 11, and married her, whereby the plaintiff lost the profit of her marriage.

It is doubtful if the Court exercised any jurisdiction over infants, as such, before the reign of Elizabeth.

Injunctions.—1396–1403; case 70. The plaintiff took certain lands in execution for a debt due on a statute staple; the defendants have interfered, so that the tenants dare not occupy or till their lands. The plaintiff asks for an injunction that defendants shall not 'intermeddle or disturb' him, his servants, or farmers.

1396-1403; case 86. An injunction seems to be the only remedy applicable to this case, though it is not specifically asked for.

1415-1417; case 112. An interim injunction to restrain the Treasurer of Calais from parting with certain moneys in his possession is asked for.

1432-1443; Cal. i. xxiv. The plaintiff prays the Chancellor to restrain the defendant by oath from using 'the craftys of enchantement, wychecraft and sorcerye,' whereby 'he brake his legge and foul was hurt.' We are not surprised to find it stated that 'the comyn lawe may nou3t helpe.'

1461-1467; Cal. i. lxii. See *Waste*.

Marriage Settlements.—After 1398; Case 40. See *Specific Performance*.

1414-1417; case 114. See *Specific Performance*.

1456; case 142. See *Specific Performance*.

Mistake.—1417-1424; Case 119. See *Fraud*.

1454-1455; Cal. i. xlviii. The plaintiff's father enfeoffed defendant and another on trust to refeoff him or his heirs; the plaintiff, after his father's death, having continued them his feoffees, and having commenced an action against one S, for trespass, the defendant gave to S a general release of all actions, &c., whereby the plaintiff's action is abated.

1458; Cal. i. li. The plaintiffs are the executors of A, to whom the defendant owed 40*l.* on a bond. The defendant afterwards became servant to B, one of the plaintiffs, who, when he quitted his service, gave him a general release, which release the defendant pleaded in bar of an action brought by all the plaintiffs on the bond.

Mortgages.—1456; case 141. The plaintiff borrowed 80*l.* from the defendant, giving as security (1) a feoffment of the manor of S, with a clause of refeoffment on payment of 100*l.* in six years, the defendant receiving the rents and profits, which will amount to 85 marks; (2) a bond for 300*l.* to perform the conditions of the feoffment; certain indentures of defeasance of the bond were agreed upon, but have not yet been made. The defendant has sued on the bond. The plaintiff claims relief. In his replication he offers to pay the 80*l.* and all reasonable costs. Judgment: that as the 80*l.* has been paid in Court, the defendant shall reconvey the manor, and the bond shall be cancelled.   Nothing is said about interest or costs.

1463 ; Cal. i. lxvii.   The plaintiff seeks to recover certain lands, which, as he alleges, were only mortgaged to the defendant.   The plaintiff also says that the mortgage money has been fully paid off and more by the rents and profits, taken by the defendant for ten years.   General remedy asked for.   Bill dismissed on the grounds that the plaintiff has not proved his allegations, and that the defendant has shown sufficient title ' in lawe and conscience.'

Partition.—1432–1443 ; case 136.   The plaintiff and the defen dant, brothers, are joint tenants of certain lands under their father's will.   The feoffees to the uses of the will attempted to assign part of the lands to each, but the defendant, the elder son, has occupied the whole.   Prays that the defendant may be directed to make partition.

The earliest cases quoted by Spence are of the reign of Elizabeth.

Perpetuation of Testimony.—1486–1500 ; Cal. i. cxx.   Bill by John, Earl of *Oxford*, to perpetuate testimony relating to his mother's property, she having been compelled to part with her ' live lode ' to Richard III.

Rescission of Contract.—1396–1403 ; case 56.   The plaintiff had agreed with one X for the exchange of their benefices, one being parson of a church and the other master of a hospital.   X was duly ∨ presented to the church by the patron, but the patron of the hospital refused to present the plaintiff.   He asks for a writ against X and that he may be restored to his benefice, that is, a rescission of the agreement.

Specific Performance.—After 1398 ; case 40.   An agreement for a marriage was made between the father of the intended husband (the plaintiff) and feoffees of the mother of the intended wife ; the feoffees refuse to settle certain property as covenanted.   General remedy asked for.

1396–1403 ; case 83.   The plaintiff and defendant agreed that the defendant should sue for certain lands, purchased by the plaintiff, and should afterwards enfeoff the plaintiff therein for life.   The exact nature of the transaction is not clear, but it was probably a recovery or something of that sort.   The defendant having refused to ' fulfill his covenant,' the plaintiff asks that he may be compelled to do so.

1413–1417 ; case 114.   The defendant refuses to enfeoff the plaintiff and his wife in certain lands, according to the terms of a marriage settlement.   General remedy asked for.

Undated ; case 127.   See *Trusts.*

xxxvi SELECT CASES IN CHANCERY

1456; case 142. Specific performance of an agreement by a father to settle land on his daughter immediately after her marriage was decreed. As the daughter had since died leaving issue, the land was ordered to be settled on the husband (plaintiff), and the heirs of the body of the wife by him.

1424-1426; Cal. i. xx. The plaintiff complains of the non-delivery of certain goods bought by him from the defendant. He asks for right to be done, specific performance being evidently in his mind.

1460-1465; Cal. ii. xl. Specific performance of an agreement for the sale of a manor is asked for.

1467-1473; Cal. ii. liv. Defendant made a contract with plaintiff's father to build a house, as specified in an indenture, to be finished by a certain day. Defendant refuses to complete the house.

Stay of Proceedings.—After 1396; case 18. The plaintiff complains of a multiplicity of actions brought by the defendant. He asks the Chancellor to ordain a remedy so that he be not utterly ruined.

1396-1403; case 57. The plaintiff alleges that the defendants have maliciously caused him to be indicted of felony. He asks for a ' good remedy,' which seems to include stay of proceedings.

1396-1403; case 58. The plaintiff asks for a writ to the defendant ' to cease altogether from the suit which he had moved against the suppliant in the court of D.'

1432-1443; Cal. i. xxxiv. Stay of proceedings at Lancaster in respect of the arrears of an annuity is the remedy wanted, though it is not asked for in so many words.

1482; Cal. i. cviii. Stay of proceedings is asked for in these words: 'to injoin him or his attourney noo ferther to procede in the seid suyt.' No injunction appears to have been decreed, but it is ordered that the plaintiff shall be absolutely discharged from the debt in respect of which he had been sued.

1484; Cal. i. cxiii. An interlocutory injunction was awarded by the Chancellor and the authority of the Court of Chancery under a penalty of £1,000.

Trusts.—After 1393; case 45. A enfeoffed three persons in certain lands to the uses of his will, viz., upon trust for his wife, B, for life, remainder to his brother, C, and the heirs of his body; in default of issue, the lands to be sold and proceeds given to charitable uses, viz., masses for testator's soul. Two of the feoffees released to the third, who fraudulently sold the premises. The widow and her second husband ask that she may have her right in the said lands and tenements.

After 1398 ; case 40. See *Specific Performance*.

1399–1413 ; case 98. See *Will*.

1396–1403 ; case 71. A enfeoffed the defendants in certain lands, upon trust to re-enfeoff himself or his heirs when called upon ; the plaintiff is son and heir of A ; the defendants refuse to enfeoff him. He asks for a general remedy.

1396–1403 ; case 72. The plaintiff, an infant, is son and heir of A, who enfeoffed the defendant and others in certain lands and gave him certain goods and chattels, to the use of the plaintiff. The defendant has sold many of the lands and appropriated the money, and has wasted all the goods. General remedy asked for.

1399–1413 ; case 99. See *Fraud*.

1399–1413 ; case 100. See *Ward*.

1417–1424 ; case 117. Feoffees to uses on trust to enfeoff the plaintiff when he is eighteen years old, refuse to do so. Plaintiff asks that they may be made to declare why.

1417–1424 ; case 118. The grandson and heir of a last surviving feoffee to the uses of a will enfeoffs new feoffees. The plaintiff, who is entitled under the limitations of the will, requests the feoffees to enfeoff him. Three of them do so, but the remaining two refuse. The plaintiff asks that they may be compelled to enfeoff him.

1422–1426 ; case 122. Testator gave a manor to feoffees to the uses of his will, viz., to convey it to a priory in mortmain or to sell it and hand over the money. The surviving feoffee, having kept the profits for 26 years, has now sold it, and retains the purchase money. General remedy asked for.

1422–1429 ; case 135. The plaintiff enfeoffed the defendant in her lands, for trust and succour ; he tried to force her to sell them to him much below their value.

1441 ; case 138. The plaintiffs are sisters and heirs of X, who enfeoffed the defendant and others to the use to refeoff him or his heirs when required to do so. X died before any refeoffment and without issue. The defendant admits the feoffment, and says that no will of X has ever been brought to his knowledge, and that his only reason for refusing to enfeoff the plaintiffs was that he wished to see if X had left any will affecting the property. Since the issue of the writ the defendant has released all his interest to the plaintiffs.

Undated ; case 123. X gave lands to feoffees upon trust for sale and to pay out of the proceeds 40*l.* to his heir. The feoffees refuse to pay. The plaintiff, who is heir at law of X, cannot get relief at common law, which did not recognise uses, nor in the Ecclesiastical Courts, because the matter was not a testamentary one.

Undated ; case 127. X gave lands to feoffees to the uses of his will, and by his will declared the use to be for his son and his heirs. The son sold to the plaintiff, the feoffees consenting and agreeing to convey to the plaintiff in fee when required by him to do so. The purchase money was to be paid by instalments, most of which have been paid ; and the plaintiff is ready to give security for the balance. The feoffees refuse to convey.

1456 ; case 143. Feoffees to uses sold part of the land and received 50 marks for it, and also received the rents of other part for sixteen years without accounting for them. The cestui que use recovers from the executor of the last surviving feoffee. A claim for waste, in allowing the tenements to fall into bad repair, is ignored in the judgment.

1471 ; case 147. The plaintiffs say that the defendant was enfeoffed by A of a manor to their use. The defendant denies this, and says that he bought it of A. Judgment for the defendant.

1413–1416 ; Cal. i. xiii. The plaintiff was carter to Henry V., and went abroad with him, but before doing so enfeoffed his wife and two others in all his lands ; these two (the defendants), against plaintiff's will and without his knowledge, let his lands and gave away his goods.

1432–1443 [?] ; Cal. i. xxxv. The plaintiff's father, A, enfeoffed certain persons in certain manors, &c., to the uses of his will, which he subsequently declared by deed to be to his younger son (the plaintiff) and the heirs of his body. After A's death his eldest son B, the plaintiff's brother, entered as heir at law, notwithstanding the feoffment. B enfeoffed the defendants to the uses of his will, which he declared in a letter to be that an estate should be made to the plaintiff according to the will of their father. The defendants refuse to enfeoff the plaintiff, who asks that they may be compelled to do so.

The feoffment to uses was no very new thing at the time when the Court of Chancery came into existence. It had been employed by the Franciscan Friars and others, and we may perhaps be surprised that a system having so many obvious advantages should have been so long in spreading to the ordinary landowner. Whatever may have been the cause of this, it is not until the reign of Richard II, when the Court of Chancery was in full swing, that feoffments to uses became general.[1] In these printed cases we find numerous examples during that reign, and the growth of the custom can be traced about the same period in almost any good collection of charters. What gave an enormous impetus to feoffment to uses, was doubtless the discovery that by its means land could practically be devised by will.

Unfortunately, as in so many cases, we are without data as to the exact time when this was first done.

Villeinage.—A considerable number of cases occur in which the defendant claims the plaintiff as his villein.

1392-1396; Cal. i. ii. The plaintiff, 'a freeman and of free condition,' has been seized and imprisoned by the defendant as being a nief appurtenant to his manor of C.

1432-1443; Cal. i. xxii. The plaintiff complains that the defeudants have invaded her manor of G, and carried off a nief of the abbess of W, out of the franchise of the manor; whereas there is an ancient custom there that all natives who choose to live within the manor 'shall be received to dwell there freely and peaceably without claim or impeachment of their bodies, tenements, goods, or chattels.'

1413-1417; case 113. The plaintiff had entrusted sheep, cattle, &c., to one A to keep for him. The defendant falsely claimed A as his villein and seized the plaintiff's goods. Plaintiff claims damages.

1443-1450; case 139. The plaintiff complains of forcible entry into his house, imprisonment, and seizure of his goods and chattels. The defendant by his answer claims the plaintiff as his villein, which the plaintiff denies by his replication.

Cir. 1464; case 145. False claim of villeinage.

1465-1467; case 146. The plaintiff, a villein, had agreed with his lord, the defendant, for manumission, the deed of which was to be kept by A until the money was paid. This having been done, A has of malice given the deed back to the defendant, who refuses to deliver it to the plaintiff.

Wards.—1401; case 47. The plaintiff was grantee of the wardship of A, who was lord of the manor of B, which was held in capite. Defendant took possession of the manor. Plaintiff asks, at the suit of the King as well as his own, that the defendant may make satisfaction both to the King and to the plaintiff.

After 1401; case 49. The mother of an infant tenant in socage, as his guardian, complains of trespass, &c.

1399-1413; case 100. The plaintiff is testamentary guardian of the body and lands of her infant daughter, under the will of her late

---

[1] But see stat. 50 Edw. III, cap. 6.

husband. The defendant, one of the feoffees to uses of the said lands, has removed the infant from her mother's custody, and also takes the profits of the lands to his own use. The plaintiff asks that the wardship may be restored to her, with the mesne profits of the lands.

1413–1417 ; case 115. The plaintiff had been appointed manager of a manor; the heir of the manor is an infant and in ward to the King, who assigned the wardship to the Chancellor. The defendants broke up certain pastures and closes in the manor and turned them into commons, to the prejudice of the ward and the damage of the plaintiff.

1420–1422 ; case 121. The plaintiff's wife has an infant daughter and heir-apparent by a former husband ; which infant was in the custody of A, to whose care she had been committed by the plaintiff. The defendant took her out of A's custody, and declines to give her up to the plaintiff without ransom. The plaintiff asks for restitution of the infant and for damages.

1417–1422 ; Cal. i. xv. The plaintiff is grantee of the wardship of A by assignment from the Mayor of London, who was entitled to the wardship by the custom of the City. The plaintiff had arranged to marry the ward to his daughter, but the ward's mother and others have got possession of the ward and intend to marry him to some one else. General remedy asked for, including the examination of the infant.

1467–1473 ; Cal. i. lxxxvi. The defendants have possession of two infant co-heiresses, the King's wards ; the plaintiff, ' which suyth for oure Lord kyng in this party,' asks for the wards to be given up to the King. The defendants appeared before the King, the Chancellor, and others of the Council, and were ordered to deliver up the wards by the Chancellor in the King's presence, by a certain day. This not being done, the defendants were, by the Chancellor, with the advice of the justices, serjeants-at-law, the attorney, and others of the Council, committed to prison. This order was made in ' le Chekker Chambre.'

Waste.—1461–1467 ; Cal. i. lxii. The defendant, a feoffee to uses, refuses to make an estate according to the wishes of his feoffor, and has also cut down trees to the value of 40*l*. The bill asks that the defendant may ' be ruled to relese his right   . to his said cofeffees, to thintent that he may have noe power to do noe more wast upon the said place, and to make . . . . satisfaccion for the said wode so sold and feld.'

Wills.—After 1393 ; case 45. Feoffees to uses of a will. See *Trusts.*

1399–1413 ; case 98. The plaintiffs, who are feoffees to the uses of a will, complain of disseisin by the defendants, on the ground that it will delay the execution of the will.

1399–1413 ; case 100. See *Ward*.

1417–1424; case 118. Feoffment to uses of will. See *Trusts*.

1432–1443; case 136. See *Partition*.

1454; case 140. The plaintiff filled some office in the King's Household ; one A, late Bishop of S, threatened to have him removed, but accepted twenty marks as an inducement not to stir the King in the matter. By his will A directed that 'if he had vnduely offended eny man or injustly receyued the goodes of eny persone, that his executours shuld duely satisfie theym therfore as right wold.' The defendant, the executor of A's will, refuses to refund the twenty marks. The judgment is not recorded.

1429; Cal. i. xxi. The plaintiff seeks to recover certain rights under a will from the feoffees to uses of the will. The defendants appeared and were examined, and the bill was dismissed. No details of the answers are given.

1432–1443 [?] ; Cal. i. xxxv. See *Trusts*.

1456–1460; Cal. i. l. Bill against executors for refusing to carry out the directions of a verbal will with regard to plate and jewels deposited for safe custody with the testator.

1473 ; Cal. i. xciii. The plaintiffs are executors of the will of A, who, without any writing or specialty, lent money to B. They claim to recover against B's executors, having no remedy at common law because ' there was never especialte therof maide.'

Unclassified Cases.—1410–1412 ; case 104. An action of detinue will not lie at common law because the plaintiff has no 'specialty,' which here seems to mean merely written evidence, not necessarily under seal.

1413–1417 ; case 116. Detinue will not lie at common law where the goods are already in the hands of a third party without ' privity.' [1]

1432–1443; Cal. i. xxxii. The defendants, late Sheriffs of Norwich, have imprisoned and greatly oppressed the plaintiff for making tallow candles with wicks of flax instead of cotton, when by so doing he could sell them $\frac{1}{4}d.$ a pound cheaper, ' to gret refresshyng of the seid pouer people ;' and also for buying and selling by the standard weight of the Exchequer, instead of by the Norwich weights.

1477 ; Cal. i. xcix. The plaintiff has been appointed to a rectory. His predecessor had allowed the choir of the church and also the

---

[1] See Jacob's *Law Dict.* s.v. ' Privies.' Privity in blood or in representation is   what is referred to in this case.

parsonage house to become very dilapidated; to prevent any claim
against his representatives, he made no will, but gave all his goods
and chattels to the defendant by a deed of gift.   The plaintiff claims
to recover against the late rector's estate, as he has no remedy at
common law under the circumstances.   Judgment for the plaintiff for
twenty-six marks.

7. Particular Cases.

A few of the cases here printed seem to require comment at more
length than is possible in footnotes.

Cases 3, 9, 18, 42, 55, 103, 125, and 129 are cases in which one
or both parties to the suit were *aliens*.   The Council always assumed
jurisdiction in cases between aliens or between aliens and subjects,
the reason being, no doubt, that an alien plaintiff could not sue in the
ordinary law courts, while in the case of an alien defendant it would
be difficult in most cases, and impossible in many, to enforce a judgment by ordinary process.   Thus, in Case 3, where both parties were
aliens, the only remedy open to the plaintiff if he had not been an
alien would seem to be trespass on the case; but, apart from that, it
would be an immense advantage to have the defendants examined
on oath.

The cases of mercantile reprisals—Nos. 23, 34, 42, and 55—present some peculiar features.   The remedy sought was very often not
against the party actually offending, but against some person or
persons from the same town who had accidentally come within the
jurisdiction.

Thus, in case 34, some citizens of Bristol seized a ship from
Waterford in revenge for some wine taken from a Bristol ship at
Waterford under a right of prisage.

In case 55, the plaintiff's husband having been arrested at Sluys,
reprisals are asked against two men of Sluys who have been arrested
at Portsmouth.

In case 125, the plaintiff was owner of certain merchandise, which
was seized by pirates on the high seas, and brought to England, and
there sold.   The defendants were purchasers from the pirates; and,
as it is not alleged that they had any notice of the seizure, we may
assume that they were bona-fide purchasers without notice.   The
question as to how far the absence of notice affects the rights of the
parties is a difficult one, as nothing is said about market overt, but
there is a case in the Calendar which suggests that the bona-fide
purchaser, without notice, would have been protected.   In that case

(Cal. i. xl.) the defendant had purchased part of a cargo of salt which had been taken at sea, *after notice* that it belonged to the plaintiff. Here the fact that the notice is pleaded, and that considerable stress is apparently laid upon it, seems to give some ground for supposing that the absence of notice would have affected the plaintiff's claim.

The singular case against the surgeon, No. 128, is chiefly interesting from the fact that the plaintiff asks for the King's surgeons and other sufficient surgeons to be called as expert witnesses. Apparently both trespass and assumpsit lay at common law in such cases. A case in 1433, in which assumpsit was brought, is mentioned in a note (p. 124, n. 3). That case was one of a broken leg, which the defendant, described as a 'leche,' had undertaken to cure in consideration of 40s. The leg mortified, in consequence of the surgeon's neglect according to the plaintiff, or because of the patient's wilful disregard of directions according to the defendant. The case went to a jury, but the judgment has not been found.

Another case of a similar nature between 1492 and 1500, will be found in the Calendar (i. cxxiv.). The plaintiff is a surgeon. The defendant's child was 'diseased in the ie wᵗ a pynne and a webbe;' he requested the plaintiff to cure it. The plaintiff undertook to do so if the defendant would see that the child did not touch or rub it; this was not done, and the plaintiff was unable to save the eye. The defendant thereupon brought an action of trespass before the Sheriffs of London. The plaintiff prays for a certiorari.[1]

Case 134, 1337. A translation of this highly curious bill is given in Palgrave's *Council*; it was thought of sufficient interest to reprint here with the text. Apart from its interest as relating to the extinct science of alchemy, the offer to perform experiments before the Council is probably the earliest instance known of scientific evidence.

8. Historical and Social Aspects.

A few remarks on the historical and social aspects of these cases may not be considered out of place.

One or two cases contain historical references, though none of them of very great importance. Case 112, for instance, where two soldiers sought the help of the Chancellor in obtaining their share of the

[1] Certiorari was usually asked for where the action complained of was brought in the Sheriffs' Court. See the cases collected, Seton, *op. cit.* 62. The use of it by the Chancery was not confined, as might have been expected, to equitable causes or to courts of equity.

ransom of certain persons taken prisoners by them at the battle of
Agincourt.   A curious piece of information is that the king was
entitled to a proportion of the ransom.   In the Black Book of the
Admiralty (vol. i. p. 288) we learn that a soldier had to pay ‘to his
capitene or maistre’ one-third ‘of all maner wynnynges of werre.’
Nothing, however, is there said about any proportion being paid to
the king, but possibly the captains had also to account in turn to
their leaders, and so on until the king ultimately received a certain
proportion.

Case 111 mentions Sir John Oldcastle, Lord Cobham, and his ‘sect,’
that is, the Lollards, and it is stated that the defendant, a citizen and
tailor of London, and ‘one of the greatest sustainers of the evil sect
aforesaid,’ had been privy to Lord Cobham’s escape from the Tower.

The various truces in the French wars of Henry IV are mentioned in cases 96 and 103.

We get some interesting details of the social condition of the
country.   The extent to which force of arms was carried in private
affairs is truly astounding.   Every man seems to have appealed to
his friends and neighbours to help him *vi et armis* on the smallest
provocation, and to have set at defiance the laws of the realm, if not
with impunity, at any rate regardless of consequences.   This, no
doubt, was partly if not principally owing to the weakness of the
central authority, and to the constant wars, both civil and foreign,
which disturbed the latter part of the fourteenth and the early part
of the fifteenth centuries.   To these factors we must add the abuse of
office by sheriffs, constables, and others in authority, abundantly illustrated in the first part of this volume.   The series of charges against
the Sheriff of Lincolnshire, cases 24 to 30, and case 54 against a constable, are good examples.

Cases of forcible entry are very numerous.   This particular offence
had been provided against in 1381 by the statute 5 Ric. II, stat.
1, c. 8, the punishment there laid down being imprisonment and
ransom at the king’s will.   This statute apparently was of little
effect, for ten years later it was found necessary to pass a more
stringent measure, 15 Ric. II, c. 2, which gave power to the Justices
of the Peace, upon complaint, to raise the *posse comitatus*, and to
arrest and imprison the offenders, who were to remain in prison,
apparently without being tried, until they had paid fine and ransom.
That this statute, notwithstanding its severe penalty, had as little
effect as its predecessor, is shown by the numerous cases printed
both here and in the Calendar.

In this connection may be mentioned those cases concerned with brawls and other unseemly behaviour in churches, cases 31, 52, 81, 91, 92 and 97. Priests were compelled to take off their vestments (31), deprived of their devotional books and assaulted (92), arrested in church (97), and in various ways interfered with in the performance of divine service.

Indirectly connected with these church cases, may be mentioned case 20, where the customs of a Cornish parish as to mortuaries were the cause of a series of disputes and assaults. The rector claimed the best garment of each parishioner at his death, or the second best beast of those parishioners who owned cattle. The troubles of the unfortunate cleric and the interference with divine service are very graphically described.

Case 132 is also concerned with the disputes between a rector and his parishioners. The rector had placed an image in the church in such a way as to impede the view of the chancel, and threatened to excommunicate any one who interfered. He also tried to stop the custom of ringing a bell to assemble the tenants for the purpose of collecting the king's rents.

Another interesting case that deserves special mention is that of the poor herring hawker from Scarborough, travelling up into Huntingdonshire, and there assaulted by his local rivals (case 23).

9. General Conclusions.

We may here state a few of the general conclusions to which we have been led by the evidence that has come before us.

The Chancellor's jurisdiction is an offshoot from that of the Council.

The cleavage had begun certainly in the reign of Richard II and probably in that of Edward III.

It was probably not complete and absolute until the statute of 3 Henry VII.

The equitable jurisdiction began with the Council, and not with the Chancellor.

It became exclusively the Chancellor's, probably by delegation from the Council, towards the end of the fifteenth century, but the details are unknown.

It was augmented from time to time by statute, but principally by the extension of its general principles by individual Chancellors.

LIST OF CHANCELLORS, 1363–1467.

(*From* Foss)

1363, Feb. 19.	Simon Langham, Bishop of Ely.
1367, Sept.	William of Wykeham, Bishop of Winchester.
1371, March 16.	Sir Robert de Thorpe.
1372, July 5.	Sir John Knyvet.
1377, Jan. 11.	Adam de Houghton, Bishop of St. David's.
1378, Oct. 29.	Sir Richard le Scrope.
1379, July 4.	Simon de Sudbury, Archbishop of Canterbury.
1381, Aug. 10.	William de Courteneye, Bishop of London.
Nov. 18.	Sir Richard le Scrope.
1382, Sept. 20.	Robert de Braybroke, Bishop of London.
1383, March 13.	Sir Michael de la Pole, afterwards Earl of Suffolk.
1386, Oct. 24.	Thomas de Arundel, Bishop of Ely.
1389, May 4.	William of Wykeham, Bishop of Winchester.
1391, Sept. 17.	Thomas de Arundel, Archbishop of York.
1396, Nov. 23.	Edmund de Stafford, Bishop of Exeter.
1399, Aug.	Thomas de Arundel, Archbishop of Canterbury.
Sept.	John de Scarle.
1401, March 9.	Edmund de Stafford, Bishop of Exeter.
1403, Feb.	Henry Beaufort, Bishop of Lincoln.
1405, Feb. 28.	Thomas Langley, afterwards Bishop of Durham.
1407, Jan. 30.	Thomas de Arundel, Archbishop of Canterbury.
1410, Jan. 31.	Sir Thomas Beaufort.
1412, Jan. 5.	Thomas de Arundel, Archbishop of Canterbury.
1413, March 21.	Henry Beaufort, Bishop of Winchester.
1417, July 23.	Thomas Langley, Bishop of Durham.
1424, July 6.	Henry Beaufort, Bishop of Winchester.
1426, March 16.	John Kempe, Bishop of London, afterwards Archbishop of York.
1432, March 4.	John Stafford, Bishop of Bath and Wells, afterwards Archbishop of Canterbury.
1450, Jan. 31.	John Kempe, Archbishop of York.
1454, April 2.	Richard Neville, Earl of Salisbury.
1455, March 7.	Thomas Bourchier, Archbishop of Canterbury.
1456, Oct. 11.	William Waynflete, Bishop of Winchester.
1460, July 25.	George Neville, Bishop of Exeter, afterwards Archbishop of York.
1467, June 20.	Robert Stillington, Bishop of Bath and Wells.

SELECT CASES IN CHANCERY

Part I.

EARLY CHANCERY PROCEEDINGS
BUNDLE 3

1   [1] A Chaunceller nostre seignur le Roi

1385 Monstre et se pleint Clement Lauender de sire Johan Hilton, person del esglise de Haüerhill,[2] Clerc de la Chauncellerie nostre seignur le Roi, de ce que l'auant dit Johan a tort ne luy rend resonable acompt del temps q'il estoit receiuour de les deniers du dit Clement en Londres, et pur ce atort que l'auantdit Johan le primer iour de Marche l'an [de nostre] seignur le Roi E. aiel nostre seignur le Roi q'ore est quarant primer, en la paroch du Seint Benet ioust Pouleswarf en Loundres en la Warde de Baynardeschastell resceut del dit Clement . . . lxj li. viij d. par my mayn de Monseignur Lionell Duc de Clarence al oeups et profit le dit Clement et au profit et loial acompt au dit Clement ent rendre, par quoy souent . . . et luy pria du ce acompt rendre, et il acompter ne voilloit ne vnquore ne voet einz countredit a tort et as cez damages de C li. dont il prie remedy.[3]

               Plegges de pursuer :
                 Simond atte Naxe
                 Johan Pigeon

Indorsed.   Infrascriptus Johannes ponit loco suo Simonem Gaunstede ad lucrandum vel perdendum in loquela infrascripta.

Infrascriptus Clemens, nono die Decembris anno regni Regis Ricardi secundi post conquestum nono,[4] in propria persona sua in Cancellaria eiusdem Regis comparuit petendo sibi iusticiam fieri de omnibus in ista billa contentis. Et super hoc Johannes de Hilton

---

[1] Early Chancery Proceedings, bundle 3, No. 1. The right margin of this document is rather worn.

[2] Partly in Suffolk and partly in Essex.

[3] The Court of Chancery assumed jurisdiction in matters of account at an early date, notwithstanding that an action lay at common law. The chief advantage of going

To the Chancellor of our Lord the King,

1385 Showeth and complaineth Clement Lavender of Sir John Hilton, Parson [Rector] of the church of Haverhill and Clerk of the Chancery of our lord the King, that the said John doth wrongfully refuse to render him a reasonable account of the time when he was the receiver of the moneys of the said Clement in London, and that the said John on the first day of March in the 41st year of our lord King Edward the grandfather of our lord the King who now is, [1367,] in the parish of S. Benet near Paul's Wharf in London in the ward of Baynard's Castle, received £61 0s. 8d. by the hand of my lord Lionel, Duke of Clarence, to the use and profit of the said Clement, and the same to the profit and a lawful account thereof should render to the said Clement, by whom he hath often [been urged] and prayed to render an account of this, and he will not account for the same, nor yet hath done so, but refuseth wrongfully and to [the plaintiff's] damages of £100; for the which he prayeth remedy.[3]

Pledges for the prosecution :

SIMON ATTE NAXE AND JOHN PIGEON.

Indorsed. The within written John puts in his place Simon Gaunstede to gain or lose in the within written plaint.

The within written Clement on the 9th day of December, 9 Richard II, appeared in his proper person in the King's Chancery, praying that justice might be done to him concerning all things contained in

to the Court of Chancery was that that court could obtain discovery, on oath, of either facts or documents. This case, however, was within the common law jurisdiction of the Chancellor, inasmuch as the defend-ant was a clerk of the Chancery.

[4] 1385.

[5] Appointed March 13, 1383; removed Oct. 23, 1386.

infrascriptus per Simonem Gaunstede attornatum suum eodem die
in predicta Cancellaria similiter comparuit. Et de assensu parcium
predictarum datus est eis dies vsque ad octabas Sancti Hillarii proximo
futuri in s^tatu quo nunc.

2   [1] A mon treshonore seignur, mons^r le Chan-
              celler d'Engletere,

1386 Monstre vostre clerk Johan de Brampton, persone del esglise de Seint
      Dunstan West de Londres, que come il bailla a Johan Seymour
      attourne vne relees le primer iour de Juyn darrein passe sur condicion
      q'il dust aver deliuere a dit Johan de Brampton mesme le iour xx
      Marez d'esterlings ou deux obligacions, continantz l'un obligacion xl li.
      que fuist fait a Gunnore Horn de Londres que mort est a qi Johan fitz
      Nicol Horn de Londres est executour, ꝉ l'autre xij li. fait a dit Johan
      Seymour en noun de dit Johan Horn, oue vne lettre d'attourne
      desouth le seal de dit Johan Seymour ensele, et vn testament de dit
      Gunnore Horn, quex le dit Johan Seymour auoit en sa garde mesme
      le iour, come acorde fuist a celle iour parentre le dit Johan fitz Nicol
      Horn de Londres, a qi la duete de ditz obligacions estoit et est, et le dit
      Johan Seymour adonqes son attourne, dont l'acorde estoit eut fait
      parentre eux en la grant sale de Westm'; le quel Johan Seymour
      maliciousement et fausement ymachina a deceyuer le dit Johan de
      Brampton luy monstra xx Marcz en oor en sa mayn, et manda de luy
      le dit relees ; le quel le dit Johan de Brampton luy deliuera en espoier
      dauer receu de luy a celle oure les ditz xx Marcz come acorde fuist,
      nient entendant ascune fraude ne male engyne ; luy quel Johan
      Seymour apres qil auoit receu le dit relees de dit Johan de Brampton
      ne voloit mye liuerer a luy les ditz xx Marez ne l'obligacion de xl li.
      ne lettre d'attourne ne le testament susditz, einz les detient en
      destruccion del estat de dit Johan de Brampton et encontre l'accorde
      susdit, nient contreesteant q'il ad este puis requis par le dit Johan de
      Brampton de luy faire restitucion des ditz relees, ou obligacion, lettre
      d'attourne et testament susditz : Que please a vostre noble seignurie
      faire venir le dit Johan Seymour deuant vous en la Cha[n]cellarie a
      vn certein iour par vous assigne a dire pur quoi il ne doit deliuerer
      les ditz relees ou obligacion, lettre d'attourne et le testament susditz
      a dit Johan de Brampton, ou a dire pur quoi il ne doit estre condempne

---

[1] Bundle 3, No. 3.

the bill. And thereupon John de Hilton, by Simon Gaunstede, his attorney, on the same day in the said Chancery, likewise appeared. And with the consent of the parties a day was given them on the octave of S. Hilary next to come, in the same state as now.

2   To my most honoured Lord, the Chancellor of England,

1386 Showeth your clerk John de Brampton, rector of the church of S. Dunstan in the West in London, that whereas he delivered to John Seymour, attorney, on the first day of June last, a release, on condition that he should have delivered to the said John de Brampton that same day 20 marks sterling or two bonds, the one being a bond for £40 made to Gunnora Horn of London, deceased, whose executor is John son of Nicholas Horn of London, and the other for £12 made to the said John Seymour in the name of the said John Horn, together with a letter of attorney sealed with the seal of the said John Seymour, and the will of the said Gunnora Horn, which [documents] the said John Seymour had in his keeping on that same day, as it was agreed that same day between the said John son of Nicholas Horn of London, to whom the duty of the said bonds ought to and does belong, and the said John Seymour, then his attorney, the which agreement was made between them in the great Hall at Westminster; and John Seymour, maliciously and falsely scheming to deceive the said John de Brampton, showed him 20 marks in gold in his hand, and demanded from him the said release, which John de Brampton gave him, hoping to have received the 20 marks, as was agreed, and not suspecting any fraud or ill device. But John Seymour, after he had received the release from John de Brampton, would not deliver to him the 20 marks, nor the bond for £40, nor the letter of attorney, nor the will aforesaid, but doth retain them, to the destruction of the estate of the said John de Brampton and contrary to the said agreement, and notwithstanding that he hath been required by the said John de Brampton to make restitution of the release, or of the bond, the letter of attorney and the will abovesaid. May it please your noble lordship to cause the said John Seymour to come before you in the Chancery on a certain day to be fixed by you to say why he should not deliver the said release, or the bond, letter of attorney and will abovesaid to the said John de Brampton, or to

par vous a dit Johan de Brampton en les lij li. contenuz en lez deux
obligacions susditz, ensemblement oue les costages ent foitz et a faire
par le dit Johan de Brampton par celle cause, depuis que l'acorde
fuist fait deins la Jurisdiccion de la Chancellarie.¹

Benedictus de Gresby clericus ⎫ plegii de
Elias Potonhale clericus   ⎭ prosequendo.

² Ricardus dei gracia Rex Anglie et Francie et Dominus
Hibernie, Johanni Seymour de London' salutem. Quibusdam certis
de causis nos concernentibus, tibi precipimus firmiter iniungentes
quod excusacione quacumque cessante et omnibus aliis pretermissis in
propria persona tua sis coram nobis in cancellaria nostra die Martis
proximo futuro vbicumque tunc fuerit, ad respondendum super hiis
que tibi tunc ibidem obiicientur ex parte nostra et ad faciendum
vlterius et recipiendum quod per nos tunc contigerit ordinari ibidem.
Et hoc sub periculo quod incumbit nullatenus omittas. Et habeas
ibi hoc breve. Teste meipso apud Westm' xv die Junii anno regni
nostri nono. [1386.]

Indorsed. Ad diem infrascriptum Johannes Seymor infrascriptus
detulit istud breve in Cancellaria Regis et de assensu Johannis de
Brampton clerici qui sequitur istud breve, Datus est eis dies vsque ad
Octabas Sancti Michaelis proximo futuras.

B. *PETITIONS ADDRESSED TO THOMAS DE ARUNDEL, BISHOP OF ELY*, 1386–1388.³

3   ⁴ A mon treshonore et tresnoble seignur et
tresreuerent Pier en Dieux l'euesque d'Ely,
Chaunceller nostre seignur le Roy,

s. d. Supplie humblement Martin van der Mere de Sounde en Almaigne,
Mariner, qi fuist mestre d'un Nief appelle le Marieknyght, qe come certeins merchantz de Gascoigne affretterent la dite Nief a Hampton des
vins pur sigler vers Sandwich ou a Kyrkle a sa droit descharge, et

<hr>

¹ The exact ground for appeal to the Chancellor in this case seems to be, as here stated, that the agreement was made within his jurisdiction, namely, within the royal palace of Westminster; but the two equi-table doctrines of *fraud* and *specific per-formance* are given in the bill as grounds for relief. I do not think the fact that the defendant was an attorney is of any sig-nificance here; attorneys were hardly yet

say why he should not be condemned by you to the said John de Brampton in the said £52 contained in the said two bonds, together with the
costs incurred and to be incurred by the said John de Brampton in the
matter, since the agreement was made within the jurisdiction of the
Chancery.[1]

Pledges for the prosecution ·
BENEDICT DE GRESBY, clerk.
ELIAS POTONHALE, clerk.

Richard, [etc.], to John Seymour of London, Greeting: For
certain causes concerning us we command you, firmly enjoining you,
that, ceasing every excuse, and all other matters laid aside, you do
come in your proper person before us in our Chancery on Tuesday
next to come, wherever it shall then be, to answer to those things
which shall then and there be objected against you on our behalf,
and further to do and receive whatever shall then be ordained by us
there. And this, under the peril which may ensue, you shall in no
wise omit. And have you there this writ. Witness ourself at Westminster, June 15th, in the 9th year of our reign. [1386.]

Indorsed. On the within written day the within written John
Seymour delivered this writ in the King's Chancery, and, with the
assent of John de Brampton, clerk, who sued out the writ, a day was
given them on the octave of Michaelmas next.

B. *PETITIONS ADDRESSED TO THOMAS DE ARUNDEL, BISHOP OF ELY*, 1386–1388.

3

To my right honoured and right noble lord
and right reverend Father in God, the Bishop
of Ely, Chancellor of our Lord the King,

s. d. Humbly beseecheth Martin van der Mere, of Sounde in Germany,
mariner, who was the master of a ship called the 'Marie-knyght,'
that whereas certain merchants of Gascony freighted the said ship at
Hampton with wines to sail for Sandwich or Kirkley[5] as her [ports of]

considered to be officers of the court to the
extent of giving the Chancellor common
law jurisdiction in all matters relating to
them.
[2] Bundle 3, No. 2.

[3] Appointed Oct. 24, 1386; consecrated
Archbishop of York, April 3, 1388.
[4] Bundle 3, No. 4.
[5] Probably Kirkley near Lowestoft, Suffolk.

couenant fuist parentre eux que lesdites merchantz a lour costages deue-
roient trouer vn suffisant lodesman pur conduer la dite Nief, par cause
qe le dit mestre n'auoit conisance de passage del mer vers la ou il
deust passer pur lui descharger, et ils allowerent vn lodesman pur la
dite bosoigne, quele lodesman par [deus iours?] [1] apres s'enfuit de
dite Nief. Sur quoi le dit mestre vint a les merchantz rehersant as
eux coment le dit lodesman fuist departiz, et dist q'il n'osa enprendre
la viage saunz auoir vn lodesman de eux come couenant fuist. Sur quoi
les ditz merchantz firent couenant oue le steresman de dite nief de la
conduer. Par quele steresman les ditz merchantz empristerent pur
parformer le dit viage, et ensi a lour peril passa auaunt la Nief; depuis
par infortune la Nief se rompi a Seford [2] en la Seignurie mon tresnoble
s[r] le Counte d'Arundell, et ore les ditz merchantz surmettans le dit
mestre estre la cause del perde de lour biens ount fait arester les biens
le dit mestre a Seford auauntdit saunz lui faire gre de son frecte, a
graunde damage de luy et defesance de son petit estate. Qe plese a
vostre tresnoble seignurie graunter vn brief de faire venir les ditz
merchantz deuant vous en la Chauncellrie pur respondre a dit mestre
si bien des ditz arest et frecte come del perde de sa Nief.[3]

4   [4] A tresreuerent pier en Dieu et tresgracious
           seignur l'Euesque d'Ele, Chaunceller d'Engle
           terre,

s. d. Suppliont voz poueres oratours Thomas Catour de Beuerley et Emme
sa femme qe come les ditz Thomas et Emme ont estez seisez de sept
mesez et sept shopes oue les appurtenancez dedeinz la Franchisez de
la ville de Beuerle en lour demesne come de fee et de droit par long
temps, c'estassauoir d'ascunes des ditz tenementz par quarrant anz
et d'ascuns par vynt anz, tanque aore a deuz anz passez qe sire
William [M]onketon,[5] sire Johan de Midelton et Robert Chappeman,
Ministres et seruantz del Erceuesque d'Euerwyk oue plousours autres
mesfesours et distourbours de la pees . . . eux par commandement et
volunte de dit Erceuesque torcenoucement ousteront [6] les ditz Thomas
et sa femme de toutz les tenementz suisditz et vncore   tenementz

[1] A hole in the document here.
[2] In Sussex; one of the Cinque Ports.
[3] It is not quite clear why the plaintiff
should have petitioned the Chancellor in
this case. The probable reason was that
as an alien he would find it difficult, if not
impossible, to proceed at common law. The
Council always assumed jurisdiction in cases
between aliens, or between aliens and Englishmen, but I am not aware that the Court
of Chancery did so. Similar petitions from
or against aliens are not uncommon, and

right discharge, and it was agreed between them that the merchants should find at their own costs a competent pilot to steer the ship, because the said master had no knowledge of the sea passage towards the place where he had to go to discharge her; and [the merchants] hired a pilot for the work, who, two days afterwards, ran away from the ship. Whereupon the master came to the merchants, telling them how the pilot had gone away, and said that he dared not undertake the voyage without having a pilot from them, as had been agreed. Whereupon the merchants agreed with the steersman of the ship to take her; by which steersman the merchants undertook to perform the voyage, and so at their peril the ship passed forward. Since which the ship has by ill fortune been wrecked at Seaford in the lordship of my right noble lord, the Earl of Arundel. And now the merchants, pretending that the master was the cause of the loss of their goods, have caused his goods to be arrested at Seaford, without making him any satisfaction for his freight, to his great damage and the defeasance of his small estate. May it please your right noble lordship to grant a writ to cause the said merchants to come before you in the Chancery to answer to the said master as well for the arrest and freight as for the loss of his ship.[3]

4   To the right reverend Father in God and right gracious Lord, the Bishop of Ely, Chancellor of England,

s. d. Beseech your poor orators, Thomas Catour of Beverley and Emma his wife, that whereas Thomas and Emma have been seised of seven houses and seven shops within the franchise of the town of Beverley in their demesne as of fee and right for a long time, that is to say, of some of the said tenements for 40 years, and of some of them for 20 years, until now two years ago Sir William Monkton, Sir John de Middleton and Robert Chapman, officers and servants of the Archbishop of York, with many other evil-doers and disturbers of the peace, . . . by the command and wish of the Archbishop, wrongfully ousted the said Thomas and his wife from all the said tenements; and they still hold [the said] tenements, and have chased the said

they form an additional argument that the Chancellor at this period had no judicial functions apart from the Council. See Introduction.

[4] Bundle 3, No. 5.

[3] The left margin of the document is torn.

[4] A very frequent source of complaint, especially when of a tortious or *quasi*-criminal character.

tiegnont et enchaseront les ditz Thomas et sa femme hors de la dite
ville de Beuerley et les ditz Thomas et sa femme vnque pus . . . et
pur doute de mort la dit ville de Beuerley ne lour ditz tenementz
approcher.   Qe plese a vostre tresgracious seignurie de maunder pur
les ditz sire William, sire Johan [et Robert] par briefs de la Chauncellerie directz a eux seueralment sur graunt peyn d'estre deuant
vous a certein iour en la dite Chauncellerie pur monstre et declarer
. . . de lour ditz entre et occupacion des tenementz avantditz considerant qe les ditz Thomes et Emme nul remedie purront auoir par
la comune ley a cause [qe les] ditz tenementz sont dedeinz la dite
Franchise de Beuerle dont le dit Erceuesque est seignur.   Pur dieu
et en eouere de charite.[1]

C. *PETITIONS ADDRESSED TO THOMAS DE ARUNDEL, ARCHBISHOP OF YORK*, 1388–1389, 1391–1396.[2]

5   [3] Au Chaunceller nostre seignur le Roy

1388   Monstre humblement Johan Biere de Bodmyn del Counte de Cornewaille et soy pleint de Rogger Mule, Rogger Trewry, Johan Forde,
Rauf Hawkyn, Dauy Taillour de Bodmyn et Johan Misthewed del
dite ville de ceo q'ils oue autres de lour couyne viendrent noett-
andre [oue] force et armes le samady en demy qaresme darrein
passe l'an du Roy Richard seconde puis le conqueste vnzisme en la
maison du dit Johan Biere a Bodmyn et en lez seruantz du dit Johan
Biere illeoqes assaut fistrent et eux naufrerent et malement treteront
et la dite maison cercheront pur le dit Johan Biere auoir malmenee
s'ils l'eussent trouee, et soy giseront en agait noites et iours de le dit
Johan Biere endamage si auant q'il couenist au dit Johan soun dit
paijs guerpier,[4] et pur doute de mort ne lose vnqore approchier.   Et
outre ceo les auantditz mesfesours deteigner font la marchandise et
lez biens du dit Johan en sa dite pais q'il ne lez poet auoir ne son
prou ent faire par la ou le dit Johan n'ad autre meistier de soi mein-
tenir sinoun sa marchandise ; et lez auantditz mesfesours ount acroche
a eux plusours autres meyntenours et de la pees le Roy destourbours
de lour couyne, si auant q'ils ne voillent par le viscomte de mesme le

---

[1] One of the commonest reasons alleged
for the interference of the Chancellor is
that the plaintiff has no remedy at common
law.

[2] Appointed Chancellor Oct. 24, 1386,
then Bishop of Ely; consecrated Archbishop of York April 3, 1388 ; William of
Wykeham, Bishop of Winchester, appointed

Thomas and his wife out of the town of Beverley, and the said Thomas and his wife never since . . [and dare not] for fear of death approach the said town of Beverley nor their said tenements. May it please your most gracious lordship to send for the said Sir William, Sir John and Robert by writs from the Chancery directed to them severally on great pain to be before you on a certain day in the Chancery, to show and declare [the cause?] of their said entry and occupation of the said tenements, considering that Thomas and Emma can have no remedy at common law because the said tenements are within the franchise of Beverley, of which the Archbishop is lord. For God and in way of charity.[1]

C. *PETITIONS ADDRESSED TO THOMAS DE ARUNDEL, ARCHBISHOP OF YORK*, 1388-1389, 1391-1396.

5   To the Chancellor of our Lord the King,

1388 Humbly showeth John Biere of Bodmin in the County of Cornwall, and complaineth of Roger Mule, Roger Treury, John Forde, Ralph Hawkyn, Davy Tailor of Bodmin and John Misthewed, of the said town, for this, that they, with others, of their covin came by night with force and arms on the Saturday in mid-Lent last past, 11 Richard II, [1388,] into the house of the said John Biere at Bodmin, and there assaulted the servants of the said John Biere and beat and ill-treated them, and searched the house for John Biere himself to have maimed him if they had found him, and they lay in wait day and night to damage the said John Biere, in so much that it behoved the said John to desert his said country [abandon the district], and for fear of death he dare not come near it. And besides this, the said evil-doers have detained the merchandise and goods of the said John in his said country, so that he cannot have them, and can make no profit of them, whereas the said John has no other calling to maintain himself except his merchandise; and the said evil-doers have of their covin gathered to themselves many other maintainers and disturbers of the King's peace; Insomuch that they would not be justified by

---

Chancellor May 4, 1389; Arundel reappointed Sept. 17, 1391; his successor appointed Nov. 23, 1396.

[1] Bundle 3, No. 8.
[4] Modern French *déguerpir*, to abandon.

Counte encontre lour gree estre iustifiez, ne a nul temps serront deuaut
qe nostre seignur le Roy soy preigne a eux greuousement. Douut le
dit suppliant vous prie de remedie et qe vous pleise mander brief al
dit viscounte de Cornewaile d'amonestier chescun dez ditz malfesours
d'estre deuant vous a lez oeptaues de la seinte Trinite suz la peine de
CC marcz a respoundre sibien a nostre seignur le Roy come al dit
Suppliant et d'estre iustifie solonc qe la lay demande et a trouer suf-
fisante surete deuant vous q'ils ne mesferront al dit suppliant et qe
sez biens luy soient deliuerez, pur Dieu et en oepre de charite.[1]

[2] Memorandum quod duodecimo die Maij anno regni Regis Ricardi
secundi post conquestum vndecimo, Rogerus Rogger et Walterus Bloyghawe de Com' Cornub', Johannes Haddon et Willelmus Bygayn de
London' in Cancellaria domini Regis apud Westm' personaliter constituti manuceperunt pro Johanne Biere de Bodmyn quod ipse certis
personis in quadam peticione huic cedule consuta nominatis pro expensis et dampnis suis faciendis satisfaciat si idem Johannes Biere
intencionem suam de omnibus et singulis in eadem peticione contentis
versus ipsas personas probare non poterit, videlicet, quilibet manucaptorum predictorum sub pena quadraginta librarum, ac prefatus
Johannes Biere assumpsit sub eadem pena; que quidem persone
habent diem essendi coram prefato domino Rege in Cancellaria predicta ad respondendum prefato Johanni Biere super premissis in quindena Sancti Johannis Baptiste proximo futura.[3]

6   [4]A Chaunceller nostre Seignur le Roi

1388 Monstront Johan Skernyng et Adam Hullok, Conestables de la pees
nostre Seignur le Roi de la Hundryd de Knaueryng[5] en le Counte de
Norff' faitz par monsire Johan Holt, Justic de l'assise, pur garder le
pees et autrez chosez affere qe apartyent a lour office de conesta-
blerye, c'estassauoir, qe come lez auauntditz conestables furunt requis
par vn Johan Godefrey et Stephan Catfeld de mesme le hundryd pur
arrester Maude iadys seruaunt Simond Bukmonggere et Cecile la file
Johan Spenser de mesme le hundryd qils furunt a largez hors de
chescun yseruices nient eiant terres tenementz ne autres chateux

---

[1] The ground for interference of the Chancellor in this case is that the ordinary civil process of the country was insufficient to deal with it. 'They will not be justified against their will' meaning 'they will not appear unless they choose.'

[2] Bundle 3, No. 9.

[5] The ground of this complaint is the

the Sheriff of the County against their will, nor will they at any time unless our lord the King betakes himself against them seriously. Of which the said suppliant prayeth you for a remedy, and may it please you to send a writ to the Sheriff of Cornwall to warn each cf the sa evil-doers to be before you on the octave of Holy Trinity under pain of 200 marks to answer the said suppliant as well as the King, and to be justified as the law demands, and to find sufficient surety before you that they will not do harm to the said suppliant, and that his goods may be delivered to him. For God and in way of charity.[1]

Be it remembered that on the 12th day of May, 11 Richard II [1388,] Roger Rogger and Walter Bloyghawe of the County of Cornwall and John Haddon and William Bygayn of London, personally appearing in the King's Chancery at Westminster, undertook on behalf of John Biere of Bodmin that he would satisfy certain persons named in the petition sewn to this schedule for their expenses and damages to be incurred [in this matter], if the said John Biere shall fail to prove his assertion against those persons touching all and singular [the matters] contained in the said petition, that is to say, each of the said mainpernors under a penalty of £40, and the said John Biere has also undertaken [the same] under the same penalty. Which said persons [the defendants] have a day [fixed] to be before the King in the Chancery to answer the said John Biere touching the premises, in the quindene of S. John the Baptist next to come.[3]

6   To the Chancellor of our Lord the King,

1388 Show John Skernyng and Adam Hullok, constables of the peace of our lord the King for the Hundred of Clavering[?] in the County of Norfolk, appointed by Master John Holt, Justice of Assize, to guard the peace and to do other matters appertaining to their office of constabulary, that is to say, that whereas the said constables were required by one John Godfrey and Stephen Catfield, of the same Hundred, to arrest Maude, formerly servant of Simon Buckmonger, and Cecily, the daughter of John Spenser, of the same Hundred, who were at large out of their services, not having lands or tenements, nor

inability of the common law to punish the defendants owing to their maintainers and strong power in the county. Cases of this class were at a later date heard in the Star Chamber.   [4] Bundle 3, No. 7.
          [3] Probably Clavering.

dount viuere pount, la veindront William Hacoun, William Sekdele et Johan Deneys de la Counte de Suff' et autres ouesque eux de lour couyn et assent et lez auauntditz seruauntz Matill' et Cecile estiaunt en la possession de lez ditz Conestables par voie de arrest priterount en le Counte de Norf' et ameneront en le Counte de Suff' en contre le statut [1] et volunte dez ditz Conestables, et le Mesoun le dit Adam brusseront, et outre ceo lez auauntditz William Hacoun, William Sekdele, Johan Peper, et Johan Deneys et les autres mesfesours par vn iour et vn noet fisteront vn nouell surreccion en le ville de Beklys en la Counte de Suff' ensigerount oue graunt nombre des gentz armez oue hauberks, gantez de feer, espees, boklers et autres armurs arraies encountre la pees nostre seignur le Roi, et la ou les ditz conestables oue deux hommes ouesque eux, c'est assauoir, Johan Godefrey et Stephan Catfeld tanque Robert Duk oue certeyns hommes vient ouesque lui a la auauntdit ville de Beklys en aide de eux et en saluacion de lours vies et lez ditz conestables et les autrez deux mesnerunt hors de la dit ville pur doute de leurs vies. Pur qi please a vostre tresgracious signurie pur mander pur lez auauntditz mesfesours a respoundre deuant vous de lours male faitz et trouere seurte de la pees et lours bone portz, qar autrement lez ditz conestables n'osount mye de faire lour office si autrement ne soit ordeigne pur eux.[2]

[3] Memorandum quod xiij die Maij anno regni Regis Ricardi secundi a conquestu vndecimo Rogerus de Walsham, Ricardus Butte, Johannes Dorwen et Thomas Botolf de Com. Norff' coram domino Rege in Cancellaria sua personaliter constituti manuceperunt pro Adam Hullok, Johanne Skernyng, Johanne Godfrey, et Stephano Catfeld quod ipsi certis personis in quadam peticione huic cedule consuta nominatis in casu quod iidem Adam, Johannes Skernyng, Johannes Godfrey et Stephanus Catfeld intencionem suam de omnibus et singulis in eadem peticione contentis versus ipsas personas probare non poterunt pro expensis et misis suis in hac parte apponendis satisfaciant, videlicet, quilibet manucaptorum predictorum sub pena. xl li. ac prefatus Johannes Skernyng assumpsit sub eadem pena. Que quidem persone habent dies essendi coram domino Rege et consilio suo in Cancellaria sua predicta ad respondendum prefatis Ade, Johanni Skernyng, Johanni Godfrey et Stephano Catfeld de premissis.[4]

---

[1] 12 Ric. II. cap. 3. No servant shall depart from one hundred to another without a testimonial under the King's seal, on pain of being set in the stocks. See also 23 Edw. III. cap. 2; 34 Edw. III. cap. 10, 11.

[2] See note 3, p. 6.

other chattels of which they could live, there came William Hacoun, William Sekdele and John Deneys, of the County of Suffolk, and others with them, of their covin and assent, and seized the said servants, Maude and Cecily, in the County of Norfolk, being in the possession of the said constables by way of arrest, and brought them into the County of Suffolk, contrary to the statute, and against the will of the constables, and broke the house of the said Adam [Hullok], and moreover the said William Hacoun, William Sekdele, John Peper and John Deneys, and the other evil-doers, for a day and a night made a new insurrection in the town of Beccles in the County of Suffolk, besetting it with a great number of people armed with hauberks, iron gloves, swords, bucklers, and other arms, arrayed against the peace of our lord the King; and then, the said Constables [having] with them two men only, that is to say, John Godfrey and Stephen Catfield, Robert Duck and certain men with him came to the said town of Beccles to the aid of [the constables], and in salvation of their lives brought the constables and the other two out of the said town in fear of their lives. Wherefore may it please your most gracious lordship to command the said evil-doers to answer before you for their evil deeds, and to find surety [to keep] the peace and for their good behaviour. For otherwise the said constables dare not perform their office if it be not so ordained for them.

Be it remembered that on the 13th day of May, 11 Richard II, [1388,] Roger de Walsham, Richard Butte, John Dorwen and Thomas Botolf, of the County of Norfolk, before the King in his Chancery personally appearing, undertook on behalf of Adam Hullok, John Skernyng, John Godfrey and Stephen Catfield, that they would satisfy certain persons named in the petition sewn to this schedule for their expenses and costs to be incurred in this matter, in case the said Adam, John Skernyng, John Godfrey and Stephen Catfield shall fail to prove their assertion against those persons touching all and singular [the matters] contained in the said petition; that is to say, each of the said mainpernors under a penalty of £40; and the said John Skernyng has also undertaken [the same] under the like penalty. Which said persons [the defendants] have a day [fixed] to be before the King and his Council in the Chancery to answer the said Adam, John Skernyng, John Godfrey and Stephen Catfield touching the premises.

³ Bundle 3, No. 6.
⁴ See note 3, p. 6. Note especially in this case that the defendants are to appear before the King *and his Council* in the Chancery, and this notwithstanding that the petition is addressed to the Chancellor.

7   [1] Au Chaunceller nostre seignur le Roy

1388   Supplie Robert Dane, citeseyn et mercer de Loundres, qe come il estoit en alaunt vers sez partiez en le Counte de Kent pur surveier certeyns terres et tenementz en ycelles partiez, la vynt vn Thomas Holbein oue xx archiers bien arrayez et autres plusours gentez lour mentenauntez en tapison a Egethoyn en la dit Counte et gisaunt en agait de luy auoir tuez et destruz encontre la pees nostre seignur le Roy: Please a vostre noble seignourie de grauntier bref direct au dit Thomas de luy faire venir deuaunt vous en la Chauncellrie nostre seignur le Roy pur trouer seurte de la pees et de soun bone porte; en ouere de charite.[2]

[3] Ricardus [etc.] Thome Holbein, salutem. Quibusdam certis de causis nos et consilium nostrum intime mouentibus, tibi precipimus firmiter iniungentes quod omnibus aliis pretermissis et excusacione quacumque penitus cessante in propria persona tua sis coram nobis et dicto consilio nostro die sabbati proximo futuro vbicumque tunc fuerit [*sic*] ad respondendum super hiis que tibi obicientur tunc ibidem ex parte nostra et ad faciendum vlterius et recipiendum quod Curia nostra considerauerit in hac parte. Et hoc sub pena centum librarum nullatenus omittas. Et habeas ibi tunc hoc breve. Teste me ipso apud Westm' xxiiij die Octobris, anno regni nostri duodecimo.[4]

Indorsed. Robertus Dane Ciuis et Mercerus London' sequitur hoc breve.

8   [5] A mon treshonoure, tresgraciouse et tresreuerent seignur, le Chaunceler d'Engletere,

1388   Supplie humblement vne Johan Milner de Takileye [6] del Counte d'Esex et monstre coment il fuist pris et enprisone al suit de mon sire Nichol Brambre de Loundres,[7] en quel prison il fuist constreine d'acounter la ou il ne fuist acountable, par vne Nichol Leche, Seneschal au dit mon sire Nichol Brambre, auditour de mesme le acounte; en quel acount, il fuist charge de xxxvj li. al suit de mon sire Nichol suisdite, et puis le dit mon sire Nichol [en]presens de mon

---

[1] Bundle 3, No. 10.
[2] There seems very little reason here for an appeal to the Chancellor.
[3] Bundle 3, No. 11.
[4] See note 3, p. 6. The defendant is to appear, not before the Chancellor, but before the Council.

7   To the Chancellor of our Lord the King,

1388   Beseecheth Robert Dane, citizen and mercer of London, that as he
       was going towards his own part of the County of Kent to survey cer-
       tain lands and tenements in those parts, there came one Thomas
       Holbein, with twenty archers well arrayed and many other people
       supporting them in concealment at Egethoyn in the said County,
       lying in wait to have killed and destroyed [the complainant], against
       the peace of our lord the King: May it please your noble lordship to
       grant a writ directed to the said Thomas to cause him to come before
       you in the Chancery of our lord the King, to find surety for the peace
       and for his good behaviour; in way of charity.[2]

           Richard [etc.] to Thomas Holbein, Greeting: For certain causes
       nearly moving us and our Council, we command you, firmly enjoin-
       ing you that, all other matters laid aside and all excuse whatso-
       ever wholly ceasing, you do come in your proper person before us and
       our said Council on Saturday next wheresoever it shall then be, to
       answer to those things which shall then and there be objected against
       you on our behalf, and further to do and receive whatever our Court
       shall consider in that behalf.   And this on a pain of £100 you shall
       in no wise omit.   And then have you there this writ.   Witness ourself
       at Westminster, October 24th, in the 12th year of our reign [1388].[4]

           Indorsed. Robert Dane, citizen and mercer of London, sued out
       this writ.

8   To my most honoured, most gracious and most
           reverent Lord, the Chancellor of England,

1388   Beseecheth humbly one John Milner of Takeley in the County of
       Essex, and showeth how he was taken and imprisoned at the suit of
       Sir Nicholas Brambre of London, in which prison he was constrained
       to account where he was not accountable by one Nicholas Leche,
       steward to the said Sir Nicholas Brambre, auditor of the same
       account; in which account he was charged with £36 at the suit of the
       said Sir Nicholas; and then the said Sir Nicholas, in the presence of

---

[5] Bundle 3, No. 14.   [7] Lord Mayor in 1377 and 1383 to 1385.
[6] Takeley, near Stansted Mountfitchet.

seignour de Notyngham [1] et de Nicholas Exton, adonkis Mayre de Loundres,[2] pardonast al dit suppliant toutz maners d'accions, du quel pardoune le dit suppliant auoit vne preue seal de nostre seignour le Roy directe al dite Maire de Loundres pur sa deliuerance; et, mon seignour, deuaunt qe le preue seal viendroit al dite Mayre, vne Nicholas Leche de Loundres, Seneschal au Nichol Bambre suisdite, viendroit au mesme cesty suppliant, desanz au ly qe vnkis ne viendroit hors du dit prison, sance ceo q'il voderoit conistre le dette suisdite estre duez au ly; Et en cas q'il voderoit ceo faire, q'adonkis le dit suppliant serroit deliuerrez mesme cel iour, paiantz al dit Seneschal xl s. pur tout la summe; sure quel promise, mesme cest suppliant fuist menuz al Countour de Loundres, et la par [mal?] imaginacion et cohercion du dit Nicholas Leche mesme cel suppliant conuste les xxxvj li. suisditz estre duez au dit Nichol Leche; Et quant cest conusance fuist faite le dit suppliant fuist amesnez au prison arier, et la ad demurre et vnqore demurte et demurra taunqe les ditz xxxvj liuers soient paiez, s'il n'eit aide de dieu [ou] de vous: Sure quoy, mon treshonoure tresgraciouse et tresreuerent seignour, plese a vostre tresgraciouse seignourie d'enuoier pur le dit Nichol Leche et moy auxsint, qu'est suppliant et prisoner et nous ambedeux examiner et la verite de cest matier serchier et sure ce faire qe loy et reson demandent; pur dieu et en oeur de charite.[3]

[4] Ricardus [etc.] Vicecomitibus London', salutem. Precipimus vobis firmiter iniungentes quod omnibus aliis pretermissis et excusacione quacumque penitus cessante, Habeatis coram nobis in Cancellaria nostra die lune proximo futuro vbicumque tunc fuerit Johannem Milner de Takiley in Comitatu Essex' per vos in prisona nostra de Neugate sub aresto detentum vt dicitur, vnacum causa arestacionis et detencionis sue. Et hoc sub incumbenti periculo nullatenus omittatis, hoc breve vobiscum deferentes. Teste me ipso apud Westm' xix die Nouembris, anno regni nostri duodecimo.

Indorsed. Responsio Thome Austyn et Ade Carlill', Vicecomitum. Executio istius brevis patet in cedula huic brevi consuta.

[5] Ante adventum brevis domini Regis nobis directi et presentibus consuti, Johannes Milner infrascriptus captus fuit et prisone domini

---

[1] Thomas Mowbray, created Earl of Nottingham Feb. 12, 1383.

[2] Lord Mayor in 1386 and 1387.
[3] The cancellation of the cognovit, ob-

my Lord of Nottingham and Nicholas Exton, then Mayor of London, pardoned to the said suppliant all manner of actions, through which pardon the said suppliant had a writ of Privy Seal of our lord the King directed to the said Mayor of London for his deliverance; And, my lord, before the Privy Seal came to the Mayor, one Nicholas Leche of London, steward to the said Nicholas Brambre, came to this same suppliant, saying to him that he would never come out of prison unless he would confess the said debt to be due to him, and in case he would do this, then the said suppliant should be delivered that same day on paying to the said steward 40s. for the whole sum; Upon this promise, the said suppliant was brought to the Counter of London, and there by the evil design and coercion of the said Nicholas Leche, the said suppliant acknowledged the said £36 to be due to the said Nicholas Leche; [6] And when this acknowledgment was made, the said suppliant was brought to prison again, and there has dwelt and still dwelleth and will dwell until the said £36 be paid, if he have not God's aid or yours: Whereupon, my most honoured, most gracious and most reverend lord, may it please your most gracious lordship to send for the said Nicholas Leche and for me also, who am a suppliant and a prisoner, and to examine us both before you, and to search out the truth of this matter, and thereupon to do what law and right demand; for God and in way of charity.[3]

Richard [etc.], to the Sheriffs of London, Greeting: We command you, firmly enjoining you that all other matters laid aside and all excuse whatsoever wholly ceasing, you do have before us in our Chancery on Monday next, wherever it then shall be, John Milner of Takeley in the county of Essex, now detained under arrest by you in our prison of Newgate, as it is said, together with the cause of his arrest and detention, And this under the peril which may ensue, you shall in no wise omit, bringing with you this writ. Witness ourself at Westminster, November 19th, in the 12th year of our reign [1388].

Indorsed. The answer of Thomas Austyn and Adam Carlisle, the Sheriffs:—

The execution of this writ appears in a schedule sewn thereto.

Before the coming of the King's writ directed to us and sewn to these presents, the within written John Milner was seized and

tained by fraud and false pretences, is here the ground for the Chancellor's interference.
[4] Bundle 3, No. 12.

[3] Bundle 3, No. 13.
[6] *I.e.* signed a *cognovit.*

Regis de Neugate commissus ad sectam Nicholai Brembre militis in
quodam placito compoti super receptum c li. in Curia domini Regis
coram Willelmo Venour nuper vno Vicecomitum London'; Et similiter
ad sectam Ricardi Asshewell' in quodam placito debiti super debitum
xl s. in eadem Curia; Et similiter idem Johannes Milner detentus
est in prisona predicta pro xxxvij li. xvj s. ixd. quos Nicholaus Leche
versus eum recuperavit in quodam placito debiti in eadem Curia.
Attamen ipsum Johannem Milner coram vobis in Cancellaria
prompte habemus prout in dicto brevi precipitur et prout idem breve
requirit.

9   [1] Reuerendissimo in Christo patri gratio-
      sissimo et misericordissimo Archiepiscopo
      Ebor. et Cancellario Anglie,

89 Servitor vester Bernardus Edwardus de Reco humiliter supplicat
intuitu caritatis, quod si possibile sit facere id quod vobis peto per
misericordiam vestram breue sit, quia sunt sex menses elapsi quod
isti Mercatores tenent denaries meos et eos michi reddere nolunt, et
nauis mea remanet defracta in fossato, et eam aptare non valeo, nec ire
possum neque durare ad longam prosecucionem, et illis quibus debeo
in London' volunt esse soluti, Vnde reverendissime pater et domine,
vos qui estis mater iusticie, sibi digna prouidere racionem et iusticiam
et placeat sanctitati vestre mittere pro predictis Mercatoribus quod
compareant coram vobis ad soluendum id quod iustum fuerit dicto
Bernardo secundum discrecionem vestram.[2]

[In another hand.]

Reynaldus Grelus, Siprianus de Mare et Benedictus Lomelyn.

[3] Ricardus dei gracia Rex Anglie et Francie et Dominus Hibernie,
Reginaldo Grille, Cipriano de Maris, Benedicto Lomelyn, mercatoribus
de Janua, salutem. Quibusdam certis de causis nos et consilium nostrum intime moventibus, vobis precipimus firmiter iniungentes quod
omnibus aliis pretermissis et excusacione quacumque penitus cessante
in propriis personis sitis coram nobis et dicto consilio nostro in Cancellaria nostra hac instante die Veneris proximo futuro ubicumque tunc
fuerit, ad respondendum super hiis que vobis obicientur tunc ibidem
ex parte nostra, et ad faciendum ulterius et recipiendum quod curia

---

[1] Bundle 3, No. 16.   [2] This bill seems to refer to a former

committed to the King's prison of Newgate at the suit of Nicholas
Brembre, knight, in a plea of account on the receipt of £100, in the
King's Court before William Venour, late one of the Sheriffs of
London ; And also at the suit of Richard Asshewell in a plea of debt of
40s. in the same Court ; And. also the said John Milner was detained
in the said prison for £37 16s. 9d. which Nicholas Leche recovered
against him in a plea of debt in the same Court.   Nevertheless we
will promptly have the said John Milner before you in the Chancery
as is enjoined in the said writ and as the said writ requireth.

9   To the most reverend, gracious and merciful
       Father in Christ, the Archbishop of York
       and Chancellor of England,

1389 Humbly beseecheth your servant Bernard Edward de Reco of your
charity that if it be possible to do that which I crave of you, of your
mercy let it be speedy, because six months are now elapsed since
those merchants held my moneys and would not return them to me,
and my ship remains unfreighted in the dock, and I cannot load her,
and I cannot go, nor yet stay for a long prosecution, and my creditors
in London wish to be paid ; Wherefore, most reverend father and lord,
you who are the mother of Justice, deign to provide right and justice,
and may your holiness please to send for the said merchants that they
may appear before you to pay to the said Bernard what shall seem
just according to your discretion.[2]

     Writ directed to Reginald Grille, Ciprian de Maris and Benedict
Lomelyn, merchants of Genoa, commanding their appearance before
the King and his Council in the Chancery, on Friday next, to answer,
etc., on pain of our grave indignation and the peril which will thereby
ensue.   Dated, 15 Feb. 1389.

complaint made to the Chancellor, and to
urge expedition in the matter.   The three
names at the end are probably those of the
merchants complained of.   The plaintiff
was an alien (see p. 4, note 3).
    [2] Bundle 3, No. 15.

nostra consideraverit in hac parte; Et hoc sub gravi indignacione et
periculis incumbentibus nullatenus omittatis.   Et habeatis ibi hoc
breve.   Teste me ipso apud Westm' xv die Febr', anno regni nostri
duodecimo.

Indorsed. Bernardus de Reco Januensis sequitur hoc breve.

10   [1] A tres reuerent pier en Dieu l'Erceuesque
             d'Euerwyk, Chanceller,

1393 Supplie Henry Glanuylle, vn des poueres lieges nostre seignur le Roy
      de Countee de Deuenshire, qe come vn Richard Chaumbernoun,
      chiualer, de mesme le Counte, enpreignant sur luy Roial poair,
      comanda et enuoia plusours malefesours de ses seruantz pur arestier
      le dit suppliant sanz cause resonable ou processe de ley; par vertue
      de quel commandement lez ditz malefesours luy pristreront et mistre-
      ront en cippes a Wodelegh [2] deinz soun seignurie demesne [2] en le
      Contee suisdit, et illoeqes luy detyndreront tanqe le dit suppliant auoit
      fait fyne et raunsioun al volunte del dit Richard Chaumbernoun, et
      auxi tanqe le dit Henry auoit trouez quatre plegges, chescun de eux
      liez en Cent marcz pur estier al gard et iuggement del dit Richard,
      qar autrement il ne purroit mye estre deliuerez; et apres le dit
      suppliant n'oisa demurer en le dit Countee pur dout de mort, maes
      est venuz a uostre tresgracious seignurie pur auoir remedie et redresse
      en celle partie, qar nulle n'oise pursuer enuers luy come le commune
      ley demande par cause de sa grante maintenance : Sur quoy pleise a
      vostre tresgracious seignurie de considerer la dite matiere et de gran-
      tier de vostre benigne grace brief directe al dit Richard sur greuouse
      peyne pur luy faire venir deuant vous en la Chauncellarie a respondre
      sibien a nostre dit seignur le Roy del contempt issint fait en preiudice
      de sa corone come al dit suppliant de les tortz greuancez et oppressions
      suisditz, pur Dieu et en oeuere de charitee.[3]

      [4] Ricardus [etc.] dilectis et fidelibus suis Willelmo Rykhill et
      Willelmo Brenchesle, Justiciariis suis ad assisas in Com' Deuon'
      capiendas assignatis, et eorum alteri, salutem.   Quandam peticionem
      nobis per Henricum Glanuylle exhibitam vobis mittimus presentibus
      interclusam, mandantes quod inspecta peticione predicta et materia

---

[1] Bundle 3, No. 22.   Kingsbridge.
[2] Perhaps Woodleigh, Devonshire, near   [3] No remedy at common law, for fear of

10   To the most reverend Father in God, the
Archbishop of York, Chancellor,

1393 Beseecheth Henry Glanville, one of the poor lieges of our lord the
King in the County of Devonshire, that whereas one Richard
Champernoun, knight, of the same County, taking upon himself
royal power, commanded and sent many evil-doers of his servants
to arrest the said suppliant without reasonable cause or process of
law; by virtue of which command, the said evil-doers took him and
put him in the stocks at Woodleigh within his own lordship[5] in the
said County, and there detained him until the said suppliant had
made fine and ransome at the will of the said Richard Champernoun,
and also until the said Henry had found four pledges, each of them
bound in 100 marks, that he would abide the award and judgment
of the said Richard, for otherwise he would not have been released;
and afterwards the said suppliant dared not dwell in the said County
for fear of death, but hath come to your most gracious lordship to
have remedy and redress in this matter, for no one dare bring suit
against [Champernoun] as the Common Law demands, because of his
great maintenance: Whereupon may it please your most gracious
lordship to consider the said matter and to grant of your benign
grace a writ directed to the said Richard, on grievous pain, for him to
come before you in the Chancery to answer to our said lord the King
for the contempt so done in prejudice of his crown, as well as to the
said suppliant for the torts, grievances and oppressions aforesaid.
For God and in way of charity.[3]

Richard [etc.] to his beloved and faithful William Rykhill and
William Brenchesley, his Justices assigned to take assizes in the County
of Devon, and to either of them, Greeting. We send you inclosed in
these presents a certain petition exhibited to us by Henry Glanville,
commanding you, after having inspected the said petition and fully

the defendant—a typical Star Chamber   [4] Bundle 3, No. 21.
allegation.   [5] The complainant's, apparently.

eiusdem plenius intellecta, vocatisque coram vobis eis quos in hac parte
fore videritis euocandos, super omnibus et singulis articulis in peticione
predicta contentis diligentem facere inquisicionem, Et eam distincte
et aperte factam nobis in Cancellariam nostram sub sigillis vestris et
sigillis eorum per quos facta fuit sine dilacione mittatis et hoc breve.
Teste [etc.] 27th June, 17 Ric. II.

[1] [Inquisicio capta apud] Exon' coram Willelmo Rykhill et
Willelmo Brenchesley Justiciariis domini Regis ad assisas in [Comi-
tatu Deuon' capiendas] assignatis virtute cuiusdam brevis domini
Regis eisdem Willelmo et Willelmo directi et huic [inquisicioni consuti . . .] tunc ibidem pro domino Rege Ricardo Whitelegh, juniori,
ad informandum pro domino Rege super sacramentum suum onerato,
die veneris proximo post festum Sancte Margarete virginis [2] anno regni
regis Ricardi secundi decimo septimo per [sacramentum Warini] [3]
l'ercedekene, chivaler, Willelmi Asthorp, chivaler, Johannis Prideaux,
chivaler, Michaelis l'ercedekene, chivaler, [Roberti Corun], [3] chivaler,
Walteri Reynald, Johannis Nywynham, Willelmi Ferers, Edwardi
Boson, Thome Halghewille, Johannis Wotton et Willelmi Clifford, Qui
dicunt super sacramentum suum quod omnia contenta in ista billa per
Henricum Glaunuyle porrecta ad reuerendum in Christo patrem dominum Archiepiscopum Ebor. Cancellarium domini Regis Anglic, apposita
super Ricardum Chambernoun, Chiualer, et huic brevi vna cum Billa
predicta simul consuta tam in parte quam in toto sunt irrita et falsa
et nichil facta per cognicionem, mandatum, missionem, seu aliquo
alio modo per predictum Ricardum Chambernoun, Chiualer, prout in
illa Billa supponitur et continetur, nec idem Ricardus in nullo est
inde culpabilis. In cuius rei [etc.]

11 [4] Al treshonore et treshonorable seignur
Chaunceler d'Engletere,

1394 Supplie Edward Bokelond, qe come le dit Edward ad este long temps
seise de diuers Mees terrez et tenementz en la ville de Bristuit, la
vient Johan Bount et Johan Bruggewatere ouesque graunt nombre
dez gentz disconuz le Mecurdy proschin apres le fest de Purificacion de
nostre Dame darein passe, et lez huses en la meison del dit suppliant ou
il fuist demurant en mesme la ville a temps qe le dit suppliant fuist a
Londres debruserunt ouesque haches et altrez instrumentz et en la dit

---

[1] Bundle 3, No. 24. The top left-hand
corner is torn off. A jury panel, No. 23, is   attached.
[2] This feast is on July 20

understood the matter thereof, and having called before you those whom you shall think meet, to make diligent inquiry upon all and singular the articles contained in the said petition, and to send the same without any delay, openly and distinctly made, together with this writ, to us in our Chancery, under your seals and the seals of those by whom it was made. June 27th, 17 Richard II [1393].

Inquisition taken at Exeter before William Rykhill and William Brenchesley, the Justices of our lord the King assigned to take assizes in the County of Devon, by virtue of a certain writ of our lord the King, directed to the said William and William and sewn to this inquisition . . . Richard Whitelegh junior being then present and bound on his oath to inform on behalf of the King, on the Friday next after the feast of S. Margaret the Virgin,[2] 17 Richard II [1393,] by the oath of Warin Archdeacon, knight, William Asthorp, knight, John Prideaux, knight, Michael Archdeacon, knight, Robert Corun, knight, Walter Reynald, John Newnham, William Ferers, Edward Boson, Thomas Haliwell, John Wotton and William Clifford, who say upon their oath that all the contents in the bill exhibited by Henry Glanville to the Reverend Father in Christ, the Lord Archbishop of York, our lord the King's Chancellor of England, against Richard Champernoun, knight, and sewn to this writ together with the said bill, are vain and false, as well in the part as in whole, and not done by the knowledge, command, or commission of the said Richard Champernoun, knight, nor in any other way by him, as in the bill is supposed and contained, nor is the said Richard in any way guilty thereof. In witness, etc.

11   To the most honoured and most honourable, the Lord Chancellor of England,

1394 Beseecheth Edward Bokelond, that whereas the said Edward has been seised for a long time of divers messuages, lands and tenements in the town of Bristol, there came one John Bount and John Bridgewater, with a great number of people unknown, on the Wednesday next after the feast of the Purification of our Lady last past, and broke the doors of the said suppliant's house where he was dwelling in the same town, with hatchets and other instruments, while the said sup-

---

[2] These names are supplied from the jury panel.
[4] Bundle 3, No. 20.

meison entrerount et cez cofres en le dit meison esteantz debruserunt, et cez Chartres munymentz et autres biens illeoque trouez al value de C. li. pristerent et enporterount ; dez qeux malefeseurs susditz ascuns vnqore sountz demurountz oue fort mayn en foire de guere en le dit meison encontre la voluntee le dit suppliaunt ; et ascuns dez ditz malefeseurs par le chymyn parentre cy et la ville de Bristuit giseuntz en agayt pur tuer le dit suppliaunt en cas q'il veigne al dit ville de Bristuit ; pur qi le dit suppliaunt n'osa aler a l'ostiel a son meison dismene pur dout de mort.

Qe pleise a vostre tresgracious seignurie de grauntier a dit suppliaunt vne Brief directe a dit Johan Bount, sour peyne de deux C. li. d'estre devaunt vous en la Chauncellarie nostre seignur le Roi le lundy proschin deuant le fest de seint Edward le Roi.   Et vne autre Brief directe al dit Johan Bruggewatere d'estre deuant vous a mesme le iour sour mesme le peyne, de respondre a lez mesfaitz et tortz susditz, et ceo pur Dieux et en oeuere de charitee.

¹ M[anucaptores] Edwardi Bokeland ad prosequendum peticionem suam in Cancellaria

            Johannes Vrban de Com' Cornub'
            Johannes Lake de Com' Berk'

   ² Ricardus [etc.] Johanni Bount, salutem.   Quibusdam certis de causis coram nobis et consilio nostro propositis tibi precipimus firmiter iniungentes quod omnibus aliis pretermissis et excusacione quacumque cessante in propria persona tua sis coram nobis et dicto consilio nostro die lune proximo ante festum Sancti Edwardi Regis et Martiris proximo futurum ad respondendum super hiis que tibi obicientur ex parte nostra tunc ibidem et ad faciendum ulterius et recipiendum quod per nos et dictum consilium nostrum de te contigerit ordinari ; et hoc sub pena centum librarum nullatenus omittas, Et habeas ibi hoc breue.   Teste me ipso apud Westm' xxiiij die Febr' anno regni nostri decimo septimo.

12   ³ A Chanceller nostre seignur le Roi

1394 Supplient humblement les Mair et Citezeins de Cicestre qe come ils teignent la dite Cite a fee ferme de nostre dit seignur le Roi oue vn port appelle Horemuth ⁴ ensemblement oue toutz maners custumes de merchandises venantz a dit port, come en leur chartre en fait est

---

¹ Bundle 3, No. 18.   ³ Bundle 3, No. 25.
² Bundle 3, No. 19.   ⁴ Part of Chichester Harbour was an-

pliant was at London, and entered into the said house, and broke his coffers in the said house, and took his charters, muniments, and other goods there found to the value of £100 and carried them away; some of which evil-doers aforesaid are still living in the said house with strong hand and in manner of war, against the will of the said suppliant; and some of the said evil-doers are lying in wait by the road between here and Bristol to kill the said suppliant in case he come to the said town of Bristol; on account of which the said suppliant dare not go home to his own house for fear of death.

May it please your most gracious lordship to grant to the said suppliant a writ directed to the said John Bount, under a pain of £200, to be before you in the Chancery of our lord the King on the Monday next after the feast of S. Edward the King, and another writ directed to the said John Bridgewater to be before you on the same day and under the same pain, to answer for their misdeeds and torts aforesaid: And this for God and in way of charity.

Mainpernors of Edward Bokeland for prosecuting his petition in the Chancery,

JOHN URBAN of Cornwall,

JOHN LAKE of Berkshire.

Writ directed to John Bount, commanding his attendance before the King and his Council on the Monday before the feast of S. Edward, King and martyr, then next, under a penalty of £100. Dated, 24 Feb. 1394.

12   To the Chancellor of our Lord the King,

1394   Humbly complain the Mayor and citizens of Chichester, that whereas they hold the said city to fee-farm of our said Lord the King, together with a port called Horemouth, and together with all manner of customs of merchandise coming to the said port, as in their charter is

ciently so called. See Dallaway's *Sussex*, i. 208. The Port and customs were granted to the city by Hen. II., and confirmed by

Edw. III. *Rot. Pat.* 50 Edw. III. pt. 1, m. 11.

contenuz plus a plein, et les Mair et Baillifs de mesme la Cite les ditz
custumes ount pris apres la date de dite chartre tanqe encea tanqe
ore tard qe Wauter Stubbare, Richard Stubbare et William Hamond
venantz illoeqes oue grantz routes des gentz armez les Baillifs du dite
Citee desturberent de prendre les ditz custumes d'une Barge chargez
oue pessoun esteant deyns la dite port, et mesmes les Baillifs de vie et
de membre manacerent et lour arks enuers eux treterent q'ils a peyne
oue lour vies eschaperent ; a grant damage des ditz Mair et Citezeins
et arerissement del paiement de la fee ferme auant dite : Qe plese
pur dieu et en oeure de charite ordeigner remede as Mair et Citezeins
suisditz des dam[a]ges et tortz auantditz.

[1] Noverint vniuersı nos Maiorem ac Ciues Ciuitatis Cicestre attor
nasse et loco nostro posuisse dilectum nobis Willelmum Neel Conciuem
nostrum Ciuitatis predicte ad placitandum et prosequendum coram
domino Rege in Cancellaria sua tam pro nobis quam pro se ipso versus
Willelmum Hamond, Walterum Stubbare et Ricardum Stubbare pro
eo quod ipsi magna multitudine armatorum Balliuos dicte Ciuitatis
custumas vnius bargie piscibus carcate infra quendam portum vocatum
Horemuth existentis nobis et successoribus nostris per cartas quondam
Regum Anglie et litteras domini Regis nunc de confirmacione vna
cum Ciuitate predicta ad feodi firmam concessas capere impediuerunt,
dictis Balliuis tantas minas vite et membrorum imponendo et arcus
suos versus eosdem Balliuos tractando quod ipsi viui vix euaserunt,
ad graue dampnum nostrum et retardacionem solucionis feodi firme
predicte. Damus eciam et concedimus prefato Willelmo Neel per
presentes plenam potestatem et facultatem generalem ad faciendum
attornatos vel attornatum quos vel quem voluerit in Cancellaria
predicta ad lucrandum vel perdendum in premıssıs, Ratum et
gratum habituri quicquid predictus Willelmus Neel in premissis
duxerit faciendum.   In cuius rei testimonium sigillum nostrum
commune Ciuitatis predicte presentibus est appensum. Datum in
Gihalda nostra Cicestr' primo die Marcii anno regni Regis Ricardi
secundi post conquestum decimo septimo.

Indorsed on the bill. Willelmus Nele de Cicestr', Johannes Frenche,
Thomas Pacchyng, man[uceperunt] ad satisfaciendum infrascriptis
Waltero et sociis suis sub pena in statuto inde edito [2] contenta in casu
quo querelam infra non probaverint.[3]

[1] Bundle 3, No. 26.
[2] Query if this was an Act of Parliament or merely an ordinance of the Council. See Spence, i. 345.

[3] It is difficult to see why this complaint should have been made to the Chancellor. The violence of the defendants, as in many other cases, had, no doubt, much to do with

more plainly contained, and the Mayor and Bailiffs of the same city have taken the said customs from the date of the said charter until now of late that one Walter Stubbare, Richard Stubbare and William Hamond, coming thither with great routs of armed people, have disturbed the Bailiffs of the city in taking the said customs from a barge, laden with fish, within the said port, and they have threatened the said Bailiffs of life and limb, and have drawn their bows against them, so that scarcely have they escaped with their lives ; to the great damage of the said Mayor and citizens, and the hindrance of the payment of the fee-farm aforesaid : May it please you, for God and in way of charity, to ordain a remedy to the Mayor and citizens for the damages and torts aforesaid.

Know all men that we the Mayor and citizens of the city of Chichester have attorned and put in our place our beloved William Neel, our fellow-citizen of the said city, to plead and prosecute before the King in his Chancery as well for us as for himself against William Hamond, Walter Stubbare and Richard Stubbare for this that they with a great multitude of armed men did hinder the Bailiffs of the said city from taking the customs of a barge laden with fish within the port called Horemouth, (which customs were granted to us and our successors, together with the said city, to fee-farm, by the charters of former Kings of England and by the Letters of Confirmation of the present King), by holding out to the said Bailiffs such threats of life and limb, and by drawing their bows upon the said Bailiffs, that they scarcely escaped alive, to our great damage, and to the hindrance of the payment of the fee-farm aforesaid. We do also give and grant to the said William Neel by these presents full power and general faculty to make whomsoever he will [our] attorney or attorneys in the said Chancery to gain or lose, and we will ratify whatever he shall cause to be done in the premises.

In witness, etc. Given in our Guild Hall of Chichester March 1st, 17 Richard II [1394].

Indorsed on the bill. William Neel of Chichester, John French and Thomas Pacchyng, undertook to satisfy the within written Walter and his fellows under the penalty contained in the statute[2] ordained to that effect, in case he [Neel] shall not prove his within [written] complaint.[3]

it, but it is not alleged in the bill that the plaintiffs were unable to proceed at common law The statement as to the fee-farm rent suggests the Exchequer as being a more appropriate tribunal.

13   [1]A tres gracious seignur Chaunceller d'Engleterre

1395   Supplie humblement vostre pouere seruaunt Andrew Ramseye nomme Trygg, Fisshmonger de Loundres, qe come le Mesqerdy deuaunt le fest de Pentecost l'an du regne nostre seignur le Roi [Richard qu'or'est ?][2] seszisme le dit Andrew auoit vn Nief freyctez ouesque diuersez marchaundises gisant a soun Stathe[3] en le port de Themse, la vient vn Johan Pounsehurst, wodemonger de Loundres, ouesque vn grauut showt[4] seillant [et frappa le][2] dit Nief, et luy ensi debrusa qe certaines marchandises alors esteantz deinz le dit Nief a la value de xx li. et le Nief auxi furent outrement destruytz ; Pur quel trespas le dit Andrew [se plaint a le][2] Waterbaille de Quenehithe si come le leye et vsage del ewe demandont ; le quel waterbaille deputee de lez viscountz de Loundres de leye del ewe aresta vn showt de le dit Johan pur le trespas, [et le dit Johan][2] garna par plusours diuersez foitz de veigner a la Court pur respoundre au dit Andrew de le trespas suisdite ; et il ne veigna a la dite court solonc ceo q'il estoit garne, mes il fist iiij defautes [et puis le dit][2] Johan veigna oue force et armes par iij foitz au dit Waterbaille et prist de luy le dit showt encountre sa voluntee et encountre le leye ; et come la leye et vsage del ewe demandont [qe qant vn vesselle][2] soit areste pur trespas et le awner dicelle soit appelle a sa respounce et face iiij defautes, adonqes le dit vesselle serra prise al partie pleyntif : Qe plese a vostre tres gracious seignurie comander et charger [lez ditz] viscountz et waterbaillees pur arester le dit showt qe fuist le dit Johan a le temps qe le dit trespas fuist fait a le dit Andrew, et qe le mesme showt et toutz autres biens qeux furent au dit Johan [a le temps suisdite][2] soyent preisez et executez solonc la leye et vsage tanqe pleyn gree et satisfaccion soit fait au dit Andrew de lez damages auauntditz et les costages dicelles ; pur l'amour de Dieu et en oeuere de charitee.

[5] Ricardus [etc.] vicecomitibus London', salutem. Quandam peticionem nobis in Cancellaria nostra per Andream Trygg Civem et Fisshemonger London' exhibitam vobis mittimus presentibus interclusam mandantes sicut alias mandauimus quod inspecta peticione

[1] Bundle 3, No. 30. The right margin is illegible.
[2] Supply these words or the like.
[3] A landing-place for merchandise ; a wharf (Halliwell).
[4] A small boat, nearly flat-bottomed and

13   To the most gracious, the Lord Chancellor
of England,

1395 Beseecheth humbly your poor servant, Andrew Ramsey, called
'Trygg,' fishmonger of London, that whereas on the Wednesday
before the feast of Pentecost in the 16th year of King Richard who
now is [1392], the said Andrew had a ship, freighted with divers merchandise, lying at his stathe[3] in the port of the Thames, there came
one John Pounsehurst, wood-monger of London, with a great shout[4]
sailing, [and struck the] said ship, and so battered it that certain
merchandise there, being in the said ship, to the value of £20, and
also the ship itself, were utterly destroyed ; for which trespass the said
Andrew [complained] to the Water-Bailiff of Queenhithe as the law
and usage of the water [*i.e.* the Thames] demand ; and the Water-
Bailiff, deputed by the Sheriffs of London [in matters] touching the
law of the water, arrested a shout belonging to the said John, for the
trespass, and warned [the said John] many divers times to come
to the Court to answer to the said Andrew for the said trespass ; and
he did not come to the Court as he was warned, but made four
defaults ; [and afterwards the said] John came with force and arms
on three occasions to the said Water-Bailiff, and took from him the
said shout, against his will and contrary to the law ; and as the law
and usage of the water demand [that when a vessel] is arrested for
trespass and the owner of it is summoned to make answer and makes
four defaults, then the said vessel shall be a prize to the plaintiff :
Wherefore may it please your most gracious lordship to command and
charge the said Sheriffs and Water-Bailiffs to arrest the said shout
which belonged to the said John at the time the trespass was done to
the said Andrew, and that the said shout and all other goods which
belonged to the said John [at the time aforesaid] be taken in execution, according to law and usage, until full accord and satisfaction be
made to the said Andrew of the damages aforesaid and the costs
hereof ; for the love of God and in way of charity.

    Richard [etc.], to the Sheriffs of London, Greeting. We send you
inclosed in these presents a petition exhibited to us in our Chancery
by Andrew Trygg, citizen and fishmonger of London, commanding
you, as at other times we have done, that, the petition being inspected

very light, &c. (Halliwell). 'A great shout'   [3] Bundle 3, No. 31.
is perhaps what we should call a barge.

predicta quacumque dilacione postposita eidem Andree super contentis in eadem plenum iusticie complementum fieri faciatis. Taliter vos habentes in hac parte ne in vestri defectum idem Andreas materiam habeat alias querelandi, vel causam nobis significetis quare mandatum nostrum alias vobis inde directum exequi noluistis vel non potuistis. Teste [etc.] Dated *October* 13th, 19 Richard II. [1395]

Indorsed. Nos Willelmus Shiryngham et Rogerus Elys vicecomites London' vobis significamus quod de materia in billa interius interclusa et nobis cum hoc brevi missa non est nec fuit aliqua querela ad sectam Andree infrascripti coram nobis seu balliuo nostro de Quenehithe leuata aliquo tempore, nec aliquod recordum inde coram dicto balliuo nostro habetur seu penes nos remanet aliquo modo, quapropter arestacionem appreciacionem seu execucionem secundum formam et effectum bille predicte facere non possumus nec aliquod breue preter istud inde nobis venit seu liberatum fuit postquam in officio nostro predicto extiterimus.[1]

14　　　　　[2] A Chaunceller nostre seignur le Roy,

1395　Supplie Thomas Beaupeny qe come il soit seignur del Manoir et del Hundred de Northpederton [3] de quel Manoir et Hundred vn Johan Sydenham de Morlond estoit soun baillif par trois ans procheins deuaunt le feste de Seint Laurence [4] l'an de regne le Roi qu'or'est xixme, a quel iour de Seint Laurence le dit Johan Sidenham baillif rendit soun accompt pur le temps auauntdit deuant Johan Sidenham de Briggewater et Robert *Orchard* auditours a lui assignez par le dit Thomas Beaupeny, ou il fuit troue en arreragis duez au dit Thomas de xlix li. xij s. ix d. ob., pur quoy par lez auauntditz auditours il fuit commis en la garde Roger Tyce et Henry Hoper gardeins de la gaole de Briggewater le ioesdy proschein apres le feste de Seint Laurence proschein passe sauement agarder tanqe le dit Johan Sidenham baillif vste pleinement paie lez deniers suisditz au dit Thomas Beaupeny; lez qeux lui resceuront agarder en la fourme auauntdit, et puis ils lui lesteront aler a large, gree nient fait au dit Thomas, douut il prie remedie.[5]

Datus est dies partibus coram domino Cancellario in quindenis Sancti Hillarii.

---

[1] Actual force, the alleged intimidation of the sheriffs, and the inability to obtain justice at common law seem to be the grounds for the appeal to the Chancellor in this case.

[2] Bundle 3, No. 29.

and all delay postponed, you do cause to be done to the said Andrew the full complement of justice on the contents of the same; bearing yourselves in this behalf in such wise that the said Andrew may have no matter for further complaint through your default, or else you shall show cause why you have been unwilling or unable to follow our other mandate therein directed to you. Etc.

Indorsed. We, William Shiringham and Roger Elys, Sheriffs of London, do inform you that, touching the matter in the bill inclosed within and sent to us with this writ, there is not and has not been any plaint raised at the suit of the within written Andrew, before us or our Bailiff of Queenhithe at any time, nor is any record thereof held before our said Bailiff or remaining in our possession in any way, wherefore we cannot make the arrest, appraisement, or execution according to the form and effect of the said bill, nor has any writ in the matter, except this one, come or been delivered to us since we have been in office.[1]

14   To the Chancellor of our Lord the King,

Beseecheth Thomas Beaupeny, that whereas he is lord of the Manor and Hundred of North Petherton, of which Manor and Hundred one John Sidenham of Morland was his bailiff for the three years next before the feast of S. Laurence in the 19th year of the present King [1395], on which day the said John Sidenham rendered his account for the said time, before John Sidenham of Bridgewater and Robert Orchard, the auditors assigned to him by the said Thomas Beaupeny, when it was found that there were arrears due to the said Thomas of £49 12s. 9½d., for which he was committed by the said auditors to the ward of Roger Tyce and Henry Hoper, keepers of the gaol of Bridgewater, on the Thursday after the feast of S. Laurence last past, to be safely guarded until the said John Sidenham, the bailiff, had fully paid the said moneys to the said Thomas Beaupeny; which [keepers] received him to be guarded in form aforesaid; and afterwards they let him go at large, no satisfaction having been made to the said Thomas; for which he prayeth remedy.[5]

A day is given to the parties before the Lord Chancellor on the quindene of S. Hilary.

[3] North Petherton, Somerset.
[4] August 10.
[5] It is difficult to see why the misfeasance of the gaolers, even admitting the facts as stated, should have come before the Chancellor.

[1] Ricardus, [etc.] Rogero Tyce nuper Ballivo de Briggewater, salutem. Quibusdam certis de causis nos specialiter moventibus, tibi precipimus firmiter iniungentes quod omnibus aliis pretermissis et excusacione quacumque cessante, in propria persona tua sis coram nobis et consilio nostro apud Westm' in octabis Sancti Martini proximo futuris ad respondendum ibidem super hiis que tibi tunc obicientur ex parte nostra, et ad faciendum ulterius et recipiendum quod per nos et dictum consilium nostrum de te tunc contigerit ordinari ; Et hoc sub incumbenti periculo nullatenus omittas; Et habeas ibi hoc breve. Teste [etc.] quarto die Novembr' anno regni nostri decimo nono.

A similar writ addressed to Henry Hoper, late Bailliff of Briggewater. Each is indorsed :—Thomas Beaupyne sequitur hoc breve.

15   [2] A tres reuerent piere en Dieu l'Erceuesque d'Euerwyk', Chanceler d'Engletere,

1396 Supplie Johan Hawley de Dertemouth qe come il ad achate diuerses terrez tenements et aduoucions des Esglices queux feuront a Robert Tresilian, Chiualer,[3] en le Counte de Cornewaille et qe par forfaiture de dit Robert en les mains de nostre dit seignur le Roi deuiendront ; Sur tiel condicion, qe si ascunz dez ditz terres tenements et aduoucions santz fraude ou mal engyn du dit Johan surroient recouerez ou euictz, mesme nostre seignur le Roi et sez beires ferroient due recompensacion a dit Johan et sez heires de tielx terrez tenements et aduoucions issint euictz, come en lez lettres patentz mesme nostre seignur le Roi plus pleinement appiert ;[4] Et puis apres breifs nostre dit seignur le Roi feurent directez al viscounte de Cornewaille de faire proclamacion parmye son baille qe nul liege du Roi nostre dit seignur serroit si hardy de faire entree en ascunz dez ditz terres tenements et aduoucions du dit Johan sur peyne d'enprisonement; Et nient contresteant ceu proclamacion vn Johan Poly est entre oue fort mayn en certeins terres et tenements deins le Manoir de Tresilian et Padestowe, cestassauoir, vn Mees et vint acres de terre en le dit Manoir de Tressilian, et deux Mees en Padistowe, queux feuront a dit Robert, membres a mesme le Manoir de Tressilian, et lez tient encontre la

---

[1] Bundle 3, Nos. 27, 28.
[2] Bundle 3, No. 33.
[3] Chief Justice of the King's Bench to

Richard II. (appointed 1381) and one of his favourites and advisers ; appealed of treason 1387, and executed 1388. John Hawley,

Two writs addressed respectively to Roger Tyce, and Henry Hopere, late Bailiffs of Bridgewater, commanding their appearance before the King and his Council at Westminster on the octave of Martinmas next, under grave peril. Dated Nov. 4, 1395.

15   To the most reverend Father in God, the Archbishop of York, Chancellor of England,

1396 Beseecheth John Hawley of Dartmouth, that whereas he hath purchased divers lands, tenements and advowsons of churches which belonged to Robert Tresilian, knight,[3] in the county of Cornwall, and which by the forfeiture of the said Robert had come to the hands of our said lord the King, on this condition, that if any of the said lands, tenements and advowsons should, without fraud or evil device of the said John, be recovered or 'evicted,' the King and his heirs would make due compensation to the said John and his heirs of such lands, tenements and advowsons so purchased, as in the letters patent of our said lord the King more plainly appeareth ;[4] and afterwards writs of our said lord the King were directed to the Sheriff of Cornwall to make proclamation throughout his bailiwick that no liege of the King our said lord should be so bold as to make entry on any of the said lands, tenements or advowsons of the said John on pain of imprisonment; and notwithstanding this proclamation, one John Poly hath entered with the strong hand into certain lands and tenements in the Manor of Tresilian and in Padstowe, to wit, a messuage and 20 acres of land in the said Manor of Tresilian and two messuages in Padstowe, which belonged to the said Robert [Tresilian], and are parcel of the

the plaintiff, married Tresilian's daughter. See Foss, *Judges*, iv. 102; see also *Rot. Parl.* iii. 445.
    [4] See*Rot.Pat.* 13 Ric. II. pt. 1, m. 4;

pt. 2, m. 30; pt. 3, m. 16; 1 Hen. IV. pt. 4, m. 28. The last reference is a confirmation of the previous grants.

fourme du dit proclamacion, en contempte nostre dit seignur le Roï, et grant preiudice de dit Johan Hawley :

Qe pleise a vostre tres sage discrecion d'ordeigner ent remedie sibien pur le contempte et preiudice fait a nostre dit seignur le Roi come pur ease du dit Johan Hawley; pur Dieu et en eouere de charitee.[1]

[2] Ricardus, [etc.] vicecomiti Cornub', salutem. Quibusdam certis de causis coram nobis in Cancellaria nostra per Johannem Haule de Dertemuth seniorem propositis, tibi precipimus firmiter iniungentes quod venire facias coram nobis in dicta Cancellaria nostra in quindena Sancti Michaelis ubicumque tunc fuerit Johannem Tretherf, Johannem Poly, Johannem Nicol, Thomam Spenser, Nicholaum Veysy, clericum, Johannem Repreva, Thomam Derry, Jacobum Cruclewe, Johannem Trevaswedon, Willelmum Dunne, Johannem Bosnevon alias Johannem Clerk, et Henricum Stondard, ad respondendum super hiis que sibi ex parte nostra et predicti Johannis Haule plenius exponentur tunc ibidem, et ad faciendum ulterius et recipiendum quod curia nostra considerauerit in hac parte [etc.] 26 July, 20 Ric. II.

Indorsed.   M[anucaptores] Johannis Tretherf [and six others]
Andreas Borlas, Ricardus Respreua,
Andreas Pensynton, Regle Tretherf.

Thomas Derry [and four others] infra scripti nichil habent in balliua mea per quod eos coram vobis venire facere possum, nec sunt inventi in eadem.

Willelmus Talbot, vicecomès.

16   [3] Plese a tresreuerent pere en Dieu, Thomas,
par la grace de Dieu, Erceuesque d'Euerwyk,
etc., Chanceller d'Angleterre,

s.d. Granter briefs directz a Thomas de Coluile [chivaler pere ?] et a Richard Malbys pour estre deuaut le Conseil[4] du Roy nostre seignur lendemain de l'ascencion prochain venant pour respondre a Waltier, Euesque de Duresme,[5] sur certeins griefs et horribles trespas faiz et comys dedeins sa signeurie de Crayk dedeins le conte d'Euerwyk, en la quelle signeurie le dit Euesque ad iurisdicion roiale ; et par especial

---

[1] This case seems to contain the germ of the theory that the Chancellor is keeper of the King's conscience. The King was bound to warrant, or at any rate to make due compensation. As no action would lie against the Crown, the plaintiff appeals to the Chancellor. See also a bill by the same plaintiff against John Tresilian, Robert's son, relating to an annuity claimed by the defendant; Hawley complains of mainte-

same Manor of Tresilian; and [the said John Polȳ] doth hold them, contrary to the form of the said proclamation, in contempt of our said lord the King, and to the great prejudice of the said John Hawley : Wherefore may it please your most wise discretion to ordain remedy thereof, as well for the contempt and prejudice done to our said lord the King, as for the ease of the said John Hawley; for God and in way of charity.[1]

Writ to the Sheriff of Cornwall commanding him to have John Poly and others before the King in the Chancery on the quindene of Michaelmas. Dated, 26 July, 1396.

16   May it please the most reverend Father in God, Thomas, by the grace of God, Archbishop of York, etc., Chancellor of England,

s.d. To grant writs directed to Thomas de Colville [knight, the father,] and to Richard Malbys, to be before the King's Council[4] on the morrow of the Ascension next to come, to answer to Walter, Bishop of Durham,[5] for certain grievances and horrible trespasses done and committed within his lordship of Crake within the County of York, within which lordship the said Bishop hath royal jurisdiction; and more

nance by the sheriff. Intro. to Cal. Eliz. i. 2.

[2] Bundle 3, No. 32.

[3] Bundle 3, No. 17. This document is in very bad condition; part of it is torn away, and parts are quite illegible.

[4] This is most important, as showing that the practice was well understood. The petition was to the Chancellor, the judges were the Council.

[5] Walter Skirlaw, 1388-1406.

de ce que dedeins le moys de **Juyn** darren passe lez diz Thomas et Richard acompaignez a grant nombre de gens debrusoient son park de Crayk quatre foiz et illoeques ils tuerent toute la sauuagine quilz pouount trouuer, et dessoilloient et destrusoient les blez des tenans de Crayk et mandoient par lours messages as parquiers dicel park que s'ilz fuissient si hardyz de venir au park ou passer la ville de Crayk pour eulx defayecyer de lours chaces quilz seroient mors sans nulle mercy auoir.[1]

D. PETITIONS ADDRESSED TO EDMUND DE STAFFORD, BISHOP OF EXETER, 1396–1399, 1401–1403 [2]

17   [3] A tres reuerent pier en Dieux et tres gracious seignur l'Euesque de Excestre, Chaunceller nostre seignur le Roy,

after
1396

Monstre Thomas Seyntquintyn qe come certeynes debatez furent parentre le dit suppliant et vn Roger de Wandesford son tenaunt pur homage le dit Roger par cause de quelle debate le dit Roger ad mys en agayte plusours genz desconuz et de male fame de diuerse partiez coillez et assemblez armez si bien en haberions, palettez, gauntz de fer come plates [4] et diuerse autre armure, c'est assauoire, del fest de Pentacost l'an xix[me] nostre seignur le Roy tanque al fest de Touz Seynts adonque procheyne ensuant, a Harpham en le Counte de Euerwyk, de quelle ville le dit suppliant est seignur; Sur quelle debate par mediacion des amys de l'un partie et d'autre, vn iour d'amour ceo prist pur estre tenuz cy a Westm' al oetas de Seynt Hillare ore procheyne venaunt; puis quelle iour pris, le dit Roger fauxement et disseiuablement encontre la pees nostre seignur le Roy et sa seurte, le lundy procheyne apres le fest de Concepcion nostre Dame darreigne passe, a dit ville deinz la seignurie le dit suppliant, oue Thomas, frer le dit Roger, et plusours autres mesfesours desconuz de diuerse partiez assemblez, arraiez et armez affire de guerre oue lez armurez auauntditz, soy enbusserent pur tuer et merderere le dit suppliant et sez genz deinz sa dit seignurie; par cause de quelle enbussement lez

<hr />

[1] The remainder of this document is so damaged that an intelligible transcript or translation seems impossible. An assault on the park of Durham Castle is mentioned,

when William de Elmedon, the Bishop's sheriff, was driven out and had to take sanctuary in the church.

[2] Appointed Chancellor 23 Nov. 1396;

especially for this, that within the month of June last, the said Thomas and Richard, accompanied by a great number of people, broke his park of Crake four times, and there they killed all the game they could find, and despoiled and destroyed the corn of the tenants of Crake, and commanded them by their messages to the parkers of the park that if they should be so bold as to come to the park or to pass the town of Crake to defeat them of their hunt, they should be killed without mercy.[1]

D. PETITIONS ADDRESSED TO EDMUND DE STAFFORD, BISHOP OF EXETER, 1396–1399; 1401–1403.

17   To the most reverend Father in God and most gracious Lord, the Bishop of Exeter, Chancellor of our Lord the King,

after   Showeth Thomas Saintquintyn that whereas there were certain
1396   disputes between the said suppliant and one Roger de Wandesford, his tenant, respecting the homage of the said Roger, on account of which dispute the said Roger had put in wait many persons, unknown and of ill fame, collected and assembled from divers parts, armed also with habergions, palettes, iron gloves, as well as with plate and divers other armour, to wit, from the feast of Pentecost, 19 [Richard II, 1396], until the feast of All Saints then next following, at Harpham in the county of York, of which town the said suppliant is lord; And as to this dispute, by the mediation of the friends of both parties, a love-day was agreed to be held at Westminster on the octave of S. Hilary now next coming; since which day was agreed upon, the said Roger falsely and deceitfully, against the peace of our lord the King and against his surety, on the Monday next after the feast of the Conception of our Lady last past, did, at the said town within the lordship of the said suppliant, together with Thomas, brother of the said Roger, and many other evil-doers unknown, assembled from divers parts, arrayed and armed as for war with the armour aforesaid, ambush themselves to kill and murder the said suppliant and his people within the said lordship; on account of

his successor appointed Aug. 1399. Re-   [3] Bundle 3, No. 37.
appointed 9 March 1401; his successor   [4] Plate armour seems to be meant.
appointed Feb. 1403.

constables et baillifs de la ville auauntdit de ceo apparceux, vyndront
a dit Roger et Thomas et lez autres desconuz, oue autres seruantz et
tenantz de dit suppliant deinz mesme la ville, pur arester lez ditz
mesfesours pur esteire a la pees nostre seignur le Roy, les ditz Roger
et Thomas, oue lez autres desconuz, nyut voillauntz esteir a lour arest,
mes en lez ditz conestables, baillifs, autres seruantz et tenantz le dit
suppliant, grant assaut firent, et en vn Robert Spynes et Laurence de
Brydlyngton, en eide oue lez ditz constablez venantz, setterent,
batirent, naufrerent et malement treiterent, dont les ditz Robert et
Laurence sent en espoire [1] de lour vie, par quey le dit suppliant pardy
le seruice de sez tenantz et seruantz tanque encea, dont le dit suppliant
prie remedie en saluacion de la pees nostre seignur le Roy, sa corone
et sa dignete, come a la state et greuance de dit suppliant, pur Dieux
et en ouere de charite.[2]

18   [3] A tres honure seignur et tres reuerent
        Piere en Dieu l'erceuesque [4] d'Excestre,
        Chaunceller d'Engleterre,

after Supplie humblement Campyn Pynell', Marchaunt de Luk' en Lum-
1396 bardie, q'est demurant en ceste paijs sur la protexcion nostre tres
redoute seignur le Roy, de ceo qe vn Richard Vnderwode, Taillour de
Loundres, par malice et mal ymaginacion ad feyne diuersez suytes
enuers luy, c'est assauer vn brief de Trespas de sa Femme oue sez
bienz amenez, retornable en le Banke du Roy a Notyngham al xvme
de seint Hillare l'an du Regne nostre seignur le Roy q'or'est xixme,
par quelle brief le dit suppliaunt fuist pris par lez viscountez de
Loundres et fist fyn et raunsoun pur estre maynprise pur garder soun
jour a Notyngham al xvme susdit, a quelle iour le dit Richard fuist
nounsuwy; et puis apres le dit Richard suyst vn autre brief de
trespaas de mesme la matere enuers le dit suppliaunt, Retornable en
le Banke du Roy a Lyncolne al xvme de Paske l'an du regne nostre
seignur le Roi susdit xixme, par quelle le dit suppliant fuist pris et
emprisone par lez viscountez de Loundres qi a celle tempes furent et
mys a fyn et Raunsoun pur estre maynprise pur garder soun iour en
le Banke du Roy susdit; a quelle iour le dit suppliant en propre
persone et le dit Richard en propre persone counterent enuers le dit

---

[1] An evident error for *dcspoir*.
[2] Apparently the local authorities were unable to cope with the violence of the defendants.

which ambushment, the constables and bailiffs of the said town, perceiving it, came to the said Roger and Thomas and the others unknown, with other servants and tenants of the said suppliant within the said town, to arrest the said evil-doers to stand to the peace of our Lord the King; and the said Roger and Thomas, with the others unknown, not wishing to stand to their arrest, made a great assault on the said constables, bailiffs, and other servants and tenants of the said suppliant, and did set upon one Robert Spynes and Laurence of Bridlington, coming to aid the said constables, and did beat, maim and ill-treat them, so that the said Robert and Laurence are in despair of their lives, and therefore the said suppliant hath lost the service of his tenants and servants up to this time; of which the said suppliant prayeth remedy in safeguard of the peace of our Lord the King, his crown and his dignity, as well as the estate and grievance of the said suppliant, for God and in way of charity.[3]

18 To the most honoured Lord and most reve rend Father in God, the Bishop of Exeter, Chancellor of England,[4]

after 1396 Beseecheth humbly Campyn Pynell', Merchant of Lucca in Lombardy, who is staying in this country under the protection of our most dread Lord the King, that whereas one Richard Underwood, tailor of London, by malice and evil design hath feigned divers suits against him, to wit, a writ of trespass in taking away his wife and his goods, returnable in the King's Bench at Nottingham on the quindene of S. Hilary in the 19th year of our Lord the King who now is [1396], for which writ the said suppliant was taken by the Sheriffs of London and put to fine and ransom to be mainprised to keep his day at Nottingham on the said quindene of S. Hilary; on which day the said Richard was nonsuited; and afterwards the said Richard sued another writ of trespass touching the same matter against the said suppliant, returnable in the King's Bench at Lincoln on the quindene of Easter in the 19th year of our said Lord the King [1396], for which the said suppliant was taken and imprisoned by the Sheriffs of London at that time, and put to fine and ransom to be mainprised to keep his day in the said King's Bench; on which day the said suppliant [appeared] in his proper person, and the said Richard counted against the said

---

[3] Bundle 3, No. 38. [4] *Sic.* The previous Chancellor was the Archbishop of York.

suppliaunt de sa Femme oue sez bienz amenez, le quelle surmyse le dit suppliant trauersa, sur qoi issue ioynt entre eux, et le dit suppliant vn venire facias directes as viscountez de Loundres [1] Habeas corpora et prosses par distresse enuers lez Jurours a diuersez iours come outrement est proue par le processe de icelle; et al derrein le dit suppliant suist vn 'Nisi prius' deuaunt Hugh Huls vn dez Justicez del Banke du Roy [2] a certein iour a Seint Martyn en Loundres; a quelle iour le dit Richard fuist nounsuy; et puis encea le dit Richard ad suy diuersez pleyntez deuaunt lez viscountez de Loundres de mesme la matere, Sur quels pleintez le dit suppliaunt ad estre arrestee et emprisonee et mys a fyn et Raunsoun pur soun deliueaunce auoir; et toutfoitz quaunt le dit suppliaunt appiert en Court pur respoundre, le dit Richard est nounsuwy; et ore tard le dit Richard ad feynee deux pleintez enuers le dit suppliaunt lez queux pendent vnqore, Par queux le dit Richard est en purpos par comfort q'il ad de diuersez sez meyntenours de attendre le dit suppliaunt par Jurours procurez et nient indifferentz del matere susdit, C'estassauer de sa Femme oue sez bienz aloignez, par la ou la dite Femme est deuorse de luy par vn precontract, et la deuorse solempnement fait deuaunt lez ordinaries monseignur l'euesque de Loundres: Qe plese de vostre grace especiale sur celle matere de ordiner remedie parissint qe le dit suppliant ne soit mye destruit ne anienti pur touz iours pur issint estre trauaille, emprisone et mys as costagez saunz cause; Pur Dieu et en oeure de charitee.[3]

19   [4] Au tres gracious et tres reuerent piere en Dieu l'Euesque d'Excestre, Chaunceller d' Engleterre, et autres tres sages seignours du Counseil nostre tres redoute seignour le Roy,[5]

after 1396   Supplie Andreu Hokere, Meistre del Hospital de Bek en Byllyngford en le Counte de Norff',[6] qe come vn Johan Cursoun, Chiualer, come filtz et heire Johanne qe fuist la femme William Cursoun son piere,

---

[1] Something omitted. The proceedings are not very clear.

[2] Appointed 1389 (Foss).

[3] The remedy actually sought here, though not in so many words, is an injunction to restrain the vexatious proceedings at com-mon law. From the fact that no particulars are given as to the precise nature of the remedy asked for, it may perhaps be argued that this part of the jurisdiction of the Court of Chancery was at an inchoate stage. The practice was well recognised by the time

suppliant for his wife and his goods taken away, which surmise the said suppliant traversed, whereupon issue was joined between them, and the said suppliant [sued out] a *venire facias* directed to the Sheriffs of London [with clause of] *habeas corpora*, and process by distress against the jurors for divers days, as is clearly proved by the process thereof; and at last the said suppliant sued a *nisi prius* before Hugh Huls, one of the Justices of the King's Bench, on a certain day at S. Martin's in London; on which day the said Richard was non-suited; and afterwards the said Richard hath sued divers plaints before the Sheriffs of London for the same matter, on which plaints the said suppliant hath been arrested and imprisoned and put to fine and ransom for his deliverance; and every time when the said suppliant appeared in Court to answer, the said Richard was non-suited; and now of late the said Richard hath feigned two plaints against the said suppliant, which are still pending, by which the said Richard purposeth by the assistance of divers of his maintainers to await the said suppliant with jurors procured and not indifferent to the said matter, to wit, of his wife and goods taken away, whereas the said wife was divorced from him because of a pre-contract, and the divorce was solemnly pronounced before the Ordinaries of my Lord the Bishop of London: May it please you of your especial grace of this matter to ordain a remedy, so that the said suppliant be not destroyed and annihilated for ever by so being annoyed, imprisoned and put to costs without any cause; for God and in way of charity.[3]

19 To the most gracious and most reverend Father in God, the Bishop of Exeter, Chancellor of England, and to the other most wise Lords of the Council of our most redoubted Lord the King,

after 1396 Beseecheth Andrew Hokere, Master of the Hospital of Beck in Billingford in the County of Norfolk, that whereas one John Cursoun, knight, as son and heir of Joan who was the wife of William Cursoun,

of Henry VI. See Spence's *Equitable Jurisdiction*, i. 674.
[4] Bundle 3, No. 88.
[5] This form of address is very interesting, as recognising the fact that the Council collectively were the judges, not the Chancellor.

[6] The hospital of St. Thomas the Martyr at Billingford, near East Dereham, founded *t.* Hen. III. by William de Bec for the accommodation of poor travellers. See Blomefield's *Norfolk*, iv. 365.

suyst vn brief de post disseisine vers le dit Andreu en le dit Counte
supposant q'il auoit le dit Johan disseisi apres vn recouerir taille pur
le dit Johan enuers le dit suppliant de deux mees, cent acres de terre,
dys acres de pree et vynt acres de pasture, oue les appurtenantz en
Billyngford, Byntre, Wodenorton, Hoo, Geyst, Sparham, Gestweyt,
Folsham, Wychengham beate Marie et Belagh iuxta Byntre, la ou le
dit Andreu vnqes puis le dit recouerir n'entra pas ; le quel brief fuist
direct a Thomas Cursoun, viscount du dit Counte, vncle au dit Johan,
le quel viscount pris oue luy Johan Mundeford, l'un des coroners du
dit Counte, Thomas Halle, l'autre des coroners del Countee auauntdit
nient present, la ou il duist auoir pris oue luy ambedeux les coroners ;
prist vn enquest par le quel issint pris par le dit viscount en presence
du dit Johan Mundeford l'un des coroners, troue fuist qe le dit Andreu
auoit disseisi le dit Johan Cursoun de les mees, terre, pree et pasture
auantditz, as damages du dit Johan Cursoun de xxij liures, les queux
par le dit viscount fueront agardez a la double, c'estassauoir a xliiij
liures ; par vertue du quel enquest issint erronyousement pris adiuge
fuist par le dit viscount qe le dit Johan Cursoun serreit reseisi en les
ditz mees, terre, pree et pasture auauntditz et q'il recouereit les xliiij
liures auauntditz pur ses damages et qe le dit Andreu serreit pris ;
Par force du quele Jugement certeins bienz et chateux du dit Andreu,
c'estassauoir viij^{xx} quarters de brase et plusours ses autres chatelx,
fuiront liuerez au dit Johan Cursoun et mys en execucion pur les
damages auauntditz ; Sour quei le dit Andreu, apparceiuant tiel
erreur en le dit record et processe, pursuya vn brief d'errour retornable deuaunt nostre seignur le Roy en les oeptaues de Seint Martyn
l'an de son reigne xx^e,[1] par vertue du quel brief le dit viscount del
assent et couyne du dit Johan Cursoun, Chiualer, et William Cursoun,
south viscount du dit Thomas, en deceyt du dit suppliant, maunda
vn record de dite post disseisine deuaunt nostre dit seignur le Roy,
certifiant qe l'enqueste fuist pris deuaunt luy et ambedeux les coroners,
e'est assauoir, Johan Mundeford et Thomas Halle, encountre quel
record, issint par le dit viscount del assent et couyne des ditz Johan
Cursoun et William Cursoun certifie et retourne, le dit Andreu ne poet
mye auoir trauers ne recouerir si remedie par vous ent ne soit ordeigne
sur le dit retourne, issint en desceyt de le dit Andreu fait, as damages
de l'auauntdit Andreu de CC. liures ; l'absence de quel Thomas Halle
l'un des ditz coroners al temps del prendre du dit enquest par vertue
de dit brief de post disseisine le dit Andreu est prest de prouer et

[1] 1396.

his father, sued a writ of *post disseisin* against the said Andrew in the said County, supposing that he had disseised the said John after a recovery brought by the said John against the said suppliant of two messuages, 100 acres of land, 10 acres of meadow and 20 acres of pasture with the appurtenances in Billingford, Bintre, Wood Norton, Hoo, Guist, Sparham, Guestwick [?], Foulsham, Great Witchingham, and Belaugh near Bintre, whereas the said Andrew never entered after the said recovery, which writ was directed to Thomas Cursoun, Sheriff of the said County and uncle of the said John, and the Sheriff took with him John Mundeford, one of the Coroners of the said County, Thomas Halle the other Coroner not being present, whereas he should have taken with him both the Coroners; and he [the Sheriff] took an inquest, by which, being taken by the said Sheriff in the presence of the said John Mundeford, one of the Coroners, it was found that the said Andrew had disseised the said John Cursoun of the messuages, land, meadow and pasture aforesaid, to the damage of the said John Cursoun of £22, which were awarded by the said Sheriff as double, to wit, at £44; and by virtue of this inquest, thus wrongly taken, it was adjudged by the said Sheriff that the said John Cursoun should be reseised of the said messuages, land, meadow and pasture aforesaid, and that he should recover the said £44 as his damages, and that the said Andrew should be arrested; By force of which judgment, certain goods and chattels of the said Andrew, to wit, eight score quarters of malt and many other chattels, were delivered to the said John Cursoun, and put in execution for the said damages; Whereupon the said Andrew, perceiving such error in the said record and process, sued a writ of error returnable before our Lord the King on the octave of Martinmas in the 20th year of his reign [1396], by virtue of which writ the said Sheriff with the assent and covin of the said John Cursoun, knight, and William Cursoun, Under-Sheriff to the said Thomas, in deceit of the said suppliant, sent a record of the said *post disseisin* before our Lord the King, certifying that the inquest was taken before him and both the Coroners, to wit, John Mundeford and Thomas Halle; against which record so certified and returned by the said Sheriff with the consent and covin of the said John Cursoun and William Cursoun, the said Andrew cannot have traverse or recovery, if remedy thereof be not by you ordained on the said return so made in deceit of the said Andrew and to his damages of £200; And the said Andrew is ready to prove and aver the absence of the said Thomas Halle, one of the said Coroners, at the time the said inquest was taken by the said writ of *post disseisin*, in

auerrir solonc ceo qe la Court agarde : Sur quoy plese a voz tres sages discrecions d'enuoier sibien pur le dit Thomas Cursoun viscount come pur les ambedeux coroners auauntditz, et auxint pur les ditz Johan Cursoun et William Cursoun, et eux examiner de la veritee de ceste matiere, et ent faire droyt au dit Andreu solonc ceo qe ley et reson demaundont ; pur Dieu et en oeuere de charitee.[1]

Thomas Derham } de Comitatu Norff', manucáptores predicti
Thomas Grace } Andree iuxta formam statuti, etc.[2]

20   [3] A tres gracious et tres reuerent piere
            en Dieu l'Euesque d'Excestre, Chaunceller
            d'Engleterre,

after Supplie humblement son poure oratour Thomas Raulyn, parsone del
1396   Eglise de Seynt Just en Rosland en le Counte de Cornewayle ;[4] Qe
       Pleise a vostre tres gracious seignurie d'oier et entender certeyns greuances et extorcions [faitz a] dit Thomas par Aleyn Bugules, Michel Jakke Johan [sic] et Richard Robyn, parochiens a dit parsone, et d'ent ordinere remedie, pur dieu et en oeuere de charite.

En primes l'ou la coustume du dite paroche d'auncien temps use est qe quant ascune home ou femme deins la dite paroche murera, le parsone ad ancra la meliour garnement de celly qi issint murera par noun de mortuarie, la muroust vne femme appelle Desyra qi fuist la femme a vn Jakke Johan deins la dite parochie, et le melliour garnement q'elle auoit, e'est assauer, vn sourcote de rouge pris de vj s. viij d. partenoit al parsone par le coustume suisdit, fuist carie sur le corps al esglise de Seint Just suisdit, la vint le dit Aleyn oue force et armes, c'est assaver, baston et cotelle, deyns le cymyter de dite esgle, et le garnement issint sur le dit corps esteant, le samady prochein apres la fest del assumpcion nostre dame, l'an nostre seignur le Roy q'or'est xx[me],[5] countre la volunte du dite parsone, prist et emporta.

Item la ou vne Johane, miere au dit Richard, parochiene de dit paroche, morust illoeques, paront soun meillour garnement duisse partenir al dit parsone, le dit Richard voilleit auer deliuere au dit parsone vne cote de verde pris vj s. viij d., qe fuist le meillour garne-

<hr>

[1] The inability to obtain any remedy at common law seems to be the ground for appeal to the Chancellor, though something very like fraud is imputed to the defendants.

[2] Spence (i. 345) says that the statute of 15 Hen. VI. c. 4 was the first Act of Parliament relating to sureties, but he adds 'sureties had been, in fact, required in the reign of Richard II.' If this statement is

any way that the Court shall award: Wherefore may it please your most wise discretions to send for the said two Coroners as well as for the said Thomas Cursoun, the Sheriff, and also for the said John Cursoun and William Cursoun, and to examine them touching the truth of this matter, and therein to do .right to the said Andrew as law and right demand; For God and in way of charity.[1]

THOMAS DERHAM and THOMAS GRACE of Norfolk, mainpernors for the said Andrew according to the form of the statute.[2]

20   To the most gracious and most reverend Father in God, the Bishop of Exeter, Chancellor of England,

after 1396 Humbly beseecheth your poor orator, Thomas Raulyn, parson of the church of S. Just in Roseland in the County of Cornwall;[4] May it please your most gracious Lordship to hear and understand certain grievances and extortions done to the said Thomas by Alan Bugules, Michael Jakke-John and Richard Robyn, parishioners of the said parson, and to ordain remedy thereof, for God and in way of charity.

First, whereas the custom of the parish, used of ancient time, is that when any man or woman within the said parish dieth, the parson shall have the best garment of the person so dying in the name of a mortuary, and there died a woman called Desyra, widow of one Jakke-John, within the said parish, and the best garment she had, to wit, a red surcoat worth 6s. 8d., belonged to the parson by the custom aforesaid; this was carried over the body to the church of S. Just aforesaid, when there came the said Alan with force and arms, to wit, with club and knife, within the churchyard of the said church, and took and carried away the garment, so [laid] over the said body, against the will of the said parson, it being the Saturday after the feast of the Assumption of our Lady in the 20th year of our Lord the King who now is [1396].

Also, where one Joan, mother of the said Richard and a parishioner of the said parish, died there, by which her best garment ought to belong to the said parson, and the said Richard would have delivered to the said parson a green coat worth 6s. 8d., which was

correct, the *statutum* mentioned in the text must have been simply an ordinance of the Council.

[2] Bundle 3, No. 107. This document is torn in places round the edge, and has several holes in it.

[4] In the hundred of Powder, near Falmouth.   [5] 20 Richard II., 1396.

ment q'ele auoit, la vint le dit Aleyn et manecea et comaunda le dit
Richard q'il ne deliuereit le dit cote al dit parsone en nul manere, et
qe s'il le ferreit q'il debrusereit soun test; par quel manauce le dit
Richard ne deliuera le dit cote al dit parsone eins le detynt et vnqore
deteynt, etc.

Item l'ou le dit Jakke Johan, pere le dit Michel, parochien del
dite paroche, morust illoeqes et le custume de dite paroche de tout
temps vse est tiel qe de chescum home ou femme mouriaunt deins le
dite paroche q'ad bestez, le parsone qi pur le temps serra auera le
seconde meillour best, et le dit Johan auoit bestes, issint qe al dit
parsone deuoit d'auer en cel partie vn Juuencle[1] pris vj s. viij d., le
quel Juuencle le dit Aleyn prist et amesna contre la voluntee le dit
parsone a soun hostiel tanqe a Bugules.

Item lez ditz Michel come executour a dit Jakke Johan soun piere
et Richard feurent citez, par force d'une maundement issue del
Official l'erchedekene de Cornewaille al instance le dit parsoun, de
comparer deuaunt le dit Official a certein iour, etc, pur la detenue de
lez garnementz suisditz; a quel iour et lieu ils confesseront tout le
custume suisdit et q'ils detyndront lez ditz garnementz contre le dit
custume, par qoy ils feurent comaundez et monestez et iurez par le
dit Official a deliuerer lez ditz garnementz au dit parsone a cause de
lour dit confession, sour peyn d'escomongement, et puis certeyns iours
apres la dit monycioun, et s'ils ne ferroient q'ils serroient denunciez
escomongez; et sour ceo issist vn monicion al Curatour de dit paroche
a eux denuncier escomongez s'ils ne ferroient come dessuis est dit;
lez queux Michel et Richard voillient auer deliuere au dit parsone lez
ditz garnementz pur doute de dit escomongement, la vint le dit Aleyn
et comaunda et manacea lez ditz Michel et Richard q'ils ne deliuerent
lez ditz garnementz.   sour peyn de leur vie, par quel manace et
pur doute du dit Aleyn, lez ditz Michel et Richard ne deliuerent [lez]
suys ditz garnementz solonc la monicion auauntdit, par qei lez ditz
Michel et Richard feurent [denunciez] escomongez par le dit Curatour
le dymenge proschein apres le fest de toutz seintz l'an nostre seignur
le Roi q'ore est .   . escomongez demourauntz vindront al dit esglise
le dismenge proschein deuaunt Nowel adonqe proschein ensuant
eux veiaunt illoeqes eux monesta et comaunda d'aler hors del dite
esglise issint q'il purroit aler a sez diuinez seruisez, [lez] queux
Michel et Richard ceo fair refuserent et deins la dite esglise lour

---

[1] From the Latin *juvenculus*, a diminutive of *juvencus*, a bullock or steer.

the best garment she had, there came the said Alan and menaced the said Richard, and ordered him in no wise to deliver the said coat to the said parson ; and [saying] that if he did, he would break his head ; through which menace the said Richard did not deliver the said coat to the said parson, but detained it, and still detaineth it, etc.

Also, where the said Jakke-John, father of the said Michael and a parishioner of the said parish, died there, and the custom of the said parish, used of all time, is such that the parson for the time being shall have the second best beast of every man or woman dying within the parish and having beasts, and the said John had beasts, so that the said parson ought to have in this behalf a young steer worth 6s. 8d., which steer the said Alan took and carried off to his house at Bugules, against the will of the said parson.

Also, the said Michael, as executor to the said Jakke-John his father, and [the said Richard] were cited, by force of an order issued by the official of the Archdeacon of Cornwall at the instance of the said parson, to appear before the said official on a certain day, etc., [to answer] for the detention of the said garments ; at which day and place they confessed all the custom aforesaid and that they had detained the said garments contrary to the custom, wherefore they were ordered, monished and sworn by the said official to deliver the said garments to the said parson, because of their said confession, on pain of excommunication, within certain days after the monition, and if they did not do so, they should be pronounced excommunicate ; and thereupon he issued a monition to the curate of the said parish [directing him] to pronounce them excommunicate if they did not do as above said ; The which Michael and Richard would have delivered the said garments to the said parson for fear of the said excommunication, but there came the said Alan, and ordered and threatened the said Michael and Richard not to deliver the said garments . . . on pain of their lives ; through which threat, and for fear of the said Alan, the said Michael and Richard did not deliver the said garments according to the monition aforesaid, wherefore they were pronounced excommunicate by the said curate on the Sunday after the feast of All Saints in the . . . year of the reign of our Lord the King who now is ; [and the said Michael and Richard], remaining excommunicated, came to the said church on the Sunday before Christmas then next following, [and the said Thomas,] seeing them there, monished and commanded them to go out of the said church so that he might go on with divine service, and Michael and Richard refused to do this, but kept them-

E

tyndront par confort et mayntenance de dit Aleyn, en destourbance
dez diuines seruises, paront lez parochiens aleront a l'ostel saunz
messe a cel iour, par lour destourbance, a graund damage del dit
parsone et dissese de touz lez parochiens auaunt ditz.

Item, en le fest de Nowel adonqe proschein ensuant, le dit Aleyn
vint al dite esglise oue force et armez, c'est assauoir, hastons et cotelx,
et lez ditz Michel et Richard auxint esteauntz escomongez come
deuaunt est dit, et le dit Curatour eux monesta hors de dit esglise,
issint q'il ne purroit celebrer le primer messe, come le maner est cel
iour ce faire, ne voleient, mes en l'esglise lour tyndront par tout le
iour tanqe le hore de Midy, paront le primer messe et le seconde ne
feurent celebrez, et lez parochiens feurent alez a l'ostel saunz lour
diuinez seruices, et le parson pardy ses offrendez de cel iour ; a quele
houre de Midy le dit [Curatour] quant lez ditz escomongez veiauntz
toutz lez parochiens estre aler receceront celebra vne messe, etc. ; et
mesme le iour le dit Aleyn manacea le dit parsone de luy tuer deuaunt
toutz le ditz parochiens, issint qe le dit parsoun a peyn eschapa hors
de dit esglise tanqe a soun meyson en mesme la ville, et illoeqes luy
tynt par tout le iour pur doute du dit Aleyn.

Item en mesme la manere destourberount lez ditz Aleyn, Michel et
Richard pur lour demouraunt en l'esglise lez ditz parochiens de lour
diuinez seruicez le iour de Epiphanie adonqe proscheyn ensuaunt, et le dit Aleyn a cele iour voilleit auer chace le parsoun hors
de soun chauncelle par lez fenestrez, luy disaunt q'il ne passereit hors
par le corps de l'esglise pur ce qe ce fuist a lez parochiens et nemy
a luy, paront le dit parsoun fuist tres lee d'eschaper secretement
tancome autres de la paroche treteront oue le dit Aleyn.

Item le dit Aleyn oue force et armez, e'est assauoir, especs et
bokelers, lundy proschein deuaunt le fest de Nowel, l'an du nostre
seignur le Roi q'ore est xxj, en la ville de Seynt Maudit en William
Tabyn assaut fist et luy batist, paront le dit parsone pardy le seruice
de soun dit seruaunt par long temps, et auxint la ou le dit parsoun
auoit amesne al [official] del dit Archedekne al ville de Truru,
Henry Helier, Johan Fourneys et William Coreder, parochiens de dit
paroche, pur tesmoigner et proeuer la custume suisdite touchant lez
garnementz auauntditz, la vint le dit Aleyn et eux manacea qe s'ils
tesmoignereuent rien oue le dit parsoun q'ils serreient mortez, paront
lez ditz tesmoignes n'oserent tesmoigner la verite pur le parsone
touchaunt la matere suisdite, etc.[1]

---

[1] The Chancellor's interference is asked for because of the defendants' violence, which
prevented a remedy at common law.

selves in the said church through the comfort and maintenance of the said Alan, to the disturbance of divine service, through which the parishioners went home without mass that day because of their disturbance, to the great damage of the said parson and to the incommodity of all the parishioners aforesaid.

Also, in the feast of Christmas then next following, the said Alan came to the said church with force and arms, to wit, clubs and knives, and the said Michael and Richard also, being excommunicated as aforesaid, and the said curate warned them out of the said church, so that he could celebrate the first mass, as the manner is this day to do; they would not [go], but kept themselves in the church all day until the hour of noon, through which the first mass and the second were not celebrated, and the parishioners went home without their divine service, and the parson lost his offerings that day; at which hour of noon, when the said excommunicates, seeing that all the parishioners had gone, went away, the said [parson] celebrated a mass, etc.; and the same day, the said Alan threatened to kill the said parson before all the said parishioners, so that the said parson scarce escaped out of the church to his own house in the same town, and there he kept himself the whole day for fear of the said Alan.

Also, in the same manner the said Alan, Michael and Richard disturbed the parishioners at divine service by remaining in the church on the day of the Epiphany then next following, and on that day the said Alan would have chased the parson out of his chancel by the windows, saying to him, that he should not pass out by the body of the church because that belonged to the parishioners and not to him; wherefore the said parson was very glad to escape secretly while others of the parish treated with the said Alan.

Also, the said Alan with force and arms, to wit, swords and bucklers, on the Monday before the feast of Christmas in the 21st year of the reign of our Lord the King who now is [1397], in the town of S. Maudit, assaulted William Tabyn and beat him, whereby the said parson lost the service of his said servant for a long time; and also when the said parson had brought to the official of the said Archdeacon to the town of Truro, Henry Helier, John Fourneys and William Coreder, parishioners of the said parish, to testify to and prove the said custom touching the garments aforesaid, the said Alan came and threatened them that if they gave evidence of anything with the said parson, they should be killed, whereby the said witnesses dared not testify the truth for the parson touching the matter aforesaid, etc.

21   [1] A tres honure et tres gracious seignur piere en Dieu, l'Euesque d'Excestre et Chaunceler d'Engleterre,

1397 Supplie vmblement Symon Brit del Counte de Somer', qe come il estoit en pesible possession del deux partiez de Manoir de Hwyss-chamflour et de l'auouesoun del esglise de mesme la ville en dit Counte tanqe vne Alice Colne porte vne assise de nouel disseisin deuers le dit Symon ; et pendant la dite assise la dite Alice entra en la dite Manoire par mayntenaunce et conseille de moun sire Hugh Courtenay, Chivaler ; et apres la dite Alice fit feffement de dit Manoire al dit moun sire Hugh, et ceo pendant la dite assise ; a graunt damage et nyntesement de dit Symon; et le dit Symon n'osa pursuer la comen ley enuers le dit moun sire Hugh : Please a vostre grace especial de graunter vn brief direct a moun dit sire Hugh de luy comander d'estre deuaunt le conseille [2] nostre seignur le Roy a certeyn iour sour vn certein payne, pur Dieu et houre de charitee, ou altrement le dit Symon est anienti et destruit a toutz iours.

[3] Writ directed to Hugh de Courtenay commanding his appearance *coram nobis in Cancellaria nostra* on February 13th then next, *sub pena ducentarum librarum.* Dated at Westminster, January 30th, 20 Richard II, 1397.

Indorsed. Ad quem diem infrascriptus Hugo in Cancellaria infrascripta comparuit, et predictus Simon Brit solempniter vocatus non venit, per quod consideratum est quod predictus Hugo recedat quietus de Curia.

22   [4] A tres reuerende piere en Dieu, moun tres honure et tres gracious seignur, le Chauncellier d'Engleterre,

1397 Supplie humblent Reynold Bernewell, qe come il mesmes nadgairs pursuist a vostre tres gracious seignurie par bille reherceant coment il y auoyt vne debate trois ans passez parentre luy et vn Johan Glam de Rykemershworth, qe la vn Thomas Barton, Mareschall del Mareschalsye de Hostiel nostre seignur le Roy, vst empris la dit querelle

---

[1] Bundle 3, No. 65.
[2] See p. 7, note 4.
[3] Bundle 3, No. 64; similar to No. 11, with some slight verbal differences.

21   To the most honoured and most gracious Lord and Father in God, the Bishop of Exeter and Chancellor of England,

1397 Humbly beseecheth Simon Brit, of the County of Somerset, that whereas he was in peaceable possession of two parts [thirds] of the manor of Huish-Champflower and the advowson of the church of the same town in the said County until one Alice Colne brought an assize of *novel disseisin* against the said Simon; and, pending the assize, the said Alice entered upon the said manor by the maintenance and counsel of Sir Hugh Courtenay, knight, and afterwards Alice made feoffment of the said manor to Sir Hugh, and this pending the assize; to the great damage and impoverishment of the said Simon; and Simon dare not sue at common law against Sir Hugh : May it please you of your especial grace to grant a writ directed to the said Sir Hugh, commanding him to be before the Council [2] of our Lord the King at a certain day and under a certain pain; for God and in way of charity; or otherwise the said Simon is impoverished and destroyed for ever.

   Indorsed. At which day the within written Hugh appeared in the Chancery, and the said Simon Brit, although solemnly called, did not come; wherefore it was considered that the said Hugh should go quit of the Court.

22   To the most reverend Father in God, my most honoured and most gracious Lord, the Chancellor of England,

1397 Humbly beseecheth Reginald Bernewell, that whereas he lately sued to your most gracious Lordship by bill, reciting how there had been a dispute for three years past between himself and one John Glam of Rickmansworth, and that one Thomas Barton, Marshall of the Marshalsea of the Household of our Lord the King, had taken up the

[1] Bundle 3, No. 98.

depar le dit Johan en mayntenance deuers le dit Raynald, par force
et colour de soun office ; et la dit querelle mayntena par vn an et plus,
taunque le dit Raynald soy mist en la grace de dit Thomas, et luy
appresta xij liures d'argent pur y estre eydaunt a luy sibien en ycelle
cas come en autres ;[1] et a cause de quele aprest le dit Thomas de-
uyent del counseil le dit suppliant, et ceo continua tanque ore tarde qe
le dit suppliant demaunda de luy lez ditz xij liures ; a cause de quel
demaunde le dit Thomas exita et procura vn Henry Langeley de pursuer et mouer enuers le dit suppliant diuersez querellez en la Court
del dit Mareschalsye ou le dit Thomas est Mareschall ; quex querellez
le dit Thomas emprist en sustinance et mayntenance par colour de soun
dit office, et fist retourner certeyns gentz en enquest entre le dit Henry
et le dit suppliant fauorablement a sa entent pur passer pur le dit
Henry ; et puis quant illz fuerent pristez a passer le dit Thomas fist
le dit Henry estre nounsuy, ymaginant par tiel voy a destruer le dit suppliant a touz iourz : sur quel bille issint suy a vostre tres gracious
seignurie, pur ceo qe tiel mayntenaunce par diuersez estatutz[2] est
inhibite et ouste, grauntastis vn brief direct al dit Thomas luy com-
aundant q'il ne mayntindreit nulle querelle parentre lez ditz partiez ne
nullz autrez en la dit Court sur peyn es ditz estatutz continuz ; le quel
brief y feust deliuere al dit Thomas, et puis le dit Thomas, eyaunt
graund indignacion et despite del pursute du dit brief, y diseyt apparte-
ment en presence de plusours gentz en la esglise de Rykemershworth,
q'il auoit maynteigne et susteigne les ditz querellez entre lez ditz partiez
et les maintendroit au fyn pur despendre tout ceo q'il auoyt maugre qi le
voudroit countredire non obstant le dit brief, et outre ceo manasa
sibien le dit suppliant come vn Roger Lynster, clerc du Chauncellerie
nostre seignur le Roy, q'estoyt de Counseille[3] de dit suppliant, de vie
et de membre pur le pursieut de dit brief ; et en pursuant son dit
malice acomplier, le Desmenge darreyn passe, en vn haut chemyn q'est
parenter Rykemershworth et la measoun de William Paytevyn, le dit
Thomas apparceyuant la venue le dit Roger adonque illoque y gisoyt
en agait arme a fure de guerre oue trois hommez ouesque luy, et en
le dit Roger illouque donque assaut firrent et luy bateront, naufrerent,
et malment treterent ensy qe luy lesserent giser pur mort, endisant qe
le dit suppliant y serroit encountre deuant sa venu al hostielle q'il ne

---

[1] The plaintiff seems quite ready to
accept the services of the defendant ; it
rather suggests that the maintenance complained of was merely professional assistance.

[2] Stat. 1 Ric. II. cap. 4.

said quarrel on behalf of the said John in maintenance against the said Reginald, by force and colour of his office, and had maintained the said quarrel for a year and more, until the said Reginald put himself in the grace of the said Thomas and paid him £12 in money to be helpful to him [Reginald], as well in this case as in others, and through this payment the said Thomas became of counsel with the said suppliant, and so continued until of late that the said suppliant demanded of him the said £12 ; on account of which demand the said Thomas incited and procured one Henry Langeley to sue and move divers quarrels against the said suppliant in the Court of the said Marshalsea, where the said Thomas is Marshal ; which quarrels the said Thomas took up in sustenance and maintenance, by colour of his said office, and caused to be returned on an inquest [4] between Henry and the said suppliant certain persons favourable to his intent to give a verdict for the said Henry ; and afterwards when they were ready to give their verdict, the said Thomas caused the said Henry to be non-suited, imagining in this way to destroy the said suppliant for ever : on which bill so sued to your most gracious Lordship, because such maintenance is prohibited and forbidden by divers statutes, [your Lordship] granted a writ directed to Thomas, commanding him that he should not maintain any quarrel between the parties or any others in the said Court on the pain contained in the said statutes ; which writ was delivered to Thomas, who, having great indignation and spite for the suing of the said writ, said openly in the presence of many people in the church at Rickmansworth, that he had maintained and sustained the quarrels between the parties, and he would maintain them to the end if he spent all that he had, in spite of any one who should gainsay it, and notwithstanding the said writ; and moreover he threatened as well the said suppliant as one Roger Lynster, Clerk of the Chancery of our Lord the King, who was of counsel [3] with the said suppliant, of life and limb, for the suing of the said writ ; and in seeking to accomplish his malice on Sunday last, on the high road between Rickmansworth and the house of William Paytevyn, the said Thomas, perceiving Roger to approach, did then and there lie in wait, armed in manner of war, and three men with him, and did then and there assault the said Roger, and did beat, wound and ill-treat him, so that they left him lying for dead, saying that the said suppliant should be encountered before coming to his house so that he never

---

[3] This is interesting as showing that the clerks of the Chancery acted as counsel. The defendant, Marshall of the Marshalsea of the Household, also acted in that capacity.

[4] I.e. to serve on the jury.

vendret iames a soun hostielle; et tout pur le pursieut du dit brief :
Que plese a vostre tres gracious seignurie considerer touz lez maters
auantditz et sur ceo grauntier vn brief par vertu de quel le dit Thomas
poet estre areste et amesne deuant vous pur respondre sibien a nostre
seignur le Roy du contempt come al dit suppliant dez tortz et
greuauncez suisditz, et pur trouer suffisaunt seurte de pees as ditz
suppliant, Roger, et tous altres liegez nostre dit seignur le Roy ; Pur
Dieu et en oeuere de charite.[1]

   [2] Writ dated at Westminster, March 23rd, 20 Richard II [1397],
and addressed to Thomas Barton of Rykemeresworth, ordering his
appearance *coram nobis in Cancellaria nostra die Martis proximo
futuro.*

23   [3] A son tres honure et tres gracious seignur,
            le Chanceller d'Engleterre

1397 Monstre vostre pouere seruant, William Lonesdale de Scardeburgh,
Merchant, qe l'ou le dit William ad mesne diuerses foitz par le meer
et par terre diuerses merchandises, c'est assauoir, haranc, sore et
blank,[4] et autres pessons et vitailles, del port de Scardeburgh en le
Counte d'Euerwyke tanque a la ville de Yakesle en le Counte de Hunt',
a uendre illoesqes, come luy bien list, a grande releuement de toute
la pais environ la dite ville de Yakesle ; et a cause qe le dit William
venda ses ditz merchandises a meindre pris come autres merchantz de dite ville de Yakesle fesoient la, Richard Suffyn, Thomas
Clement et William Childe de Yarwell, et plusours autres mesfaisours
de lour coueine gisoient en agait oue force et armes pur tuer le
dit William Lonesdale, et la luy naufreront, bateront et malement luy
treteront, et luy rem[i]steront illoesqes come mort, issint qe le dit
William Lonesdale feust en despoir de sa vie : Qe pleise a vostre tres
graciouse seignurie d'envoier pur les ditz parties par briefs nostre
seignur le Roi, pur respondre en sa Chancellerie pur y respondre
sibien des ditz mesfaitz comes des autres choses qe a eux lors serront
surmys; pur Dieux et en oeuere de charitee.[5]

   [6] Writ dated at Westminster, May 20th, 20 Richard II [1397], and
directed to Richard Suffyn of Yakesle and Thomas Clement of
Yakesle, ordering their appearance *coram nobis et consilio nostro in
Cancellaria nostra in Crastino ascensionis domini proximo futuro.*

   [1] The contempt of court in disobeying   be the chief ground of complaint here.
and slighting the previous writ seems to   [2] Bundle 3, No. 97. The writ is similar

should get to his house; and all this because of the suing of the
said writ: May it please your most gracious Lordship to consider
all the matters aforesaid, and thereupon to grant a writ by virtue of
which the said Thomas may be arrested and brought before you, to
answer as well to our Lord the King for the contempt, as to the said
suppliant for the said torts and grievances, and to find sufficient
surety for the peace towards the said suppliant, the said Roger
[Lynster], and all other lieges of our Lord the King; For God and in
way of charity.[1]

23   To his most honoured and most gracious
Lord, the Chancellor of England,

1397 Showeth your poor servant, William Lonesdale of Scarborough, merchant, that whereas the said William hath divers times by sea and by
land brought divers merchandise, to wit, herring, kippered and salted,[4]
and other fish and victuals from the port of Scarborough in the County
of York to the town of Yaxley in the County of Huntingdon, to sell
them there, as well he might, to the great relief of all the country
round the said town of Yaxley; and because he sold his merchandise
at a less price than other merchants of the said town of Yaxley did
there, Richard Suffyn, Thomas Clement and William Childe of Yarwell,
and many other evil-doers, of their covin, lay in wait with force and
arms to kill the said William Lonesdale, and they assaulted him, beat
him and ill-treated him, and left him there for dead, so that he
despaired of his life: May it please your most gracious Lordship to
send for the said parties by writs of our Lord the King, to answer
in his Chancery, as well for the said misdeeds as for other things which
then shall be alleged against them; For God and in way of charity.[5]

---

in form to No. 2, with some slight verbal
differences.

   [3] Bundle 3, No. 96.

   [4] 'White fish,' according to Halliwell,
sometimes means fresh fish, and sometimes

salted fish; here it evidently means the
latter.

   [5] This seems hardly a Chancery matter.

   [6] Bundle 3, No. 95. Similar to No. 2,
with some slight verbal differences.

24 [1] A Chaunceller nostre seignur le Roi,

1397 Supplie humblement Sibille qe feust la femme Robert Dercy, Chiualer, qe come Johan de Skipwyth eit purchace diuerses terres et tenementz en la ville de Manby en les queux la dite Sibille ad sa dower assigne a la value de qatre marcz et demy par an et la myst a ferme a certeins gentz, le dit Johan par malice ne vorroit soeffrer les ditz fermours prender [2] les rentes et profites ent issantz et provenantz, mes les manassa de batre et tuer s'ils ne la susrendrent; et sur ceo les ditz fermours lesseront la dite ferme, et puis celle temps le dit Johan ad retenuz les profitz du dite dower par oept ans et plus, et vnquore retient en ses mayns propres par maistre ent ascun au rien ou poy a sa volunte rendant. Et auxi la ou la dite Sibille deuoroit auoir dower en les villes de Petit Carleton et Catdale de droit de son Baron, vnqes n'oisea ne vnquore ose demaunder ne pursuer pur la dite dower pur doute de dit Johan, mes il prist et long temps ad pris les profitz ent prouenantz, rien a ele rendant pur ycelle, a grant damage et anientissement de dite Sibille. Sur queles greuantz et plusours autres el vorroit auoir pursue a Nicol en le Bank nostre seignur le Roy et ne purroit trouer ascun homme qe oisaist estre ouesque lui pur doute et malice du dit Johan. Issy qe ele ne purra auoir droit ne recouere a commun ley si ele ne soit especialment remediez et eidez celle partie: Qe pleise a vostre tres gracious seignurie considerer les greuances auauntditz et ent ordener vostre gracious remedie, pur Dieu et en eoure de charitee, (par oier et determiner ou par special enqysicion).[3]

Indorsed. Inquisicio capta apud Lincoln' die Jouis proximo post festum Sancti Petri quod dicitur aduincula anno regni regis Ricardi secundi post conquestum Anglie vicesimo primo [4] coram Willelmo Thirnyng et Willelmo Waldeby, Justiciariis ad assisas in codem Com' capiendas assignatis virtute brevis domini Regis eisdem Justiciariis directi et huic inquisicioni consuti ad inquirendum de Johanne Skypwyth pro transgressione infra billa contenta, per sacramentum Willelmi Leueryke [etc.], Qui dicunt et presentant quod predictus Johannes Skypwyth die lune proximo post festum Sancti Michaelis

---

[1] Bundle 3, No. 55. This bill and the following, up to and including No. 30, form a series of complaints against the same defendant, John de Skipwith. The writ, No. 30, relates to all six bills. The allegations of violence and inability to obtain adequate remedy at common law are typical of the Star Chamber, as is also the

24   To the Chancellor of our Lord the King,

1397 Humbly beseecheth Sibil, widow of Robert Darcy, knight, that whereas John de Skipwith had purchased divers lands and tenements in the town of Manby, in which the said Sibil hath her dower assigned to the value of four marks and a half yearly, and which are let to farm to certain persons, the said John of malice would not suffer the said farmers to render the rents and profits issuing and forthcoming there- from, but threatened to beat and kill them if they did not surrender it [the land]; and thereupon the said farmers left the said farm, and since that time the said John hath retained the profits of the said dower for eight years and more, and still retaineth in his own hands something for the management thereof, and giveth her little or nothing, at his own pleasure. And also whereas the said Sibil ought to have dower in the towns of Little Carlton and Catdale in right of her hus- band, she did not dare and dare not now demand or sue for the said dower for fear of the said John, for he taketh and for a long time hath taken the profits forthcoming thereof, yielding nothing to her for it, to the great damage and impoverishment of the said Sibil. For which grievances and many others she would have sued at Lincoln in the Bench of our Lord the King, but could not find any one who dared to be [of counsel] with her for fear of the malice of the said John. So that she can have no right nor recovery at common law, if she be not specially righted and aided in this behalf: May it please your most gracious Lordship to consider the said grievances and to ordain your gracious remedy therefor, for God and in way of charity, by oyer and terminer or by special inquiry.

Indorsed. Inquisition taken at Lincoln on the Thursday after the feast of S. Peter which is called *ad vincula*, 21 Richard II, before William Thirnyng and William Waldeby, the Justices assigned to take assizes in the said County, by virtue of the King's writ directed to the said Justices and sewn to this inquisition [directing them] to inquire touching John Skipwith and the trespass contained in the bill, by the oath of William Leveryke [etc.], Who say and present that the said John Skipwith on the Monday after Michaelmas, 16 Richard II, at

relief asked for, namely, a special commis- sion of oyer and terminer. Mr. Bruce, it is true, says that this practice fell out of use in the reign of Edward III (*Archaeo- logia*, vol. xxv.), but it is evident from this case that his statement must be modified.

* *Sic*; probably a clerical error for *render*.

* The words in brackets added after- wards.   4 Thursday, August 2, 1397.

anno r' r' Ricardi secundi sexto decimo [1] apud Petit Carleton et
Catdale expulsit Sibillam infrascriptam de diuersis terris et tenementis que fuerunt assignate Sibille infrascripte nomine dotis, que
quidam terras et tenementa predictus Johannes occupavit et adhuc
occupat de anno predicto vsque diem huius presentacionis, ita quod
predicta Sibilla dotem suam que ei assignata fuit in predictis villis
propter metum ipsius Johannis non fuit ausa occupare nec ad firmam
dimittere. Item dicunt quo ad redditum de Manby quem ei assig-
natum fuit nomine dotis quod predictus Johannes retinet quadraginta
et quinque solidos quos debet soluere prefate Sibille pro terminis
Natalis domini, Pasche et Sancti Botulphi [2] de anno r. r. Ric' II
vicesimo,[3] et quod predicta Sibilla non audet distringere pro redditu
predicto propter metum predicti Johannis. In cujus rei [etc.][4]

25 [5] A tres reuerent seignur, Chaunceller
d'Engleterre,

1397 Monstre vne [*sic*] Johan de Rouseby de Bardenay, qe vne [*sic*] Johan
Skypwyth le lundy prochein apres le feste de seint Johan le Baptistre,
l'an de regne nostre seignur le Roy q'or'est dis et noifisme,[6] adonqes
esteant viscont de Nicole, par colour de soun office aresta le dit Johan
Rouseby et lui enprisona horriblement en soun hostiel a Nicole, et lui
mist en ceppes et mist sez mayns aderere soun dorse, et sur sez mayns
vne paire de pyrwykes,[7] et lui manassa qe ia ne serroit deliuerez hors de
prisoun s'il ne voudroit doner a lui sa terre ou dis marcz ; et issint lui
en prisoun detient tanque il fuist deliuerez pur fyne de xls. ; a graunt
damage de dit suppliant et encountre droit et resoun ; Dount il prie
a vostre hautesse remedie pur Dieu et en oenre de charite : Considerant
qe sufficiant effect de comon ley ensy oppressee par dit Johan Skypwith ouesque sez aidourz deins le counte de Nicole et aliourz qe sufficiant
execucion de comon droit a cause de ceo n'est sembleable de availer
a dit suppliant, ne a plusourz greindrez de soy, s'il ne soit aydee de
special remedie par especial oyer et determiner ou special inquisicion
en sez bosoignz.

 Indorsed. Inquisicio [etc., as before, No. 24]. Qui dicunt super
sacramentum suum quod billa ista in omnibus infracontentis est vera.
In cuius rei [etc.]

---

 [1] Monday, September 30, 1392.   [4] No. 61 is the jury panel.
 [2] June 17. [3] 1396 and 1397.   [5] Bundle 3, No. 59. See note 1, p. 29.

Little Carlton and Catdale, did expel the within written Sibil from divers lands and tenements which had been assigned to the within written Sibil as her dower, which lands and tenements the said John did and doth still occupy, from the year aforesaid up to the day of this presentment, so that the said Sibil dared not occupy nor let to farm her dower which was assigned to her in the said towns, for fear of the said John. Also, as to the rent of Manby which was assigned to her as dower, that the said John retaineth 45s. which he ought to pay the said Sibil for the terms of Christmas, Easter and S. Botolph, 20 Richard II, and that the said Sibil dare not distrain for the said rent, for fear of the said John. In witness, etc.

25   To the most reverend Lord, the Chancellor of England,

1397 Showeth one John de Rouseby of Bardney, that one John Skipwith on the Monday after the feast of S. John the Baptist in the 19th year of the reign of our Lord the King who now is, being then Sheriff of Lincoln, by colour of his office arrested the said John Rouseby and imprisoned him horribly in his house at Lincoln, and put him in stocks and fastened his hands behind his back, and put a pair of handcuffs [7] on his hands, and threatened him that he should not be delivered from prison unless he would give him his land or 10 marks ; and so he kept him in prison until he was delivered for a fine of 40s. ; to the great damage of the said suppliant, and against right and reason ; Of which he prayeth a remedy from your highness, for God and in way of charity : considering that the due effect of the common law is so overborne by the said John Skipwith and his supporters in the county of Lincoln and elsewhere, that sufficient execution of common right is therefore not likely to avail the said suppliant, nor many others greater than he, if he be not aided by special remedy in his need, either by special oyer and terminer or by special inquiry.

Indorsed. Inquisition [etc., as before, No. 24], who say on their oath that the bill is true in all its contents. In witness [etc.]

---

[6] 1395.   [7] The meaning seems obvious, but I cannot find the word anywhere.

26   [1] A tres honure et tres reuerent seignur, le
            Chaunceler d'Engleterre

1397 Monstre Adam Wyot, Clerke, qe com Johan de Skypwyth oue xlviij
      homes d'armez et archerez, arayez a fair de guere, vient a la vile de
      Grymoldby le lundy proschen apres le fest del Ascension nostre seignur,
      l'an nostre seignur le Roy qe ore est diszime,[2] et le mayson dez ditz
      [sic] suppliant oue force et armez illeqes debrisa, et toez lez bienz et
      chatieux illeqes trouez aresta, et lez issint arestiez detient tanque le
      dit suppliant figth fyne pur diz et noef marez et demi ou le dit Johan
      pur deliuerance auoir de sez bienz et chatieux auant ditz; et puis
      apres a tort il disseysoyt le dit Adam de vn mees ou vn boef de terre
      ou lez apurtenancez en le dit vile, et lez vnqore ocupie encountre droit
      et reson; et le dit suppliant n'osoit pursuer le comon ley enuers le
      dit Johan de lez ditz tortz et greuancez a ly faitz pur manace et doute
      le dit Johan; Dount le dit Adam supplie a vostre tres graciouse seign-
      urie ent de ordiner remedy, pur Dieux et en oeure de charite. Con-
      siderant [etc., as in No. 25].

      Indorsed. Inquisicio [etc., as before, No. 24]. Qui dicunt super
   sacramentum suum quod billa ista in omnibus infra contentis est vera.
   In cuius rei [etc.]

27   [3] A tres honure et tres reuerent seignurie,
            le Chaunceller d'Engleterre,

1397 Monstre Benett Rogersone de Alesby, qe Johan Skypwyth adonqes
      esteaunt viscount de Nicole par colour de soun office aresta le dit
      suppliaunt a Alesby et ly issint en areste detient et luy fesoist estre
      menuz a Nicole en la Resceit, et illoeqes le dit Johan demandoit de
      dit Benett l'argent qe a luy fuist done par vne arbitracion fait
      parentre luy et Johan de Skrelsby des diuers greuaunces qeux le dit
      Johan Skrelsby auoit a dit Benett fait; et le dit Johan Skypwyth
      disoit qe ceo fuist vn extorcion et tout qe si fuist cynk liures estoit
      la soenz, qare disoit qe toutz maners extorcions a soi aparteignent;
      et par tielle colour encountre droit et reson et encountre la volunte de

26 To the most honoured and most reverend
Lord, the Chancellor of England,

1397 Showeth Adam Wyot, clerk, that whereas John de Skipwith with 48
men-at-arms and archers, arrayed as if to make war, came to the
town of Grimoldby on the Monday after the feast of the Ascension of
our Lord, in the 10th year of our Lord the King who now is, and
there, with force and arms, broke the house of the said suppliant, and
seized all the goods and chattels there found, and detained the [goods
and chattels] so seized until the said suppliant made a fine of 19½
marks with the said John in order to have deliverance of his said
goods and chattels ; and afterwards he wrongfully disseised the said
Adam of a messuage and a bovate of land with the appurtenances in the
said town, and still occupieth the same, against right and reason ; and
the said suppliant dare not sue at common law against the said John
for the said wrongs and grievances done to him, because of the
menace and fear of the said John ; Of which the said Adam prayeth
your most gracious Lordship to ordain a remedy, for God and in way
of charity. Considering [etc., as before, No. 25].

Indorsed. Inquisition [etc., as before, No. 24], who say upon their
oath that the bill is true as to all its contents. In witness [etc.]

27 To his most honoured and most reverend
Lordship, the Chancellor of England,.

1397 Showeth Benett Rogerson of Aylesby, that John Skipwith, being then
Sheriff of Lincoln, by colour of his office arrested the said suppliant
at Aylesby, and detained him under arrest, and caused him to
be brought to Lincoln in the Receipt,[4] and there the said John demanded of the said Benett the money which had been given to
him on an arbitration between him and John de Scrivelsby [?]
concerning divers grievances which the said John Scrivelsby [?]
had done to the said Benett ; and the said John Skipwith said
that this was an extortion, and that all [the money] so given,
£5, was his, because all manner of extortions appertained to him ;
and by such colour, against right and reason, and against the

_____
[4] Apparently some building in Lincoln ; it cannot now be identified.

dit Benett prist de soi vj*s.* viij*d.* et ceo vnqore a lui detient ; [1]et si soit roberie ou nemy [1] : Please a si haut parsone de regarder dount il prie remedy, par Dieux et en oeuere de charite ; Consideraunt [etc., as before, No. 25].

Indorsed. Inquisicio [etc., as before, No. 24]. Qui dicunt super sacramentum suum quod transgressiones vnde infra fit mencio facte fuerunt die Mercurii proximo post festum Sancti Marci Euangeliste [2] anno r. r. Ricardi secundi decimo octavo, et quod billa ista in omnibus infracontentis est vera, excepta clausula de roberia infra contenta que non est vera et que infra cancellatur. In cuius rei [etc.]

28   [3] A tres reuerent et tres gracious seignur, Chaunceller d'Engleterre,

1397 Monstrent Sibelle atte Kirke de Skydbroke et William atte Kirke soun fitz, tenauntz a nostre tres redoute seignur le Roy, qe come les ditez Sibelle et William ont estez droituelement et peisiblement seisez de certein rent issant de certeinz tenementz en Garmethorpe, dont vn Richard Ramet est tenaunt, le quel Richard ne voet paier le dit rent as ditz Sibille et William par maintenance de Johan Skipwyth ; et a cause qe les ditz Sibille et William ne voillent estre obligez a dit Johan en xl liures pur esteier a l'agarde et ordinance de dit Johan touchant le dit rent, le dit Johan procura certeinz de sez seruantz et autres de s'affinite pur enditer le dit William de diuerses felonies et trespas deuaunt Justices de Banke nostre dit seignur le Roy a Nicol nient veritablement ; et outre il manasse le dit William de vie et membre de iour en autre, issint q'il n'oise demurer deinz le seignurie nostre dit seignur le Roy illeoqes pur malice et doute de dit Johan ; dont ils priont a vostre tres graciouse seignurie d'ordeigner remedy, pur Dieu et en oeure de charite : Considerantz [etc., as before, No. 25].

Indorsed. Inquisicio [etc., as before, No. 24]. Qui dicunt super sacramentum suum quod transgressiones vnde in billa ista fit mencio faete fuerunt apud Lincoln' die Jovis proximo ante festum Pentecost' anno r. r. Ricardi secundi decimo nono,[4] et quod billa ista in omnibus infracontentis est vera. In cujus rei [etc.]

---

[1]—[1] This portion is struck out : see indorsement.

will of the said Benett, he took from him 6s. 8d., and still detaineth him ; [he demandeth] if this be robbery or not : May it please so high a person to regard [this matter], of which he prayeth remedy, for God and in way of charity ; considering [etc., as before, No. 25].

Indorsed. Inquisition [etc., as before, No. 24], who say upon their oath that the trespasses within mentioned were done on the Wednesday after the feast of S. Mark the Evangelist, 18 Richard II, and that the bill is true in all its contents, except the clause of robbery contained therein, which is not true, and is cancelled [in the bill]. In witness [etc.]

28   To the most reverend and most gracious Lord, the Chancellor of England,

1397 Showeth Sibil at Kirk of Skidbrook and William at Kirk her son, tenants to our most redoubted Lord the King, that whereas the said Sibil and William have been rightfully and peaceably seised of certain rent, issuing from certain tenements in Garthorpe, of which one Richard Ramet is tenant, which Richard would not pay the said rent to the said Sibil and William through the maintenance of John Skipwyth ; and because the said Sibil and William would not be bound to the said John in £40 to be at the award and ordinance of the said John touching the said rent, the said John procured certain of his servants and others of his kin to indict the said William of divers felonies and trespasses before the Justices of the Bench of our Lord the King at Lincoln, untruthfully ; and moreover he menaced the said William of life and member from day to day, so that he dared not dwell within the Lordship of our Lord the King there for the malice and doubt of the said John ; Of which they pray your most gracious Lordship to ordain a remedy, for God and in way of charity. Considering [etc., as before, No. 25].

Indorsed. Inquest [etc., as before, No. 24], who say on their oath that the trespasses whereof mention is made in this bill were done at Lincoln on the Thursday before the feast of Pentecost, 19 Richard II, and that the bill is true in all its contents. In witness, etc.

---

[2] April 25, 1395, a Sunday.   p. 29.
[3] Bundle 3, No. 56.   See   note 1,   [4] Whit Sunday, 1396, was May 21.

29   [1] A tres reuerent seignur, Chaunceller d'Engleterre,

1397 Monstre vne Johan Palet qe par la ou le dit Johan pursuist vne assise de freshe force en la Court nostre tres excellent Dame, Anne, nadgairs Roigne d'Engleterre, qe Dieu assoile, en Garmethorp, enuers vne Rauf Melle, chapelein, Wauter Melle et Alain Melle, des tenementz en Somercotes en le Countee de Nicole, et vne Johan Skipwyth, viscont de mesme le Countee adonque esteant, feust au dit suppliant conseillant et eidant en le matire susdit; Et puis lez ditz Rauf Melle, Wanter et Alain, eux doutantz qe l'assise passereit enuers eux, viendrent a Johan Skypwith viscont susdit, et lui granteront tout lour droit q'ils auoient en les ditz tenementz par le dit Johan Palet issint demaundez; a cause de quele graunt vient Johan Skipwyth viscont susdit le merkirdy prochein apres la feste de Marie Magdalene l'an de regne nostre seignur le Roi dis et noifismc,[2] en la dit Court, et a dit suppliant comaunda q'il ne serroit si hardiz de pursuer auant la dite assise enuers les ditz Rauf Melle, Wauter et Alain, et dit qe si le dit suppliant pursuist plus outre qe ly vorroit amesner a la Gaole de Nicole susdit; issint pur manace et doute du dit Johan Skypwith le dit Johan Palet n'osa ne encore ose pursuer ent soun droit; a graunt anientissement, destruction et disheritance du dit suppliant, dont il prie a vostre hautesse remedie, pur Dieu et en oeure de charite. Considerant [etc., as before, No. 25].

    Indorsed. Inquisicio [etc., as before, No. 24]. Qui dicunt super sacramentum suum quod billa ista in omnibus infracontentis est vera. In cuius rei [etc.]

30   [3] Ricardus [etc.] Justiciariis suis ad assisas in Com' Lincoln' capiendas assignatis, Salutem.

1397 Quasdam peticiones coram nobis et Consilio nostro in Cancellaria nostra per Johannem Palet, Johannem de Rousby de Bardenay, Adam Wyot, clericum, Benedictum Rogereson de Alesby, Sibillam atte Kirke de Skydbroke et Willelmum filium eius, et Sibillam que fuit uxor Roberti

----
[1] Bundle 3, No. 60. See note 1, p. 29.

29   To the most reverend Lord, the Chancellor of England

1397 Showeth one John Palet, that whereas the said John sued an assize of *novel disseisin* in the Court of Garthorpe of our most excellent Lady, Anne, late Queen of England, whom God assoil, against one Ralph Melle, chaplain, Walter Melle, and Alan Melle, concerning tenements in Somercotes in the County of Lincoln, and one John Skipwith, then Sheriff of the same County, counselled and helped the said suppliant in the said matter; And afterwards, the said Ralph Melle, Walter and Alan, fearing that the assize would go against them, came to John Skipwith, the Sheriff, aforesaid, and granted to him all the right that they had in the said tenements so demanded by the said John Palet; In consequence of which grant, John Skipwith, the Sheriff aforesaid, on the Wednesday after the feast of S. Mary Magdalene in the 19th year of the reign of our Lord the King, came to the said Court, and commanded the said suppliant that he should not be so bold as to sue the said assize any further against the said Ralph Melle, Walter and Alan, and said that if the said suppliant proceeded any further, he would bring him to the Gaol of Lincoln aforesaid; So, by threats and for fear of the said John Skipwith, the said John Palet did not, and yet doth not, dare to sue his right thereof; to the great annihilation, destruction and disinheritance of the said suppliant, of which he prayeth a remedy from your highness, for God and in way of charity. Considering [etc., as before, No. 25].

Indorsed. Inquisition [etc., as before, No. 24], who say on their oath that the bill is true in all its contents. In witness [etc.]

30   Richard [etc.] to his Justices assigned to take assizes in the County of Lincoln, Greeting.

1397 We send you inclosed in these presents certain petitions exhibited before us and our Council in our Chancery by John Palet, John de Rousby of Bardney, Adam Wyot, clerk, Benedict Rogerson of Aylesby, Sibil at Kirk of Skidbrook, and William her son, and Sibil

---

¹ 1395.   ² Bundle 3, No. 54. See Note 1. p. 29.

Dercy, chiualer, exhibitas certa dampna iniurias et transgressiones sibi per Johannem Skipwyth separatim vt dicitur illata continentes, vobis mittimus presentibus interclusas, mandantes vt inspectis peticionibus predictis super omnibus et singulis in eisdem peticionibus contentis per sacramentum proborum et legalium hominum de Com' predicto per quos rei veritas melius sciri poterit diligentes faciatis inquisiciones, et eas distincte et aperte factas nobis in Cancellariam nostram sub sigillis vestris et sigillis eorum per quos facte fuerint sine dilacione mittatis et hoc breve vna cum peticionibus predictis, vt vlterius inde fieri faciamus prout de iure et secundum legem et consuetudinem regni nostri Anglic fuerit faciendum. Teste [etc.], May 26, 20 Ric. II [1397].

31   [1] A tres honourable et tres reuerent pier en Dieu, l'Euesque d'Excestre et Chaunceller d'Engleterre,

after 1397 Se pleynt son poure Chapleyn, David Vsqe, iadys vikere de l'esglise de Poulet el Counte de Somerset, qe come vn William Bawe, persone de l'esglise de Greynton el Counte suisdit, le vendredy proscheyn deuant le fest de Pentecoust la an nostre seignur le Roi Richard q'ere est vintisme, [oue] force et armes vient luy mesmes, et sys autres hommes disconuz de ses adherentz oueke luy, pleignement arraies en armes en manere de guerre, a le dit esglise de Poulet, qant le dit Dauid estoit a sa messe vestuz, deuant q'il auoit dit le Ewangelie de seynt Johan q'est appelle 'In principio;' et en le Chauncell de mesme l'esglise commanderont le dit Dauid esteant a son autere vestuz, d'oustere ses vestementz et parlier oueke eaux; le quelle Dauid respondy et disoit a eaux q'il ne voliest houstier ses vestementz tanqe q'il sauoit lour volente; le quelle William Bawe et autres de sa couyne diseront ex-pressement q'ils voedrent decoller le dit Dauid s'il ne voliest faire fyne oueke eaux pur Cent marez; pur doute de quelle manasse le dit Dauid fist fyne et raunson oueke le dit William et sa compaignie en saluacion de sa vie pur x liures d'esterlynges. Et depuis qe le dit William et sa compaignie ont raunsonez le dit Dauid en le manere suisdite, le dit William et ses adherentz firont le dit Dauid iurer in verbo sacerdocii q'il deuoit alere oueke eaux hors de son englise auant-dit tanqe a le ville de Briggewater; et illeoqes luy firont fere a eaux

[1] Bundle 3, No. 41.

widow of Robert Dercy [Darcy], knight, containing certain damages, injuries and trespasses done to them severally by John Skipwith, as it is said; commanding you that, having inspected the said petitions, you do make diligent inquiries by the oath of proved and lawful men of the County aforesaid, by whom the truth of the matter may better be known, as to all and singular contained in the said petitions, and such inquests, distinctly and openly made, you do send without delay to us in our Chancery, under your seals and the seals of those by whom they shall be made, and also this writ and the said petitions, so that we may proceed in the matter as of right and according to the law and custom of our realm of England ought to be done. Witness [etc.], May 26th, 20 Richard II [1397].

31   To the most honourable and most reverend Father in God, the Bishop of Exeter, Chan cellor of England,

after
1397

Complaineth his poor chaplain, David Usqe, formerly Vicar of the church of Pawlett in the County of Somerset, that whereas one William Bawe, Parson of the church of Greinton in the said county, on the Friday before the feast of Pentecost in the 20th year of our Lord King Richard who now is [1397], with force and arms, and six other men unknown, his adherents, with him, fully arrayed in arms in warlike manner, came to the said church of Pawlett when the said David was vested for mass, before he had said the Gospel of S. John which is called *In principio*; and in the chancel of the said church he commanded the said David, who was at his altar, vested, to take off his vestments and to speak with them; the which David answered and said unto them that he would not take off his vestments until he knew their will; the which William Bawe and the others of his covin said expressly that they would cut off his head if he would not make fine with them for 100 marks; and for fear of this menace, the said David made fine and ransom with the said William and his company for £10 sterling in order to save his life. And after the said William and his company had ransomed the said David in manner aforesaid, the said William and his adherents made the said David swear on his priestly word to go with them out of his said church to the town of Bridgewater; and there they forced him to make a bond to them for

vne obligacion de xx liures, sour condicion de paiere les x liures auantdit le vendredy proscheyn adonc ensuant ; Et apres qe le dit Dauid auoist fait l'obligacion auantdit, le dit William et ses adherentz compelleront le dit Dauid deliuerer a eaux pur defaute d'autre paiement en pris pur son raunson auantdit touz ses herþies, ses agnelles, ses porkes et ses autres biens, le samedy en le veil de Pentecoust proscheyn ensuant apres le vendredy auantdit ; a quelle iour le dit William et sa compaignie pristeront les biens du dit Dauid et a luy deliueront son obligacion auantdit. Et les ditz berbies, agnelles, et autres biens asmeneront a le meson du dit William de Aluerton, et vnquore illeoqes sont en garde, en grante destruccion et anientissement de son poure estate, et encontre tout ley et reson : Qe plese a vostre tres graciouse seignurie grantere a dit Dauid vn brief de quibusdam certis de causis [1] de faire le dit William venir deuant vous a vn certeyn iour sour certayn payne deyns mesme le brief compris a respondre a cest bille ; pur Dieu et en eouere de charite. Eiant consideracion qe le dit William est si riche et si forte d'amys en pays la ou il est demourant qe le dit Dauid iames n'auera recouerer de luy par la commun ley s'il n'eyt eide de vostre tres gracious seignurie.[2]

Factum est inde breve predicto Willelmo Bawe de essendo coram Rege in Cancellaria sua in quindena sancti Martini proximo futura.

32   [3] A tres reuerent piere en Dieu et son tres gracious seignur, l'Euesque d'Excestre, Chaunceller d'Engleterre,

after 1397

Supplie humblement Johan Stenby de Staunford qe come il pursue solonc la commun ley vn brief de trespas enuers certeins tenauntz du Johan Hellewell de Stenby pur certeins trespasses a luy faitz par les ditz tenauntz ; par cause de quele pursuite le dit Johan Hellewell ore tarde, c'estassauoir le septisme iour d'Auerill, l'an de nostre tres redoute seignur le Roy Richard vyntisme, en la haute chymyn pres la ville de Bytham en le Counte de Nicol, gisoit en agayte arme en vn hauberk ouesque vn chapel de ferre et vne espee, ouesque autres mesfaisours en sa compaignie arraiez en manere de guerre, pur auoir

---

[1] The writ *quibusdam certis de causis* was not quite the same as the *subpoena*, inasmuch as no penalty was mentioned ; see an example in Case 35. It was probably the older writ of the two. See Palgrave, *King's Council*, 131.

£20, on condition to pay the said £10 on Friday then next following; And after the said David had made the said bond, the said William and his adherents compelled the said David to deliver unto them, in default of other payment, as the price of his said ransom, all his sheep, his lambs, his pigs, and his other goods, on the Saturday in the eve of Pentecost following next after the aforesaid Friday; on which day the said William and his company took the goods of the said David and delivered up to him his said bond. And the said sheep, lambs, and other goods, they brought to the house of the said William at Alverton,[4] and they are still there in ward, to the great destruction and annihilation of the plaintiff's poor estate, and against all law and right: May it please your most gracious Lordship to grant the said David a writ *de quibusdam certis de causis*, to make the said William come before you at a certain day and under a certain pain contained in the writ, to make answer to this bill; for God and in way of charity. Having consideration that the said William is so rich and so strong in friends in the country where he dwelleth, that the said David will never recover from him at common law, if he have not aid from your most gracious Lordship.[2]

A writ thereof was made [commanding] the said William Bawe to be before the King in his Chancery on the quindene of Martinmas next to come.

32   To the most reverend Father in God, and his most gracious Lord, the Bishop of Exeter, Chancellor of England,

after 1397   Beseecheth humbly John Stenby of Stamford [?], that whereas he sued a writ of trespass at common law against certain tenants of John Hellewell of Stainby, for certain trespasses done to him by the said tenants; because of which suit, the said John Hellewell lately, that is to say, on the 7th day of April, in the 20th year of King Richard [1397], our most redoubted Lord, did lie in wait on the high road near the town of Bytham in the County of Lincoln, armed with a hauberk and an iron cap and a sword, and having other evil-doers in his company arrayed in warlike manner, in order to

---

[2] The reason for applying to the Chancellor appears sufficiently from the last paragraph. No doctrine of equity seems to be involved.

[3] Bundle 3, No. 46.

[4] I cannot identify this place.

tue le dit suppliant ; et le dit Johan Hellewell, treant hors son espee,
ouesque les autres mesfaisours suisditz, ou graunt ire et rancour
encontre la pees, firent assaut en le dit suppliant, chiuachant en la
dite haute chymyn vers la dite ville de Staunford, pur luy auoir tue ;
Sur qoi le dit suppliant seiant la grant poair des ditz mesfaisours,
pur dout de sa mort et en saluacion de sa vie, cheast a la terre sur
ses genules deuaunt le dit Johan Hellewell luy proferant tout q'il
auoit a sa volunte, et luy criant mereye q'il voudrast sauuer sa vie ;
la quele le dit Johan Helewell ne voudroit luy grauntier deuaunt qe
luy fist iurer qe iammes ne pursuera outre la commun ley par brief
ne sanz brief, enuers luy ne ses tenauntz sanz son congie, et q'il
paieroit a ses ditz tenauntz tout l'argent qe le viscount et autres
officers eussent pris de eux a cause del dite pursuite ; Et apres le dit
serement issint fait, le dit Johan Hellewell amesna le dit suppliant al
Chastelle de Bytham pur luy auoir mys illoeqes par destresse en
agarde de certeins amys et bienvoillantz du dit Johan Hellewell de
toutes les trespasses faitz au dit suppliant, sibien par les ditz mesfaisours come par les tenauntz auauntditz ; Et pur ce qe mesme le
suppliant, quant il fuist en le dit Chastelle, ne voudroit assentir
d'estre mys en agarde de les amys et bienvoillantz du dit Johan
Hellewell en la forme auauntdite, et puis mesme le suppliant par
l'eide et socour de ses amys departa hors del dit Chastelle, vnqore le
dit Johan Hellewell ouesque pluseurs autres de sa couyne gist en
agayte pur tuer le dit suppliant en la manere suisdite ; issint q'il
n'oise aprocher a son hostelle s'il n'eit vostre socour et graciouse
eide en celle partie : Plese a vostre tresgraciouse seignurie d'enuoier
pur le dit Johan Hellewelle d'estre deuaunt vous et le Conseil nostre
dit seignur le Roy en la Chauncellerie a la quinszein du Pasque
proschein venaunt a respondre de les choses auauntdites ; pur Dieu et
en oeuere de charite, Considerantz tres honure seignur coment les
dites choses sont ouertment faitz encontre nostre dit seignur le Roy
et sa corone et encontre sa pees come auauntdit est.[1]

---

[1] The suggestion is, though it is not so stated in actual words, that the common law was not able to cope with the violence and power of the defendant and his friends.

have killed the said suppliant; and the said John Hellewell, drawing his sword, together with the other evil-doers aforesaid, with great wrath and rancour and against the peace, did assault the said suppliant, who was riding on the said high way towards the said town of Stamford, in order to have killed him; whereupon the said suppliant, knowing the great power of the said evil-doers, and for fear of death and to save his life, fell on the earth on his knees before the said John Hellewell, offering him all that he had to dispose of at his will, and crying him mercy, so that he would spare his life; which the said John Hellewell would not grant him until he did swear that he would never again sue at common law, by writ or without writ, against [Hellewell] himself or his tenants, without his leave, and that he would repay his said tenants all the money that the Sheriff and other officers had taken from them on account of the said suit; And after the said oath was so made, the said John Hellewell brought the said suppliant to Bytham Castle in order to force him through distress to submit to the award of certain friends and well-wishers of the said John Hellewell, in regard to the trespasses done to the said suppliant, as well by the said evil-doers as by the tenants aforesaid; [2] And because the same suppliant, when he was in the said Castle, would not consent to submit to the award of the friends and well-wishers of the said John Hellewell in the form aforesaid, and [because] afterwards the same suppliant, by the aid and succour of his friends, did depart out of the said Castle, the said John Hellewell, with many others of his covin, did again lie in wait to kill the said suppliant in manner aforesaid; so that he dare not approach his house if he have not your succour and gracious aid in that behalf: May it please your most gracious Lordship to send for the said John Hellewell to be before you and the Council [3] of our said Lord the King in the Chancery on the quindene of Easter next to come, to answer touching the matters aforesaid; For God and in way of charity. Considering, most honoured Lord, how the said things are openly done against our said Lord the King and his crown and against his peace, as is aforesaid.

---

[2] This seems to be the meaning of the text, which is somewhat obscure.

[3] Another variation from the usual form; the fact that the Chancellor and the Council are both mentioned is especially interesting.

33   [1] A tres reuerent piere en Dieu et son tres gracious Seignur, l'Euesque d'Excestre et Chaunceller d'Engleterre,

after
1397
Monstre tres humblement et soy pleynt Richard le Yong, clerke, d'un Nicholas Charwode, de ceo qe le dit Nicholas a tort luy deteint et ne pas a luy render xl marcz d'argent les queux il luy doit; et pur ce a tort qe le xxiij iour de Feuerer, l'an du regne nostre seignur le Roy q'ore est xxme, en la paroche de Seint Clement hors de la Temple Barre, mesme cesti Nicholas par son fait connist estre oblige a la dit Richard en les auantditz xl marcz, a paier al feste de Pasche adonqes prochien ensuant, a quele iour il ne paia point; par quoy mesme cesti suppliant vient al dit Nicholas, et luy pria pur luy paier les auantditz xl marcz; et il paier ne voilloit, ne vnqore ne voet, einz luy detient a tort et as damagez du dit suppliant de x liures; par quoy prie le dit Richard qe le dit Nicholas, ore present en court, respoigne a dit Richard selonc les previleges de mesme la court de son dette auantdit, de si come le dit Richard est vn des Clerks de Chauncellerie, pur Dieu et en oeure de charite.

    [2] Plegii de prosequendo:

           Hugo Bauent,
           Johannes Brokholes.

34   [3] A tres gracious seignur et tres reuerent pere en Dieu, l'Euesque d'Excestre, Chan celler d'Engleterre,

1398
Supplie humblement William Foxhill, Mair et Citezein de la Cite de Waterford en Irland, qe come les progenitours nostre seignur le Roy par lour chartres eiont grauntez a lez Citezeins du dite Cite, qe de chescune niefe qe vindra a dite Cite oue vins chargez, qe les Baillifs

---

[1] Bundle 3, No. 83; No. 84 is a dupli-
cate.

[2] No. 84 only.

[3] Bundle 3 No. 115.

33   To the most reverend Father in God and his most gracious Lord, the Bishop of Exeter, Chancellor of England,

after 1397   Showeth most humbly and complaineth Richard le Young, clerk, of one Nicholas Charwoode, of this, that the said Nicholas wrongfully detaineth from him and will not pay him 40 marks, which he oweth; and that wrongfully, because on the 23rd day of February, 20 [Richard II., 1397], in the parish of S. Clement without Temple Bar,[4] the same Nicholas by his deed confessed to be bound to the said Richard in the said 40 marks, to be paid at the feast of Easter then next, at which day he paid nothing; wherefore the said suppliant came to the said Nicholas, and besought him to pay the said 40 marks; and he would not pay them, and will not yet do so, but detaineth them, wrongfully and to the damage of the said suppliant of £10; wherefore the said Richard prayeth that the said Nicholas, now present in court,[5] may answer the said Richard, according to the privileges of the same Court, touching his debt aforesaid, since the said Richard is one of the clerks of the Chancery:[6] For God and in way of charity.

Pledges to prosecute ·

Hugh Bavant,
John Brockholes.

34   To the most gracious Lord and most reverend Father in God, the Bishop of Exeter, Chancellor of England,

1398   Beseecheth humbly William Foxhill, Mayor and citizen of the city of Waterford in Ireland, that whereas the progenitors of our Lord the King have by their charters granted to the citizens of the said city[7] that, from every ship coming to the said city laden with wine, the

[4] S. Clement Danes.
[5] This is very curious, and almost suggests a verbal petition afterwards reduced into writing. It is difficult to explain otherwise how the plaintiff could possibly know that the defendant would be present when his petition was presented. See Case 47, where the defendant is also stated to be present in the Chancery.

[6] This brings the matter within the common law jurisdiction of the Chancellor.
[7] See Smith's *State of the County and City of Waterford*, 1746, p. 205. The 'predecessors' who granted charters to Waterford were John (1205), Henry III (1232), Edward II. (1309), and Edward II (1328, 1356, 1364, 1372, and 1377)

de la dite Cite, en presence del Prouost de mesme la Cite, deussent
eslire deux tonelles de vin de chescune nief, c'est assauoir, vne deuant
la mast et l'autre aderere, paiant pur le tonel xx$s$.; des queux tonelles
les ditz Citezeins ancront vne en releuacion et eide de lour ferme du
dite Cite, reseruant l'autre tonel al oeps nostre seignur le Roy; les
queux chartres de ses progenitours nostre seignur le Roy de sa grace
especiale ad ratifie et conferme, come par ses lettres patentes pleinement appiert; les queux Citezeins, par vn Henry Bruer lour Baillif,
en presence del Mair du dite Cite, d'une nief appelle ' la Trinitee ' de
Bristuyt, de quele nief Markys Spaynoll et Johan Palmer sont possessours, charge oue les vins d'un Nichol Compayng et des autres Marchantz, pristrent et eslierent a Waterford deux tonelles de vin solonc
les grauntz et confirmacion auantditz; nientmains l'euantdit Nichol,
vn Robert Tydbroke et autres Marchantz, par cause del dite prise fait
a Waterford come deuant est dit, firent arester vne nief du dit suppliant a Bristuyt chargez oue peux lanutz et autres marchandises, et en
arest detenir tanque le dit suppliant paia lez ditz Nichol et Robert
xxviij marz, encontre droit, et anientisement del franchise auantdite,
et graunt damage du dit suppliant: Qe plese a vostre tres gracious
seignurie considerer la matier auantdit, et graunter briefs directz a les
Mair, Baillifs et Viscount de Bristuyt, pur faire le dit suppliant re-auoir
et d'estre repaiez de ce qe il ad paie a les auantditz Nichol et Robert,
ou d'enuoier pur les ditz Nichol et Robert d'estre deuant vous a certein
iour pur respondre a le dit suppliant en le matier susdit : Pur Dieu et
en oeuere de charite.

Indorsed. Le vintisme iour d'Auerille l'an, etc., vint et primer.
Accordez est par le Counsail que briefs soient faitz desouz le grant seal
sur la contenue de ceste peticion.

Presens Messeignurs les
- Chanceller,
- Tresorer,
- Gardein du priue seal,
- Le Clerc des roules,
- Messires Johan Bussy,
- Henri Grene,
- Johan Russell et
- Robert Faryngton, clerc.[1]

[1] This list of the members of the Council before whom the bill came is of the highest importance. The Chancellor, it is true, was present, but apparently only as an *ex officio* member of the Council. The Clerk of the Rolls is the same as the Master of the Rolls. See *Proc. and Ord. of the Privy Council*, vol. i., where all these names will be found except Faryngton's.

Bailiffs of the said city, in the presence of the Provost of the said city, should choose two tuns of wine from each ship, one before the mast and the other abaft,[2] paying 20s. for the tun; and of these tuns the said citizens shall have one in relief and aid of their farm of the said city, reserving the other tun for the use of our Lord the King; and these charters of his progenitors our Lord the King hath of his especial grace ratified and confirmed, as by his letters patent plainly appeareth;[3] And the citizens, by one Henry Bruer their Bailiff, in the presence of the Mayor of the said city, took and chose at Waterford two tuns of wine, according to the grants and confirmation aforesaid, from a ship called the 'Trinity' of Bristol, of which ship Markys Spaynoll and John Palmer are owners, laden with wine of one Nicholas Compayng and others, merchants; Nevertheless the said Nicholas, and one Robert Tydbroke, and other merchants, because of the said taking at Waterford, as aforesaid, have caused to be arrested at Bristol a ship of the said suppliant's laden with wool-fells and other merchandise, and they kept [the same] in arrest until the said suppliant paid the said Nicholas and Robert 28 marks, contrary to right, and to the destruction of the franchise aforesaid, and to the great damage of the said suppliant: May it please your most gracious Lordship to consider the matter aforesaid, and to grant writs directed to the Mayor, Bailiffs and Sheriff of Bristol, [commanding them] to cause the said suppliant to have again and be repaid what he hath paid the said Nicholas and Robert, or to send for the said Nicholas and Robert to be before you on a certain day to answer the said suppliant in the matter aforesaid: For God and in way of charity.[4]

Indorsed.—April 20th, 21 [Richard II., 1398]. It is agreed by the Council that writs be sent under the great seal concerning the matter contained in this petition.

Present, my Lords
- The Chancellor,
- The Treasurer,
- The Keeper of the Privy Seal,
- The Clerk of the Rolls,
- Messieurs, John Bussy,
- Henry Grene,
- John Russell and
- Robert Faryngton, clerk.

[2] This is the usual rule in cases of prisage. See Jacob, *Law Dict.* I cannot suggest any explanation, unless it was the custom to load different kinds of wine in different parts of the ship.
[3] In 1380.

[4] It seems doubtful if the plaintiff had any remedy at common law; but, apart from that, these mercantile reprisals were probably treated as affairs of state, which seems sufficient to account for the application to the Chancellor and Council.

35 [1] A Chanceller nostre Seignur le Roy,

1398 Supplie humblement Hugh de Bisleye, qe come Thomas Walweyn, Johan Hikcokkes, Richard Monemouth et Thomas Sodegroue, oue plusours autres nient conuz, encontre la pees en manere de guerre, c'est assauoire, oue espees, bokelers, arkes et setes, viendront a Strode deinz le Hundred de Byseley, la ou lez iurrours d'une enquest furent assignez par le Viscont de Gloucestre et le Baillif de Franchise del Manoir de Byseley, par le brief nostre dit seignur le Roy, pur extendre lez terres de monsire Richard de Talbot, Chiualer, qui Dieu assoile, pur vne certeine somme contenuz en vn estatut de l'estaple en le quel le dit monsire Richard feust tenuz a monsire William Heron, Chiualer, et autres; et lez ditz iurrours manasseront, issint q'ils ne osent procedre en celle partie, et a le dit Hugh illoeqes assaut firont; et le dit Thomas Walweyne manasa le dit Hugh, qe si le dit Hugh serroit si bardiz de pursuer, medler ou seer [sic] outre en ceo cas, ou de pursuer par la ley vn Richard Grenhull, q'adonqes le dit Hugh ne serroit si hardys a demurer en sa maison demesne q'il ne serroit occye; a grant damage et preiudice sibien au dit Hugh come a dit monsire William, s'ils n'eyent vostre graciouse remedie en celle partie: Pleise a vostre graciouse seignurie grantier briefs directz a lez mesfaisours susditz de venier deuant vous a vn certeigne iour pur respondre en cele cas, ou autrement nulles briefs ne mandementz du Roy serront seruiz, ne iurrours n'oesent faire lour deuoir en ycelles parties.

[2] Ricardus [etc.] Ricardo Monemouth, salutem: Quibusdam certis de causis coram nobis in Cancellaria nostra per Hugonem Bisleye propositis, tibi precipimus quod in propria persona tua sis coram nobis in dicta Cancellaria nostra in octavis Sancti Martini proximo futuris vbicumque tunc fuerit, ad respondendum super hiis que tibi ex parte nostra et ipsius Hugonis tunc ibidem plenius exponentur, et ad faciendum vlterius et recipiendum quod Curia nostra considerauerit in hac parte, Et hoc sub graui indignacione nostra ac periculo quod incumbit nullatenus omittas. Teste [etc. 24 October, 22nd year, 1398].

[3] Similar writ of same date addressed to Thomas Sodegroue.

---

[1] Bundle 3, No. 123. [2] Bundle 3, No. 121. [3] Bundle 3, No. 122.

35   To the Chancellor of our Lord the King,

1398   Humbly beseecheth Hugh de Bisley, that whereas Thomas Walweyn,
John Hikcokkes, Richard Monmouth and Thomas Sodegrove, with
many others unknown, against the peace and in warlike manner, to
wit, with swords, bucklers, bows and arrows, came to Stroud in the
Hundred of Bisley, where the jurors of an inquest were assigned by
the Sheriff of Gloucester and the Bailiff of the Liberty of the manor
of Bisley, by the writ of our Lord the King, to make an extent of the
lands of Sir Richard de Talbot, knight, whom God assoil, for a certain
sum contained in a statute staple in which the said Sir Richard was
bound to Sir William Heron, knight, and others; and they threatened
the said jurors, so that they dared not proceed in that behalf, and
they there assaulted the said Hugh; and the said Thomas Walweyn
threatened the said Hugh, that if he should be so bold as to prosecute,
meddle, or sue anything further in that case, or to prosecute at law one
Richard Grenhull, then he had better not be so bold as to live in his
own house, for he would be killed; to the great damage and prejudice
of the said Hugh as well as of the said Sir William [Heron], if they
have not your gracious remedy in this behalf: May it please your
most gracious Lordship to grant writs directed to the evil-doers
aforesaid [commanding them] to come before you at a certain day to
answer in this case, for otherwise no writs or orders of the King will
be obeyed and no jurors will dare to do their duty in those parts.[4]

Richard [etc.], to Richard Monmouth, Greeting: On account of
certain causes put before us in our Chancery by Hugh Bisley, we
command you to be before us in our said Chancery in your proper
person on the octave of Martinmas next to come, wherever it [the
Chancery] shall then be, to answer those things which on behalf of us
and of the said Hugh shall then and there be fully explained to you,
and further to do and receive what our Court shall consider in that
behalf, And this ye shall in no wise omit under our grave indignation
and the peril which shall ensue. Witness [etc.] October 24th, 22
Richard II. [1398].

---

[4] There seems no particular reason for applying to the Chancellor, except the statement in the last paragraph that the King's writ would not be obeyed.

[1] A tres reuerent et tres graciouse Seignur, l'Euesque d'Excestre, Chaunceller d'Engliterre,

1398 Supply vn Thomas de Bridsall qe come il estoit ore tarde seissi et en peisible possession de deux mees et sisz carwes de terre oue lours appurtenantz en Leuenyng en le Counte d'Euerwyke, la venyst vn Johan de Bulmer, par ordeignance, ymaginacion et auyse de vn Robert Bulmer [2] son piere et William son frere, en la vigile de toutz seintz ore darrein passe, par noet, par bone estimacion parentre oeptz et neofz hours del cloke, a faire de guerre, ouesque trentz gentz de lour couyne, arraiez ; a force et armes et forciblement entreround en les tenementz auantditz, oue le dit suppliaunt ouesque ses seruauntz par longe temps deuant auoit demurez, et lez ditz tenementz vnqore forciblement reteignent ; et le dit suppliaunt et toutz sez seruauntz et partie de sez bienz et chateux ousteround, et graunde partie de lez ditz biens et chateux arderound, defoileround, et degasteround ; Sur qoy, tres graciouse seignur, y pleyse a vostre tres noble discrecion d'ordeigner remedie en ceste matire, en tiel manere qe lez tres bones leyes nostre tres redoute seignur le Roy et de son noble Roialme puissent estre honestment gardez, et virtuez enhanciez, et peichez et oppressionez du le pople punyez et chastiez ; pur Dieu et en ouere du charite.

Indorsed. Memorandum quod decimo septimo die Nouembris anno regni Regis Ricardi secundi xxij°, Walterus de Askham et Willelmus Skyren de Comitatu Ebor' coram domino rege in Cancellaria sua personaliter constituti, manuceperunt pro infrascripto Thoma quod ipse satisfecerit infrascripto Roberto et Willelmo de dampnis custubus et expensis suis quas in hac parte sustinebunt si idem Thomas intencionem suam versus ipsos Robertum et infrascriptum Willelmum probare non poterit secundum tenorem et effectum huius bille.[3]

37   [4] A tres reuerent piere en Dieu, l'Euesque d'Excestre, Chaunceler d'Engleterre,

after Supplie humblement vostre pouere seruant [5] Johan Barnabe de
1397 Nouelle Salisbury, qe come il mesmes nadgairs suist vn brief de Scire

---

[1] Bundle 3, No. 119. See Case 91, where the bill appears to be supplemental to this one.

[2] It will be noticed here, and in other cases in this volume, that the *de* was already dropping out of use in surnames of local origin.

[3] No reason appears why the Chancellor

36 To the most reverend and most gracious Lord, the Bishop of Exeter, Chancellor of England,

1398 Beseecheth one Thomas de Bridsall, that whereas he was now of late seised and in peaceable possession of two messuages and six carucates of land with their appurtenances in Leavening in the County of York, there came one John de Bulmer, by the order, scheme and advice of one Robert Bulmer his father and William his brother, in the eve of All Saints now last past, at night, by good estimation between eight and nine o'clock, with thirty people of their covin, arrayed in manner of war ; and with force and arms they forcibly entered on the said tenements, where the said suppliant with his servants had dwelt for a long time before, and they do still forcibly retain possession of the said tenements ; and they have ousted the said suppliant and all his servants and part of his goods and chattels, and have burnt, damaged and wasted a great part of the said goods and chattels · Wherefore, most gracious Lord, may it please your most noble discretion to ordain a remedy in this matter, in such a way that the very good laws of our most redoubted Lord the King and his noble realm may be honestly kept, virtues exalted, and crimes and op-ⲣressions of the people punished and chastised ; For God and in way of charity.[3]

Indorsed. November 17th, 22 Richard II. [1398]; Walter de Askham and William Skyren of the County of York became sureties [mainpernors] for the plaintiff.

37 To the most reverend Father in God, the Bishop of Exeter, Chancellor of England,

after 1397 Humbly beseecheth your poor servant John Barnabe of New Salisbury, that whereas he lately sued out a writ of *scire facias* against John

should be asked to interfere in this case.
[4] Bundle 3, No. 114. No. 113 is a dupli-cate, with slight verbal differences, but

w:thout the indorsement.
[5] *Orator*, No. 113.

facias enuers Johan Harengeye et Thomas Berwyke, executours du testament de Robert Harengeye, nadgairs Citezein et Mercer de Loundres, d'auoir restitucion de certeins terres et tenementz queux le dit Robert auoit en execucion deuers le dit suppliaunt par force d'une reconusaunce del estatut de staple; le quel brief fuist retourne ycy en la Chauncellarie deuant vous le terme del Trinite darrein passe; a quel temps lez ditz executours, qi furent garny, firent defaute, par qe le dit suppliaunt auoit iuggement d'auoir restitucion de sez terres et tenementz autres foitz par force du dite reconusaunce extenduz; et sur ceo brief issist al viscount de Suth' de luy liuerer les terres et tenementz auauntditz, et luy furent liuerez. Puis quel temps vn Thomas Lysle, veiaunt la graund pouert et impotence du dit suppliaunt, et nient voillaunt suffrer le iuggement renduz deuant vous estoier en sa force, fresshement saunz droit ou title oue forte mayn ousta le dit suppliaunt, au fin q'il mesme purroit tenir les ditz terres et ent prendre les profitz dicelle, et mettre le dit suppliaunt de suer la commune lay, sachaunt bien qe le dit suppliaunt est si pouere q'il n'ad de qoi viure ne pursuer; et les tenementz vaillent bien par an xx marcz. Et auxi la ou le dit Thomas ad pris diuers distresses dez tenauntz du ditz tenementz pur le rente dez ditz tenementz, briefs de Replegiare ount estee suez deuers luy, et alias [et] pluries, et sy auant qe Withername fuist agarde, et le viscount ne puist rien trouer dez biens le dit Thomas pur ent faire execucion. Et auxi le dit Thomas manace le dit suppliaunt et sez seruauntz et attournez de vie et de membre a cause du dite pursute: Qe plese a vostre tresgraciouse seignurie considerer toutz les matiers auantditz et la graund pouert et impotence du dit suppliaunt, et sur ceo graunter vn brief directe au dit Thomas d'estre deuant vous a certein iour de monstrer pur quoi il ne voilloit suffrer le dit suppliaunt auoir ses terres et tenementz come il les ad recouere, et auxi pur trouer surte du pees au dit suppliaunt et sez seruauntz sur graund peyne; pur Dieu et en oenere de charite.

Indorsed. Transgressiones infrascripte faete fuerunt die lune proximo post festum Sancti Michaelis anno xxj°,[1] et die Martis proximo post festum Natalis Domini eodem anno.

---

[1] 1397.

Harengeye and Thomas Berwyke, executors of the will of Robert Harengeye, late citizen and mercer of London, in order that he might have restitution of certain lands and tenements which the said Robert had in execution against the said suppliant by force of a recognisance on a statute staple ; and the said writ was returned here in the Chancery before you in Trinity Term last past ; at which time the said executors, who had been warned, made default, by which the said suppliant had judgment to have restitution of his lands and tenements formerly extended by force of the said recognisance ; and thereupon a writ was issued to the Sheriff of Southampton to deliver to the plaintiff his lands and tenements aforesaid, and they were delivered to him. Since that time one Thomas. Lysle, seeing the great poverty and weakness of the said suppliant, and not wishing to suffer the judgment given before you to be of any force, did oust the said suppliant anew, without right or title and with the strong hand, to the end that he himself might hold the said lands and take the profits thereof, and put the said suppliant to sue at common law, knowing well that the said suppliant is so poor that he hath not wherewithal to live nor to sue ; and the tenements are well worth 20 marks yearly. And also whereas the said Thomas [Lysle] hath taken divers distresses from the tenants of the said tenements for the rent thereof, and writs of replevin have been sued against him, and *alias* and *pluries* writs, and so on until withernam was awarded, [but] the Sheriff could not find any goods of the said Thomas of which to make execution.[2] And also the said Thomas threateneth the said suppliant, his servants and attorneys, of life and limb because of the said suit : May it please your most gracious Lordship to consider all the matters aforesaid, and the great poverty and weakness of the said suppliant, and thereupon to grant a writ directed to the said Thomas, [commanding him] to be before you on a certain day to show wherefore he would not suffer the said suppliant to have his lands and tenements as he had recovered them, and also to find surety of the peace towards the said suppliant and his servants, under a great pain ; For God and in way of charity.

Indorsed. The trespasses within written were done on the Monday after Michaelmas in the 21st year, and on the Tuesday after Christmas in the same year.

[2] The text is rather obscure. The *alias* writ is a second writ issued after a first writ has proved abortive ; the *pluries* is a third writ after the failure of the *alias*. *Wither-nam* is where the goods as to which replevin is ordered cannot be found, and the Sheriff is thereupon, by a *capias in Withernam*, ordered to seize other goods of the defendant's to the like value.

38   [1] A tres gracious et tresage seignur, l'Euesque
de Excestre et Chaunceller d'Engletre,

after Supplie humblement Johan Charleton, qe par l'ou l'an du regne nostre
1398   seignur le Roi Richard q'or'est xxj,[2] vn son noef appelle 'la Marye de
Plymmouth' pris de ij^c liures,oue diuersez biens et marchaundisez des
soens et des autrez en sa garde esteantz et deinz la dite noef contenuz
a la value de ij^c liures, fuist passant par le mere enuers la porte de
Plymmouth, la, vn William Benteley, adonqes lieutenaunt del Admirall
nostre seignur le Roi, par colour de son office et saunez cause resonable
arresta la dite noef, et amesna deinz la porte de Plymmouth; et
illoeqs vn Esteuene Derneford l'eisne, Johan Sampson le puisne,
Henry Crese et le dit William, ymaginauntz coment ilz purront
anienter l'estat le dit suppliant par conspiracye entre eux ewe, fause-
ment et desceiuablement ensemble conspirerount, et issint qe le dit
Esteuene afferma vn pleint de dette en absence du dit suppliant vers
le dit suppliant, deuant le dit Henry Crese, adonqes Waterbailly de
la ville de Plymmouth, de la somme de v^c marez lez qeux il duist auoir
rescieu d'un enfaunt Denys al oeps le dit Esteuene; et en affermance
de lour fauce conspiracye, le dit Johan Sampson forgea vne faux
acquitance fait al dit enfaunt Denys par le dit suppliant, en prouant
la resceite auantdite; par l'ou le dit suppliant nulle denier du dit
enfaunt Denys onqes resceust, ne nulle acquitance ne fist; mes en
absence du dit suppliant saunz due proces de ley le dit Henry Waterbailly, sour le faux proue le dit Esteuene denant lui fait de la somme
auantdite, fist preiser la dite noef et touz lez biens contenuz deinz
mesme la noef, et liuera les a le dit Esteuene pur la somme suisdite,
forspris le veile cablez et autrez apparailez du dit noef, queux le dit
Henry prist a son oeps en claymant de cheschun liure xij*d.* pur son
fee par cause suisdite, torcenousement encountre ley et droit, a grand
anientisment du dit suppliant; dount il prie remedye pur Dieux et en
oeure de charyte.

---

[1] Bundle 3, No. 118.   [2] 1397-8.

38   To the most gracious and most wise Lord,
            the Bishop of Exeter, Chancellor of England,

after Humbly beseecheth John Charleton, that whereas in the 21st year of
1398 our Lord King Richard who now is, a ship of his called the 'Mary of
      Plymouth,' worth £200, together with divers goods and merchandise
      of his own and of others in his keeping and contained in the said
      ship to the value of £200, was passing on the sea towards the port of
      Plymouth, one William Bentley, then Lieutenant to the Admiral of
      our Lord the King, by colour of his office and without any reasonable
      cause, arrested the said ship, and brought her within the port of
      Plymouth; and there one Stephen Derneford the elder, John Sampson
      the younger,[3] Henry Crese and the said William [Bentley], scheming
      how they could destroy the estate of the said suppliant by a conspi-
      racy had between them, did falsely and deceitfully conspire together,
      so that the said Stephen lodged a plaint of debt against the said sup-
      pliant in his absence, before the said Henry Crese, then water-bailiff
      of the town of Plymouth, for the sum of 500 marks which he ought
      to have received from one Child Denys [4] to the use of the said Stephen;
      and in confirmation of their false conspiracy, the said John Sampson
      forged a false acquittance made to the said Child Denys by the said
      suppliant, proving the receipt aforesaid; whereas the said suppliant
      never received one penny from the said Child Denys, and never made
      any acquittance; but in the absence of the suppliant and without due
      process of law, the said Henry the water-bailiff, upon the false proof
      of the said Stephen made before him as to the said sum, caused the
      said ship to be seized and all the goods contained therein, and delivered
      them to the said Stephen for the sum aforesaid, excepting the old
      cables and other fittings of the said ship, which the said Henry took
      to his own use, claiming for his fee in the said cause 12d. in each
      pound, wrongfully and against law and right, and to the great destruc-
      tion of the said suppliant; Of which he prayeth remedy for God and
      in way of charity.[5]

[3] See a bill of complaint by him in the
Admiralty Court; *Selden Soc.* vi. no. 1.

[4] I use this translation with some mis-
giving. Ordinarily one would translate
'from a youth, one Denys;' but here the
word *enfant* is used each time before *Denys*,
in a way which seems quite unnecessary,
and suggests some sort of title or appella-
tion. For many examples of Child used in

this way, see *N. E. D.*

[5] As to the Chancellor's jurisdiction in
Admiralty cases, see *Selden Soc.* vol. vi.
This case, however, seems hardly an
Admiralty case, notwithstanding that the
lieutenant of the admiral is mentioned.
The alleged fraud is the ground for the
Chancellor's interference.

39   [1] A tres honurable et tres reuerent seignur et piere en Dieux, l'Euesque d'Excestre et Chauncellere d'Englitere,

after 1398 Supplie William Sysel, vn dez lieges nostre seignur le Roy, qe come nadgeres Johan Burdeyn, le priour le Liez en le Counte d'Essex,[2] par son escript endente et par assent de son Couent, granta au dit suppliant vn corrodie a prendre annuelment en le dit priourie, come en certeynz endentours parentre le dit priour et le dit suppliant pluis de pleyn fuist contenuz ; le quele corrodie par vertu del grant susdit le dit suppliant fuist peisiblement possessionez tanqe le jouedy proscheyn apres le Purificacion nostre Dame, l'an nostre seignur le Roy xxj[me],[3] qe certeynz gentz par assent del dit priour entrierunt en le meson de dit William deinz le dit priourie encovntre son gree et son volunte, et le dit meson debruserunt, et lez fetz, euidencez et autres munimenz tuchant le dit corrodie et autres dettes parentre le dit suppliant et le dit priour pristerunt et emporterunt par le dit priour oue force et armez ; dount le dit suppliant a cause dycelle est ennitize, et pardu le substance de son viuere : Qe plese a vostre graciouse seignurie grauntier brif nostre tres redoute seignur le Roy directe a dit priour d'estre deuant vos en le Chauncerie al xv[me] del Trinite proschein auenir, de respoundre a ceste matier, et solone ceo q'est troue par examinment oue par averment fere ceo qe reson et ley et bon foy demandont ; pur Dieux et en ouere de charite.

40   [4] A tres reuerent piere en Dieu, Euesque d'Excestre, Chaunceller d'Engleterre,

after 1398 Monstre et soy compleynt Thomas Wace de Waynflet, qe come le lundy proscheyn apres le fest de Seint Hillare, l'an nostre seignur le Roy q'ore est vynt et primer,[5] en la ville de Freston en la Counte de Nicolle, accorde se prist parentre Johan Wace, piere l'auantdit Thomas suppliant, d'un part, et Johan Brasse de Freston, William Leuerton, William Bealuncle de Stykeney et Robert Belle de Benyngton, d'autere

[1] Bundle 3, No. 109.
[2] Little Leighs, Lighes, or Leezparva, 5¼ miles from Braintree. See *Mon. Ang.* ii. 362; Morant's *Essex*, ii. 100. The Priory was one of Augustine Canons.
[3] Richard II. ; 1398.
[4] Bundle 3, No. 104.
[5] Richard II. ; 1398.

39   To the most honourable and most reverend Lord and Father in God, the Bishop of Exeter and Chancellor of England,

after 1398   Beseecheth William Sysel, one of the lieges of our Lord the King, that whereas lately John Burdeyn, Prior of Leighs in the county of Essex, by his writing indented, and with the assent of his convent, granted to the said suppliant a corrody [6] to be taken yearly in the said Priory, as in certain indentures between the said Prior and the said suppliant was more fully contained; of which corrody the said suppliant was peaceably possessed, by virtue of the said grant, until the Thursday after the Purification of our Lady in the 21st year of our Lord the King [1398], when certain persons, with the assent of the said Prior, entered the house of the said William within the said Priory against his consent and will, and broke the said house, and, with force and arms, took and carried off the deeds, evidences, and other muniments touching the said corrody and other debts between the suppliant and the said Prior, by [the direction of ?] the said Prior; whereby the said suppliant is ruined, and [hath] lost the substance of his living: May it please your most gracious Lordship to grant a writ of our most redoubted Lord the King directed to the said Prior [commanding him] to be before you in the Chancery on the quindene of Trinity next to come, to answer to this matter, and according to what is found by examination or by averment, to do what right, law and good faith demand; For God and in way of charity.[7]

40   To the most reverend Father in God, the Bishop of Exeter, Chancellor of England,

after 1398   Showeth and complaineth Thomas Wace of Wainfleet, that whereas on the Monday after the feast of S. Hilary in the 21st year of our Lord the King who now is, in the town of Frieston, in the County of Lincoln, an agreement was made between John Wace, father of the said Thomas the suppliant, of the one part, and John Brasse of Fries-ton, William Leverton, William Bealuncle of Stickney, and Robert

---

[6] A right to certain allowances of food, and sometimes lodging and raiment; they were common in most English monasteries, and were frequently commuted for a money payment.

[7] No equitable doctrine appears in this case, unless *discovery* is implied in the prayer. *Specific performance* is not asked for, although it might have been expected.

part, qe le dit Thomas duist espouser Maude, la file Aleyn Williamsone de Stykeneye, et paier dis marcs a lez ditz Johan Brasse, William, William et Robert pur ent faire distribucion pur l'alme Agnes, la Miere cesty Maude, et auxi trouer vn Chapeleyn diuynz seruicez en l'esglise de Stykeney de iour en iour par trois anz continuelment chauntand pur l'alme l'auantdite Agnes, le terme comensant a la fest de seint Michelle l'an nostre seignur le Roy q'ore est vynt et seconde; [1] et les auantditz Johan Brasse, William, William et Robert dussent enfeffer lez ditz Thomas et Maude, apres lez espousels parentre eux celebres, en touz lez terrez et tenementz les quex ils auoient del done et feffement la dite Agnes en Benyngton et Boterwyke, a auer et tener a ditz Thomas et Maude et a les heirs Maude a toutz iours ; As touz quex chosez et couenauntz a parforner et parimpler les partiez [2] lez iour, an et lieu auantditz, foialment et saunz fraude ou male engyne promystrent et eux obligerunt. Puis quelle temps le dit Thomas, voillant et desirant de parforner les condicions et couenantz suisditz de sa part a parimpler, solonc ceo qe droit et reson le demande, prist a femme la dite Maude, et les dis marcs pleynement paia, et de trouer vn Chapeleyn come auant est dit par son escript obligatorie soy obliga ; et longe temps deuant ore le dit Thomas ad troue vn Chapeleyn, et vncore a ces costages demesne luy troue, solonc ceo qe l'accorde . . . le demande ; et le dit Thomas souent-foith puis les ditz espousels ad requis les auantditz Johan Brasse, William, William et Robert de faire le feffement des terres et tene-mentz auantditz solonc l'effecte et la nature d'accorde auantdit, et eux le faire refuserunt et contradierunt, et vncore refusunt et contra-diunt, a tort et as damages de dit suppliant de CC liures et a graunt areresment de son estate ; . . il prie remedie pur Dieu et en oeure de charite.

41   [3] A tres reuerent piere en Dieu et tres gracious seignur, l'Euesque d'Excestre et Chaunceler d'Engleterre,

1399 Supplie humblement Symond Helgeye, parson de l'esglise de Helgeye, qe par la ou il ad charge et cure dez almes de mesme la paroche, et

[1] 1398.
[2] A hole in the document.
[3] Bundle 3, No. 99. Nos. 100 and 101   are duplicates, but with some slight verbal differences.

Belle of Bennington, of the other part, that the said Thomas should marry Maude, the daughter of Alan Williamson of Stickney, and pay 10 marks to the said John Brasse, William, William and Robert, to be distributed for the soul of Agnes, mother of the said Maude, and also to find a chaplain to chant divine services in the church of Stickney for the soul of the said Agnes continually from day to day for three years, the term to commence at Michaelmas in the 22nd year of our Lord the King who now is; and also that the said John Brasse, William [Leverton], William [Bealuncle] and Robert [Belle] should enfeoff the said Thomas and Maude, after the marriage was celebrated between them, in all the lands and tenements which they had of the gift and feoffment of the said Agnes in Bennington and Butterwick, to have and to hold to the said Thomas and Maude and the heirs of Maude for ever; and the parties [aforesaid], the day, year, and place aforesaid, promised and bound themselves to perform and fulfil all those matters and covenants, faithfully, and without fraud or evil device. Since which time the said Thomas, wishing and desiring to perform the conditions and covenants aforesaid on his part to be fulfilled, as right and reason demand, took the said Maude to wife, and fully paid the said 10 marks, and bound himself by his writing obligatory to find a chaplain as aforesaid; and long before this time the said Thomas hath found a chaplain, and still findeth him at his own costs, as the said agreement demandeth; and many times since the said marriage, the said Thomas hath required the said John Brasse, William [Leverton], William [Bealuncle] and Robert [Belle] to make the feoffment of the said lands and tenements according to the effect and nature of the agreement aforesaid, and they have refused to do so, and have denied [that they ought to do so], and still do refuse and deny, wrongfully, and to the damages of the said suppliant of £200, and to the great detriment of his estate; [for which] he prayeth remedy for God and in way of charity.[4]

41   To the most reverend Father in God, and most gracious Lord, the Bishop of Exeter, Chancellor of England,

1399   Beseecheth humbly Simon Hilgay, parson of the church of Hilgay, that whereas he hath charge and cure of souls of the same parish,

[4] *Specific performance* of the agreement is asked for, but besides this, the defendants were feoffees to uses, that is, trustees, and though there is no question of any equitable estate, yet they were bound to fulfil the terms of their trust, which could

est manase par vn Robert de Wesnam, et Johan atte Gotere,[1] Johan
Bilney, Johan Walmere, Robert Walmere, Johan Mody et Henry
atte Fenne, au dit Robert [2] associez et confederez, et luy manasent de
iour en autre issint q'il n'ose en cest tres seint temps de qaresme a sa
dite parsonage approcher pur oier lez confessions de sez parochiens,
pur pour de sa mort sanz soun desert ; et en purpos de lour male
parfournier, le dit Robert de Westnam, ouesque lez autres desuis
nomez, le Marsdy en la primer semaigne de qaresme [3] darrein passe,
enchaseront et pursueront le dit suppliaunt oue force et armes, c'est
assauoir, espees nuez treez, bastons et bokelers, de la ville de Fyn-
cham en le Countee de Norff' iesqes a la ville de Crympelsam, qe
sont distantz par deux lieukes, pur luy tuer, et vn Johan Ouere a
celle temps en sa compaignie esteaunt illeosqes bateront ; Et en outre
consideraunt qe le dit Robert de Wesnam ad tantz de malfaisours a
luy associez et confederez et est de tiel horrible mayntenaunce issint
qe le dit suppliaunt iammez ne viendra a soun recouere par la commune ley deuers luy et lez autres sanz vostre tres gracious eide : Qe
pleise a vostre tres gracious seignurie de considerer la matere auantdite et ent faire remedie [4] au dit suppliaunt, solonc vostre tres sage
discresion ; Pur Dieu et en oeure de charitee.

Indorsed. Virtute istius supplicacionis Simon Helgeye persona
ecclesie de Helgeye infrascriptus habet quatuor brevia directa personis
infrascriptis de essendo coram ipso Rege et Consilio suo in Cancellaria
sua die Jovis proximo post festum Sancti Gregorii proximo futurum
ad respondendum super contentis.[5]

42   [6] A tres gracious seignur et tres reuerent
            piere en Dieu, l'Euesque d'Excestre, Chaun-
            celler d'Engleterre,

Ric. II. Supplient tres humblement Henry Mayn et William Mayn, son
friere, Marchauntz de Dertemouthe, qe come le disme iour d'Augst,
l'an du regne nostre seignur le Roy Richard q'or'est quatorszisme,[7]
en temps de peas, mesmez lez suppliantz chargerent vne nief a
Dertemouthe, appellee le George, oue draps de layne de diuersez

only be enforced in Chancery. It is true
that the terms of the deed of feoffment, or
the deed to uses, are not set out, but there
can be little doubt that a feoffment to
Maude and her heirs was one of them.

The earliest bills of this nature cited by
Spence are of the reign of Hen. V. *Equit.
Jur.* i. 443.
[1] Gottere ; Nos. 100 and 101.
[2] *Add* de Wesnam ; No. 101.

and is menaced by one Robert de Wesnam,[3] and by John at Gotere, John Bilney, John Walmer, Robert Walmer, John Mody and Henry at Fen, associated and confederated with the said Robert de Wesnam; and they do menace him from day to day, so that he dare not, in this most holy time of Lent, approach his said parsonage to hear the confessions of his parishioners, for fear of unmerited death; and for the purpose of their evil design, the said Robert de Wesnam, with the others above named, on the Tuesday in the first week of Lent last past, 22 Richard II. [1399], chased and pursued the said suppliant with force and arms, to wit, naked swords drawn, clubs and bucklers, from the town of Fincham in the County of Norfolk to the town of Crimplesham, which are two leagues distant, in order to have killed him, and there they did beat one John Ouere, who was in his company at that time; And moreover, considering that the said Robert de Wesnam hath so many evil-doers associated and confederated with him, and is of such horrible maintenance, so that the said suppliant can never come to his recovery against him and the others at common law without your most gracious aid: May it please your most gracious Lordship to consider the matter aforesaid and thereof to make right and remedy for the said suppliant according to your most wise discretion; For God and in way of charity.

Indorsed. By virtue of this supplication the within written Simon Hilgay, parson of the church of Hilgay, hath four writs directed to the persons within written, [commanding them] to be before the King and his Council in his Chancery on the Thursday after the feast of S. Gregory next to come, to answer upon the contents [hereof].[9]

42   To the most gracious Lord and most reverend Father in God, the Bishop of Exeter, Chancellor of England,

Ric. II. Most humbly beseech Henry Mayn and William Mayn his brother, merchants of Dartmouth, that whereas on the 10th day of August in the 14th year of the reign of our lord King Richard who now is, in time of peace, the said suppliants loaded at Dartmouth a ship, called the 'George,' with woollen cloth of divers colours, images of alabaster,

<hr>

[3] No. 101 has 'l'an vint et second.'
[4] Droit et remedie; No. 100.
[5] On No. 100 only.
[6] Bundle 3, No. 44. Nos. 43 and 45 in the same bundle are duplicates of this bill.

[7] 1390.   [8] Probably Weasenham.
[9] No remedy at common law. Note that the defendants are to come before the King and his Council, not before the Chancellor.

colours, ymagez d'alabastre, et autres marchandizes, al value de mille
liures, pur auoir passee le meer enuers lez partiez de Cyuylle graunt,
la vient vn Piers Laurence, come vn laron de meer, et maistre d'une
nief de Jene,[1] oue plousours de sa couiegne, oue force et armes ; et la
dite nief appellee Seint George [sic], et touz les marchandizes icelle
trouez et esteauntz, prist et emporta et a sa paijs amesna, saunz
vnqez gree ou restitucion a lez ditz suppliantz fait ; Pur quelle trespaas le samady[2] prochein deuant le feste de Seint Johan le Baptistre,
l'an du regne nostre dit seignur le Roy Richard disnoefisme,[3] le dit
Henry fesoit le dit Piers Laurence en la ville de Southampton arrester
et amesner deuant Johan Boteller, adonqe Baillyf du dite ville, et
illeoqez le dit Piers Laurence fuist examine, et par l'examinacion tout
le trespasse graunta et confessa, et profera de faire[4] gree et restitucion
al dit Henry, et lui pria de grace et mercie ; et sur ceo fuist commys
a prison tanqe al lendemayn, qe le dit Baillif amesna le dit Piers al
Guyhalde deuant Johan Flete, Mair de mesme la ville de Southampton, et illeoqez l'auantdit Henry en plein court outrement empria et
requera lez ditz Mair et Baillif depar le Roy, come ils auoient lez
loys nostre dit seignur le Roy illeoqez a gouernir, de lui faire reason
et loy come a tiel trespassour et malfaisour est ordeignee et appent,
enataunt qe le dit Piers auoit toute la dite trespasse outrement
grauntee et confessee ; Et de quelle trespasse lez ditz Mayr et Baillyf
nulle remedie ne loy faire ne volient, mais torcenousement encountre
droit et loye comaundont ij Sergeauntz de tenir en prison le dit
Henry en lour Guyhalde tanqe le suisdit Piers Laurence fuist escapee et
passee le meer ; Issint par desceyt et fausyne dez ditz Mayr et Bayllif les
suisditz suppliantz ount perduz touz lour biens auantditz pur touz
iours sinon qe remedie par vous tresdroiturel seignur soit fait et ordeignee : Please a vostre tres graciouse seignurie grauntier a lez ditz
suppliantz vne brief directe a lez suisditz Johan Botyller et Johan Flete,
eaux commandant et chargeant d'estre deuant vous a certein iour
en mesme le brief limitee, a respoundre a les suisditz suppliantz de
la matiere suisdite, Et enoutre eaux examiner de toute la veritee touchant la dite matiere, Et sur iceo qe soit trouee deuaut vous par examinacion ou par confession pur ent ordeigner due remedie ; pur Dieu et en
oeure de charitee.[5]

---

[1] Gene ; No. 43.
[2] Dismenge ; No. 43.   [3] 1395.
[4] *Add* amendes ; No. 43.
[5] Seint charite ; No. 43.

and other merchandise, to the value of £1,000, in order to have crossed the sea towards the parts of Great Seville, there came one Piers Laurence as a sea-robber and the master of a ship of Genoa, with many others of his covin, with force and arms, and seized the said ship called the ' S. George' [sic] and all the merchandise found and being therein, and carried them off and brought them to his own country, without any recompense or restitution made to the said suppliants ; for which trespass the said Henry caused the said Piers Laurence to be arrested in the town of Southampton on the Saturday before the feast of S. John the Baptist, 19 Richard II., and brought before John Botiller, then Bailiff of the said town ; and there the said Piers Laurence was examined, and on the examination admitted and confessed all' the said trespass, and offered to make recompense and restitution to the said Henry, and besought him to have grace and mercy; and thereupon he was committed to prison until the morrow, when the said Bailiff brought the said Piers to the Guild Hall before John Flete, Mayor of the said town of Southampton, and there the said Henry in full court fully besought and required the said Mayor and Bailiff on behalf of the King, since they have to enforce there the laws of our said lord the King,[6] to do him right and law, as to such a trespasser and evil-doer is ordained and belongs, inasmuch as the said Piers had fully admitted and confessed all the said trespass ; And of this said trespass, the said Mayor and Bailiff would do [the said suppliants] no remedy nor law, but tortiously, against right and law, commanded two serjeants to keep the said Henry in prison in their Guild Hall until the said Piers Laurence had escaped and passed the sea ; So, by the deceit and falsity of the said Mayor and Bailiff, the said suppliants have lost all their goods aforesaid for ever, if a remedy be not made and ordained, most righteous lord, by you : May it please your most gracious lordship to grant the said suppliants a writ directed to the said John Botiller and John Flete, commanding and charging them to be before you on a certain day in the said writ to be limited, to answer the said suppliants concerning the said matter, and further to examine them [the defendants] as to the whole truth concerning the said matter, and to ordain due remedy upon whatever may be found before you by examination or confession ; for God and in way of charity.[7]

---

[6] This probably refers to the statute of 27 Edward III., cap. 13, giving restitution of goods on proof of ownership. On the subject of piracy generally in relation to English tribunals, see *Selden Soc.* vol. vi. *passim.*

[7] It is very difficult to see why the plaintiffs should have come to the Chancellor with their complaint against the Mayor and Bailiff. But, on the other hand, the complaint against Piers Laurence, he being an alien, was properly within the Chancellor's, or rather the Council's, jurisdiction. See p. 4, note 3.

43   [1] A tres honurable et tres reuerent piere en Dieux, l'Euesqe d'Excestre, Chaunceler nostre seignur le Roi,

Ric. II. Supplie humblement vostre poure oratour, William Kele de Newerk, qe come vn William Courteys de Gedlyng et Margerie sa femme come en droit Margerie sueront vne assise de nouelle disseisine d'un mees oue les appurtenauntz en Newerk el Counte de Notyngham le Judy proschein apres le feste del Cluse de Paske[2] l'an du Reigne le Roi Edward, aiel nostre dit seignur le Roi, dys et neofysme, deuaunt Roger Bankewelle et Thomas Sybethorpe adonqes Justices as assises prendre el dit Counte assignez, enuers Robert Stoke et Alice sa femme et Thomas Snowe, Chapeleyn, et auters, processe tant sue deuaunt mesmes les Justices qe les ditz William Courteys et Margerie recouer-eront, les queux William et Margerie deuaunt execucion ent suy demeront; Et puis le dit suppliaunt pursui qe le dit record fuist fait venir en la Chauncellarie nostre dit seignur le Roi, et d'illeoqes maunde el Commune Banke nostre dit seignur le Roi; hors de quel record le dit suppliant come cosyn et heir l'auantdite Margerie, c'estassauoir, filz Thomas filz Elizabeth soere Thomas piere l'auant-dite Margerie, suyst vn scire facias enuers Richard de Stoke et Alice sa femme adonqes tenauntz de mesme le mees, l'an nostre dit seignur le Roi treszime, deuaunt Monsire Robert de Cherlton et ses compaignouns, adonqes Justices de mesme le Banke, retornable al quinszime de la Trinite, l'an nostre dit seignur le Roi quatorszime, processe tant suy qe le dit suppliant recouerist et suyst execucion et ent fuist en pesible possession par force de mesme le recouerer tanqe il fuist oste par Johan Pollard, Johan Burton de Newerk et Johan Tymworth, sanz processe de ley oue forte mayn: Qe vous plese de vostre tres graciouse seignurie graunter al dit suppliant briefs sur certein peyne directez as ditz Johan Pollard, Johan Burton et Johan Tymworth d'eux faire venir deuaunt vous el dit Chauncellarie de respoundre illeoqes del oster suisdit, Considerant qe le dit suppliant est si poure q'il ne poet en nulle manere enuers eux la commune ley pursuyer, et ceo pur Dieu et en eouere de charite.

---

[1] Bundle 3, No. 93.
[2] Clausum Paschae, or Low Sunday, is the first Sunday after Easter.

43   To the most honourable and most reverend Father in God, the Bishop of Exeter, Chancellor of our Lord the King,

Ric. II. Beseecheth humbly your poor orator, William Kele of Newark, that whereas one William Courteys, of Gedling, and Margery his wife, as in right of Margery, sued an assize of *novel disseisin* of a messuage with the appurtenants in Newark in the County of Nottingham, the Thursday next after the feast of Low Sunday in the 19th year of the reign of King Edward, grandfather of our said Lord the King [1345], before Roger Bankwell [3] and Thomas Sibthorpe,[4] then the Justices assigned to take assizes in the said county, against Robert Stoke and Alice, his wife, and Thomas Snowe, chaplain, and others ; and process was sued before the same Justices, so that the said William Courteys and Margery recovered [their seisin], the which William and Margery died before execution was sued thereof ;[5] and afterwards the said suppliant sued that the said record should be brought into the Chancery of our said Lord the King, and from thence sent into the Common Bench of our said Lord the King ; out of which record the said suppliant, as kinsman and heir of the said Margery, to wit, son of Thomas, son of Elizabeth, sister of Thomas, the father of the said Margery, sued a *scire facias* against Richard de Stoke and Alice, his wife, then tenants of the same messuage, 13 [Richard II, 1389-90], before Master Robert de Charlton and his fellows, then Justices of the said Bench, returnable on the quindene of Trinity, 14 [Richard II, 1390], process so sued that the said suppliant recovered [seisin] and sued execution thereof, and was in peaceable possession thereof by force of the same recovery, until he was ousted by John Pollard, John Burton of Newark and John Tymworth, with the strong hand and without process of law : May it please you of your most gracious Lordship to grant to the said suppliant writs, under a certain pain, directed to the said John Pollard, John Burton, and John Tymworth, to cause them to come before you in the said Chancery to answer there of the said ouster, considering that the said suppliant is so poor that he can in no wise pursue the Common Law against them ; and this for God and in way of charity.[6]

[3] Appointed a Justice of the King's Bench before Easter 1341 ; he is mentioned in the Year Books as late as 23 Edw. III., 1349-50. Foss.

[4] Not mentioned by Foss. He was probably a commissioner of Assize merely.

[5] Possibly in the Black Death of 1348.

[6] The poverty of the suitor was recognised as a valid reason for the interference of the Council as early as the reign of Edward I. (*Rot. Parl.* i. 372, 380), and in the 'articles' of 5 Hen. VI. the 'unmyght' of the plaintiff is expressly mentioned (*ibid.* v. 407). Many instances will be found in this Volume.

44 [1] A tres noble et tres gracious seignur, l'Eu
esqe d'Excestre, Chaunceller d'Engleterre,

Ric. II. Supplie humblement vostre pouere oratour, William Hamelyn, qe
come vn Johan Isbury le puisnee et Thomas Isbury en le feste del
assumpcion nostre dame, l'an de regne nostre seignur le Roy q'or'est
xvj[e], giseront en agayt del dit suppliant a Maleburgh en le Countee de
Wiltes', et en le dit suppliant assautes firont et ly bateront et
naufreront issint q'il fust en dispeir de sa vie ; et cez biens et chateux,
c'estassauer, boefs, vaches, blees et autres biens al value de vint liueres,
pristront et amesneront et lez ditz biens en lour garde vnqore detien-
drant ; Et outre lez ditz Johan et Thomas manassont le dit suppliant
continuelment de iour en autre pur ly occier, issint q'il ne ose mye
son pays aprochier ne deuers eux a la comune ley pursuer pur doute
de mort : Sur qoi pleise a vostre tres gracious seignurie de grantier a
dit suppliant briefs directz a lez ditz Johan et Thomas pur venir
deuant vous en vostre place sur vn certein peyne encontre lez treys
symeignes de Seint Michel proschein auenir, pur respondre a lez
matiers suisditz ; considerant, tres gracious seignur, qe lez ditz
Johan et Thomas sont si grandz de consanguineteez, alliancez et
amistez, en lour pays, qe le dit suppliant n'auera mye droit deuers
eux par ascun pursuite a la comune ley ; Les queux briefs vous pleise
grantier al dit suppliant pur Dieu et en oeure de charite.

Plegii de prosequendo :

> Johannes Melhede de Com' Somers'
> Walterus Hamelyn de Com' Deuon'

Sub pena x li.

45 [2] A tresreuerent piere en Dieu et tres
gracious seignur, l'Euesque d'Excestre,
Chaunceller d'Engleterre,

1393 Supplient tres humblement Thomas Godwyne et Johanne sa femme
nadgairs femme a Piers atte More de Suthewerk, qe come en le feste
de seint Michel en l'an du regne nostre tressexcellent seignur le Roy
Richard q'or'est xvij[e] le suisdit Piers atte More en sa viuount enfeffa
Thomas Profyt, parsone del eglise de seint George en Suthewerk,

---

[1] Bundle 3, No. 82.   [2] Bundle 3, No. 40.

44   To the most noble and most gracious lord,
the Bis o of Exeter, Chancellor of England,

ic. II.   Beseecheth humbly your poor orator, William Hamelyn, that whereas
one John Isbury the younger and Thomas Isbury on the feast of
the Assumption of our Lady, 16 Richard II. [1392], lay in wait for
the said suppliant at Marlborough in the County of Wilts, and
assaulted the said suppliant, and beat him and wounded him, so
that he despaired of his life ; and did seize and carry off his goods
and chattels, to wit, oxen, cows, corn, and other goods, to the value
of £20, and the said goods do yet detain in their custody ; and further, the said John and Thomas do continually threaten the said
suppliant from day to day to kill him, so that he dare not approach
his own country nor sue them at Common Law for fear of death :
Wherefore may it please your most gracious lordship to grant your
said suppliant writs directed to the said John and Thomas [command-
ing them] to come before you in your place [3] on a certain pain before
the three weeks of Michaelmas next, to answer concerning the said
matters ; considering, most gracious lord, that the said John and
Thomas are so great in their country in kinsmen, alliances and
friends, that the said suppliant cannot have right against them by
any suit at Common Law; the which writs may it please you to
grant the said suppliant for God and in way of charity.[4]

Pledges to prosecute :
    John Malhede of the County of Somerset,
    Walter Hamelyn of the County of Devon.
Under a penalty of £10.

45   To the most reverend Father in God, and
most gracious Lord, the Bishop of Exeter,
Chancellor of England,

ter
1393   Beseech most humbly Thomas Godwyne and Joan his wife, late wife of
Peter at More of Southwark, that whereas at Michaelmas in the 17th
year of our most excellent Lord King Richard who now is,[5] the said
Peter at More in his lifetime enfeoffed Thomas Profyt, parson of
S. George's Church, Southwark, Richard Saundre and John Denewey,

---

[3] Evidently the Chancery is meant.   [4] No remedy at Common Law.   [5] 1393.

Richard Saundre et John Denewey en vn tenement oue sez appurtenantz assis en Suthwerk, vynt et quatre acres de terre et sis acres
de pree en mesme la paroche de seint George, et en la parosche de
nostre Dame de Newnton, sur tiels condicions q'ensuient, c'estassauoir,
qe lez suisditz trois feffetz, mayntenaunt apres la mort du dit Piers,
duissent enfeffer la dite Johanne en touz les ditz terres et tenementz
oue touz ses appurtenauntz a terme de vie du dite Johanne, la remeyndre apres soun decesse a vn Nichol atte More, frere a dit Piers,
a auer a luy et a ses heirs de soun corps engendres, et pur defaute
d'issue la remeyndre outre pur estre vendu par quatre bonnes gentz
du dit parosche, et la monoye pur yceux receu, doner a seinte esglise
pur s'alme[1]; Sur quey le dit Piers murrust; apres qy mort deux des
dites feffetz, Richard et Johan, pur procurement d'un Johan Solas,
relesseront al dit Thomas Profyt tout lour estate dez ditz terres et
tenementz sur lez ditz condicions, pur la graunt affiaunce q'ils auoient en le dit Thomas Profyt qi fuist lour confessour, et q'il voleit parfourmer la volunte du dit Piers en fourme desuisdite; et ceo bien et
loialment faire mesme le Thomas Profyt iura par soun Verbum Dei lez
suisditz condicions en touz poyntz de parfourmer; apres quelle reles
ency faite, le dit Thomas Profyt par ymaginacion et fauxe couyne du
dit Johan Solas ad vendu a mesme le Johan Solas touz lez terres et
tenementz auauntditz pur toutz iours; Et le dit Johan Solas est
oblige al dit Thomas Profyt en cent liures par vne obligacion a faire
defence des ditz terres et tenementz par brocage et maynteynaunce
enuers chescuny; issint par lour fauce interpretacion et conspiracion
la dite Johanne Nichol et seinte eglise sount en poynt d'estre disherites
et dismettes de lour estate et droit, come desuis est dit, pur touz iours
torcenoucement, encountre lez condicions suisditz, et encontrariaunt
la volunte de dit Piers: Que plese a vostre tresdroiturel seignurie
pur comaunder lez ditz Thomas Profyt, Richard Saundre et Johan
Denewey venir deuaunt vous, et eux examiner pur la dire de verite de
toute la matere suisdit, issint qe la dite Johanne, qi n'ad de quoy
viuere, purra auoir soun droit en lez ditz terres et tenementz, come
par l'examinacion deuaunt vous, tresgracious seignur, serra troue et
proue; pur Dieu et en oeure de seint charite.

---

[1] This appears to be an abbreviation for 'sa alme.' I may mention here that apostrophes are not used at all in these documents.

in a tenement with the appurtenances situated in Southwark, and 24 acres of land and 6 acres of meadow in the said parish of S. George and in the parish of our Lady of Newington, on the conditions following, to wit, that the said three feoffees should, immediately after the death of the said Peter, enfeoff the said Joan in all the said lands and tenements with all their appurtenances for the life of the said Joan, with remainder after her decease to one Nicholas at More, brother of the said Peter, to hold to him and the heirs of his body begotten, and for default of issue, then to be sold by four worthy people of the said parish, and the money to be received for the same to be given to Holy Church for his soul; whereupon the said Peter died; and after his death two of the said feoffees, Richard [Saundre] and John [Denewey], by the procurement of one John Solas, released all their estate in the said lands and tenements to the said Thomas Profyt, on the said conditions, out of the great trust that they had in the said Thomas Profyt, who was their confessor, that he would perform the will of the said Peter [at More] in form aforesaid; and this well and lawfully to do the same Thomas Profyt swore on his *Verbum Dei* and to perform the said conditions in all points; and since the release was so made, the said Thomas Profyt, through the scheming and false covin of the said John Solas, hath sold all the lands and tenements aforesaid to the same John Solas for ever; And the said John Solas is bound to the said Thomas Profyt in £100 by a bond to make defence of the said lands and tenements by brokage [2] and maintenance against every one; and so by their false interpretation and conspiracy the said Joan, Nicholas, and Holy Church are like to be disinherited and put out of their estate and right, as is above said, for ever, tortiously, against the said conditions, and contrary to the will of the said Peter [at More]: May it please your most righteous Lordship to command the said Thomas Profy̆t, Richard Saundre, and John Denewey to come before you, and to examine them to tell the truth of all the said matter, so that the said Joan, who hath not wherewithal to live, may have her right in the said lands and tenements, as by the examination before you, most gracious Lord, shall be found and proved; for God and in way of holy charity.[3]

---

[2] The usual meaning of this word in early documents is the corrupt farming or jobbing of offices, or the price or bribe paid unlawfully for any office or place of trust; in the text its meaning seems to be equivalent to maintenance.

[3] A purely equity matter. Feoffees to uses were known in England as early as the twelfth century. The plan was largely adopted by the Franciscan Friars (who came here *cir.* 1224), because the rules of their order forbad them to own anything. See Pollock and Maitland, *Hist. of English Law*, ii. 229, and the cases cited, pp. 232, 233.

46 ¹ A tres reuerent piere en Dieux et soun tres honure seignour, l'Euesque d'Excestre et Chaunceller d'Engleterre,

Ric. II. Monstre vostre bachiler, Robert Yeluerton, Chiualer, et se pleint de Rauf Trenewith del Counte de Cornewaille, qe come le dit Robert soit seignur del Manoir de Trenewith et Trewishannes come del droit Johanne sa femme et qe les auncestrez la dite Johanne eient graunte as auncestrez le dit Rauf en la taille comune de pasture a certein nombre des bestez et resonable estouers deins le dit Manoir come piert par vn fin leue en temps le Roi E, aiel nostre seignour le Roi q'or'est, la vient le dit Rauf qi n'ad riens el dit Manoir forsqe la dite comune et resonable estouers, oue graunde nombre des gentz ouesque lui oue arkez, setes, espees, bokelers, bastouns, souent foitz countre la pees, et graund quantite du bois du dit Robert abatise par colour des ditz comune et resonablez estouers, et les arbres issint abatu vendi et dona as diuerses gentz du dit pais ; et auxi ad pris deins le dit bois cere et mel qatient au dit Robert ; et auxi l'ou le dit Robert ad vn profit deins le dit Manoir appelle Tyntol, le dit Rauf l'ad pris a soun oeps demesne, encountre la ley, si come il fuist seignur del soil ; et auxi l'ou le dit Robert par ces seruauntz ad vendu pasture as diuerses gentz du pais, come bien lui luis sauant as comuners sufficiant comune, la vient le dit Rauf come deuant est dit, et prist les ditz bestez issint agistez et les emparka tanqe les possessours des ditz bestez lui ount fait fin a sa volunte, par ount le dit Robert ne purroit nul profit prendre ; et auxi ascuns des bestez issint agistez ad tue et d'autres trespassauntz deins le dit Manoir prist amendez a soun oeps demesne, si come il fuist seignur du soil, a graund anientisment du dit Robert ; et en les seruauntz du dit Robert de mesme le Manoir assaut fist, batise et malement treta, c'estassauoir Johan Nicol, Johan Eursdon, et autres, par qi nul homme apeine est hardi de seruir le dit Robert deins le dit Manoir, par qi le dit Robert pardist le profit q'il poet auoir pris de soun dit Manoir ; les queux articlez sount notories et bien conuz el dit pais : Please a vostre gracious seignurie grauntier brief direct al dit Rauf d'estre deuant le tres sage counseil nostre seignur le Roi de

¹ Bundle 3, No. 116.

46   To the most reverend Father in God and his most honoured Lord, the Bishop of Exeter and Chancellor of England,

Ric. II   Showeth your bachelor,[2] Robert Yelverton, knight, and complaineth of Ralph Trenewith of the County of Cornwall, that whereas the said Robert is lord of the manor of Trenewith and Trewishannes in right of Joan his wife, and the ancestors of the said Joan had granted to the ancestors of the said Ralph, in tail, common of pasture for a certain number of beasts and reasonable estovers within the said manor, as appeareth by a fine levied in the time of King Edward, grandfather of our Lord the King who now is, there came the said Ralph, who hath nothing in the said manor except the said common and reasonable estovers, and a great number of people with him, with bows, arrows, swords, bucklers, and staves, many times against the peace, and cut a great quantity of the said Robert's wood by colour of the said common and reasonable estovers, and sold and gave the trees so cut down to divers persons of the said country; And also he [Ralph] hath taken wax and honey belonging to the said Robert within the said wood; and also, whereas the said Robert hath a profit called ' Tin-toll '[3] within the said manor, the said Ralph hath seized it to his own use, contrary to law, as if he were lord of the soil; And also, whereas the said Robert [Yelverton], by his servants, hath sold pasture to divers persons of that country, as well he might, saving sufficient common for the commoners, there came the said Ralph [Trenewith] as aforesaid, and seized the beasts so agisted, and impounded them until the possessors of the said beasts made fine with him at his will, whereby the said Robert could not take any profit; And also he [Ralph] hath killed some of the beasts so agisted, and of other [beasts] trespassing within the said manor he hath taken amends to his own use, as if he were lord of the soil, to the great destruction of the said Robert; And hath assaulted, beaten and ill-treated the said Robert's servants in the said manor, to wit, John Nicol, John Fursdon, and others, so that scarce any one is bold enough to serve the said Robert within the said manor, whereby the said Robert hath lost the profit he would have taken from his said manor; Which articles are notorious and well known in the said country: May it please your most gracious Lordship to grant a writ directed to the said Ralph, [commanding him] to be before the most

[2] The word is still used in this sense when we speak of a Knight Bachelor.
[3] Probably the same as ' Tin-penny,' a   tribute paid for the liberty of digging in tin mines. Cowell.

de charite.

A l'onurable piere en Dieu, l'Euesque
d'Excestre, Chanceller d'Engleterre

1401 Monstre Johan Prophete, Clerc, greuousement en compleinant qe combien qe le Manoir de Ansty en Countee de Warr' par la mort de Johan
Deyncourt, Chiualer, (qi tenoit le dit Manoir de Richard, nadgairs
Roy d'Engleterre, par seruice de Chiualer, come du Manoir de Cheilles-
more), et a cause du meindre age de Roger Deyncourt, fitz et heir au
dit Johan, estoit seisez es mains du dit nadgairs Roy; et sur ce par
ses lettres patentes il eust grantez a Monsire William d'Arundell la
garde du dit Manoir de Ansty durante la meindre age de l'auantdit
Roger; et apres la mort du dit Monsire William d'Arundell, Dame
Agnes, qe feust sa femme et executrice de son testament, eust donez
et grantez au dit Johan Prophete la garde du dit Manoir durante la
meindre age de mesme celuy Roger, ensemblement ouec les issues et
profitz du Manoir susdit duz de temps passez, come par lettres de la
dite Dame Agnes ent faites, et par nostre souerain seignur le Roy
q'ore est² ratifyes et confermees, purra plus pleinement apparoire.
Nientmaine vn Roger Smart, durante la meindre age du dit heir, ad
entrez en le dit Manoir de Ansty, et pris les issues et profitz dycelle
par vn an et plus, non obstant qe le dit heir n'eit vncore lineree de
mesme le Manoir hors des mains du Roy; quel entre et occupacion
est fait sibien en contempt du Roy et disheriteson du dit Roger Deyncourt come a damage et preiudice de l'auantdit Johan Prophete a la
value de xxx liures et plus. Par quoy supplie le dit Johan Prophete
qe please au dit Chanceller comander au dit Roger Smart, ore esteant
present en la Chancellerie, d'esteere a son response sur les materes
desusdites tant al suit du Roy come du dit Johan Prophete, saunz
lesser le dit Roger Smart departir tanque il eit fait gree au Roy et au
dit suppliant siauant come ley et reson demandent; et q'il troeue
suffissante seuretee qe desore enauant il n'attemptera riens contre le

¹ Bundle 3, No. .78. This and the   of Exeter's second Chancellorship, 1401 to
following eight bills belong to the Bishop   1403.   ² Henry IV.

wise Council of our Lord the King to answer the said Robert as to the articles aforesaid; For God and in way of charity.[3]

47   To the honourable Father in God, the Bishop of Exeter, Chancellor of England,

1401 Showeth John Prophete, clerk,[4] grievously complaining that whereas the manor of Ansty in the county of Warwick, by the death of John Deyncourt, knight (who held the said manor of Richard, late King of England, by knight service, as of the manor of Cheylesmore), and because of the nonage of Roger Deyncourt, son and heir of the said John, was seized into the hands of the said late King; and thereupon he [Richard] by his letters patent granted the wardship of the said manor of Ansty, during the nonage of the said Roger, to Sir William de Arundel; and after the death of the said Sir William de Arundel, Dame Agnes, who was his wife, and executrix of his will, gave and granted the wardship of the said manor, during the nonage of the said Roger, together with the issues and profits of the said manor [accrued] due for time past, to the said John Prophete, as by the letters of the said Dame Agnes made thereof, and ratified and confirmed by our Lord the King who now is,[2] may more plainly appear. Nevertheless one Roger Smart, during the nonage of the said heir, hath entered on the said manor of Ansty, and hath taken the issues and profits thereof for a year and more, notwithstanding that the said heir hath not yet [sued his] livery of the same manor out of the King's hands ; the which entry and occupation is done as well in contempt of the King and to the disinherison of the said Roger Deyncourt as to the damage and prejudice of the said John Prophete to the value of £30 and more. Wherefore the said John Prophete beseecheth that it may please the said Chancellor to command the said Roger Smart, who is now present in the Chancery,[5] to stand to his answer touching the matters aforesaid, as well at the suit of the King as of the said John Prophete, not allowing the said Roger Smart to go away until he hath made accord to the King and to the said suppliant so far as law and right demand ; and that he may find sufficient surety that henceforward he will not attempt

---

[3] The violence and power of the defendant seem to be the only reasons for approaching the Chancellor.

[4] He was Clerk of the Privy Council under Richard II. and Henry IV., which probably accounts for his petition to the Chancellor. See *Proc. and Ord. of the Privy Council*, i. *passim*.

[5] See p. 37, note 5.

Roy, ne le dit Johan Prophete, touchant le dit Manoir, tancome il
auera la garde de mesme le Manoir par vertue du grant auantdit.

Indorsed. Memorandum quod primo die Decembris anno regni
Regis Henrici quarti post conquestum tercio,[1] Ricardus Merbroke et
Thomas Archer coram domino Rege in Cancellaria sua personaliter
constituti manuceperunt de habendo infrascriptum Roger Smart in
Cancellaria predicta in Octabis Sancti Hillarii proximo futuri vbicunque
tunc fuerit, videlicet, vterque predictorum Ricardi et Thome sub pena
quadraginta librarum, quas concesserunt et vterque eorum per se
insolidum concessit de terris et catallis suis ad opus ipsius domini
Regis leuari in casu quo ipsi prefatum Rogerum in Cancellaria predicta
ad diem predictum in forma predicta non habuerint.

48   [2] Al tres reuerent piere en Dieu, l'Euesque
                 d'Excestre, Chanceller d'Engleterre,

1402 Suppliet humblement Johan Frank, vn des Clerks del Chancellerie
nostre seignur le Roi, qe come par presentement Richard nadgairs Roi
d'Engleterre, qi de patronage del esglise de Lutton fuit sesy en son
demesne come de fee, fuit vn William Vpton, autrement appellee
William Hile, admys a mesme l'esglise, et institut et induct en ycelle;
le quelle continua sa possession ans et iours tanque a sa moriant,
apres qi mort fuit vostre dit suppliant, par force del presentement
nostre seignur le Roi q'ore est,[3] fait en son droit roiale, duement
institut et induct en l'esglise auantdite, come par les institucions et
induccions ent faitz purra pleinement apparoir; et sa possession ent
peisiblement continua tanque vn Robert Rodelane, Chapellein, John
Symond, Chapellein, et Nicholl Lauerence, le dymenge proschein
denant le fest de Seint Martyn darrein passee viendrent al dite esglise,
et sur la possession le dit presentee nostre dit seignur le Roi en mesme
l'esglise tortenousement, et par maistrie, et sanz due proces, entrerent
et ent luy ousterent, et les oblacions, dismes, rentes des tenantz, et
toutz autres profitz du dite esglise, le meene temps prouenantz et a
ycelle appurtenantz, pristrent et vncore preignent, et la possession de
mesme l'esglise maliciousement teignont vncore, et font tiele manace
qe les procuratours ne seruantz le dit presentee nostre dit seignur le
Roi n'osent approcher sa dite esglise; a tres grande preiudice, reproof
et damage nostre dit seignur le Roi et de son clerk auantdit: Plese

---

[1] 1401.   [2] Bundle 3, No. 79.   [3] Henry IV.

anything against the King, nor the said John Prophete, touching the said manor, so long as [the said John Prophete] shall have the custody of the same manor by virtue of the grant aforesaid.

Indorsed. Be it remembered that on December 1, 3 Henry IV.,[1] Richard Merbroke and Thomas Archer personally appearing before the Lord King in his Chancery, undertook to have the within written Roger Smart in the Chancery aforesaid on the octave of S. Hilary next, wherever it shall then be, that is to say, each of them, the aforesaid Richard and Thomas, under a penalty of £40, which they have granted, and each of them for himself alone hath granted, to be levied of their lands and chattels to the King's use, in case they shall not have the said Roger in the Chancery aforesaid, at the day aforesaid, in form aforesaid.

48   To the most reverend Father in God, the Bishop of Exeter, Chancellor of England,

1402 Humbly beseecheth John Frank, one of the Clerks of the Chancery of our Lord the King, that whereas by the presentation of Richard, late King of England, who was seised in his demesne as of fee of the patronage of the church of Lutton, one William Upton, otherwise called William Hile, was admitted to the same church, and instituted and inducted therein ; who continued his possession thereof for years and days until his death, after whose death your said suppliant, by force of the presentation of our Lord the King who now is, made in his royal right, was duly instituted and inducted into the said church, as by the institutions and inductions made thereof may plainly appear ; and he continued his possession thereof peaceably until one Robert Rodelane, chaplain, John Symond, chaplain, and Nicholas Laurence, on the Sunday before the feast of S. Martin last past, came to the said church, and entered on the possession of the said presentee of our said Lord the King in the same church tortiously and by mastery, and without due process [of law], and therefrom did oust him, and took and do still take the oblations, tithes, rents of tenants, and all other profits of the said church arising in the mean time and appurtenant thereto, and they do still maliciously hold possession of the said church, and do make such menace that the proctors and servants of the said presentee of our said Lord the King dare not approach the said church ; to the great prejudice, reproof and damage of our said Lord the King, and of

a vostre tres noble et tres graciouse seignurie ordeigner due punisse-
ment et remedie en ceste partie, en saluacion del droit, honour et
estat nostre seignur le Roi et de son dit clerk; pur Dieu et en oepre
de charitee.

      Termino Hillarii anno tercio Regis Henrici quarti.[1]

   Indorsed.   Dies datus est per dominum Cancellarium infrascripto
Roberto Rodelane quod compareat coram domino Rege in Cancellaria
sua in quindenis Pasche anno tercio Regis Henrici in propria persona
sua sub pena viginti librarum responsurus materiis infracontentis.

49   [2] A tres bonure et tres reuerent pier en Dieu,
l'Euesque d'Excestre, Chaunceller d'Engle
terre,

After   Suppliont humblement Thomas Walker et Juliane sa femme, qe come
1401   la dite Juliane, tanceme ele fuist sole, fuist seisi de la garde des
certeins terres et tenements oue les appurtenauntz appellez Swannes-
dyche en Tonneworthe, par cause de meindre age de Johan fitz et heir
a Thomas de Bernes come proschein amy, c'estassauoir, miere au dit
Johan, pur ceo qe la dite terre est teunz en socage, la vient vn Thomas
Archer, oue force et armes, le Lundy proschein apres le feste de la
Natiuite de nostre Dame, l'an de regne nostre seignur le Roy q'ore est
seconde,[3] et a fort main sur la dite Juliane en la dite terre entra, et
sez bleez et herbes, c'estassauoir, frument, oue arkes, setees, espees,
bokelers, ouesque graunt nombre des gents, illeoqes cressantz a la
value de xx liures, scia et emporta; et vn taure, vne vache pris de
deux marcz de dite Juliane, illeoqes trouez, prist et amesna; Et en
vn Thomas Arnald, seruant as ditz suppliantz, illeoqes assaut fist, et
luy batist, et deux marcz d'argent de dit Thomas Arnald par extorcion
prist; a tort et as damages les ditz suppliantz de xl liures : Please a
vostre tres gracious seignurie considerer les ditz graundes extorcions
par le dit Thomas Archer faitz, et de ceo faire droit as ditz suppliantz,
pur Dieu et en oeure de charitee.

---

[1] 1402. This is written at the head of the document in a different hand.

[2] Bundle 3, No. 77. See Case 51.

[3] Henry IV., 1401. The feast is Sept. 8.

his clerk aforesaid : May it please your most noble and most gracious Lordship to ordain due punishment and remedy in this behalf, in salvation of the right, honour and estate of our Lord the King and of his said clerk ; For God and in way of charity.

Hilary Term, 3 Henry IV.

Indorsed. A day is given by the Lord Chancellor to the within written Robert Rodelane to appear before the Lord King in his Chancery, on the quindene of Easter, 3 Henry [IV.], in his proper person, under a penalty of £20, to answer the matters within contained.[4]

49 To the most honoured and most reverend Father in God, the Bishop of Exeter, Chan cellor of England,

After 1401 Humbly beseech Thomas Walker and Juliana his wife, that whereas the said Juliana while she was sole was seised of the wardship of certain lands and tenements with the appurtenances, called 'Swans' Ditch,' in Tonworth, by reason of the nonage of John son and heir of Thomas de Bernes, [she being] his next friend, to wit, mother of the said John, because the said land is held in socage, there came one Thomas Archer, with force and arms, on the Monday after the feast of the Nativity of our Lady, in the second year of the reign of our Lord the King who now is, and with the strong hand against the said Juliana entered on the said land, and cut and carried away her corn and grass there growing, to wit, wheat, to the value of £20, [being armed] with bows and arrows, swords and bucklers, and with a great number of people ; and seized and took away a bull and a cow of the said Juliana's there found, price 2 marks ; and there assaulted one Thomas Arnald, servant of the said suppliants, and beat him, and took two marks of silver by extortion from the said Thomas Arnald ; [and this] wrongfully, and to the damages of the said suppliants of £40 : May it please your most gracious Lordship to consider the said great extortions made by the said Thomas Archer, and thereof to do right to the said suppliants, for God and in way of charity.[5]

[4] The plaintiff being a Clerk of the Chancery, the case comes within the Chancellor's common law jurisdiction. No principle of equity is involved.

[5] There seems no particular reason for applying to the Chancellor in this case, except the defendant's violence. The infancy of the tenant in socage has, apparently, nothing to do with it.

50   ¹ A tres reuerent pier en Dieu, et tres
          gracious seignur, l'Euesque d'Excestre,
          Chaunceler d'Engleterre,

After   Monstront humblement Robert Faryngton et Johan Brokholes,
1401   Clerkis del Chaunselerie nostre seignur le Roy, q'un Water Welryngton
        a tort vient, et oue force et armes, c'est assauoir, espeez, boclers et
        bastons, le xxᵐᵉ iour de Julij, l'an nostre seignur le Roy q'ore est ijᵈᵉ,²
        et les closez et les maisons de les auantditz Robert et Johan a
        Londres en le paroch de toutz seintz de Berkyngcherch en le garde de
        Touerstrete debrusa, et lour tenantz la demurantz, c'est assauoir,
        William Chaundeler, Johan Vndirhill, Johan Chenore, et Richard
        Prendigest, Frutour, de lour vies et membres manassa et vnqore de
        iour en autre manasse ; et les ditz tenantz entant qe les rentz, fermes,
        et seruicez as auantditz Robert et Johan pur les tenurez des ditz
        tenantz duez paier ne purront desturba ; et autres graundes tortz a
        eur [sic] et a lour ditz tenantz fist, a tort et encontre le pees nostre
        seignur le Roy, et as damages des ditz pleintiffs de C. liures ; Sur quoi
        les ditz Robert et Johan supplient a vostre tres graciouse seignurie
        due remedie en celle partie, pur Dieu et en oeure de charite.

51   ³ A tres bonure et tres reuerent piere en
          Dieux, l'Euesque d'Excestre et Chaunceller
          d'Engleterre,

After   Supplient humblement Thomas Walker et Juliane sa femme qe,
1401   come ils furent seisez de certeins terres et tenementz en Tonne-
        worthe et eux lesseront a vn Johan Notehurst a terme de x ans
        rendant par an as ditz suppliantz sept marcz, la vint Thomas
        Archer oue plusours autres a force et armes le lunedy prochein de-
        nuant le fest de Nowelle derrein passe, et l'auauntdit Johan manasse
        q'il ne poet la dite terre gayner ne ocupier durant son terme auauntdit
        ne son rent as ditz suppliantz paiere par doute de sa morte par le
        dit Thomas Archer et sez mayntenours ; ne nulle autre les auaunt-
        ditz terres n'oyse prendre par mesme la cause ; as damages des
        ditz suppliantz xx liures ; Et que mesme Thomas Archer oue force et
        armes le vendredy prochein deuaunt le fest de la Natiuitee de nostre

---

¹ Bundle 3, No. 89. See Case 49.   ² Henry IV., 1401.   ³ Bundle 3, No. 76.

50   To the most reverend Father in God and most gracious Lord, the Bis o of Exeter, Chancellor of England,

After
1401

Humbly show Robert Farington and John Brockholes, Clerks of the Chancery of our Lord the King, that one Walter Welrington wrongfully came with force and arms, to wit, swords, bucklers and clubs, the 20th day of July, in the 2nd year of our Lord the King who now is, and broke the closes and houses of the said Robert and John in London in the parish of All Hallows Barking, in the Ward of Tower Street, and threatened their tenants there dwelling, to wit, William Chandler, John Underhill, John Chenore and Richard Prendigast, fruiterer, of their lives and limbs, and still doth threaten them from day to day; and hath so disturbed the said tenants that they cannot pay the rents, farms, and services, due to the said Robert and John by the tenures of the said tenants ; and hath done other great wrongs to them and to their said tenants, wrongfully and against the peace of our Lord the King, and to the damages of the said plaintiffs of £100 ;   Whereupon the said Robert and John beseech from your most gracious Lordship due remedy in this case, for God and in way of charity.[1]

51   To the most honoured and most reverend Father in God, the Bishop of Exeter and Chancellor of England,

After
1401

Humbly beseech Thomas Walker and Juliana his wife, that whereas they were seised of certain lands and tenements in Tonworth,[5] and leased them to one John Notehurst for a term of ten years, yielding yearly to the said suppliants 7 marks, there came Thomas Archer, with many others, with force and arms, on the Monday before Christmas last past, and menaced the said John so that he could not till nor occupy the said land during his term aforesaid, nor pay his rent to the said suppliants, for fear of his death by the said Thomas Archer and his maintainers ; and no other person dared take the said lands for the same cause ; to the damages of the said suppliants of £20 ;   And that the same Thomas Archer, with force and arms on the Friday next before the feast of the

[1] The plaintiffs being Clerks of the Chancery, the case comes within the Chancellor's common law jurisdiction.

[5] Probably either Tamworth, co. Staffs., or Tanworth, co. Warwick.

dame, l'an du regne nostre seignur le Roy q'ore est second,[1] lour
seueral ewe a Tonneworth pisca et les pessons illeoqes troues a le
valu de x liures prist et emporta, as damages des ditz suppliantz x
liures : Please a vostre tres gracious seignurie considerer a les grandes
damages et extorcions par le dit Thomas Archer faitz as ditz suppli-
autz et nomement de ceo q'il est si grand mayntenour, extorcioner et
conducour des enquestes en sa pays issint qe nulle n'osa contredire
le dit Thomas Archer ; pur Dieux et en ouere de charite.[2]

52   [3] A tres reuerent pier en Dieu et tres
          graciouse seignur, l'Euesque d'Excestre et
          Chaunceller d'Engleterre,

After Supplie vostre poure oratour William de Egremond, parsone de
1401 Wirkyngton en le countee de Cumbr', qe come Richard Orfeure,
Richard de Lamplogh, William de Syngilton et Nicol Harras et
plusours autres disconuz par abbettement le dit Richard Orfeure,
en le veile de seynt Mare Magdalene, l'an nostre seignur le Roi
q'or'est second,[4] oue force et armes viendront a Wirkyngton suisdit
dedeinz la Franchise de sa esglise suisdit en le dit suppliant horriblement de lour tort demesne ossaut firent, et le dit suppliant vou-
dront auoir pris ou tuez sy noun q'il feust a mesme le temps reneste
pur diuinez seruicez faire ; et Richard de Wodhall, William Clerke,
Richard de Bromfeld, Thomas Diconson, Richard Diconson, et Johan
Carpenter, seruantz al dit suppliant, illoeqes pristeront, et ouesque
eux amesneront tanque a Egremond, et illoeqes lez emprisoneront, et
en prisone detiendront par viij semaignes et plus, tanq'ils firent fyne
oue le dit Richard Orfeure et lez autres de x li. pur lour deliuerance
auoir ; Et nient obstante qe diuerses briefs de part nostre seignur le
Roy et honurables lettres de part nostre seignur le prince feurent
diliuerez al dit Richard Orfeure come Baillif le seignur Fitz Wauter
de Egremond pur certifier la cause del emprisonement suisdit, le dit
Richard Orfeure en grande dedignacion et despit lez ditz briefs et
lettre resceust et rien pur ceux ne voilloit my faire, einz par cause dez
briefs et lettre suisditz feust plus haynouse et horible q'il ne feust
vnqes a deuant en disobeisance et contempt de lez mandementz et
la lettre suisditz ; et la malice le dit Richard Orfeure et les autres

---

[1] Henry IV., 1401. This feast is Sept. 8.   [2] The suggestion is that the plaintiffs

Nativity of our Lady, in the second year of the reign of our Lord the King who now is, fished in their several water at Tonworth, and the fish there found he did take and carry away to the value of £10, to the damage of the said suppliants of £10 : May it please your most gracious Lordship to consider the great damages and extortions done by the said Thomas Archer to the said suppliants, and especially of this, that he is so great a maintainer, extortioner and conducer of inquests in his country that no one dare contradict the said Thomas Archer ; For God and in way of charity [2]

52   To the most reverend Father in God and most gracious Lord, the Bishop of Exeter and Chancellor of England,

After 1401   Beseecheth your poor orator, William de Egremont, parson of Workington in the County of Cumberland, that whereas Richard Goldsmith, Richard de Lamplugh, William de Singleton and Nicholas Harras, and many others unknown, by the abetment of the said Richard Goldsmith, on the eve of S. Mary Magdalene in the second year of our Lord the King who now is,[4] with force and arms, did come to Workington aforesaid, and within the franchise of his said church did horribly assault the said suppliant, of their own wrong, and would have taken or killed the said suppliant if he had not been at that time vested for divine service ; and there they did seize Richard de Woodhall, William Clerke, Richard de Bromfeld, Thomas Diconson, Richard Diconson and John Carpenter, servants of the said suppliant, and did take them away with them to Egremont, and there did imprison them, and did keep them in prison for eight weeks and more, until they made fine with the said Richard Goldsmith and the others for £10 to have deliverance ; And notwithstanding that divers writs on behalf of our Lord the King and honourable letters on behalf of our Lord the Prince were delivered to the said Richard Goldsmith, as Bailiff of Egremont for Lord FitzWalter, to certify the cause of the said imprisonment, the said Richard Goldsmith received the said writs and letter in great contempt and despite, and would do nothing in compliance therewith, but by reason of the said writs and letter was more malicious and horrible than ever he was before, in disobedience and contempt of the commandments and letter aforesaid ; And the malice of

could get no remedy at common law through fear of the defendant's violence and power.

[3] Bundle 3, No. 30.
[4] Henry IV., July 21, 1401.

prison tanque gree serroit fait al dit Hamond del dite somme, Et en prison demura del feste auantdit tanque al fyn d'une moys adonqes prochein ensuant, qe le dit Mair luy lessa d'aler a large, gree ou satis-faccion del somme auantdit al dit suppliant nient faitz, a tort et a sez damages de x liures ; dount il prie remedie pur Dieu et en oeoure de charitee.

Plegii de predicto Willelmo ·

Oliuerus

Ricardus Michell.

Indorsed.   Dies datus est partibus vsque ad quindenam Sancte Trinitatis proximo future.

54   [1] A tres reuerent piere en Dieux et tres gracious seignur, Euesqe de Excestre, Chan-celler d'Engleterre,

1402   Monstre humblement Johan Bartelot, vn dez seruants en la Recept del Escheqer nostre seignur le Roy, et soy compleint sur vn William Russell, q'est chief Conestable del Hundred de Bekyngtre en le Counte de Essex, de ceo qe le dit William par graunde malice et par mainte-nance de Dann Herman, Abbe de Monken Stratford, en le dymenge le xxijº iour de ceste moys de Januer, l'an tierce del regne nostre seignur le Roy Henri,[2] ouesqe autres de son couigne, oue force et armes, en les champes de Esthamme gesoit en agayt sur le dit Johan pur luy auoir oeeis ; et sureeo mesme le iour et an, sicome le dit Johan estoit venant de son esglise parochiel de Esthamme auantdit vers son hostel, l'euantdit William onesque autres encontre la pes en les champes auantditz, oue gleyues, baselardes et bastons, assaut en le dit Johan fist et ly malement batist, et luy voloit auoir occis, s'il ne vst este socoure et rescue par certeins de sez veisines ; Et outre ceo le dit William ouesque quatre autres gents, par maintenance del Abbe susdit, oue force et armes et encontre la pes come desus est dit mesme le dymenge apres noon ala quere l'euantdit Johan en diuerses mesons de la ville de Esthamme pur auoir oeeis l'euantdit Johan si ills luy puissent auoir troue : Qe plese a vostre tres graciouse seignurie con-siderer qe le dit William est le pluis graund oppressor del poeple et

---

[1] Bundle 3, No. 42.   [2] 1402.

which he [Martyn] was committed to prison until satisfaction should be made to the said Hamond of the said sum ; And in prison did he remain from the feast aforesaid for a whole month thence next following, when the Mayor did wrongfully let him go at large, no accord or satisfaction of the sum aforesaid having been made to the said suppliant, and to his damage of £10 ; Of which he prayeth remedy, for God and in way of charity.[3]

Pledges for the said William :

Oliver

Richard Mitchell.

A day is given to the parties on the quindene of Trinity next.

54   To the most reverend Father in God and most gracious Lord, the Bis o of Exeter, Chancellor of England,

1402   Humbly showeth John Bartelot, one of the servants of the Receipt of the Exchequer of our Lord the King, and complaineth of one William Russell, who is Chief Constable of the Hundred of Becontree in the County of Essex, that the said William, by great malice and by the maintenance of Dom Herman, Abbat of Monks Stratford,[4] on Sunday, the 22nd day of this month of January, in the third year of the reign of our Lord King Henry, with others of his covin, with force and arms, did lie in wait for the said John in the fields of East Ham, in order to have killed him ; and thereupon, the same day and year, as the said John was coming from his parish church of East Ham aforesaid towards his house, the said William and others, against the peace, did assault the said John in the fields aforesaid, with glaives, baslards, and clubs, and did beat him sore, and would have killed him, if he had not been succoured and rescued by certain of his neighbours ; And moreover, the said William, with four other persons, by maintenance of the said Abbat, with force and arms and against the peace, as aforesaid, on the same Sunday, after noon, did go to seek the said John in divers houses in the said town of East Ham, in order to have killed him if they could have found him : May it please your most gracious Lordship to consider that the said William is the greatest oppressor of the people and disturber of

---

[3] There seems no reason why this matter should be brought before the Chancellor.

[4] Now known as Stratford-Langthorne. The Cistercian Abbey was founded about 1135.

destourbour del pees en les marches illeoqes, et pur ceo vous plese luy
faire venir deuant vous et luy punisser come la ley demande et son dit
mayntenour auxi, et auxi eux faire trouer sufficeant suirte du pees pur
eux et touz lours, en saluacion del vie le dit Johan, et en oeuere de
charite.

55   ¹ A tres reuerent piere en Dieu et tres
            gracious seignur, l'Euesque d'Excestre,
            Chauncellere d'Engleterre,

Query,   Supplie tres humblement Agneys la femme d'un William Wykham,
Ien. IV. Citezein de la cite de Loundres, qe come le dit William venoit
par voie marchandise en la terre de Flaundres et prist son hostelle
en la ville de Sclus,² et illeoqes vendist certeynes marchaundises
as diuerses gentz de mesme la ville; et qant il duist estre
paie, les ditz gentz par faux ymaginacion et conspiracie fesoient
arester le dit William et luy mistrent en prison deins le chastelle de
Sclus, la ou il gist, et ne poet my estre deliuere tanque il paia CC
Frankz pur son raunson et chescun iour xijd. de moneye d'Engleterre
pur ses costages; Et pur cele cause, tres reuerent piere, deux certeyns
hommes de mesme la ville sont arestes a Portesmouth : Que plese a
vostre tres reuerent paternite et tres gracious seignurie de graunt vn
brief direct a les Baillifs de Portesmouth auantdit eux comandant de
safment garder les ditz gentz issint arestes, sanz ascun deliuerance
tanque le dit William soit deliuere hors du prison ; pur Dieu et en
oeure de charite.

Indorsed. Soit fait brief as Baillif et Conestables de la ville de
Portesmuth d'auer Henrik et Poul Kengyard du paiis de Flaundres,
estant en lour garde, deuant le Counsail nostre seignur le Roy a West-
menstre en la viele de Seint Jake l'apostre prochein venant, pur
certeins causes le dit Counsail moeuantes, ensemblement ouesque la
cause de lour prise et detenue.   Par le Conseil ; presens,
            Messeignurs le Chanceller,
                    Tressorer,
                    Gardein du prive seal,
                    J. Scarle,
                    [J.] Prophete,
                    Johan Doreward,
                et Johan Frome.

¹ Bundle 3, No. 44.   ² Near Flushing.

the peace in the marches there, and may it therefore please you to make him come before you, and to punish him as the law doth demand, and his said maintainer also,[3] and also to make them find sufficient surety for the peace for them and all theirs, in salvation of the life of the said John, and in way of charity.[4]

55   To the most reverend Father in God and most gracious Lord, the Bis o of Exeter, Chancellor of England,

Query, Ien. IV Beseecheth most humbly Agnes, wife of one William Wykham, citizen of the City of London, that whereas the said William came in way of trade to the country of Flanders, and made his abode in the town of Sluys, and there sold certain merchandise to divers people of the same town; and when he ought to have been paid, the said people by false scheming and conspiracy caused the said William to be arrested and put in prison within the Castle of Sluys, where he [still] doth lie, and he cannot be delivered until he pay 200 francs for his ransom, and 12d. a day, of English money, for his expenses; And for this cause, most reverend Father, certain two men of the same town have been arrested at Portsmouth: May it please your most reverend paternity and most gracious Lordship to grant a writ directed to the Bailiffs of Portsmouth aforesaid commanding them safely to keep the said two men so arrested, without any deliverance until the said William be delivered out of prison; For God and in way of charity.[5]

Indorsed. Let a writ be made to the Bailiff and Constables of the town of Portsmouth, [directing them] to have Henrik and Paul Kengyard, of the country of Flanders, being in their custody, before the Council of our Lord the King at Westminster on the eve of S. James the Apostle next coming, for certain causes moving the said Council, together with the cause of their arrest and detention. By the Council.

Present, my Lords	J[ohn] Scarle,
The Chancellor,	J[ohn] Prophete,
Treasurer,	John Doreward, and
Keeper of the Privy Seal,	John Frome.

[2] The Abbat of Stratford.
[4] As in the two preceding cases and many others, the violence and power of the defendants seem the only excuse for the Chancellor's interference.
[5] An interesting example of the jurisdiction of the Council with regard to aliens, as to which see Dicey, *Privy Council,* 56.

56   [1] A soun tres honore et tres gracious seignur, l'Euesque d'Excestre, Chaunceller d'Engleterre,

s d. Supplie humblement vostre pouere oratour et seruant, Johan Bernard, nadgairs persone de l'esglise de Idelstre en la diocese de Nichole, qe come il et vn William Tamworth, Meistre del Hospital seinte Marie Magdaleine de Clothale ioust Baldok en mesme le diocese, nadgairs estoient assentuz et accordez de parmutier ensemblement lour ditz benefices canonikement, et apres ceo le dit William estoit teunz et obligez par soun fait au dit Johan en dys liures pur accomplier et parfourner l'accorde du parmutacion auantdit ; sur quelle assent et accord le dit William estoit presentez au dite esglise par l'abbe de seint Albone, patron de mesme l'esglise, et duement institut et induct en ycelle esglise par l'ordinarie de mesme le lieu ; et combien qe le dit Johan [Bernard] pursuez longement a vn Johan Burwell, patron du dit Hospital, pur ent auoir collacion de luy a cause du dite parmutacion, la quelle collacion le dit Johan Bernard ne purroit r.e vnqore poet auoir tanque encea, sique le dit Johan Bernard est ore destitut outrement de soun benefice, a grand damage de luy et enpouerissement de soun estat, s'il ne soit eidez par vous en ce cas : Par quoy pleise a vostre tresgraciouse seignurie grantier brief de faire venier le dit William deuant vous en la Chauncellerie nostre seignur le Roy pur y estre examinez de celle matiere, et enoutre ordeigner graciousement qe le dit Johan Bernard puisse estre restitut a soun dit benefice issint q'il ne soit ensy destitut de soun vinere, pur Dieux et en oeuere de charitee.

57   [2] A tres reuerent pier en Dieu et son tres gracious seignur, l'Euesque d'Excestre, Chanceller nostre seignur le Roy,

s. d. Supplie humblement Johan Steven, nadgeirs vn des Conestables de la ville de Mysne deinz la fee de Kyrketon in Lyndesey, qe come nadgeirs pur vne debate faite par vn Thomas Nowell et William son fitz en la dite ville de Mysne deinz la dite fee, encontre la peex nostre

[1] Bundle 3, No. 34. This and the following bills are addressed to the Bishop of Exeter, but there is nothing to show whether they belong to his first or second Chancellorship.

[2] Bundle 3, No. 35.

56 To his most honoured and most gracious Lord, the Bishop of Exeter, Chancellor of England,

s.d. Beseecheth humbly your poor orator and servant, John Bernard, late parson of the church of Idlestray[3] in the diocese of Lincoln, that whereas he and one William Tamworth, Master of the Hospital of S. Mary Magdalene of Clothall near Baldock,[3] in the same diocese, lately consented and agreed to exchange their benefices canonically, and afterwards the said William by his deed became held and bound in the sum of £10 to the said John to fulfill and perform the said agreement of exchange; on which consent and agreement the said William was presented to the said church by the Abbat of S. Alban's, the patron of the said church, and was duly instituted and inducted into the same by the Ordinary of the same place; and although the said John [Bernard] hath long besought one John Burwell, the patron of the said Hospital, to have collation thereof because of the said exchange, the said John Bernard hath not been able to have the same, nor yet hath it up to this present time, so that he is now deprived altogether of his benefice, to his great damage and to the impoverishment of his estate, if he be not aided by you in this case : Wherefore may it please your most gracious Lordship to grant a writ to cause the said William to come before you in the Chancery of our Lord the King to be there examined touching the matter, and moreover graciously to ordain that the said John Bernard may be restored to his benefice, so that he be not so deprived of his livelihood, for God and in way of charity.[4]

57 To the most reverend Father in God and his most gracious Lord, the Bishop of Exeter, Chancellor of our Lord the King,

s.d. Beseecheth humbly John Steven, late one of the Constables of the town of Misson[5] within the fee of Kirton in Lindsey, that whereas of late for a strife made by one Thomas Nowell and William his son in the said town of Misson within the said fee, against the peace of our Lord the

[3] Co. Hertford.
[4] The plaintiff was in somewhat awkward case; he could not ask for *specific performance*, for Burwell was not a party to the agreement, and Tamworth was powerless in the matter. The only course left seems to be to have the agreement of exchange rescinded, which is what the Chancellor is asked to do.
[5] Co. Notts.

seignur le Roy, le dit Johan, come a luy appartient par reasoun de son office, aresta les ditz Thomas et William, mesmes les Thomas et William oue force et armes debruserent la dit arest et ne veulleient ascunement obeier a icelle ; et par le ou le dit Johan ouesque l'autre conestable de la dite ville de Mysne voloit autrefoitz auoir arestuz pur la dite debate les ditz Thomas et William, mesmes les Thomas et William alerent a vne meason deinz la dite ville de Mysne, et la lour tiendroient dedeinz oue forte mayn, et ne voilleient estere a celle arest, ne lour soeffrer ent ascunement estre iustifiez, encontre la peex nostre dit seignur le Roy et en grant destourbance des lieges le Roy illeoqes ; et puis apres les ditz Thomas et William, par enemytee et de lour malice, ont fait enditer le dit Johan de felonie deinz le Contee d'Euerwyk a grant damage du dit suppliant et anientissement de son pouer estat : Plese a son dit tresgracious seignur d'ent ordeiner bone remede, pur Dieu et en oeuere de charitee.

58   [1] A tres reuerent piere en Dieux et tresgracious seignur, l'Euesque d'Excestre, Chaunceller d'Engleterre,

s.d. Supplie vostre humble subget, Johan Swelle, Marschall del honurable sale nostre tres redoute seignur le Roy, Que comme y pleust a vostre tres gracious seignurie de grauntier a dit suppliant vne brief directe a Johan Haukyn de Stallesfeld pur oustrement cesser de la suyt q'il auoit moue deuers le dit suppliant en la Courte de le Chastell de Douer, sur certeins causes reisonables et suggestions a vous mounstres par supplicacion mys en escript ; quelle brief au temps q'une certein valet [2] le bailleroit a dit Johan Haukyn de part nostre dit seignur le Roy, c'est assauoir, en le presence de pluseurs persoues recorde [3] en l'esglise de Otryngden, il ne dedeignast mye ses mains oouerer pur le dit brief resceiuer, ne nulle aultre reuerence faire a ycelle, qomme deuoit a chescune maundement roial, mais le ietta desoubz ses pieds[?] ou il gisoit par vne certein temps, ledement defoule, tanque aultres le pristerent suise et le metterent sur le founte du la dite esglise ; et de

---

[1] Bundle 3, No. 36.

[2] A difficult word to translate at any time on account of its Various meanings ; here it seems to mean an officer of the Court, but whether a serjeant-at-arms, a special messenger, or what, it seems impossible to say.

[3] *Sic*, but probably an error for *recoile*, assembled.

King, the said John, as appertained to him by reason of his office, arrested the said Thomas and William, the said Thomas and William with force and arms broke the said arrest and would not in any wise obey it ; and whereas the said John [Steven], together with the other constable of the said town of Misson, another time would have arrested the said Thomas and William for the said strife, the same Thomas and William went to a house in the said town of Misson, and there kept themselves within with the strong hand, and would not stand to the arrest, nor suffer themselves in any way to be justified, against the peace of our Lord the King and to the great disturbance of the King's lieges there. And since then the said Thomas and William, through their enmity and malice, have caused the said John to be indicted of felony within the County of York, to the great damage of the said suppliant and the diminution of his poor estate : May it please his most gracious Lord to ordain a good remedy thereof, for God and in way of charity.[4]

58   To the most Reverend Father in God and most gracious lord, the Bishop of Exeter, Chancellor of England,

s.d. Beseecheth your humble subject, John Swelle, Marshall of the honourable Hall of our most redoubted Lord the King, that whereas your said suppliant applied to your most gracious Lordship to grant him a writ directed to John Hawkin of Stalisfield,[5] [ordering him], for certain reasonable causes and suggestions shown to you by the plaint and put in writing, to cease altogether from the suit which he had moved against the said suppliant in the court of Dover Castle ;[6] which writ, when a certain messenger delivered it to the said John Hawkin on behalf of our said Lord the King, to wit, in the presence of many persons assembled in the church of Otterden,[5] he would not deign to open his hands to receive the same, and did no reverence to it, as he ought to every royal mandate, but he threw it under his feet where it lay for some time, vilely trampled upon, until others took it up and placed it on the font of the said church ; and of this contempt

[4] As to the first part of the plaint, the inability of the ordinary processes of common law to cope with the defendants' violence is the only reason for bringing the matter before the Chancellor. In the second part of the plaint, a stay of the proceedings at York is distinctly suggested, though not asked for in so many words. See Spence, i. 673-675, where several early instances of stay of proceedings at common law are given, though none earlier than Henry VI.

[5] Co. Kent.

[6] An early instance of an injunction to stay proceedings at common law. See note 4 supra.

ceste contempt fait par le dit Johan Haukyn, le dit suppliant vouché
recorde a Johan Chilmelle, Johan Clement et Johan Grafte, de la dite
ville de Stallesfeld, alors presentz ; n'oustre ceo le dit Johan Haukyn
ne voet cesser vncore de durement pursuer le dit suppliant [nient con-
tresteant] le roial maundement suisdit : Que pleise a vostre tres
graciouse seignurie et tres reuerent paternite de faire venir le dit
Johan Haukyn en vostre honurable presence par vertue d'une tiel
brief qe vous semble reisonable en ceste cas, pur illeoqes respondre
et estre iustifie de se contempt et disobeisaunce auantditz comme
la ley demande, pur Dieux et en oeuere de charitee.

Indorsed. Breve inde factum retornabile die Veneris proximo post
festum Purificacionis beate Marie proximo futurum.

.

59   [1] A tres reuerent pier en Dieu, l'Euesque
          d'Excestre et Chauncellir d'Engleterre,

s.d. Supplie humblement William Coriton del Counte de Deuens' qe come
il est sei[sit] de deux mees et certeins terres a ycelles appurtenauntz
del value de dys marcz par an en Alphington et Topsham, come de
droit Cristien nadgairs sa femme, la reuersion ent regardaunt a
Andreu Coriton fitz et heir du dite Cristine [*sic*], la possession des
qeux tenementz le dit suppliaunt ad pesiblement continue par trent
ans et pluis, tamque ore tard q'un Adam Baron, Henry Baron,
Richard Baron, Henry Inthehaye, Johan Marschell de Alphington et
Thomas Monk atte Weye, oue plousours autres mesfaisours desconuz,
y veignent oue forte mayn et graunt riot des gentz sour mesme la
terre pur oustier le dit suppliaunt hors de sa possession, le quele riot
le ditz mesfaisours continuent de iour en autre. Et auxi les ditz
mesfesours a dit suppliaunt onut fait diners assautes et luy ount
batuz, naufreez, et malement treteez, et vn de ces bras debruseez ;
et vnquore luy manassent de iour en autre de vie et de membre, par
qe le dit suppliaunt est en despoir de sa vie ; les qeux mesfesours
ount si graund maintenaunce et sustinaunce en lour parties qe le dit
suppliaunt ne peot auoir droit ne resoun enuers eux : Qe pleise a
vostre tresgracious seignurie considerir les riotes et manesceez
auauntditz, et sour ce grauntier briefs directez as ditz Adam, Henry,
Richard, Henry, Johan et Thomas, pur y estre deuaunt vous en la
Chauncellarie a vn certein iour sour graund peyne, pur respoundre

[1] Bundle 3, No. 47.

committed by the said John Hawkin, the said suppliant doth vouch to record John Chilmelle, John Clement and John Grafte, of the said town of Stalisfield, then present ; and besides this, the said John Hawkin doth not cease still to sue the said suppliant [notwithstanding] the said royal mandate : May it please your most gracious Lordship and most reverend paternity to cause the said John Hawkin to come into your honourable presence by virtue of such a writ as to you shall seem reasonable in this case, there to answer and to be justified of his contempt and disobedience aforesaid as the law demands, for God and in way of charity.

Indorsed. Let a writ thereof be made, returnable on the Friday next after the feast of the Purification of Blessed Mary next to come.

59 To the most reverend Father in God, the Bishop of Exeter, and Chancellor of England,

s. d. Beseecheth humbly William Coriton of the County of Devon, that whereas he is seised of two messuages and certain lands appurtenant thereto, of the yearly value of 10 marks, in Alphington[2] and Topsham[2] in right of Christine, his late wife, the reversion whereof belongs to Andrew Coriton, son and heir of the said Christine, the possession of which tenements the said suppliant hath peaceably continued for thirty years and more, until now of late that one Adam Baron, Henry Baron, Richard Baron, Henry In-the-hay, John Marshall of Alphington and Thomas 'Monk atte Weye,' with many other evil-doers unknown, came thither with the strong hand and a great riot of people, upon the same land, to oust the said suppliant from his possession ; the which riot the said evil-doers do continue from day to day. And also the said evil-doers have made divers assaults upon the said suppliant, and have beaten, wounded and ill-treated him, and have broken one of his arms ; and they still threaten him from day to day of life and limb, through which the said suppliant is in despair of his life; the which evil-doers have so great maintenance and sustenance in their own parts that the said suppliant can have no right nor reason against them :[3] May it please your most gracious Lordship to consider the riots and menaces aforesaid, and thereupon to grant writs directed to the said Adam, Henry, Richard, Henry, John and Thomas, [commanding them] to be before you in the Chancery, on a certain day and under a great pain, to

[1] Co. Devon.   [3] That is, at common law.

sibien a nostre seignur le Roy come a dit suppliaunt des riotes de forcible entreez auauntditz, Et auxi pur trouer suffisaunt assurtee du pees a dit suppliaunt; Pur Dieu et en eouere de charite.

60   [1] A tresreuerent pier en Dieu, l'Euesque d'Excestre, Chaunceller d'Engleterre,

s. d. Monstre et soy pleint Johan Lyndewode, Marchant, qe come le dit Johan le Lundy en le quinszime de Pasque darreyn passe, en chiuachant par Chesthunt vers Loundres pur y soun custume paier a l'Escheker nostre seignur le Roy, la viendront Johan Esmondesseruaunt Fauconer de Chesthunt, William Brit, Johan Baker, Johan Milner l'esne, Johan Milner le puisne, Robert de Pantry, Johan Bredon, et Thomas Ferrour de Chesthunt, et plusours autres de mesme la ville nient conuz, ascunes de eux arraiez en draps femyneles, oue espies, arkes, bastones et plusours autres harnois; et le dit Johan Lyndewode aresteront, et espee du dit Johan Lyndewode hors trereront, et [en] Robert Chestrefeld seruant a dit Johan Lindewode assaut firent et luy bateront, naufreront et malement treieront,[2] par qay le dit Johan Lyndewode soun seruice de soun seruant prodist del iour auauntdite tanque en cy; et plusours autres ledes a dit Johan Lyndewod firent a tort et damage du dit Johan Lyndewode de cent liures: Qe pleise a vostre tresgracious seignurie ent orden remedie.

61   [3] A tres reuerent Piere en Dieu et tres noble seignur, l'Euesque d'Excestre, Chaunceller d'Engleterre,

s. d. Supplie tres humblement Margarete Grymmesby de Straesburgh en Duchelond qe come Reignold Cobham, esquier, le xiiij[e] iour d'Octobre darrein passe, prist a femme la dite Margarete affirmaunt q'il n'auoit autre femme; lui quel Reignold soi auaunta q'il estoit le fitz de Seignur de Cobeham et coment il auoit tres graund enheritaunce en Engleterre, et issint par ses fraudes paroles il auoit la dite Margarete et ses biens al value de cc liures ouesque lui hors du dite ville de Straes-

[1] Bundle 3, No. 48.   [3] Bundle 3, No. 49.
[2] *Sic*, for *treteront*.

answer to our Lord the King as well as to the said suppliant, for the said riots and forcible entries, and also to find sufficient surety [to keep] the peace towards the said suppliant ; for God and in way of charity.[4]

60   To the most reverend Father in God, the Bishop of Exeter, and Chancellor of England,

s. d. Showeth and complaineth John Lyndewode, merchant, that whereas, while the said John on the Monday in the quindene of Easter last past [was] riding from Cheshunt to London to pay his custom at the Exchequer of our Lord the King, there came John, the servant of Edmond Falconer of Cheshunt, William Brit, John Baker, John Milner the elder, John Milner the younger, Robert of the Pantry, John Bredon and Thomas Ferrour of Cheshunt, and many others unknown of the same town, some of them arrayed in female clothes, with swords, bows, clubs and other harness ; and they seized the said John Lyndewode, and drew the sword of the said John Lyndewode, and assaulted Robert Chesterfield, servant to the said John Lyndewode, and did beat, maim and ill-treat him, by which the said John Lyndewode hath lost the service of his said servant from the day aforesaid even until now ; and they did many other injuries to the said John Lyndewode wrongfully, and to his damage of £100 :   May it please your most gracious Lordship to ordain remedy thereof.[5]

61   To the most reverend Father in God and most noble Lord, the Bis o of Exeter, Chancellor of England,

s. d. Beseecheth most humbly Margaret Grimsby, of Strasburg in Germany, that whereas Reginald Cobham, esquire, on October 14th last past took to wife the said Margaret, affirming that he had no other wife ; which Reginald boasted himself to be the son of the Lord of Cobham and how he had very great inheritance in England,[6] and so by his fraudulent words he got the said Margaret and her goods to the value of £200 with him out of the said town of Strasburg

---

[4] No remedy at common law on account of the defendants' power and violence.
[5] It seems to be implied that the common law was unable to deal with the matter.
[6] Lord Cobham of Sterborough at this period had a son Reginald.

burgh tanque al ville de Tilleburi en le Countee d'Essex, et illoesqes demurreit ouesque la dite Margarete tanque al xx^e iour de Nouembre darrein passe, a quel iour le dit Reignold toutz les ditz biens du dite Margarete al value de cc liures illoesqes troues prist et ouesque lui apporta, disaunt q'il auoit autre femme allostielle : [1] Plese a vostre tres noble seignurie graunter comission a vn sergeaunt d'armes pur prendre et amesner le corps de dit Reignold deuaunt vous a respoundre a iceste cas, en oenere de charite.

62   [2] A tres reuerend piere en Dieux, l'Euesque
d'Excestre, Chaunceller d'Engleterre,

s. d. Supplient humblement Johan Gedneye de Flete et William Gedneye de Flete qe come deuaunt ceux heures les ditz Johan et William ount estee manacez par vn Henry Rocheford, esquier, pur quele manace les ditz Johan et William eux doutount graundement de lour mort ne osont mye aler hors de lur meison ; q'il plese a vostre tresgracious seignurie de maunder pur le dit Henry et luy faire trouer sufficeant seurtee de la pees as ditz Johan et William deuaunt vous pur eux et touz les soens sur peyne d'une graunde summe d'argent, come la ley demaunde, issint qe lez ditz Johan et William et les soens puissent estre en pees ; pur Dieux et en oeure de charitee.

63   [3] A son tres honourable, tres gracious seignur,
et tres benigne pier en Dieu, l'Euesqe
d'Excestre et Chaunceller d'Engleterre,

s. d. Monstre tres humblement vostre pouere oratour Johan Arnesby de Turlyngton et se pleynt de Thomas Bouylle de mesme la ville, esquier, qe come le dit Thomas, par assent et maintenaunce de Richard de Bosworth de Harbargh, pristront vn chartre de feoffement du dit Johan de iiij liures xvj s. del value par an de terre, son droit heritage, sur surrance de luy deliuerer la dite chartre arier sur peyne de M liures, la quele le dit Thomas detient oue tout la terre, la ou il ne doit rendre ent par an, mes vn liure de piper al meer du dit Thomas ; et sur ceo ils ne voillent seoffrer sez bestes aler en le commun du dit

[1] *Al hostiel.*   [3] Bundle 3, No. 51.
[2] Bundle 3, No. 50.

unto the town of Tilbury in the County of Essex, and there he dwelt with the said Margaret until the 20th day of November last past, on which day the said Reginald took all the said goods of the said Margaret there found to the value of £200, and carried them away with him, saying that he had another wife at home: May it please your most noble Lordship to grant a commission to a serjeant at arms to take and bring the body of the said Reginald before you to answer in this case; In way of charity.[4]

62   To the most reverend Father in God, the Bis o of Exeter, Chancellor of England,

s. d. Beseech humbly John Gedney of Fleet and William Gedney of Fleet that whereas aforetime the said John and William have been menaced by one Henry Rocheford, esquire, on account of which menace the said John and William have greatly feared their deaths, and dared not go out of their houses; May it please your most gracious Lordship to send for the said Henry, and make him find sufficient surety for the peace towards the said John and William before you for themselves and all theirs, on pain of a great sum of money, as the law demandeth, so that the said John and William and theirs may be at peace; For God and in way of charity.[5]

63   To his most honourable and most gracious Lord and most benign Father in God, the Bishop of Exeter, Chancellor of England,

s. d. Showeth most humbly your poor orator, John Arnesby of Tur Langton[6] [?], and complaineth of Thomas Bovylle of the same town, esquire, that whereas the said Thomas, with the consent and maintenance of Richard de Bosworth of [Market] Harborough, took a charter of feoffment from the said John touching land of the annual value of £4 16s., his rightful heritage, upon assurance to deliver the said charter again to him on pain of £1000, and the said Thomas detaineth the same with all the land, whereas he [Arnesby] ought not to render anything except a pound of pepper yearly to Thomas's mother; and moreover they will not suffer his beasts to go on the

[4] No reason appears why the plaintiff should apply to the Chancellor, unless the fact that the plaintiff is an alien supplies one.

[5] No reason is shown for application to the Chancellor.   [6] Leicestershire.

ville ; et par cause qe le dit Johan luy pleyne, le dit Thomas oue son chapelleyne Robert son seruaunt et autres encontra le dit Johan, l'endemaigne de le feste d'exaltacion seint Croiee darreyne passe a Turlyngton et luy bata, naufra, debrusa et mahayme et pur morte luy lessa, nonobstant qe le dit Johan auoit pris vn brief appelle *supplicauit* sur le dit Thomas, et al a sa maison et sez pottes, pannes et autres biens emporta ; et luy ad chasa hors del pais, q'il n'ose approcher sa dite maison ne pursuir la commun ley enuers le dit Thomas pur dout de sa vie et maintenaunce du dit Richard : Qe plese a vostre tres gracious seignurie enuoier pur lez ditz Thomas et Richard par brief a respondre a ceste matier deuaunt vostre tres noble et tres haute presence et sur ceo ordinir due remedie soloncq ceo qe droit et reson demande ; al honour de Dieu et en sauacion de droit et maintenaunce de pees et lez leyes.

64   [1] Au reuerent Pere en Dieu et tres honnore Seignur, l'Euesque de Excestre Chaunceller d'Engleterre,

s. d. Supplie William de Beauchamp, Que come il soit saisi du manoir de Spellesby [2] oue les appurtenaunces joust la foreste de Whichewode et hors de l'anciene bounde de mesme la foreste, deins quel manoir le dit William et tous ceaux qui estat il ad en le dit manoir du temps dont memoire ne court, ont paisiblement fait leur proufit auxi bien de lour boys come de lour autres commoditees deins mesme le manoir, sanz inquietacion ou destourbance des officers ou ministres de la dite foreste, tanqe ore tard qe les ditz ministres ont arrestee le boys qe le dit William ad fait vendre deins le dit manoir, a grant damage de luy : Plaise a vostre reuerente paternite et graciouse seignurie commander brief directe as ditz officers et ministres et a chescun de eaux qe si ainsi soit come dessuis qu'ils souffrent le dit William faire son proufit du boys suisdit sans inquietacion ou destourbance par eaux ou aucun de eaux au contraire ; en oeure de charite.

[1] Bundle 3, No. 52.   [2] Probably an error for ' Spellesbury.'

common of the said town; and because the said John complained thereof, the said Thomas, with his chaplain, Robert, his servant, and others, [assaulted] the said John at Tur Langton on the morrow of the feast of the Exaltation of Holy Cross last past, and did beat, wound, bruise and maim him, and did leave him for dead (notwithstanding the said John had taken a writ called *supplicavit*[3] against the said Thomas), and went to his house and carried away his pots, pans, and other goods; and he hath chased [the said suppliant] out of the country, so that he dare not approach his said house nor sue the common law against the said Thomas for fear of his life and of the maintenance of the said Richard: May it please your most gracious Lordship to send for the said Thomas and Richard by writ to answer touching this matter before your most noble and most high presence, and thereupon to ordain due remedy according to what right and reason demand; To the honour of God, and in salvation of right, and maintenance of peace and the laws.[4]

64 To the most reverend Father in God and most honoured Lord, the Bis o of Exeter, Chancellor of England,

s. d. Beseecheth William de Beauchamp, that whereas he is seised of the manor of Spelsbury[5] with the appurtenances, near the forest of Wychwood, and outside the ancient boundary of the forest, within which manor the said William, and all those whose estate he hath in the said manor, have, from time of which the memory runneth not, peaceably made their profit, as well of their wood as of their other commodities within the same manor, without annoyance or disturbance by the officers or ministers of the said forest, until now of late that the said ministers have seized the wood which the said William had sold within the said manor, to his great damage: May it please your most reverend Paternity and gracious Lordship to order a writ [to be] directed to the said officers and ministers and to each of them [commanding them] that, if it be so as [stated] above, they shall suffer the said William to make his profit of the wood aforesaid without annoyance or disturbance by them or any of them to the contrary; In way of charity.[6]

[3] A writ for taking sureties of the peace, upon articles filed on oath, when one was in danger of being hurt in his body by another.—Wharton.
[4] No remedy at common law because of the defendants' violence.

[5] Co. Oxon. Roger de Beauchamp held it, 3 Ric. II. *Inq. p. m.* Chancery, No. 5.
[6] It is difficult to see why the Chancellor should be applied to. The right of taking wood is mentioned in the Hundred Rolls, ii. 746.

65   [1] A tres honoûre et tres graciouse seignur, Mestre Esmon Stafford, l'Euesque d'Excestre et Chaunceller d'Engleterre,

s. d. Supplie tres humblement Johan Harecourt qe come il ad certeinz terres et tenementz appellez Smalbroke et Morton deinz le Isle de Wyght des queux il est disseise par Thomas Russel, William Dale, et William le fitz du dit Thomas et luy manasceront q'il n'osa approcher son droit terres et tenementz auantditz pur doute d'estre occis par lour grand manace, et pour ceo vous plese d'enuoier pur les ditz Thomas, William et William fitz du dit Thomas, et faire venir deuaunt vous et trouer ioinctement et seueralment suffisant seurte sur vn grand pein de porter loialment pees enuers le dit Johan ; pur Dieu et en oeure de charite.

Concordatum fuit per Consilium quod brevia inde dirigerentur prefatis Thome, Willelmo et Willelmo sub pena quadraginta librarum ad comparendum coram domino Cancellario in Cancellaria domini Regis ad ibidem inueniendum sufficientem securitatem pacis prefato Johanni in forma predicta.

66   [2] A tres reuerent pier en Dieux, l'Euescque d'Excestre, Chauncellier d'Engleterre,

s. d. Supplient l'Abbe et Couent de Westm' qe come diuerses gentz [al nombre] de lx persones, oue force et armes, encountre la pees nostre seignur le Roy, ont bruses, gastez et comburez les haies et l'enclosures del copice du dit Abbe . . . lour bois appelle Horewelle Wodde en le Countee de Wircestre : Please a vostre tres graciouse seignurie grauntier vn commission a Johan . . . nostre seignur le Roy, Waulter Cokeson, chiualer, Richard Ryhale, Johan Derhurst, Robert Whityngton, Henry Haggeley, Thomas Throkmerton,   Wircestre et Johan Bras, viscont de Wircestre, d'enquerer de les maufesours auauntditz, et certifier nostre dit seignur le Roy en soun Conseil   [3]

---

[1] Bundle 3, No. 53. See No. 74.
[2] Bundle 3, No. 72 ; much damaged on the right margin.

[3] As to special commissions, see p. 29, note 1. The commission asked for in this case, however, was not one of *oyer et*

65   To the most honoured and most gracious
          Lord, Master Edmond Stafford, Bis o of
          Exeter and Chancellor of England,

s. d. Beseecheth most humbly John Harcourt, that whereas he had certain lands and tenements, called Smallbrook and Morton, in the Isle
of Wight, of which he is disseised by Thomas Russel, William Dale,
and William son of the said Thomas, and they menace him so that he
dare not approach his own lands and tenements aforesaid for fear of
being killed through their great menaces; And therefore may it please
you to send for the said Thomas, William, and William son of the
said Thomas, and to make them come before you, and jointly and
severally to find sufficient surety under a great pain to keep the peace
lawfully towards the said John ; for God and in way of charity.[4]

It was agreed by the Council that writs should be directed to the
said Thomas, William, and William [commanding them] under a penalty
of £40 to appear before the Lord Chancellor in the Chancery of our
Lord the King, there to find sufficient security for the peace towards
the said John, in form aforesaid.[5]

66   To the most reverend Father in God, the
          Bishop of Exeter, Chancellor of England,

s. d. Beseech the Abbat and Convent of Westminster, that whereas divers
persons [to the number] of sixty, with force and arms, against the
peace of our Lord the King, have broken, wasted, and burnt the
hedges and inclosures of the coppice belonging to the said Abbot [and
Convent in] their wood called Horewell Wood in the County of Worcester: May it please your most gracious Lordship to grant a commission to John . . . of our Lord the King, Walter Cokeson, knight,
Richard Ryhale, John Derhurst, Robert Whityngton, Henry Haggeley,
Thomas Throkmerton, . . . of Worcester, and John Bras, Sheriff of
Worcester, to inquire as to the malefactors aforesaid, and to certify
our Lord the King in his Council.

---

terminer, but of inquiry only.
[4] It seems implied that the plaintiff
could have no remedy at common law because of the defendants' violence.

[5] Note that the decision is by the Council. The defendants are to appear before
the Chancellor, but not in his judicial
capacity.

67   [1] A tres reuerent pier en Dieu, l'Euesque d'Excestre, Chaunceller d'Engleterre,

s. d. Monstre et soi pleint Thomas Byflet, esquier, qe come il fuist seisit en soun demesne come de fee et de droit del maner de Canesford oue les appurtenancz en le Contee de Somers', la viendront monsire Johan Loterell, chiualer, Richard Popham et Johan Bradeford, seruantz de dit monsire Johan, et par soun commandement et plusours autres maisfeisours le Meskerdie proschein apres le Dymenge des Palmes flores darrein passe, oue fort mayn et en faire de guerre armez, et pur maintenir vn Gilbert Basynge, qi a tort et sanz ascun cause droiturelle clayme le dit Manoir oue les appurtenances ; et le dit Thomas hors del dit Manoir engetteront, et a ses hommes et seruantz illoeqes esteantz, c'est assauoir, Wanter Bannok, et as autres ses seruantz, assaut firont, et eux emprisoneront, et en prison deteigneront tanque eux auoient faitz fyne d'un tonele de vyne price de viij marez ; et le dit Thomas et ses hommes et seruantz de iour en autre manasont de eux batir, maihemir et tuer si eux a dit Manoir approcher voillont ; parount le dit Thomas et ses ditz hommes et seruantz soun dit Manoir mainouerer ne approcher pur dout de mort ne oisent point ; a graund damage de dit Thomas et arrerment de soun estat : Plese a vostre tresgracious seignurie considerer le tort fait a dit Thomas en forcible manere, et le graund peril et mort des hommes qe poet legerement auenir en cest partie, auxi le graund damage du dit Thomas, pur maunder pur les ditz monsire Johan Loterell, Richard Popham et Johan Bradeford d'estre deuaunt vous sur certein pein a certein iour par vous a limiter pur estre examine sur cest matier et toutz les circumstances dicelle, et de faire droit et due remedie a dit Thomas en cest partie ; [2] Considerant q'il n'ad nulle hastius remedie a luy done par le comun ley.[2] Pur Dieu et en eouere de charite.

68   [3] A tres reuerent piere en Dieu et soun tresgracious Seignur, l'Euesque d'Excestre et Chaunceller d'Engletre,

s. d. Supplie humblement vostre pouere Chapellein et Oratour, Nichol Boteler, vikair de l'esglise de Wesbury, qe come ore tarde vn Richard

---

[1] Bundle 3, No. 63. No. 62 relates to the same matter, but the details are not given so fully.

[2] In No. 62 only.

[3] Bundle 3, No. 66.

67   To the most reverend Father in God, the Bishop of Exeter, Chancellor of England

s. d. Showeth and complaineth Thomas Byflet, esquire, that whereas he was seised in his demesne as of fee and right of the manor of Canesford with the appurtenances in the County of Somerset, there came Sir John Loterell, knight, and Richard Popham and John Bradeford, servants to the said Sir John, by his order, and many other evil-doers, on the Wednesday after Palm Sunday last past, with the strong hand and armed in warlike manner, in order to maintain one Gilbert Basynge, who, wrongfully and without any righteous cause, claimeth the said manor with the appurtenances; and they ejected the said Thomas from the said manor, and assaulted his men and servants who were there, to wit, Walter Bannok and his other servants, and imprisoned them, and kept them in prison until they made fine of a tun of wine, price 8 marks; And they do from day to day threaten to beat, maim, and kill the said Thomas, his men and servants, if they approach the said manor; and on this account the said Thomas and his said men and servants dare not till nor approach his said manor for fear of death, to the great damage of the said Thomas and the detriment of his estate: May it please your most gracious Lordship to consider the wrong done thus forcibly to the said Thomas, and the great peril and death of his men which might easily happen in this behalf, and also the great damage to the said Thomas, and to command the said Sir John Loterell, Richard Popham, and John Bradeford to be before you, under a certain pain, and at a certain day by you to be limited, to be examined on this matter and all the circumstances thereof, and to make right and due remedy to the said Thomas in this behalf. Considering that he hath no speedy remedy given to him by the common law.[4] For God and in way of charity.

68   To the most reverend Father in God and his most gracious Lord, the Bishop of Exeter, Chancellor of England,

s. d. Humbly beseecheth your poor chaplain and orator, Nicholas Boteler, Vicar of the church of Westbury [on Severn], that whereas of late one

---

[4] The plaintiff was anxious to avoid the delays of an action at common law.

Stawr, par conseil et procurement de William Stawr del Hundred de Wesbury, debrosa les mesons et les portes de sa vikarage et hors prist des ditz mesons vn cheual de value de xxx *s.* et vnqore detient tortenousement et sanz processe de loye, et prist de iour en autre les profites del dit esglise a soun profet demesne, sanz aucune restitucion ou paiement faire a dit Nichol ycelx ; Et auxi les ditz Richard et William gisont en agait de iour en autre pur tuer le dit suppliant et ses seruantz, issint q'il n'ose mye approcher a sa dite esglise pur faire dinine seruise ; Et combien qe le dit suppliant auoit ore tarde vn brief de manace[1] direct a les Justices de la pees illoeqes et feust deliueree a Robert Wbytyngton, vn des ditz Justices, pur faire execucion dicel ; et il enuoia vn precept a le Conestable del Hundred de Wesbury pur parner seurete de la pees des ditz Richard et William ; Et depuis cel temps le dit Nichol enuoia ses seruantz a sa dit vikarage pur faire ses affaires illoeqes, supposant qe les ditz Richard et William anoient trouez seuretee de la pees come le brief demanda ; mesmes les Richard et William ouek autres de lour couyn viendront a la dite vikarage oue force et armes et firent assaut a ses ditz seruantz deinz le dit vikarage, et les veullent auoir tuez : Qe plese a vostre tres graciouse seignurie considerer ceste matiere et qe le dit Nichol est tenuz et obligez pur faire residence personel a sa dite vikarage, le quel il n'ose my pur doute de morte, et graunter briefs directz a le viscont de Glone' pur auoir les ditz Richard et William deuaunt vous en la Chancellerie sur certeine peyne pur y trouer seuretee de la pees a dit Nichol et ses seruantz; pur Dieu et en oenre de charitee . Consirant [*sic*], tres gracious seignur, q'il n'ose deuaunt cel temps q'ils aient trouer seurtee de la pees approcher ne venir a sa dit vikarage.

69.   [2] A tres reuerent pier en Dieu, l'Euesque d'Excestre, Chanceller d'Engleterre,

s. d.   Supplie tres humblement William, Priour de Spyneye, qe come il pur luy et ses Conchanons et seruantz ore tard troua sufficeant seurete denant vous de la pees enuers Johan Peyton et Thomas Peyton, Esquiers, del Conte de Cantebr', et sur ceo vous grantastez vn brief direct a le viscont du dit Conte luy comandant de surseier de l'execu-

---

[1] The same as the writ *de securitate pacis* or *supplicavit.* See *F.N.B.* 79, and   p. 64, note 3.
[2] Bundle 3, No. 67.

Richard Stawr, by counsel and procurement of William Stawr of the Hundred of Westbury, broke the houses and doors of his Vicarage, and took out of the said houses a horse worth 30s., and still detaineth it wrongfully and without process of law, and doth from day to day take the profits of the said church to his own profit, without any restitution or payment made thereof to the said Nicholas; And also the said Richard and William do from day to day lie in wait to kill the said suppliant and his servants, so that he dare not approach his said church to perform divine service; And although the said suppliant had lately a writ of menaces directed to the Justices of the peace there, which was delivered to Robert Whytyngton, one of the said Justices, to do execution thereof; and he [Whytyngton] sent an order to the Constable of the Hundred of Westbury to take surety for the peace from the said Richard and William; And after that time the said Nicholas sent his servants to his said Vicarage to do his business there, supposing that the said Richard and William had found surety for the peace as the writ demanded; the said Richard and William with others of their covin came to the said Vicarage with force and arms, and made assault on the said servants within the said Vicarage, and would have killed them: May it please your most gracious Lordship to consider this matter, and that the said Nicholas is bound and obliged to make personal residence in his said Vicarage, which he dare not do for fear of death, and to grant writs directed to the Sheriff of Gloucestershire to have the said Richard and William before you in the Chancery under a certain pain, there to find surety for the peace towards the said Nicholas and his servants; for God and in way of charity. Considering, most gracious Lord, that until they have found surety for the peace, [the said Nicholas] dare not approach or come to his said Vicarage.[3]

69 ## To the most reverend Father in God, the Bishop of Exeter, Chancellor of England,

s. d. Most humbly beseecheth William, Prior of Spinney,[4] that whereas he, on behalf of himself, his Canons and servants, of late found sufficient surety before you for the peace towards John Peyton and Thomas Peyton, esquires, of the County of Cambridge, and thereupon you granted a writ directed to the Sheriff of the said County, commanding

---

[3] The violence and power of the defendants seem the only excuses for applying to the Chancellor.

[4] Co. Cambridge.

cion sibien de tous maniers briefs de manasses [1] come de qeconqes autres garrantz des Gardeins de pees du dit Conte pur trouer seurete de pees a les ditz Johan et Thomas, come en le dit brief est contenuz pluis aplain ; Nientmains le dit viscont ne voet mye surseser de l'execucion des ditz briefs et garrantz, mes detient ascuns de Conchanons et seruantz suisditz en prison, et fait cercher de iour en autre de prendre et arrester les autres, encontre le tenure du dit brief ; parensi qe les ditz Priour, et ses Conchanons et seruantz q'apresent ne sont arrestuz, n'osent demurrer en lour measons ; en contempt nostre seignur le Roy, et a tres grant damage et perpetuel anientisment du dit suppliant et de soun Priorie : Qe plese a vostre tres graciouse seignurie grant brief direct a dit viscont luy comandant soubz certein peyne par vous a limiter de surseer de l'execucion des briefs et garrants suisditz, et enoutre de apparoir deuant vous lendemayn de la Natiuite de Nostre Dame proschein auenir pur respondre par quele cause il ne vorreit obeier le mandement le Roy auantdit ; pur Dieu et en eoure de charitee.

70   [2] A tres reuerent piere en Dieu et tres gracious seignur, l'Euesque d'Excestre, Chaunceller d'Engleterre,

s. d. Supplie humblement Esmon Fraunceys, Grocer, Citezein de Loundres, qe come le dit Esmon par deux ans passez auoit execucion dez certeins terres et tenementz qe iadys furent a Johan Madesden, Dier de Loundres, en la paroche de Madesden en le Counte de Gloucestre, pur certein dette a luy due par vertue d'une Estatut del Estaple de Westm' de la somme de lviij liures, Et dez ditz terres et tenementz auoit liuere par brief du Roy, come la comun ley demandast ; Et ore est ency qe, par maintenance et conspiracye de James de Clifford et Hugh de Byslee de mesme le Counte, nulle homme ne fermer del dit Counte n'oise pur poar et meintenance et procurement dez ditz James et Hugh occupier ne gouerner lez ditz terres et tenementz pur le oeps et profit de dit Esmon : Please a vostre tres noble et tres graciouse seignurie graunter brief nostre seignur le Roy direct al viscount du dit Counte et as Justices de la peas de mesme la paijs lour comandantz de charger et comander lez ditz James et Hugh depar nostre dit seignur

---

[1] See p. 67, note 1.   [2] Bundle 3, No. 68.

him to stay the execution of all manner of writs of menaces,[1] as well as of all other warrants of the guardians of the peace of the said County for [the said suppliant] to find surety for the peace towards the said John and Thomas, as in the said writ more fully is contained; Nevertheless the said Sheriff will not stay the execution of the said writs and warrants, but detaineth some of the said Canons and servants in prison, and maketh search from day to day to take and arrest the others, contrary to the tenor of the said writ; so that the said Prior, and his Canons and servants who are not yet arrested, dare not live in their houses; in contempt of our Lord the King, and to the very great loss and perpetual impoverishment of the said suppliant and his Priory: May it please your most gracious Lordship to grant a writ directed to the said Sheriff commanding him, under a certain pain by you to be limited, to stay the execution of the writs and warrants aforesaid, and moreover to appear before you on the morrow of the Nativity of our Lady next to come, to answer wherefore he would not obey the King's commandment aforesaid; for God and in way of charity.

70   To the most reverend Father in God and most gracious Lord, the Bishop of Exeter, Chancellor of England,

s. d. Humbly beseecheth Edmund Fraunceys, grocer and citizen of London, that whereas the said Edmund for two years past hath had execution of certain lands and tenements which lately belonged to John Madesden, dyer, of London, in the parish of Madesden, in the County of Gloucester, for a certain debt, due to him by virtue of a Statute of the Staple of Westminster, of the sum of £58; and he had livery of the said lands and tenements by a writ of the King, as the common law demands; And now so it is that by the maintenance and conspiracy of James de Clifford and Hugh de Byslee of the same County, no man nor farmer of the said County dare occupy or till the said lands and tenements to the use and profit of the said Edmund, through the strength, maintenance and procurement of the said James and Hugh: May it please your most noble and most gracious Lordship to grant a writ of our Lord the King directed to the Sheriff of the said County and to the Justices of the Peace of the same country, commanding them to charge and command the said James and Hugh on behalf of

le Roy sur perille q'appent de suffrer le dit Esmon, sez seruantz et fermers, de occupier et gouerner lez ditz terres et tenementz issint a luy extentez par ley, sanz ascun entremeller ou destourbance dez ditz James et Hugh ; issint qe le dit Esmon pura auoir son auauntage dez ditz terres et tenementz, come il eux ad recouere par la ley, pur Dieu et en oeure de charitee.[1]

71   [2] A tres reuerent pier en Dieu et son tres gra cious seignur, l'Euesque d'Excestre, Chaun celler d'Engleterre,

s.d. Supplie hoemblement William Holt, esquier, qe come Estene Holt son piere, qi deuia ore tard deuaunt la feste de Saynt Michel darrein passe, et en sa vie purchasa certeynes terres, rentes et tenementes en le Countee de Sussex et de ent fist enfeffer mestre Johan Debenham, Richard Monek, Johan Holt, William Goldsmyth, clercz, Andrew Blake, Johan Bedeford, et aultres, al entent de luy enfeffer ou ses heirs quaunt ils feuront requis ; apres qi mort le dit William come fitz et heir a dit Esteue son piere, il les requira de luy enfeffer solonc l'en tente dil dit feffement ; & ils refuserent et ne voillent le faire, mais les ditz terres, rentes et tenementes tiegnent en lour mayns par graunt extorcion et graunt arerisement du dit supplient : Qe please a vostre tresgraciouse seignurie de eux faire venir deuaunt vous par brief nostre seignur le Roy de certeyne peyne pur eux examiner de là verite, et de faire ce qe reson et bone foy demaunde, et qe nul tiel extorcion ne fauste soit suffre ; pur Dieux et en oenre de charite.

72   [3] A tres reuerent piere en Dieu, l'Euesque d'Excestre et Chaunceller d'Engleterre,

s. d. Supplie humblement Johan Chelmewyke, fitz et heir a Richard Chel- mewyke q'est a dieu comande, le quele Johan est deins age, qe come le dit Richard son piere enfeoffa Roger Hay et certeins autres persones en certeins terres et tenementz queux feurent a mesme son piere, al oeps du dit supplient, et auxi lessa diuerses biens et chateux en la

---

[1] The violence and power of the defen- dants seem to be the only reasons for applying to the Chancellor.

[2] Bundle 3, No. 69.

[3] Bundle 3, No. 70.

our said Lord the King, that they, on peril which may ensue, shall suffer the said Edmund, his servants and farmers, to occupy and till the said lands and tenements so extended to him by law, without any intermeddling or disturbance by the said James and Hugh ; so that the said Edmund may have his advantage of the said lands and tenements, as he had recovered them by the law ; for God and in way of charity.[1]

71   To the most reverend Father in God and his most gracious Lord, the Bishop of Exeter, Chancellor of England,

s. d. Humbly beseecheth William Holt, esquire, that whereas Stephen Holt, his father, who died lately before Michaelmas last, in his lifetime purchased certain lands, rents and tenements in the County of Sussex, and thereof enfeoffed Master John Debenham, Richard Monek, John Holt, William Goldsmith, clerks, Andrew Blake, John Bedeford, and others, to the intent [that they should] enfeoff him or his heirs when they should be required [to do so]; after whose death, the said William, as son and heir to the said Stephen, his father, required them to enfeoff him according to the intent of the said feoffment ; and they refused, and will not do it, but keep the said lands, rents, and tenements in their hands, by great extortion, and to the great damage of the said suppliant : May it please your most gracious Lordship to cause them to come before you by writ of our Lord the King, under a certain pain, and to examine them of the truth, and to do what right and good faith demand, so that no such extortion nor deceit be suffered ; for God and in way of charity.[4]

72   To the most reverend Father in God, the Bishop of Exeter, Chancellor of England,

s.d. Humbly beseecheth John Chelmewyke, son and heir to Richard Chelmewyke, who is commended to God, which John is within age, that whereas the said Richard, his father, enfeoffed Roger Hay and certain other persons in certain lands and tenements, which belonged to his said father, to the use of the said suppliant, and also left divers

[4] A purely equity matter   As to feoffments to uses, see p. 49, note 3.

garde du dit Roger agarder al oeps de mesme celuy Johan; et ensy soit qe le dit Roger ad alienez plusours des ditz terres et tenementz et ent pris a son oeps demesne diuerses graundez sommes, en desheritison du dit suppliant; et auxi ad gastez toutz les ditz biens et chateux en ouert destruccion de l'estat de mesme le suppliant : Plese a vostre graciouse seignurie grauntier au dit suppliant vn brief direct au dit Roger d'estre deuaunt vous a les oeptaues de Seint Hillere proschien auenir sur peine de C. liures, et qe a mesme le iour le dit Roger soit examine des matiers susditz et des autres matiers qe luy serront surmys a mesme le temps pur profit de nostre seignur le Roy; pur Dieu et en oenre de charite.

73   [1] A tres reuerent pier en Dieu et son tres gracious seignur, l'Euesque d'Excestre, Chanceller d'Engleterre,

s d. Supplie tres humblement vostre pouere oratrice Agnes, qe fu la femme
cir. Richard Bales, qe com nadgairs ele soi purpoisa d'auoir passe le meer
1394 vers les parties de Frisland a son dit baron adonqes la esteant quaunt il vesquist en la port de Chichestre, en la quele lieu la dite Agnes de sa dit passage estoit destourbe, et toutz sez biens la trouez a la value de xl liures, com en vne sedule ent fait et prest a demonstrer est contenuz pluis au plein, furent arestuz par cause qu'ele n'auoit lors brief de passage, et mesmes les biens par Thomas Hyne et William Farnehirst de mesme la ville issint arestuz la par eux furent mys a sire Thomas Frie, vicare de West Wyghteryng pur saluement estre gardez al oeps du dite Suppliant, com par lettres tesmoignales desoutz les seales du ditz Thomas Hyne et William et autres gentz du dite ville ent faitz pluis pleinement appiert; Et ore le dit vicair les ditz biens ad aloignes et ne les voet deliuerer a dite suppliant com reson demande, mes soi absent et voidit de lieu en autre, issint q'ele nulle recouere ne remedie vers luy ent puisse auoir par commun ley nautrement si ele ne soit recouerez et securez par vostre gracious eide : Qe pleise a vostre tres gracious seignurie graunter brief de faire venir deuaunt vous sibien les ditz Thomas Hyne et William qi mesmes les biens aresteront,

---

[1] Bundle 3, No. 71. No. 102 is a duplicate.

goods and chattels in the keeping of the said Roger to be kept for the use of the same John; and so it is, that the said Roger hath alienated many of the said lands and tenements, and for the same hath taken to his own use divers great sums, to the disinheritance of the said suppliant; and he hath also wasted all the said goods and chattels in open destruction of the estate of the said suppliant: May it please your most gracious Lordship to grant the said suppliant a writ directed to the said Roger [commanding him] to be before you on the octave of S. Hilary next, under a penalty of £100, and that on the same day the said Roger may be examined touching the matters aforesaid and other matters which shall be charged against him at the same time for the profit of our Lord the King; for God and in way of charity.[2]

73 To the most reverend Father in God, and his most gracious Lord, the Bishop of Exeter, Chancellor of England,

s.d.
cir.
1394
Most humbly beseecheth your poor oratrix Agnes, widow of Richard Bales, that whereas she of late purposed to have crossed the sea to the parts of Friesland to her said husband, who was then there, when he lived in the port of Chichester, at which place [Chichester] the said Agnes was prevented of her said passage, and all her goods there found, to the value of £40, as in a schedule made thereof and ready to be shown is more fully contained, were arrested because she had not then a writ of passage;[3] and the same goods, so there arrested by Thomas Hyne and William Farnehirst of the same town, were sent by them to Sir Thomas Frie, Vicar of West Wittering, to be safely kept to the use of the said suppliant, as by evidential letters made under the seals of the said Thomas Hyne and William and other people of the said town more fully appeareth; And now the said Vicar hath carried away the said goods and will not deliver them to the said suppliant as right doth demand, but absenteth himself and departeth from place to place, so that she can have no recovery nor remedy against him at common law, nor otherwise unless she be recovered and secured by your gracious aid: May it please your most gracious Lordship to grant a writ to cause to come before you as well the said Thomas Hyne

---

[2] A purely equity case like the last. See p. 49, note 3.

[3] The king's licence to go beyond the seas. See 5 Ric. II. stat. 1, cap. 2.

com le dit vicáre a qi les furent deliuerez, pur respondre de les biens et malefaites auantditz ; pur Dieu et en oeure de charite.

74   [1] A tres reuerent piere en Dieu, l'Euesque d'Excestre, tres honoure et tres gracious seignur, le Chauncellir d'Engleterre,

s. d. Supplie humblement Johan Harcourt qe come vn Thomas Breidynge, Stephen Wenyl et Adam Wenyl ount deseisez le dit suppliant de certeins terres et tenementz en l'isle de Wyght, et la ad vn Richard Birton, sachant lez ditz terres et tenementz estre en debate et le dit suppliant hors de la possession dicelle, achate lez ditz terres et tenementz du dit suppliant a champarte pur cent marcz, encountre la forme dez ordinancez autrefoitz en ceo cas purueu ; Et outre ceo le dit Richard par son exitacion et abettement ad fait le dit suppliant faire vne reconusance a luy de cent liueres par estatuyt marchaunt, promittaunt a luy qe certeins condicions de defesaunce dicelle estatuyt entre eux accordez serroient engrossez, c'estassauoir, qe le dit Richard [2] denst venir as costages du dit Richard ou lez ditz terres et tenementz y sount, et duist entrer et deliuerer la possession a dit Richard, et ceo par garnyssement affaire a dit Richard par le dit suppliant par oept iours deuant, et qe adonque le dit estatuyt serroit voide et tenuz pur nulle, et autrement esterroit en sa force ; puis quele reconusaunce faite le dit Richard ne vorroit engrossier lez condicions suisditz, mez il lez countredit et ce a cause q'il vorreyt auoir execucion enuers le dit suppliant sanz respounce et sanz auauntage auoir dez ditz condicions, a fynal destruccion et anientesment du dit suppliant a touz iours ; Et puis le dit suppliant pur acomplier lez condicions de sa parte ad garny le dit Richard de venir ou lez ditz terres et tenementz y sonnt et q'il vorreyt entrer et luy liuerer la possession acordant a son couenaunt ; et le dit Richard ne voet point : Qe plese a vostre tres graciouse seignurie d'examiner le dit Richard sibien del purchas issint fait a champarte come dez condicions suisduitz, et sour

---

[1] Bundle 3, No. 73. See No. 65.   [2] Probably a mistake for *suppliant*.

and William, who arrested the same goods, as the said Vicar, to whom they were delivered, to answer as to the goods and the misdeeds aforesaid ; for God and in way of charity.

74   To the most reverend Father in God, the Bis o of Exeter, the most honoured and most gracious Lord, the Chancellor of England,

s. d. Humbly beseecheth John Harcourt, that whereas one Thomas Brading, Stephen Wenyl and Adam Wenyl have disseised the said suppliant of certain lands and tenements in the Isle of Wight, and there one Richard Birton, knowing that the said lands and tenements were in dispute and that the said suppliant was out of possession thereof, hath bought the said lands and tenements of the said suppliant by champerty for 100 marks, against the form of the ordinances formerly provided in this case;[3] And, moreover, the said Richard, by his incitement and abetment, induced the said suppliant to make a recognizance of £100 to him by statute merchant, promising him that certain conditions of defeasance of the said statute agreed upon between them should be engrossed, to wit, that the [? suppliant] should come at Richard's expense where the said lands and tenements are, and that he should enter and deliver possession to the said [Richard], and this on notice to be given by the said suppliant to the said Richard eight days beforehand, and that then the said statute should be void and held for null, otherwise it should be in force ; And after the recognizance was made the said Richard would not engross the said conditions, but denied them, because he wished to have execution against the said suppliant without his having any answer or any advantage of the said conditions, to the final destruction and impoverishment of the said suppliant for ever ; And afterwards the said suppliant, to fulfil the conditions on his part, gave notice to the said Richard to come where the said lands and tenements are, so that he might enter and deliver possession to [Richard] according to his covenant; and the said Richard would not : May it please your most gracious Lordship to examine the said Richard, as well touching the purchase so made by champerty, as touching the conditions aforesaid, and thereupon to

[3] The principal statutes against champerty were 13 Ed. I. stat. 1, cap. 49 ; 33 Ed. I. stat. 3 ; 4 Ed. III. c. 11 ; 7 Ric. II. c. 15.

ceo par vostre tres haut discrecion ordeigner qe le dit suppliant soit eyde en cest mischiefe ; pur Dieu et en oeure de charite.

75   [1] A tres reuerent piere en Dieu et tres noble seignur, Euesque de Excestre et Chauncellere d'Engleterre,

s. d. Monstre tres humblement William Pecoc, citein [*sic*] et Pessonere de Loundres, coment il recouera en le Court de la Marchalsye de vn Richard Pecot, Esquier, xvij marcz et dimi, oue quelle Richard issynt condempnez Thomas Barton, Mareschall de dit Court, fust charge ; quelle Richard est deliuere hors de prison et le dit William nient paye ; quelle William ad pursue a dit Thomas d'estre paye ou altrement d'auoir le dit Richard en prison ; et a cause de dite pursute le dit Thomas Barton et Johan Preston ount rebuckez et manasez le dit William issynt q'il ne osa pluys outre pursuer : Que plese a vostre tres noble et tres graciouse seignurie de considerere ceste matere et le tort al dit William feate, et ent ordeignere remedye, pur Dieu et en oeure de charitee.

76   [2] A tres honurable et tres reuerent pier en Dieu, l'Euesque de Excestre, Chauncellier d'Engleterre,

1397 Monstre si vous plese Johan Wisdam qe come Johan de Morley fuist teuuz a dit Johan Wisdam en oept marcz et dimid' par vn obligacion a pair a dit Johan Wisdam a certeyn iour, come en l'auauntdit obligacion ent fait pleynement apert ; a quelle iour du paiement assigne le dit Johan Wisdam enuoia vn Johan Godeman ouesque l'auauntdit obligacion pur receyuer les ditz oept marcz et dimid', par vn lettre de atturne, a cause qe le dit Johan Wisdam a celle temps fuist alez en Irland ; a quelle temps vn John Scothorpe, seruaunt au dit Johan de Morley, omprist l'auauntdit obligacion oue fors hors del mayne d'une Johan Hosier encontre sa volunte et le emporta ; et puis apres les ditz oept

---

[1] Bundle 3, No. 74.
[2] Bundle 3, No. 75.
[3] This case is very obscure, and there is clearly a mistake in the text somewhere.

The plaintiff and the defendant may perhaps have been trying to take advantage of Brading and the others by means of a colourable sale and entry. The relief asked

ordain in your most high discretion that the said suppliant may be aided in this mischief; For God and in way of charity.[3]

75   To the most reverend Father in God and most noble Lord, the Bishop of Exeter and Chancellor of England,

s.d. Most humbly showeth William Peacock, citizen and fishmonger of London, how he recovered 17½ marks in the Court of the Marshalsea from one Richard Pecot, esquire, and Thomas Barton, Marshal of the said Court, was charged with [the custody of] the said Richard, so condemned; which Richard is delivered out of prison, and the said William not paid; and William hath sued the said Thomas to be paid or otherwise to have the said Richard [kept] in prison; And because of the said suit the said Thomas Barton and John Preston have rebuked and menaced the said William, so that he dare not sue any further: May it please your most noble and most gracious Lordship to consider this matter and the wrong done to the said William, and thereof to ordain remedy, for God and in way of charity.[4]

76   [5]To the most honourable and most reverend Father in God, the Bishop of Exeter, Chancellor of England,

1397 Showeth, if you please, John Wisdam, that whereas John de Morley was bound to the said John Wisdam in 8½ marks by a bond to pay [the same] to the said John Wisdam on a certain day, as in the said bond made thereof plainly appeareth; on which day assigned for payment, the said John Wisdam sent one John Godeman with the said bond to receive the said 8½ marks, with a letter of attorney, because the said John Wisdam at that time had gone to Ireland; at which time one John Scothorpe, servant to the said John de Morley, forcibly took the said bond out of the hand of one John Hosier against his will, and carried it away; And afterwards the said 8½

for seems to be specific performance of the Verbal conditions of defeasance of the statute merchant.

[4] There seems no particular reason why this matter should be brought before the Chancellor.

[5] This case has been accidentally misplaced.

marcz et dimid' furent paiez et deliueres a dit Johan Godeman, come al atturne du dit Johan Wisdam; et sur ceo vient vn Thomas Maudesley, baillif nostre seignur le Roy en celle Wapentake, et les ditz oept marez et dimid' prist et aresta pur vn pleint feyne de trespas al suit du dit Johan Morley par colusion fait parentre le dit baille et les auauntditz Johan de Morley et Johan Scothorpe son seruaunt; le quelle pleint puis apres fuist demande, et la vient l'auauntdit Johan Godeman, par son lettre de atturne, et vodroit auoir respoigne au dit pleint pur le dit Johan Wisdam, soi adonqes esteant en Irland, et la Courte la ne luy vodroit resceyuer; pur qei il purchasa vn recordare pur remouer le dit plee, ils le remouer ne vodroient, mes le dit Johan Wisdam en apres sur le dit pleint demanderent de iour en autre, et sur ceo ount liure les ditz oept marez et dimid' a dit Johan de Morley sanz due proces de ley; dont supplie le dit Johan Wisdam a vostre tres haute et tres gracious seignurie de ont ordigner due remedie en cest cause, pur Dieu et en oeure de charite, et vn brief de peyne directez au ditz Johan de Morley et a son seruaunt Johan de Scothorpe, et le dit baille, pur estre deuaunt vous le Mekyrdy prochein deuaunt le feste del Pasche flore.

Indorsed.—Memorandum quod tercio die Februarii anno regni Regis Ricardi secundi xx¹ Thomas Wicherley de Com' Staff' et Thomas Mapurley de Com' Notyngh', coram domino Rege in Cancellaria sua personaliter constituti, manuceperunt pro Johanne Wisdam infrascripto quod ipse satisfaciet infrascriptis Johanni Morley, Johanni Scothorpe et Thome Maudesley pro expensis suis si contenta in ista billa vera esse non probauerit prout Curia considerauerit.

77   ² A tres honouree et tres reuerent piere en Dieux et mon tres gracious seignur, le Euesque d'Excestre, Chaunceller d'Engleterre,

s. d.   Supplie tres humblement Henry Solyng, mestre de la nief dit Ever³ de Lubyk, qe come la ou il venoit hors de Lubyk susdit en le dit nief chargee oue diuerses biens et marchaundises al entent d'auoir arriue al Escluce⁴ en Flaundres, soit ensi qe le vj^{me} iour de Juyn darrein

---

¹ 1397.
² Bundle 3, No. 81.
³ Probably 'Eber,' the Boar.
⁴ Sluys, near Bruges.
⁵ See p. 40, note 2.
⁶ A writ of *recordari facias loquelam*

marks were paid and delivered to the said John Godeman, as attorney of the said John Wisdam ; and thereupon came one Thomas Maudesley, bailiff of our Lord the King in that wapentake, and seized and arrested the said 8½ marks upon a feigned plaint of trespass at the suit of the said John Morley,[5] by collusion made between the said bailiff and the said John de Morley and John Scothorpe his servant ; which plaint was afterwards called on, and there came the aforesaid John Godeman, by his letter of attorney, and would have answered the said plaint for the said John Wisdam, he being then in Ireland, and the Court there would not receive him ; wherefore he purchased a *recordare* to remove the said plea,[6] [but] they would not remove it, but afterwards demanded the said John Wisdam from day to day on the said plaint, and thereupon have delivered the said 8½ marks to the said John de Morley without due process of law ; for which the said John Wisdam beseecheth your most high and most gracious Lordship to ordain due remedy in this cause, for God and in way of charity, and a writ of *sub poena* directed to the said John de Morley and to his servant, John de Scothorpe, and to the said bailiff, to be before you on the Wednesday next before Palm Sunday.

Indorsed.—Be it remembered that on the third day of February, 20 Richard II, Thomas Wicherley of the County of Stafford and Thomas Mapurley of the County of Nottingham personally appeared before the King in his Chancery and undertook for the within written John Wisdam that he would satisfy the within written John Morley, John Scothorpe and Thomas Maudesley as to their expenses if he shall not prove the contents of the bill to be true, as the court shall consider.[7]

77   To the most honoured and most reverend Father in God and my most gracious Lord, the Bis o of Exeter, Chancellor of England,

s.d. Most humbly beseecheth Henry Solyng, master of the ship called 'Ever' of Lübeck, that whereas he came out of Lübeck aforesaid in the said ship laden with divers goods and merchandise intending to have arrived at Sluys in Flanders, so it is that on the 6th day of

directed to the sheriff ; the plea referred to was probably in the County or Wapentake Court.

[7] The fraud and conspiracy of the defendants and the difficulty of getting at the facts of the case without their answers on oath seem to be the reasons for the Chancellor's interference here.

passe il encountra en la meer ouesque le Admiralle del North d'Engleterre, quelle fiste prendre mesme la nief et tous les biens et
marchaundises esteantz en icelle et ceo fist amesner al ville de
Kyngeston sur Hulle; et le dit Suppliaunt ne sciet pas pur quelle
cause; Et yest bien conuz as plusours bons gentz qe le dit nief oue
les biens et marchaundises est des biens des gentz de Lubyk et de
Pruee et de nulles autres: Que please a vostre tres reuerent paternite
et haut seignurie considerer qe gentz de Lubyk et de Pruce sount
bons amys as gentz d'Engleterre, et sur ceo luy graunter vn garraunt
sufficeaunt pur auoir deliueraunce de dit nief ouesque les biens et
marchaundises, ou autrement ordeigner par vostre tres sage discrecion
qe la dite nief ouesque les biens et marchaundises soit mys en sauf
garde tanque la veritee diceste matiere soit deuaunt nostre tres
excellent seignur le Roy et son tres sage Counsaille terminee; pur
Dieux et en oeure de charitee.

78   ¹ Plese a tres reuerent piere en Dieu, l'Euesque
          de Excestre et Chaunceller d'Engleterre,

s.d. De mettre remedie a Wanter Broun et Margarete sa femme de
cir. certeyns terres, tenementz en Wenfryth, Saltford et aillours en le
1394 Countee de Somers', donut ils sonnt deforcez a cause d'un retardacion
      de execucione d'un iuggement done en Bank le Roy pur les dit Wanter
      et Margarete, come le droit heritage le dite Margarete come fille et heire
      d'un Johan Basset, qi morust seisy, come estoit troue par vn office pris
      deuant le Eschetour de Somers' par vertue d'un brief de mandamus;
      q'est ore de pleyn age et xx ans outre, par accion trie deuers vn Esmond
      Basset; par force de quele iuggement le Roi auoit possessioune de garde
      et terres a cause de noun age de dite Margarete par soun prerogatiue;
      et par le dit recouerer dez ditz terres tenuz de seignur le Spencer de la
      Manoir de Lassebergh tenuz de Roy en chief; de queles terres issint
      recouerez le Roy ad eut les profitz longe temps nient contresteiaunt
      les comaundementz le Roy de ses lettres secretz et de soun priue
      seale: Sur quoy les ditz suppliantz vous humblement requerent
      d'auoir liuere dez ditz terres et tenementz par vostre auys et le Chief
      Justice le Roy, le quele dona iuggement sur verdit d'enquest come la

¹ Bundle 3, No. 86.   Council as a matter of State. For similar
² This case clearly came before the   cases see *Selden Soc.*, 6, xlvii, xlviii.

June last past he encountered on the sea the Admiral of the North of England, who caused the said ship to be seized and all the goods and merchandise therein, and caused it to be brought to the town of Kingston on Hull; and the said suppliant knoweth not wherefore; and it is well known to many good folk that the said ship with the goods and merchandise is the property of people of Lübeck and Prussia and of no others: May it please your most reverent paternity and high Lordship to consider that the people of Lübeck and of Prussia are good friends to the people of England, and thereupon to grant a sufficient warrant to have deliverance of the said ship with the goods and merchandise, or otherwise to ordain in your most wise discretion that the said ship with the goods and merchandise may be put in safe keeping until the truth of this matter may be determined before our most excellent Lord the King and his most wise Council; For God and in way of charity.[2]

78   May it please the most reverend Father in God the Bis o of Exeter and Chancellor of England,

s.d.   To provide a remedy to Walter Brown and Margaret his wife touching
cir.   certain lands and tenements in Winford, Saltford, and elsewhere in
1394   the County of Somerset, of which they are deforced because of the
       delay in the execution of a judgment given in an action against one
       Edmund Basset in the King's Bench for the said Walter and Margaret,
       in respect of the rightful inheritance of the said Margaret as daughter
       and heir of one John Basset, who died seised thereof, as was found by
       an office taken before the Escheator of Somerset, by virtue of a writ
       of mandamus; [which Margaret] is now of full age and 20 years more;
       and by force of that judgment the King had possession of the wardship
       and lands because of the nonage of the said Margaret, by his pre-
       rogative, and by the said recovery of the said lands held of Lord le
       Spencer [and] of the manor of Lasborough[3] held of the King in chief,
       of which lands so recovered the King had the profits for a long time
       notwithstanding the commandments of the King by his letters close
       and by his privy seal; Whereupon the said suppliants humbly request
       to have livery of the said lands and tenements by your advice and that
       of the Chief Justice of the King, who gave judgment on the verdict of

                              [3] Co. Glouc.

droit de dite Margarete et profit le Roy quele pent deuaunt vous en la Chauncellerie ; eiant regard, tresgracious seignur, qe le dit Esmond est foringe dez ditz terres par le dit recouere, et qe nulle autre person estrange cleyme tytle de droit, considerant, tres gracious seignur, q'il n'ad rien douut viuer ne meynteyne sa femme ne ses siz iuueniz enfantz ; Pur Dieu et en eoure de charite ; considerant qe le Roi ad pris les profitz des ditz terres par siz ans et pluis apres la pleyn age de dite Margarete, q'amonte iiij^{xx} liures et pluis par le dit terme.

Indorsed.—Le Roy l'ad comys a Chaunceller pur faire due remedie et droit celle partie par autorite de parlement selonc ceo qe luy semblerra melx par sa bone discrecion par anys et conseil de ceux qi luy semblerra busoignables appeller en la matier.

79   [1] A tres reuerent pier en Dieu et son tres graciouse seignur, l'Euesque d'Excestre, Chanceller d'Engleterre,

s. d. Monstre et soi pleint Nichol de Skelton, sergeant d'armes, qe come il estoit seisy des certeyns tenementz en la Citee d'Euerwyke et auoit este pessiblement possessione dicels par plusours anz passez par leie et droit de descent, tancque ore qe puis le duszisme iour de Januier darrein passe, vn Richard de Thursby et William de Otteley, clerk, par confederacion et conspiracy entre eux et certeyns persones d'une Gilde appelle la Trinite Gilde deinz la dite Citee d'Euerwyke faitz, esteant forciblement en affraye del peple nostre seignur le Roy al noumbre de deux centz ou troys des persones de la dite Gilde, arraiez afeere de guerre en routz et insurrecciouns, a cause qe lez ditz Richard et William promistrent et assurerent de doner lez ditz tenementz a lour dite Gilde en case q'ils eux voilloient mayntenir forciblement pur tenir lez ditz tenementz et eux enforcer encountre le dit Nichol en ycelle partie, ont entrez par forcibles assemblies sur le dite Nichol en lez ditz tenementz en destourbance de la comune leie et encountre la fourme de l'estatut nadgairs ent fait, et sez tenantz illoqes naufreront, bateront et male-

---

[1] Bundle 3, No. 87.

[2] That is, up to 1382 when the Inquisition was taken. Margaret was of full age, fourteen, in 1374, having been born in 1360. We can thus date the case about 1396, as Margaret says she is now more than 34, which comes within the Bishop of Exeter's first Chancellorship, 1396–1399.

[3] This case is very obscure. Edmund

the inquest, as to the right of the said Margaret and the profit of the King, which is pending before you in the Chancery; having regard, most gracious Lord, that the said Edmund is for-judged of the said lands by the said recovery, and that no other stranger claims title of right, and considering, most gracious Lord, that [the said Walter] hath nothing whereon to live' and maintain his wife and his six young children; For God and in way of charity; Considering that the King took the profits of the said lands for six years[2] and more after the full age of the said Margaret, which amounteth to four score pounds and more for the said term.

Indorsed.—The King hath commissioned the Chancellor to make due remedy and right in this behalf by the authority of parliament, according to what shall seem best to him in his good discretion with the advice and counsel of those to whom it shall seem needful to him to appeal in the matter.[3]

79   To the most reverend Father in God and his most gracious Lord, the Bishop of Exetei, Chancellor of England,

s. d. Showeth and complaineth Nicholas de Skelton, Serjeant at arms, that whereas he was seised of certain tenements in the City of York, and had been in peaceable possession thereof for many years past, by law and in right of descent, until now of late, on the 12th day of January last past, that one Richard de Thursby and William de Otley, clerk, (by confederacy and conspiracy made between them and certain persons of a Guild, called the Trinity Guild, within the said City of York, being forcibly in affray of the people of our Lord the King to the number of two or three hundred persons of the said Guild, arrayed in manner of war in routs and insurrections, because the said Richard and William promised and assured to give them the said tenements for their said Guild in case they would forcibly maintain them to hold the said tenements and enforce them against the said Nicholas in that behalf,) have entered by forcible assemblies upon the said Nicholas in the said tenements, to the disturbance of the common law and contrary to the form of the statute lately made thereof,[4] and did there assault, beat

Basset was Margaret's uncle; he claimed as heir male of John, on the ground that the lands had been settled in tail male. See Inq. *post mortem*, Chancery, 6 Ric. II, no. 16; 7 Ric. II, no. 176; 21 Ric. II, no. 105.

[4] 17 Ric. II, cap. 8.

ment treteront encountre la pees nostre seignur le Roi et le course de
la comune leie; le dit Nichol adonqes esteant en lez seruices et messages nostre dit seignur le Roy; Et mesmes lez t⋅nantz[1] lez auantditz Richard et William par force et outrageouse noumbre de lez
persones de la Gilde auantdite vncqore en routz et assemblies par
pales armure et en autre manere afeere de guerre occupiont, tiegnont
et enforsont en contempt nostre dit seignur le Roi et encountre la
puruoiance de l'estatut auantdit; Entandantz, tres graciouse seignur,
qe lez Justices du pees deinz mesme la Citee sont de mesme la Gilde
et iurrez a la fraternite dicelle, paront ils sont parties aidantz fauor-
ables et meyntenantz a lez ditz Richard et William par cause de lour
promys et assurance suisditz; Plese a vostre tres reuerent et tres
graciouse seignurie grantier briefs sur peine de centz liuers directz a
lez ditz Richard et William de venir deuant le Counseille nostre
seignur le Roy ou denaut vous[2] en la Chauncellery al quinszime de
Pasque proschein venant pur respondre a Roy et a le dit Nichol de ceo
et des autres choses qe adonqes a eux serront surmys par le dit Nichol
en la matier suisdite.

  Plegii de prosequendo iuxta formam statuti:
          Robert Saperton,
          Robert Marchall de London.

80   [3]A tres reuerent pier en Dieu l'Euesque
          d'Excestre et Chaunceller d'Engleterre,

s. d. Supplie humblement Cristine qi fuist la femme Esmond fitz Lucas
    de Bury, qe come ele estoit seise en son demesne come de fee de cer-
    teins mees, terres et rentes oue lour appurtenances en la ville de Bury,
    la vendroient Johan Bret de Cokefeld, Johan Coppyng de Bury, Adam
    Hoo de Cokefeld, Johan Boteler et William Hosteler de Bury, le Lundy
    proschein apres le feste de Seint Laurence darrein passe, ouesque
    plusours autres de lour assent, et la dite Cristine ousterent od force
    et armes de ses mees, terres et rentes auantditz, et la les biens et
    chateux du dit suppliant tanque a value de XX liures emporteront; et
    outre ceo les ditz Johan, Johan, Adam, Johan et William issint man-
    assent le dit suppliant de iour en autre de vie et de membre q'ele
    n'ose aprocher a son propre hostelle ne demurer en cele pais pur doute

---

[1] Sic, for *tenementz*.
[2] A distinction seems intended here between the Council and the Chancellor.

and ill-treat his servants, against the peace of our Lord the King and the course of the common law; the said Nicholas then being on the services and messages of our said Lord the King; And the said Richard and William, by force and by the outrageous number of the persons of the said Guild, in routs and assemblies with palisades, armour, and otherwise in warlike manner, do still occupy, hold, and enforce the said tenements, in contempt of our said Lord the King and against the provision of the statute aforesaid; Understanding, most gracious Lord, that the Justices of the Peace within the said City are of the same Guild and sworn to that Fraternity, wherefore they are parties aiding, favouring and maintaining the said Richard and William because of their promise and assurance aforesaid: May it please your most reverend and most gracious Lordship to grant writs, on penalty of £100, directed to the said Richard and William, [commanding them] to come before the Council of our Lord the King or before you in the Chancery, on the quindene of Easter next coming, to answer the King and the said Nicholas touching this and other things which shall then be charged against them by the said Nicholas in the matter aforesaid.

Pledges to prosecute according to the form of the statute,

Robert Saperton,
Robert Marshall of London.

80   To the most reverend Father in God, the Bis o of Exeter and Chancellor of England,

s.d. Humbly beseecheth Christine, widow of Edmund FitzLucas of Bury [St. Edmunds], that whereas she was seised in her demesne as of fee of certain messuages, lands and rents with their appurtenances in the town of Bury, there came John Bret of Cockfield, John Coppyng of Bury, Adam Hoo of Cockfield, John Boteler and William Hosteler of Bury, on the Monday after the feast of S. Lawrence ⁴ last past, with many others by their consent, and with force and arms ousted the said Christine from her messuages, lands and rents aforesaid, and carried off the goods and chattels of the said suppliant to the value of £20; and moreover the said John, John, Adam, John and William so threaten the said suppliant from day to day of life and limb that she dare not approach her own house nor dwell in that country for fear of

³ Bundle 3, No. 91.
⁴ August 10.

de mort: Qe plese a vostre tres gracious seignurie graunter briefs au dit suppliant de faire les ditz mailfaisours venir deuant vous a certein iour en la Chancellarie nostre seignur le Roy de respondre sibien au Roy come a dit suppliant des trespas auantditz; Entendantz, tres gracious seignur, qe, si ele ne purra auoir tiel remedie par vostre graciouse ordinance, ele vnqes n'auera remedie enuers les ditz tres-pasours, a cause q'ele n'ad rien de pursuer la comune ley enuers eux; Pur Dieu et en oeure de charitee.

81   [1] A tres reuerent piere en Dieu et lour tres graciouse seignur, l'Euesque d'Excestre, Chaunceller nostre seignur le Roi

s. d. Monstrent, s'il vous plest, Margerete Harfeld et Thomas Sohawe et se pleynent de certeyns oppressions, extorcions et iniures a eux faitz par vn Johan Shelwyke, Hygyn Wayte et Hygyn Symond, mayntenours des mesfesours encontre la pees et tranquillite de poeple nostre seignur le Roi en Brynsoppe en la Countee de Hereford; primerement coment les ditz Johan, Hygyn et Hygyn sont mayntenours de larons et homicides, et coment les ditz mesfesours oue altres venoient oue force et armes en manere de insurreccion encontre la pees nostre seignur le Roi sanz garrant, et entreront en la maison la dite Margerete, et bateront et naufront la dite Margerete a peine q'ele eschappa la mort, et la sercheront chescun angle et chambre de dite maison, issint q'ils fycherent en lytz oue lour espees nuz et daggers pur auoir tue vn des fitz la dite Margerete; et auxi vn altre foiz entrerent la clos de dite Margerete oue force et armes en manere de insurreccion, et la pristront maeresme grant plente, al value de dys liures, et firent havoke dycelle; et coment les ditz mesfesours Johan Shelwyke et ses compaignons horsbotoient la dite Margerete de ses terres et tenementz illoeqes sanz processe de ley mes par volunte, et pristrount et em-porteront grant quantite de feyn illoeqes al value de quarante soldz; et coment les ditz mesfesours oue altres estoient embusshez en manere des enemys gisantz en agayt pur le dit Thomas pres le droit haute chemyn nostre seignur le Roi, et come le dit Thomas chiuecha en la dite chemyn ils ly pristrent sanz processe ou comandement des Justices de la pees nostre seignur le Roi ou ascun altre ministre qeqanque, et ly amesneront en prison, a grant tort, damage et poaur

[1] Bundle 3, No. 92.

death : May it please your most gracious Lordship to grant the said suppliant writs to cause the said evil-doers to come before you at a certain day in the Chancery of our Lord the King to answer as well to the King as to the said suppliant for the said trespasses ; Understanding, most gracious Lord, that if she cannot have such remedy by your gracious ordinance, she can never have any remedy against the said trespassers, because she has nothing wherewith to sue the common law against them ; For God and in way of charity.[2]

81   To the most reverend Father in God and their most gracious Lord, the Bishop of Exeter, Chancellor of our Lord the King,

s. d. Show, if you please, Margaret Harfield and Thomas Sohawe, and complain of certain oppressions, extortions and injuries done to them by one John Shelwick, Higgin Wayte and Higgin Symond, maintainers of evildoers against the peace and tranquillity of the people of our Lord the King in Brinsop in the County of Hereford ; and firstly how the said John, Higgin and Higgin are maintainers of robbers and homicides, and how the said evildoers with others came with force and arms in the manner of an insurrection, against the peace of our Lord the King, without warrant, and entered the house of the said Margaret, and did beat and assault her so that she scarcely escaped death ; and they searched each nook and chamber of the said house and prodded the beds with their naked swords and daggers, in order to have killed one of the sons of the said Margaret ; And also another time they entered the close of the said Margaret with force and arms in the manner of an insurrection, and there seized timber in great quantity, to the value of £10, and made havoc thereof ; And how the said evil-doers, John Shelwick and his companions, ejected the said Margaret from her lands and tenements there, without any process of law, but by their own will, and seized and carried off a great quantity of hay there to the value of 40s. ; And how the said evil-doers with others were ambushed like enemies, lying in wait for the said Thomas near the lawful highway of our Lord the King, and as the said Thomas rode on the said highway they seized him, without any process or order of the Justices of the Peace of our Lord the King, or of any other officer whatsoever, and took him to prison, to the great wrong, damage, and

[2] As to the poverty of the plaintiff see p. 47, note 6.

a dit Thomas; et puis apres vn altre foiz coment le dit Thomas entra
en la esglise pur oier seruice de Dieu, les ditz mesfessours oue altres
de lour couyn firent assaut a dit Thomas au fyn q'ils vodroient auoir
tue le dit Thomas s'il ne isseroit hors de la dite esglise; et altres
plusours damages et tortz firent as ditz Margerete et Thomas : Par
qoi plese a vostre tresgraciouse seignurie d'enuoier par brief nostre
dit seignur le Roi pur les ditz Johan Shelwyke et ses compaignons
pur estre deuant vous en lour propres persones a vn certein iour sur
vn grande peyne pur y respounder a les articles auantditz, et sur ceo
faire remede pur Dieu et en oeuere de charite, sibien pur le profit
nostre dit seignur le Roi come pur les ditz Margerete et Thomas.

82   [1] A tres reuerent piere en Dieu et son tres
          gracious   seignur,   l'Euesque   d'Excestre,
          Chaunceller d'Engleterre,

s. d. Supplie humblement Rauf Wathe, clerk, qe come ore tarde vous, tres
gracious seignur, grauntastez a dit suppliant vn brief direct a William
Smyth et [? de] Graund Wylburgham [2] luy chargeant d'auoir com-
pareu deuant vous en la Chauncellarie pur la auoir troue seurte de
pees a dit suppliant, le quel suppliant fist deliuerer le dit brief a dit
William par vn Thomas *Prat* et William Halsey; et le dit William,
nient   [3] de dit brief et nient voillant a ceo obeire, ietta le dit
brief de luy maliciousement, endisant q'il ne vorroit rien faire pur
ycelle, en graund contempt nostre soueraigne seignur le Roy et de
son maundement auantdit : Plese a vostre tres gracious seignurie
graunter brief d'arester le dit William par son corps et luy amesner
deuant vous a respoundere de les choses suisditz, pur Dieu et en oeure
de charite.

83   [4] A tres gracious seignur et tres reuerent
          piere en Dieu, l'Euesque d'Excestre, Chaun
          celler d'Engleterre,

s. d. Monstre William by the Broke et soy pleynt de Johan Giles de
Longedon, qe par la ou lez ditz William et Johan furent accordez

---

[1] Bundle 3, No. 94.
[2] Probably Great Wilbraham, co. Cambridge.

fear of the said Thomas; And afterwards at another time as the said Thomas entered the church to hear God's service, the said evildoers, with others of their covin, assaulted the said Thomas, to the end that they might have killed him if he had not left the said church; And many other damages and wrongs they did to the said Margaret and Thomas: Wherefore may it please your most gracious Lordship, by a writ of our said Lord the King, to send for the said John Shelwick and his companions to be before you in their proper persons, at a certain day and under a great pain, to answer to the articles aforesaid, and thereupon to provide a remedy, for God and in way of charity, as well for the profit of our said Lord the King as for the said Margaret and Thomas.

82   To the most reverend Father in God and his most gracious Lord, the Bishop of Exeter, Chancellor of England,

s. d. Humbly beseecheth Ralph Wathe, clerk, that whereas now lately you, most gracious Lord, did grant to the said suppliant a writ directed to William Smyth of Great Wilbraham, charging him to appear before you in the Chancery there to find surety for the peace towards the said suppliant, which writ the said suppliant caused to be delivered to the said William by one Thomas Prat and William Halsey; and the said William Smyth not [? regarding] the said writ and not wishing to obey it, maliciously threw it from him, saying that he would do nothing for it, in great contempt of our sovereign Lord the King and of his said order: May it please your most gracious Lordship to grant a writ to arrest the said William by his body and to bring him before you to answer for the matters aforesaid, for God and in way of charity.

83   To the most gracious Lord and most reverend Father in God, the Bishop of Exeter, Chancellor of England,

s. d. Showeth William by the Brook, and complaineth of John Giles of Longdon,[5] that whereas the said William and John made an agree-

---

[3] A hole in the MS.　　　　　　　　　　　[5] Near Lichfield, co. Staffs.
[4] Bundle 3, No. 103.

deuant monsire Thomas Daston, James Arblastre et autres en l'an
darrein passe a Lichefeld en manere q'ensuyt, c'est assauoir, le dit
Johan dust pursuer la commune ley pur certeyns terres et tenementz
iadys Thomas Colman en le fee de Elmehurst, quelx le dit William
purchacea de Richard Colman, fitz et heir au dit Thomas, en
eschaunge pur dimi virge de terre naitif [1] en Longedon, sur lez costages
d'ambideux, et sur ceo le dit William releassa au dit Johan son droit
en ycellz sur ceste condicion, qe apres qe lez ditz terres furent
recouerez de William Bridde son aduersary, le dit Johan dust auoir
feoffe le dit William en ycellz a terme de sa vie; de quelx terres et
tenementz issint as costages d'ambideux recouerez le dit Johan ore ne
voet acomplier son dit couenant vers le dit William, mes ad entre
en lez ditz terres et tenementz et luy hors tient dycellz, countre
droit : Qe please a vostre tres graciouse seignurie commaunder le dit
Johan Giles de venir deuant vous et luy compeller d'acomplier son dit
couenant vers le dit William ; Pur Dieu et en oeure de charite. [2]

84   [3] A tres reuerent piere en Dieu, l'Euesque
          d'Excestre et Chaunceller d'Engleterre,

s. d. Supplie humblement Matheu Londoneis, vn de les attornees en le
Commune Banke, qe come il estoit de conseil ouesque Johan Loue [4]
en vne assise de nouelle dissesin, qe passa enuers le dit Johan, ore
tarde deuaut les Justices d'assise a Chelmesford ; et a cause qe vn
William Mepesale, vn des Jurrours el dite assise, al suggestion del
dit Matheu fesoit fyn a nostre dit seignur le Roi deuant lez ditz
Justices pur taunt q'il encountre la ley mangeast et boest depuis q'il
auoit sa charge et estoit en vne chaumbre oue ses compaignons, le dit
William meinteinant, apres lez ditz assises finez, encountra le dit
Matheu chiuachaunt a son hostielle et luy suist oue vne espee, manas-
sant de luy tuer, mes q'il a peine eschapa et returna a Chelmesford,
et vnqore luy manasse de vie et de membre : Plese a vostre tres
graciouse seignurie graunter brief direct au dit William d'estre deuant
vous au certein iour de respondre de cest haynous et mauueis fait,
et de trouer suirtee de pees a dit Matheu ; Pur Dieu et en oeuere de
charitee. Considerant, tres honure seignur, qe le dit Matheu ne ose

---

[1] Probably equivalent to the *terra nativa*   [2] An interesting and early case of *specific*
or *terra nativorum*, frequently mentioned   *performance*. See Spence, i. 644.
in manorial rolls.

ment before Sir Thomas Daston,[5] James Arblaster and others, last year at Lichfield in manner following, that is to say, the said John should sue at common law for certain lands and tenements, formerly Thomas Colman's, in the fee of Elmhurst,[6] which the said William purchased of Richard Colman, son and heir of the said Thomas in exchange for half a virgate of bond-land in Longdon, at their joint costs, and thereupon the said William should release to the said John his right in the same, on this condition, that after the said lands were recovered from William Bird, his adversary, the said John should have enfeoffed the said William therein for the term of his life ; and the said John will not now fulfil his covenant with the said William touching the said lands and tenements so recovered at their joint costs, but hath entered into the said lands and tenements and keepeth [William] out of them, against right : May it please your most gracious Lordship to command the said John Giles to come before you, and to compel him to fulfil his said covenant with the said William ; For God and in way of charity.

84   To the most reverend Father in God, the Bishop of Exeter and Chancellor of England,

s. d. Beseecheth humbly Mathew the Londoner, one of the Attorneys in the Common Bench, that whereas he was of counsel with John Love [or Lone] in an assize of novel disseisin now of late before the Justices of Assize at Chelmsford, which went against the said John ; and because one William Mepesale, one of the jurors of the said assize, was fined to our said Lord the King before the said Justices, at the suggestion of the said Mathew, for that contrary to the law he had eaten and drunk after he was charged and was in a room with his fellows, the said William now, after the said Assizes were finished, encountered the said Mathew, who was riding to his house, and followed him with a sword, threatening to kill him, so that he with difficulty escaped and returned to Chelmsford ; and [the said William] doth still threaten him [Mathew] of life and limb : May it please your most gracious Lordship to grant a writ directing the said William to be before you at a certain day to answer for this heinous and wicked act, and to find surety for the peace towards the said Mathew ; For God and in way of charity. Considering, most honoured Lord, that the said Mathew

---

[3] Bundle 3, No. 105.
[4] Or Lone.

[5] Perhaps D'Aston.
[6] Near Lichfield, co. Staffs.

mie approcher sa maison pur doute de mort tanque q'il eit sufficiant
suirtee du dit William.

85   [1] Plese a tres reuerent piere en Dieu,
          l'Euesque d'Excestre et Chaunceller d'Engle-
          terre,

s. d. Considerer coment William Couentre de Plymmouth, clerc, ad fait
diuerses faux escriptz enseales desouz son seal, sanz cognissance des
persones souz quelx nouns mesmes l'escriptz sont faitz, en desheretison
des plusours gentz du Countes de Cornwaille et Deuenshire, Et sur
ce ordeigner due remede solonc vostre tres sage discrecion ; Pur Dieu
et en oeuere de charitee.[2]

86   [3] A tres reuerent piere en Dieu, l'Euesque de
          Excester, Chauncellier d'Englitere,

Ric. H. Supplie Hugh Loterell, chiualer, qe come nostre seignur le Roy par
sez lettrez patentz [4] luy ad graute le officie et le garde del forest de
Gyllyngham,[5] ouesque toutz lez feez a le dit officie appourtenauntez,
come en lez ditz lettrez patentz plus pleynement appert, et sur ceo
Johan Hayme et Johan Clerke ount fait graunt suggestion parmy le
pais qe lez ditz lettres patentz ne feurent my grauntez par nostre
seignur le Roy ne par avys par son Conseille mez par le suggestion del
dit Hugh fait a la Chauncellier, en disclandour de la Court et en
neyntesment del dit Hugh : Qe pleise enveier pur lez ditz Johan et
Johan deuener deuaunt vous sur pene de cent liures, et sur ceo or-
degner remedy, issint qe lez foresters illoqes purront estre en pes
pur leuer lez profitestz nostre seignur le Roy et dit Hugh.

87   [6] A tres reuerent piere en Dieu et soun tres
          honoure et tres gracious seignur, l'Euesque
          d'Excestre, Chaunceller d'Engleterre,

s. d. Supplie vn pouere homme, William fitz Johan Culne,[7] qe come il soit
de frank estate et condicion, et il et toutz ses auncestres de toute

---

[1] Bundle 3, No. 106.
[2] The plaintiff's name is not mentioned.
It would be interesting to know what course
was taken by the court in the case of an
anonymous bill.
[3] Bundle 3, No. 108.

dare not approach his house for fear of death, until he have sufficient surety from the said William.

85   May it please the most reverend Father in God, the Bishop of Exeter and Chancellor of England,

s. d. To consider how William Coventre of Plymouth, clerk, hath made divers false writings, sealed with his seal, without the knowledge of the persons under whose names the same writings are made, to the disinherison of many people of the Counties of Cornwall and Devon, And thereupon to ordain due remedy according to your most wise discretion : For God and in way of charity.

86   To the most reverend Father in God, the Bishop of Exeter, Chancellor of England,

Ric. II. Beseecheth Hugh Loterell, knight, that whereas our Lord the King by his letters patent hath granted to him the office and ward of the Forest of Gillingham, with all the fees to the said office appertaining, as in the said letters patent more fully appeareth, and thereupon John Hayme and John Clerke have made great suggestion throughout the country that the said letters patent were not granted by our Lord the King nor by the advice of his Council, but by the suggestion of the said Hugh made to the Chancellor, to the slander of the Court and the destruction of the said Hugh : May it please [you] to send for the said John and John to come before you on pain of £100, and thereupon to ordain a remedy, so that the foresters there may be in peace to levy the profits of our Lord the King and the said Hugh.

87   To the most reverend Father in God and his most honoured and most gracious Lord, the Bishop of Exeter, Chancellor of England,

s. d. Beseecheth a poor man, William son of John Culne, that whereas he is of free estate and condition and he and all his ancestors time out

---

⁴ *Rot. Pat.* 22 Ric. II. pt. 2, m. 20.   ⁶ Bundle 3, No. 110.
⁵ Gillingham, co. Dorset. See Hutchins's   ⁷ Or perhaps Culve.
Dorset, iii. 199.

temps dount memoire ne court, sount et ount estes de mesme la condicion, saunz ceo qe ascun cleyme ou chalange ad estre fait de dit
William ou de ascun de ses ditz auncestres, vient ore vn Johan Shorte-
groue, fermer de certeins terres et tenementz d'un George Belamy, et
cleyme le dit William come nief appurtenaunt as ditz terres et tenementz, et ad pris et areste le dit William a Vpton en le Countee de
Hereford et luy ad amesne de dit Countee tanque en Gales, et luy
illeoqes detient en forte et dure prison en perpetuel destruccion de dit
William s'il u'eit vostre tres gracious aide: Plese a vostre tres gracious
seignurie graunter brief de faire le dit Johan venir deuant vous a certein iour sur certein peine, amesnant ouesque luy le dit William
esteant en sa garde, a respoundre de les choses suisditz, et outre faire
grace a dit William, et ordeiner q'il purra estre deliuerez par sufficiant
meinprise, d'atendre ceo qe droit et reson demaundent en ceste cas ;
pur Dieu et en oeure de charite.

88   [1] A tres reuerent piere en Dieu, l'Euesque
d'Excestre, Chaunceller d'Engleterre,

s. d. Supplient voz poueres seruantz Johan Wilton et William Goldeman,
qe come nostre tres excellent seignur le Roy nadgaires par ses lettres
patentes dona et graunta as ditz suppliantz et a lour heirs vn cotage
en Holbourne en Loundres et quatre cotages en la paroche de l'esglise
de scinte Marie atte Stronde hors le barre de Nouel Temple de Loundres oue les appurtenaunces, queux furent a Piers Ascharn, clerke, si
come en les dites littres patentes pluis pleinement appiert ; par virtue
de quelles lettres les ditz suppliantz sont en possession des ditz cotages
oue les appurtenaunces ; Et vn Johan Kemle, ore parsone du dite
esglise del Stroude, ad et detient certeins chartres, faitz, escriptz et
munimentz aunciens touchantz les ditz cotages, par quelles chartres,
faitz, escriptz et munimentz le title et le droit nostre dit seignur le
Roy de les ditz cotages oue les appurtenances purront expressement
estre coignuz et prouez et les queux chartres, faitz, escriptz et munimentz appurtenents as ditz suppliantz en affirmacion del droit nostre
dit seignur le Roy, et en saluacion de la possession des ditz suppliantz
en les cotages oue les appurtenaunces suisditz : Plese a vostre gra-

[1] Bundle 3, No. 111.

of mind are and have been of the same condition, and no claim or challenge hath been made of the said William or of any of his said ancestors, and now there cometh one John Shortegrove, farmer of certain lands and tenements from one George Belamy, and claimeth the said William as his villein appurtenant to the said lands and tenements, and he hath seized and arrested the said William at Upton in the County of Hereford, and hath brought him from that County into Wales, and there keepeth him in a strong and hard prison, to the perpetual destruction of the said William if he have not your most gracious aid : May it please your most gracious Lordship to grant a writ to cause the said John to come before you at a certain day and on a certain pain, bringing with him the said William, who is in his keeping, to answer touching the matters aforesaid, and further [please you] to do grace unto the said William, and to ordain that he may be delivered [out of prison] by sufficient mainprise, to await what right and reason demand in this case; For God and in way of charity.

88   To the most reverend Father in God, the Bishop of Exeter, Chancellor of England,

s. d. Beseech your poor servants, John Wilton and William Goldeman, that whereas our most excellent Lord the King by his letters patent latelv gave and granted to the said suppliants and their heirs a cottage in Holborn in London and four cottages in the parish of the Church of S. Mary at Strand, outside the Bar of the New Temple of London,[2] with the appurtenances, which had belonged to Peter Ascharn, clerk, as in the said letters patent more fully appeareth ; by virtue of which letters the said suppliants are in possession of the said cottages with the appurtenances ; And one John Kemle, now Rector of the said Church of the Strand, hath and detaineth certain ancient charters, deeds, writings and muniments concerning the said cottages, by which charters, deeds, writings and muniments the title and right of our said Lord the King to the said cottages with the appurtenances may be expressly known and proved, and which charters, deeds, writings and muniments belong to the said suppliants in affirmation of the right of our said Lord the King, and in salvation of the possession of the said suppliants in the cottages with the appur-

---

[2] The Bar of the Old Temple was in Holborn, near what is now known as Holborn Bars.

ciouse seignurie de faire venir le dit Johan Kemle deuaunt vous et luy
commaunder et charger de deliuerer ein la Chauncellerie toutz les
chartres, faitz, escriptz et munimentz touchantz les ditz cotages oue
les appurtenaunces esteantz en sa possession et poair, pur y estre
monstrez et deliuerez as ditz suppliantz; pur Dieu et en oeuere de
charitee.[1]

89   [2] A tres sage, tres reuerent et tres gracious
seignur, l'Euesque d'Excestre et Chaunceller
d'Engleterre,

s. d. Supplie humblement Johan, parson de l'esglise del Stronde,[3] qe come
il achata vne grande quantite de maeresme, et le dit maeresme fist
carier et metter deinz vn son mees en Holbourne, et puis vn William
Goldman, par vertue d'vn patent nostre seignur le Roy, supposant qe
vn Piers Askarne murust seisi de dit mees, ousta le dit parsone de dit
mees, et le dit maeresme et autres biens et chatieux du dit parsone
deinz le dit mees trouez a la value de x liures detient, et ne les voet
suffrer estre deliuerez en nulle manere, a grand damage du dit parsone,
dont il supplie remedie pur Dieu et en oeure de charitee.[4]

90   A tres honure et tres gracious seignur,
l'Euesque d'Excestre, Chanceller d'Engle
terre,

s. d. Suppliont humblement voz pouers Chapelleins et Oratours, l'Abbe et
Couent de Wyggemore,[5] qe come vn Thomas Stones de son grant
malice torciousement ad entrez sur les ditz Abbe et Couent en son
Manoir de Lowe en le Countee de Salop, et eux ad disseisiz et oustez
hors de lour possession du dit Manoir de sa propre auctorite et grant
meyntenance forciblement, sanz ascun droit et reson et proces de ley,
faisant en mesme le Manoir plusours et grantz gastes et destruccions,
sibien des grosses arbes [sic] et boys par lui trenchez et cariez et
apportez hors de icelle, come de toutz autres choses a dit Manoir appur-
tinantz, a grant preiudice et damage des ditz Abbe et Couent et plein

[1] See Case 89.   [3] S. Mary's.
[2] Bundle 3, No. 112.   [4] See Case 88.

tenances aforesaid: May it please your gracious Lordship to cause
the said John Kemle to come before you, and to command and
charge him to deliver all the charters, deeds, writings and muniments
in his possession and power concerning the said cottages with the
appurtenances into the Chancery, there to be shown and delivered to
the said suppliants; For God and in way of charity.

89 To the most wise, most reverend and most gracious Lord, the Bishop of Exeter and Chancellor of England,

s. d. Humbly beseecheth John, Rector of the Church of the Strand, that
whereas he bought a great quantity of timber, and had the said
timber carried and put in a house of his in Holborn, and then one
William Goldman, by virtue of a patent of our Lord the King, supposing that one Peter Askarne had died seised of the said house,
ousted the said Rector from the said house and detaineth the said
timber and other goods and chattels of the said Rector to the value of
£10, found within the said house, and will not suffer them to be
delivered in any way, to the great damage of the said Rector, of which
he beseecheth remedy for God and in way of charity

90 To the most honoured and most gracious Lord, the Bishop of Exeter, Chancellor of England,

s. d. Humbly beseech your poor chaplains and orators, the Abbat and
Convent of Wigmore, that whereas one Thomas Stones of his great
malice hath tortiously entered into their manor of Lowe in the County
of Salop against the said Abbat and Convent, and hath disseised
them and ousted them out of their possession of the said manor, of
his own authority and great maintenance, forcibly and without any
right or reason or process of law, committing many and great wastes
and destructions in the said manor, as well of great trees and wood
by him cut and carried and taken out thereof, as of all other things
appertaining to the said manor, to the great prejudice and damage of

* Bundle 3, No. 117.   * Co. Hereford.

disheritison de eux et de lour esglise, la ou ils ont este en peisible
possession de mesme le Manoir duement et loialment a eux mortisez
del an du regne le Roy Edward tierce vynt et quart,[1] sanz ascune
manere distourbance tanque ore tarde q'ils sont si oustez et spoillez
par le dit Thomas, si come par l'enroullement et recorde de mesme
le mortisement en la Chancerie nostre dit seignur le Roy lour droit
appiert plus au plein :　Qe plese a vostre dit tres gracious seignurie
granter brief de faire le dit Thomas venir deuant vous a vn certein
iour a respoundre a cestes matires, tortz et greuances par lui si faitz,
et sur ceo faire due et gracious remedie as ditz suppliantz q'ils
purront estre restitutz et mys en possession de lour dit Manoir sicome
ley et reson demandent en saluacion de lour droit et enheritance　en
celle partie ; pur Dieu et oeure de charite.

91　　　　　[2] A tres reuerent pier en Dieu, l'Euesque
　　　　　　d'Excestre, Chaunceller d'Engleterre,

s. d. Supplie Thomas de Bridsall, qi suyt auxi bien pur nostre seignur le
Roy com pur luy mesmez, qe come soit defendu par nostre seignur le
Roy en cez estatutz ore tarde proueuz[3] qe 'nulle disore ne face ne
comence de faire riotez, rumorez, inhonestez congregacions, ne in-
surreccions, ne autres chosez semblablez, sur peyne de estre iugge
traytour a luy et a son Roialme, Et auxi qe nulle ne face entre en
terrez ne tenementz oue forte mayne ne ouesqe multitude de gentz
sur payne de prisonement et de faire redempcion a nostre dit seignur
le Roy, la vient vn Johan de Bulmer par ordinaunce, ymaginacion et
auyse Robert Bulmer[4] son pier et William frere mesme celuy Johan,
en la viegile de Toutz Seintez ore darrein passe,[5] par noet par bon
estimacion parentre oeptz et neofz hours del cloke, ouesque trentz
homez et araiez a faire de guerre, c'est assauoir, oue haberions,[6]
palettez de ferre, arcuz tenduz, seetez, espeez et bokelers, et forciblement entrierunt en le meson le dit Thomas oue il ouesque cez
seruauntz par longe temps deuaut auoit demurez, et le dit meson oue
lez appurtenauncez forciblement retendrent, et le dit suppliaunt et
touz cez seruauntz et partye de cez bienz et chateux ousterunt, et
graunt party del remenant de cez bienz et chateux, c'est assauoir,

[1] 1350_1.
[2] Bundle 3, No. 120.　See Case 36, to which this bill appears to be supplemental.
[3] Stat. 15 Ric. II. cap. 2, seems to be the statute referred to.　See also 5 Ric. II. 1, cap. 8, and 4 Henry IV. cap. 8.

the said Abbat and Convent and to the complete disinheritance of them and their church; whereas they have been in peaceable possession of the same manor, duly and lawfully given to them in mortmain, since the twenty-fourth year of the reign of King Edward III., without any manner of disturbance until now of late that they are so ousted and despoiled by the said Thomas, as by the enrolment and record of the said mortgage in the Chancery of our Lord the King their right may more fully appear : May it please your said most gracious Lordship to grant a writ to cause the said Thomas to come before you on a certain day to answer as to these matters, wrongs and grievances so done by him, and thereupon to make due and gracious remedy to the said suppliants, so that they may be restored and put in possession of their said manor as law and reason demand, in salvation of their right and inheritance in this behalf; For God and in way of charity.

91 To the most reverend Father in God, the Bishop of Exeter, Chancellor of England,

s. d. Beseecheth Thomas de Bridsall, who sueth for our Lord the King as well as for himself, that whereas it is forbidden by our Lord the King in his statutes now of late provided that no one shall henceforth make or begin to make riots, rumours, dishonest assemblies, insurrections, or other like things, on pain of being adjudged a traitor to [the King] and his realm, and also that no one shall make entry upon lands or tenements with strong hand or with a multitude of people on pain of imprisonment and of making redemption to our said Lord the King; [nevertheless] there came one John de Bulmer by the ordinance, scheme and advice of Robert Bulmer his father and of William, brother of the said John, in the vigil of All Saints now last past, at night and by good estimation between 8 and 9 o'clock, with thirty men arrayed in manner of war, that is to say, with habergeons, iron palets, bows drawn, arrows, swords and bucklers, and forcibly entered upon the house of the said Thomas, where he with his servants had dwelt for a long time before, and forcibly retained the said house with the appurtenances, and ousted the said suppliant and all his servants and part of his goods and chattels, and they there burnt, trampled on and wasted a great part of the residue of his goods

⁴ See p. 40, note 2. ⁴ Probably 1398.
⁶ Habergeon, a little coat of mail, covering the head and shoulders.

maerisme, feyne et strauue, a la valu xls. illoqes arderunt, defoulerunt et degasterunt; Et outre ceo le dit Johan par ordinaunce et assent de lez ditz Robert et William lez venderdy prochein deuant le fest del Pasque, la viegile de mesme le fest, le iour de Pasque, et le lundy prochein ensuant ore darreinz passez a Leuenyng en le Counte d'Euerwyke . . . .[1] et amena ouesque luy ascun foith oeptz hommez disconuz, et ascun foitz dis ou plusours, armez a faire de guerre pur encountrier et masfeair au dit suppliaunt come il fuit enuenaunt . . . . meson de Leuenyng par vne demy leuke a sa esglise parochiel in Acclom par le temps suisdit; et plousours foitz assemblerent et estoisent en la chemyn par le quel il duyst auer passe   . Et auxi la samedy prochein auant l'assencion nostre seignur Jehu Crist ore darrein passe a Bernthorp[2] le dit Robert ouesque quater genz araiez en faire de guerre fist assaut en vn [Robert] Nauelton et luy batust et naufra qi fuit [en] enspeir[3] de sa vie; Et le dismaygne adonque prochein ensuaunt en la parochiel esglise illoqes en temps de messe, vient le dit Johan   . gentz armez et araiez a faire de guerre pur serchier vn Walter Rouclyf, pier le dit Robert Nauelton, pur luy auer masfeat ou de luy auer tue; Et la samady proschein apres le fest . . . assencion par ordinaunce et auyse de les ditz Robert Bulmer et William, vient le dit Johan en le Market de Malton ouesque xij gentz araiez oue haberions et palettez, arcuz et seettez, espeez et daggers, et tres souent passerunt et compasserunt par le dit Market et de illoqes chiuacherount ouesque arcuz tenduz; Et la samady adonque prochein ensuaunt lez ditz Robert et Johan viendront au dit Market ouesque . . gentz araiez en la manere suisdit et tres souent compasserunt et passerunt par le dit Market, et en Johan de Nauelton, esquier, illoqes assaut fierunt, et luy greuousment manasserunt; Et en la viegile de Seinte Trinite ore darrein passe sur Langeton Wolde le dit Johan oue autres masfeasours ouesque luy fist assaut au dit suppliaunt et luy appella escomenge faux . . et luy greuousment manassa; Et la marsdy adonqes prochein ensuaunt en la porche del esglise de Acelom auantdit le dit Johan fist assaut au dit suppliaunt et luy ferrist sur le corse ouesque cez poygnes; en contempt nostre dit seignur le Roy, parturbacion del poeple, et greuouse ensaumpel de insur- rexion, et damage au dit suppliaunt de CC liures: Dount y please a vostre tres sage discrecion d'ordeigner et faire remedy en cestez maters; al boneur nostre seignur Jehu Crist.

Plegii de prosequendo { Alexander Steyndrop, Johan de Hylton.

[1] The left margin is torn.
[2] Probably Barthorpe Bottoms, two or three farmhouses in the parish of Acklam.

and chattels, to wit, timber, hay and straw, to the value of 40s. ; And moreover the said John, by the ordinance and consent of the said Robert and William on the Friday before Easter, the vigil of the same feast, Easter day, and the Monday following now last past, at Leavening in the county of York . . . and brought with him at one time eight men unknown, and at another time ten or more men, armed in manner of war, to encounter and ill-use the said suppliant as he was coming . . . [from his] house at Leavening half a league to his parish church in Acklam at the time aforesaid ; and many times they assembled and stood in the road along which he ought to have passed.

. . And also on the Saturday before the Ascension of our Lord Jesus Christ last past, at Barthorpe, the said Robert, with four men arrayed in manner of war, assaulted one [Robert] Navelton, and beat him, and wounded him so that he despaired of his life; And on the Sunday following in the parish church there at the time of mass, came the said John [and with him . . .] men armed and arrayed in manner of war, to search for one Walter Rouclyf, father of the said Robert Navelton, to have ill-treated or killed him ; And on the Saturday after the feast [of the] Ascension, by the ordinance and advice of the said Robert Bulmer and William, came the said John to the market at Malton with twelve men arrayed with habergeons and palets, bows and arrows, swords and daggers, and very often they passed and re-passed through the said market, and rode away therefrom with their bows drawn ; And on the Saturday following, the said Robert and John came to the said market, with   . men arrayed in manner aforesaid, and very often they passed and re-passed through the said market, and there they assaulted John de Navelton, esquire, and grievously menaced him ; And in the vigil of Holy Trinity now last past, on Langton Wold, the said John with other evil-doers assaulted the said suppliant, and called him an excommunicate falsely [?]   . and grievously menaced him ; And on the Tuesday then next following, in the porch of the church of Acklam aforesaid, the said John assaulted the said suppliant, and struck him on the body with his fists; in contempt of our said Lord the King, to the perturbation of the people, and grievous example of insurrection, and to the damage of the said suppliant of £200 : May it please your most wise discretion to ordain and make a remedy in these matters ; to the honour of our Lord Jesus Christ.

Pledges to prosecute :—

Alexander Steyndrop,
John de Hylton.

* Sic ; apparently an error for despoir. See p. 20, note 1.

92 ·   [1] A tres reuerent pier en Dieu, l'Euesque
           d'Excestre et Chaunceller nostre seignour le
           Roy,

s. d. Monstre William Tyrell, parsone del esglise de Wynchelse, et soy
pleynt de Robert Arnold, Roger atte Gate et Johan Hermet de ceo
q'ils viendront, le dismenge en le feste del Natiuite de Seynt Johan le
Baptistre, al chapelle du Seynt Johan en mesme la paroche, oue force
et armes et encontre la pees nostre seignour le Roy, c'est assauoir,
espees, bokelers, daggers, arkes, setes, et altres maners d'armure, a
faire de guerre, et illoqes en mesme la chapelle, ou le dit suppliant
fuist esteant a misse et leant l'euangelie, assaut firont et luy bateront,
naufreront, et malement treteront issint qe le dit suppliant fuist en
despoir de sa vie ; et pristront le liure esteant deuaut luy et oblacions,
et lez emporteront ; et altres ledes luy firont a tort et as damages du
dit suppliant du C liures, dont il prie remedie pur Dieu et en eouere
du charite ; Considerant, tres gracious seignour, qe le Roy presenta
le dit suppliant al dite esglise et est son patron.

   Indorsed.—De assensu parcium datus est eis dies vsque ad quindenam Sancti Michaelis proximo futuram in statu quo nunc.

E. *PETITIONS ADDRESSED TO THOMAS DE ARUNDEL,
   · ARCHBISHOP OF CANTERBURY,* 1399, 1407–1409,
   1412–1413.[2]

93   [3] A tresreuerent pier en Dieux, l'Erceuesque
           de Cauntierburs, Chaunceller d'Engleterre,

1407 Supplie humblement le Abbe de Burgh Seint Pier, qe come vne Emme
Bodulbrigge le samady procheigne deuaunt le fest de corps de Crist,
l'an du regne nostre seignur le Roy qu'or'est oeptisme, a Burgh,
en la court de Marche le dit suppliaunt, afferma vn pleint de trespas
enuers Nicholle Semark et Thomas Semark soun fitz, par force de
quelle pleint vn Symound Tapyser de Burgh, Bailly le dit suppliaunt

---

[1] Bundle 3, No. 124.
[2] Appointed *cir.* Aug. 23 ; his successor
appointed *cir.* Sept. 5, 1399 ; appointed
Jan. 30, 1407 ; resigned Dec. 21, 1409.
Appointed Jan. 5, 1412 ; his successor appointed March 31, 1413. See Foss.

92   To the most reverend Father in God, the Bishop of Exeter, and Chancellor of our Lord the King,

s. d. Showeth William Tyrell, Rector of the church of Winchelsea, and complaineth of Robert Arnold, Roger at Gate, and John Hermit, of this, that on the Sunday in the feast of the Nativity of S. John the Baptist they came to the chapel of S. John in the same parish, with force and arms, and against the peace of our Lord the King, to wit, with swords, bucklers, daggers, bows, arrows, and other kinds of armour, in manner of war, and there, in the same chapel, where the said suppliant was standing at Mass and reading the Gospel, they assaulted him and beat him, and wounded him and ill-treated him so that the said suppliant despaired of his life; and they took the book that was before him and the oblations, and carried them away; and they did him other injuries wrongfully, and to the damages of the said suppliant of £100, of which he prayeth remedy for God and in way of charity; considering, most gracious Lord, that the King presented the said suppliant to the said church and is his patron.

Indorsed.—With the consent of the parties, a day is given them on the quindene of Michaelmas next to come, in the same state as now.

E. *PETITIONS ADDRESSED TO THOMAS DE ARUNDEL, ARCHBISHOP OF CANTERBURY,* 1399, 1407–1409, 1412–1413.

93   To the most reverend Father in God, the Archbishop of Canterbury, Chancellor of England,

1407 Humbly beseecheth the Abbat of Peterborough, that whereas one Emma Bodulbrigge on the Saturday before the feast of Corpus Christi in the 8th year of our Lord the King who now is,[4] at Peterborough in the said suppliant's Court for the [manor of] March,[5] affirmed a plaint of trespass against Nicholas Semark and Thomas Semark his son, by force of which plaint one Simon Tapyser of Peterborough,

---

[3] Bundle 3, No. 126.
[4] 1407.
[5] Doubtful. March is in the Island of

Ely, some fifteen miles from Peterborough. I am not aware that it belonged to the Abbey.

en la dite ville, attachea les ditz defendaunts par deux chiualx deins
la dite ville pur venir en la dite court a respoundre al dit pleintif en
la pleint suisdit; sur quoy les ditz Nicholle et Thomas et vn Johan
Caluerley adounqes illoeques esteauntz illoeques en le dit baillif assaut
firent et luy baterount et de les ditz chiualx rescous firent et eux
amesnerount; a cause de quelle attachement lez ditz Thomas et
Johan, c'est assauoir, le Joesdy en le fest du corps du Crist le dit an
oeptisme, a Thorpe deins la paroche de Burgh suisdit, viendrount oue
graund noumbre des gentz disconuz, et oue force et armes en manere
de guerre a la seconde houre apres la my noet, et par cause q'ils ne
purroient trouer le dit Symund, ils la meason d'un Henry Hopkyn,
seruaunt et vilein le dit suppliaunt, enuirnerount et les hoeses de dit
meason debruserount, et luy appellerount hors de soun lite, et luy
manasserount de luy auoir arde en sa dite meason s'il ne venast hors
de dite meason de parler ouesque eux; issint pur doute de arder et par
promis q'il n'aueroit male, il venast hors de sa chaumbre; et quaunt le
dit Henry fuist venuz hors de dit chaumbre, les ditz Thomas et Johan
et les autres disconuz illoeques assaut firent en le dit Henry, et la luy en
sa meason horriblement baterount, naufrerount, et maymerount, issint
qe vnques ne eidera soi mesmes; et manassauntz le dit suppliaunt, ses
moignes, sez seruauntz et teignauntz, qe si en temps a veignir aucun
pursuyt serroit fait pur le trespas auauntdit, le dit suppliaunt, sez
moignes, seruauntz et tenauntz, serroient ardez ou en semblablement
batuz et maymez; a tres graund disease et damage de dit suppliaunt
et tres male ensaumple as autres malfeasours si ne soit par vous, tres
reuerent pier, deue remedie purueu en cest cas: Que please a vostre
tres gracious seignurie de grauntier vne commissioun direct a vn
Sergeaunt d'armes et deux Esquiers et prodes hommes et sufficeauntz
queux vous pleast d'assigner, grauntaunt poiar a eux et a checun
d'eux pur arester les ditz Thomas et Johan et les amesner deuant vous
en la Chauncellarie pur respoundre a la matier suisdit et as autres
matiers queux serrount declarez a eux pur nostre dit seignur le Roy a
lour venue, et de trouer suffisaunt soertee de pees au dit suppliaunt et
toutz les lieges nostre dit seignur le Roi; Considerauntz qe les Ministres
nostre dit seignur le Roi en cels parties n'oiesent arester les ditz malfeasours, et qe les ditz malfeasours s'enfuent de Countee en Countee;
et ceo pur Dieux et en oepre du charitee.

Ricardus Denton [et] Walterus Brigge, de Com' Lincoln', Johannes
Rothewell de Com' Norh't', [et] Thomas Lynton de Com' Ebor', xxj
die Junii, anno, etc., octauo,[1] manuceperunt, videlicet, quilibet eorum

[1] 1407.

bailiff of the said suppliant in the said town, attached the said defendants, by two horses within the said town, to come to the said Court to answer the said plaintiff in the aforesaid plaint; whereupon the said Nicholas and Thomas and one John Calverley, then being there, did assault the said bailiff, and beat him, and made rescue of the two horses and took them away; and on account of the said attachment, the said Thomas and John, to wit, on the Thursday in the feast of Corpus Christi in the said 8th year, at Thorpe in the parish of Peterborough aforesaid, came with a great number of persons unknown, and with force and arms in warlike manner, at the second hour after midnight, and because they could not find the said Simon, they surrounded the house of one Henry Hopkyn, servant and villein of the said suppliant, and broke the doors of the said house, and called him out of his bed, and threatened to have burnt him in his said house if he did not come out of the said house to speak with them ; so for fear of being burnt and on [their] promise that no evil should befall him, he came out of his room ; and when the said Henry had come out of the said room, the said Thomas and John and the others unknown did there assault him, and there, in his house, they did horribly beat, wound and maim him, so that he can never help himself ; and they threatened the said suppliant, his monks, his servants and his tenants, that if in time to come any suit should be made for the trespass aforesaid, the said suppliant, his monks, his servants and his tenants, should be burnt or in like manner beaten and maimed ; to the great discomfort and damage of the said suppliant and right evil example to other ill-doers if due remedy be not provided by you, most reverend Father, in this case : May it please your most gracious Lordship to grant a commission directed to a Serjeant at arms and two esquires, honest men and sufficient, whom you shall please to assign, [and] to grant power to them and each of them to arrest the said Thomas and John, and to bring them before you in the Chancery, to answer as to the matter aforesaid and other matters which shall be declared to them on behalf of our said Lord the King at their coming, and to find sufficient surety for the peace towards the said suppliant and all the lieges of our said Lord the King ; Considering that the officers of our said Lord the King in these parts dare not arrest the said evil-doers, and that the said evil-doers do flee from County to County ; And this for God and in way of charity.

Richard Denton and Walter Brigg of the County of Lincoln, John Rothwell of the County of Northampton, and Thomas Lynton of the County of York, June 21st, in the 8th year, have undertaken, to wit,

sub pena C li., quod predictus Abbas satisfaciet predictis Thome filio
Nicholai Semark et Johanni Caluerley pro custibus suis in casu quo
idem Abbas intencionem suam versus eos probare non poterit.

94   A tres reuerent pier en Dieu et soun tres
            honure et tres gracious seignur, Thomas,
            l'Erceuesque de Canterbiers, Chanceller
            d'Engleterre,

1407 Supplie tres humblement Johan Pykworth, Esquier, qe come Thomas
      Sambroke del Counte de Somers' et Thomas Bayes de mesme le
      Counte, le xxvj^{me} iour de Juyn l'an du regne le Roy q'orest viij^{me},[2]
      . Martyn oue force et armes entrerent et sez tenantz de mesmes
      les terres et tenements en ousterent, et en Johan Blakedon vn des
      ditz tenants illoeqes assaut firent, et luy baterent, naufrerent et
      malement treterent . . vie et de membre a luy firent, et de certeins
      sez escripts et autres muniments luy espoilerent, et sez biens et
      chatelx la trouez pristerent et emporterent, paront le dit Johan
      Blakedon pur grand dolour q'il eide en ceste partie est outrement .
      [gre]uousement deuenuz hors de bone memorie, et le dit suppliant ad
      pardue son rent q'il deust auoir pris sibien del dit Johan Blakedon
      come de sez autres tenants illeoqes pris de deux ans passes ; et les
      arbres du dit suppliant . . . couperent et emporterent; et sez ditz
      terres et tenements vnqore teignent et occupiont et les rents, issues
      et profits ent prouenantz preignent et deteignent tortenousement et
      encontre son gree ; et autres ledes a luy fait a greuouse . . . de soun
      pouere estat : Plese a vostre tres reuerent paternitee et tres gracious
      seignurie considerer coment les auantditz Thomas et Thomas sount
      notores et communes extorcioners et oppressours del poeple en lour
      pais . . . et aillours en defence du roialme d'Engleterre q'il ne poet
      bien entendre a pursuyer remedie de sez greuances suisditz al
      commune ley, et sur ceo grauntier briefs seueralx directs as ditz
      Thomas et Thomas   en la Chancellarie nostre seignur le Roy a
      vn certein iour par vous a limetier, c'est assauoir, chescun d'eux sur
      peine de xl liures, pur y respondre de lez choses premesses, et de

---

[1] Bundle 3, No. 129. The margin is   [2] 1407.
torn.   [3] The plaintiff was apparently engaged

each of them in a penalty of £100, that the said Abbat shall satisfy the
said Thomas son of Nicholas Semark and John Calverley for their
costs, in case the Abbat shall fail to prove his allegations against them.

94   To the most reverend Father in God, and
     his most honoured and most gracious Lord,
     Thomas, Archbishop of Canterbury, Chan-
     cellor of England,

1407 Most humbly beseecheth John Pykworth, esquire, that whereas
Thomas Sambroke, of the County of Somerset, and Thomas Bayes of
the same county, on the 26th day of June in the 8th year of the reign
of the King who now is, . . . [? feast of S.] Martyn, with force and
arms entered, and ousted his tenants from the same lands and tenements, and there assaulted John Blakedon, one of the said tenants,
and beat him, wounded and ill-treated him, and [threatened] him of life
and limb, and despoiled him of certain writings and other muniments,
and seized and carried away his goods and chattels there found,
whereby the said John Blakedon, through the great grief that he had on
that account, hath altogether [and most grievously ?] lost his memory,
and the said suppliant hath lost his rent that he ought to have
taken as well from the said John Blakedon as from his other tenants
there for two years past; and they cut down and carried away the
said suppliant's trees; and do still hold and occupy his said lands and
tenements, and take and detain the rents, issues and profits arising
therefrom, wrongfully and against his will; and they have done him
other wrongs, to the grievous [destruction] of his poor estate : May it
please your most reverend Fatherhood and most gracious Lordship
to consider how the aforesaid Thomas [Sambroke] and Thomas
[Bayes] are notorious and common extortioners and oppressors of the
people in their country . . . and elsewhere in defence of the realm of
England [3] that he cannot well undertake to pursue a remedy for his
said grievances at common law, and thereupon to grant several writs
directed to the said Thomas [Sambroke] and Thomas [Bayes, commanding them to be] in the Chancery of our Lord the King at a certain day by you to be limited, to wit, each of them under pain of £40,
there to answer as to the premises, and further to do and receive

on some military service, possibly in Wales,   of Northumberland, was still in insur-
where Owen Glendower, aided by the Earl   rection.

faire outre et receuire ceo qe   [Pur Dieu et en] oeure de charitee.[1]

Plegii de prosequendo

    Johannes West de Com' Ebor', armiger.
    Edmundus Morle de Com' Lanc', armiger.

95   [2] A tres reuerent pier en Dieu et tres graciouse seignour, l'Ercheuesque de Canterbrys,
Chaunceller d'Engleterre,

1408 Supplie tres humblement Jasper, fitz et attourne Johan de Dent, Esquyer, d'Engleterre, ore en les cite et seignorie de Veron' demur- rant, Que come vn Phelip Gernon de la ville de Seint Botulph en le Counte de Nicole, pur les graund affeccion et affiance qe le dit Johan auoyet en sa persone, de voloir et assent du dit Johan ad resceu en noun et al oeps dicelle Johan en Engleterre de certeines persones Engloys diuerses sommes de mone dount le dit Johan a mesmes les persones auoyt fait cheuesance[3] en les cite et seignorie susditz, c'est assauoir, de Johan Dautre, chiualer, xx liures, de Chartres de Loun- dres vij liures x soulds, de Norhampton de Loundres xliij liures xv soulds, de Frere Johan Gernon xlv liures, de William Frank, Chiualer, xx liures, de Thomas Goter xx marcz, de Henry nadgairs Euesque de Norwych lxx liures, de Meistre Henry Bowet ore Ercheuesque d'Euer- wyke, ccxvj liures, de Johan Naton, chapellain, et Johan Hulle de Seint Botulph xl soulds, de William Porter, chapellain, iiij^{xx} florens, de Thomas Kyrkeby, chapellain, xl florens, et al oeps Frere Johan l florens, et du dit nadgairs Euesque de Norwich come executour de testament d'une Johan Scathelok ccccxxiij liures, sicome le dit Jasper par voyes et maners resonables est prist a monstrer; et come bien qe le dit suppliant eit souent requys le dit Phelip de luy paier en noun du dit Johan les sommes auantditz, nientmaynes le dit Phelip de paier les ditz sommes au dit suppliant ad refuse et refuse au present, a tort et a grief damage du dit Johan et arrerisment de soun pouere estate, et auxi en retraccion des bones voillours d'autres des ditz cite et seignorie cheuances as autres qi passeront par ycelles cite et seignorie en lour necessites en temps avenere fair voillantz : Que please a vostre tres reuerent paternite

---

[1] The violence and power of the defen- dants is here the primary reason for apply- ing to the Chancellor ; the secondary reason is interesting, and, although the document is unfortunately damaged at this place, there is no doubt as to its meaning. The plaintiff was evidently engaged on some military service, which made it inconvenient

what [the Court shall consider in that behalf. For God and in] way of charity.

Pledges for the prosecution :

John West of the County of York, esq.

Edmund Morle [? Morley] of the County of Lancaster, esq.

95   To the most reverend Father in God and most gracious Lord, the Archbishop of Canterbury, Chancellor of England,

1408 Most humbly beseecheth Jasper, son and attorney of John de Dent, esquire, of England, now dwelling in the city and lordship of Verona, that whereas one Philip Gernon of the town of Boston, in the County of Lincoln, through the great affection and trust which the said John had in him, hath, with the wish and consent of the said John, received in England in the name and to the use of the said John, from certain English persons, divers sums of money which the said John had lent to the same persons in the city and lordship aforesaid, to wit, from John Dautre, knight, £20, from Chartres of London £7 10s., from Northampton of London £43 15s., from Brother John Gernon £45, from William Frank, knight, £20, from Thomas Goter 20 marks, from Henry, late Bishop of Norwich, £70, from Master Henry Bowet, now Archbishop of York, £216, from John Naton, chaplain, and John Hulle of Boston, 40s., from William Porter, chaplain, fourscore florins, from Thomas Kirkby, chaplain, 40 florins, and to the use of Brother John [? Gernon] 50 florins, and from the said late Bishop of Norwich as executor of the will of one Joan Scathelok, £423, as the said Jasper by reasonable ways and means is ready to show ; and although the said suppliant hath often requested the said Philip to pay him the sums aforesaid in the name of the said John [de Dent], nevertheless the said Philip hath refused and doth now refuse to pay the said sums to the said suppliant, wrongfully and to the grievous damage of the said John and to the detriment of his poor estate, and also to the withdrawal of the goodwill of others of the said city and lordship [of Verona] willing to make loans to other persons, passing through the said city and lordship, in their necessities in time

---

for him to face the tedious delays of a trial at common law.

[superscript 2] Bundle 3, No. 135.

[superscript 3] See N. E. D. 'So estately was he of governaunce, With his bargayns and with his chevysaunce.' Chaucer, Prol. 283.

N

et tres gracious seignorie par consideracion de ceo qe dit est, et au fyne
qe le dit Johan pur sa naturesse ne soyt defait, qe Dieu ne voil
commande, de fair venir deuaut vous le dit Phelip en la Chauncellerie
a certen iour auenir par vostre brief, et illeoqes les escriptes et autres
euidences par le dit suppliant en ceste partie a monstrers oyer et
regarder, et le dit Phelip en ceste partie examiner, et sur ce fair as
parties acomplisement de iustice, pur Dieu et en oeure de charite.

Plegii de prosequendo :

Johannes Cole de London',.
Robertus Sanford de Com' Essex.

[1] Writ dated at Northflete December 8th, 10th year, directed
to Philip Gernon of S. Botolph's [Boston], commanding him to
appear ' coram nobis in Cancellaria nostra in octabis Sancti Hillarii
proximo futuri ubicumque tunc fuerit.'

[Similar to the writ in Case 2 (p. 3 ante) but with some slight
verbal differences.]

[2] Alias ad prosecucionem cuiusdam Jasper filii et attornati
Johannis Dent, armigeri, commorantis in civitate Veron' in Lumbardia,
preceptum fuit Philippo Gernon de Sancto Botulpho quod in propria
persona sua esset coram domino Rege in Cancellaria sua in octabis
Sancti Hillarii proximo preteriti vbicumque tunc foret ad respondendum super hiis que sibi obicerentur tunc ibidem, et ad faciendum
vlterius et recipiendum quod Curia domini Regis consideraret in hac
parte ; Ad quem diem tam predictus Philippus in propria persona sua,
pretextu brevis domini Regis sibi inde directi, quam predictus Jasper
in propria persona sua in Cancellaria predicta comparuerunt ; et super
hoc predictus Philippus per venerabilem patrem, Thomam, Archiepiscopum Cantuar', Cancellarium Anglie, in eadem Cancellaria
examinatus fuit super contentis in quadam petitione per prefatum
Jasper ibidem exhibita et in filaciis dicte Cancellarie residente, et
iuratus super sancta Dei euangelia de veritate dicenda in premissis ;
qua quidem examinacione sic facta, ac auditis rationibus, exceptionibus,
allegationibus et responsionibus per consilium vtriusque partis ibidem
propositis, captaque ad requisitionem earumdem parcium, pro pleniori
informatione rei veritatis in premissis, testificatione Willelmi domini
de Willughby tunc ibidem presentis in Curia, et noticiam materie
illius vt asseruerunt habentis, de auisamento Justiciariorum et
Seruientum domini Regis ad legem et aliorum peritorum de Consilio
domini Regis in eadem Cancellaria ad tunc existentium ; Consideratum

---

[1] Bundle 3, No. 133.   [2] Bundle 3, No. 134.

to come: May it please your most reverend Paternity and most gracious Lordship, in consideration of what is said, and to the end that the said John may not through his good nature be undone, which God forbid, to cause by your writ the said Philip to come before you in the Chancery on a certain day to come, and there to hear and see the writings and other evidences to be shown in this behalf by the said suppliant, and to examine the said Philip in this behalf, and thereupon to do the fulfilment of justice to the parties, for God and in way of charity.

Pledges for the prosecution:

John Cole of London.
Robert Sanford of the County of Essex.

Heretofore on the prosecution of one Jasper, son and attorney of John Dent, esquire, dwelling in the city of Verona in Lombardy, Philip Gernon of Boston was commanded to be in his proper person before the King in his Chancery on the octave of S. Hilary last past, wherever it should then be, to answer to those things which should then and there be objected against him, and further to do and receive what the Court of our Lord the King should consider in that behalf; At which day the said Philip in his proper person, by virtue of the King's writ directed to him, as well as the said Jasper in his proper person, appeared in the Chancery aforesaid; and thereupon the said Philip was examined in the Chancery by the venerable Father, Thomas, Archbishop of Canterbury, Chancellor of England, upon the contents of a certain petition exhibited there by the said Jasper and remaining on the files of the said Chancery, and was sworn upon the Holy Gospels to speak the truth in the premises; which examination being so made, and the reasons, exceptions, allegations and answers there propounded by counsel on both sides having been heard, and the evidence of William, Lord de Willoughby, then and there present in Court and having knowledge of the matter, as they asserted, having been taken at the request of the parties, for the fuller information of the truth of the matter in the premises, by the advice of the Justices and Serjeants at law of our Lord the King and of other learned men of the King's Council, then being in the said Chancery; It was con-

fuit quod predictus Philippus dimittatur de Curia et exinde recedat quietus sine die, et quod prefatus Jasper prosequatur ad communem legem pro remedio in hac parte habendo si sibi viderit expedire.[1]

96 [2] A tres reuerent pier en Dieu et leur tres gracious seignur, l'Arceuesque de Canterbirs et Chanceller d'Engleterre,

1412 Suppliont humblement Richard Gilbert et William Carswelle, possessours et vitellers d'une balingere appelle le George de Peynton, et Thomas Rake, maistre de la dite balingere, qe come certains persones esteantz en ycelle balingere nadgairs seglantz sur la meer pristeront vn vesselle charges ouesque certains tonelx de vyn des biens des Franceys, ennemys du Roy, et le dit vesselle amesneront deins le corps del Countee de Deuenshire a vn lieu appelle le Getee de Torrebaie ; la quelle prinse par les persones suisdite ensy fait, vn Johan Hauley [3] aparceiuant fist arraier en manere de insurreccion deux ses balingers oue Cent hommes ou plus armes et arraiez a faire de guerre ; les quelles hommes esteantz en les dites balingers, veiantz le dit vesselle prinsez par les persones suisdites et esteant deins le corps del Countee suisdit, eux arraieront a la guerre en manere de insurreccion, et mesmes les persones ensy esteantz en le dit vesselle en taunt de leure vie manasseront, issint q'ils pur doubte de mort lesseront le dit vesselle et aleront a la terre ; la quelle chose ensy fait les dites malefaisours pristeront encountre droit et raison le dit vesselle ensemblement ouec les vyns esteantz en ycelle, et dilleosque a le port de Dertemouth amesneront, a graund affraie des persones suisdites et de tout la pais la environ, et a damage des ditz suppliantz de CCL liures · Vous please de vostre grace especiale de grauntier vne commission [4] directe as certains persones par vous a limitier, d'oier et terminer les trespasses et insurreccion suisdites ; Pur Dieu et en oeure de charitee.

[5] Henricus [etc.] Johanni Hauley de Dertemouth, salutem : Quandam billam nobis in Cancellaria nostra per Ricardum Gilbert, Willelmum Carswell et Thomam Rake exhibitam, mencionem de certis iniuriis et grauaminibus sibi per te nuper, vt dicitur, illatis facientem, tibi mittimus presentibus interclusam, mandantes quod, inspecta billa

[1] This case is chiefly valuable from the light it throws upon the procedure of the Court of Chancery at this time. We find counsel appearing on both sides, the defendant being sworn and examined *viva voce* in Court, other evidence taken, also apparently *viva voce*, and the Chancellor sitting with Judges, Serjeants, and others *of the Council*, to give judgment. Not the least interesting point is that, the question being one of fact, the plaintiff was referred to his remedy at common law. There may also have been

sidered that the said Philip be dismissed from the Court and go there-out quit, without day, and that the said Jasper may sue at common law to have remedy in that behalf, if it shall seem expedient to him.

96   To the most reverend Father in God and their most gracious Lord, the Archbishop of Canterbury and Chancellor of England,

1412 Humbly beseech Richard Gilbert and William Carswell, possessors and victuallers of a balinger[6] called 'the George of Paynton,' and Thomas Rake, master of the said balinger, that whereas certain persons being in the said balinger lately sailing on the sea, seized a vessel laden with certain tuns of wine, the goods of the King's enemies, the French, and brought the said vessel within the body of the County of Devonshire, to a place called 'Torbay Jetty;' one John Hawley, perceiving the said prize so made by the persons aforesaid, caused to be arrayed in the manner of an insurrection two of his balingers with 100 men or more armed and arrayed in manner of war; and the men in the said balingers, seeing the said vessel taken by the persons aforesaid, and being within the body of the said county, arrayed themselves as for war in the manner of an insurrection, and threatened the persons on the said vessel of their lives, so that for fear of death they left the said vessel and went ashore; and when this was done, the said evil-doers, against right and reason, seized the said vessel, together with the wine in her, and took her thence to the port of Dartmouth, to the great dismay of the persons aforesaid and of all the country round, and to the damage of the said suppliants of £250: May it please you of your especial grace to grant a commission directed to certain persons by you to be limited, to hear and determine the trespasses and insurrection aforesaid; For God and in way of charity.[7]

Henry [etc.], to John Hawley of Dartmouth, greeting: We send you inclosed with these presents a certain bill exhibited to us in our Chancery by Richard Gilbert, William Carswell and Thomas Rake, making mention of certain injuries and grievances lately done by you to them, as it is said, commanding you that, having inspected the bill,

some difficulty in founding an action of debt on a loan made in foreign parts.
[2] Bundle 3, No. 131.   [3] See Case 15.
[4] As to special commissions, see p. 29, note 1.   [5] Bundle 3, No. 130.
[6] A small light sea-going vessel, appa-rently a kind of sloop. See *N. E. D.*
[7] If the cause had arisen outside the body of the county, it would, in theory at any rate, have gone to the Admiralty Court. See stat. 13 R. II., c. 5; 15 R. II., c. 3; 2 H. IV., c. 11.

predicta, eisdem Ricardo, Willelmo et Thome super contentis in eadem billa debitam et celerem reformacionem fieri facias, ne iidem Ricardus, Willelmus et Thomas materiam habeant nobis inde iterum conquerendi. Et si causa rationabilis subfuerit quare id facere minime debeas, tunc nos in dicta Cancellaria nostra super causa illa in octabis Sancti Hillarii proximo futuri vbicumque tunc fuerit sub sigillo tuo distincte et aperte certifices, vt vlterius inde fieri faciamus prout iusticia suadebit in hac parte. Teste [etc. December 20th, 14th year.] [1]

Indorsed.—Responsio huius brevis patet in quadam cedula presenti consuta.

[2] Memorandum quod Baro de Carrew, [3] Johannes Hawley, et plures marinarii et homines de Dertemouth habuerunt naues suas super mare modo guerrino ad destruendum inimicos Regis et regni, et apud le costes de Britaigne ceperunt quemdam craieram, oneratam de vinis et mercandisis Francorum inimicorum Regis, in et de qua quidem craiera Britones fuerunt possessores et magistri, et in eadem craiera dicti marinarii inposuerunt vj Anglicos homines ad conseruandam et ducendam dictam craieram cum vinis et mercandisis predictis usque Dertemouth; Et postea Britones predicti durante treuga inter dominum nostrum Regem et illos de Britannia noctanter interfecerunt iiij[or] Anglicos de predictis sex Anglicis; Et super hoc venit cum hominibus dicta Balingaria in billa contenta vocata le George, et ceperunt predictam prisam et illam cariauerunt et adduxerunt vsque Torrebay, in qua erat vnus de predictis sex hominibus; Et postea predicti Johannes Hawley et alii ceperunt predictam prisam pacifice vt bona et catalla sua et illam cariauerunt vsque Dertemouth; Et ibidem de omnibus premissis tam predicti Baro, Johannes Hawley et alii quam predicti supplicantes in dicta billa se submiserunt iudicio, ordinacioni et arbitrio Johannis Corpe et Johannis Foxley, electorum ex parte dictorum Baronis, Johannis Hawley et aliorum, et Johannis Carswille et Johannis Madecombe, electorum dictorum supplicantium; qui inde iudicauerunt, ordinauerunt et arbitrauerunt quod predicti Baro, Johannes Hawley et alii haberent medietatem omnium dictorum vini, bonorum et mercandisorum, et predicti supplicantes haberent inde aliam medietatem; Ad que quidem iudicium, ordinacionem et arbitrium predicti supplicantes se agreerunt, et medietatem predictam apud predictam villam de Dertemouth habuerunt de vinis, etc., predictis.

---

[1] 1412.   [2] Bundle 3, No. 132.
[3] The head of the Carew family seems to have been so called, although not a peer.

you shall cause due and speedy reformation to be made to the said Richard, William and Thomas upon the matters contained in the said bill, lest the said Richard, William and Thomas should again have matter of complaint thereof to us. And if there shall be any reasonable cause wherefore you should not do so, then you shall distinctly and openly certify us of that cause in our said Chancery, wherever it shall then be, on the octave of S. Hilary next to come, under your seal, so that we may further cause to be done therein what justice shall persuade in that behalf. Witness [etc.], December 20th, 14th year.

Indorsed.—The answer to this writ appears in a schedule sewn to these presents.

Be it remembered that the Baron of Carew, John Hawley, and many sailors and men of Dartmouth had their ships on the sea in warlike manner to destroy the enemies of the King and the realm, and they took on the coasts of Brittany a certain crayer,[4] freighted with wine and merchandise of the French, the King's enemies, of which crayer the Bretons were owners and masters, and the said sailors put six Englishmen in the said crayer to keep her and to bring her to Dartmouth with the said wine and merchandise; And afterwards, during the truce between our Lord the King and them of Brittany,[5] the said Bretons by night killed four out of the said six Englishmen; And thereupon came the said balinger with the men in the bill named, called the 'George,' and took the said prize and carried and brought her to Torbay, and in her was one of the said six men; And afterwards the said John Hawley and the others took the said prize, peacefully, and as being their own goods and chattels, and carried her to Dartmouth; And there the said Baron, John Hawley, and the others, as well as the said suppliants in the said bill, as to all the premisses submitted themselves to the judgment, ordinance and arbitrament of John Corpe and John Foxley (elected on behalf of the said Baron, John Hawley, and the others), and of John Carswell and John Madecombe (elected on behalf of the said suppliants); and they judged, ordained, and arbitrated that the said Baron, John Hawley, and the others should have one half of all the said wine, goods and merchandise, and that the said suppliants should have the other half thereof; To which judgment, ordinance and arbitrament the said suppliants agreed, and they had the said half part of the said wines, etc., at the said town of Dartmouth.

[4] A small trading vessel. See *N. E. D.*
[5] A truce with Brittany was made in 1407 for one year; it was prolonged for another year in 1408, and for two more years in 1409. See Ramsay, *Lancaster and York*, i. 108, 118, 122.

97   [1] A tres honure seignur et tres reuereut pier
en Dieu, Thomas, l'Erceuesque de Canter-
biers, Chanceller d'Engleterre,

en. IV. Supplie vostre pouere oratour, Johan de Boynton, vn des vicairs de
l'esglise Collegiale de Seint Johan de Beuerle et iadys vn des seruantz
du Johan de Burton, clerk, Gardein des Rolles de la Chauncellarie
seignur Richard nadgairs Roy d'Engleterre second puis le conquest,
qi Dieu assoille, qe come le dit suppliant en temps de mesme nadgairs
Roy fuist al prebende de Seinte Katerine en l'esglise suisdite par
vertue d'une collacion mesme nadgairs Roy a luy ent faite et institut
et induct canonykment en ycelle, et sa possession ent continua tanque
la dite prebende fuist euicte enuers luy par le dit Johan de Burton
par processe de ley, vn Johan Seggefeld alors luy pretendant title et
colour de droit al dit prebende, ou rien [il] n'auoit ent prist les fruitz
et profitz tout le temps qe le dit suppliant l'occupia, et surmettant
meyns verrayment del dit suppliant q'il, en fraude et desceyt de luy
par collusion et faux couyne entre le dit Johan de Burton et le dit
suppliant euz, resigna voluntierment le dite prebende al oeps le dit
Johan de Burton, et par celle encheson a toute sa poair machinant
nonduement greuer et molestier et entant come en luy fuist outrement destruyer le dit suppliant, enuers luy   et pursuya vne feynt
accion du trespas faite a ceo q'il dit deins la Citee d'Euerwyke, dont
vnqes ne fuist coupable, et luy fist arestier en son habite deins l'esglise
suisdite et luy amesner au prisone en despite de Dieu et de seint
esglise . . . ycelle et luy ad condempne par enquest pris al dite citee
par brief de *Nisi prius* en xvj marcz; et sur ceo processe est fait hors del
comune bank et l'exigend agarde enuers le dit suppliant, et ensi deins
brief serra utlage en finale des[truccion] et anientisment de son pouere
estat s'il ne soit purueu de remedie et secour par l'eide de vostre tres
soueraigne et tres gracious seignurie : Please a mesme vostre seignurie
considerer les graundes tort et iniurie al dit suppliant faitz celle
partie, et coment qe le dit Johan de Burton par bone et iuste title
auoit et occupia la dite prebende durant sa vie, et de faire venier le
dit Johan Seggefeld deuaut vous a vn certain iour par vous a limitier,
au fyn qe bone et resonable accord purroit estre fait en cest matier
[a] l'endempnitee du dite suppliant en vostre tres honurable presence

[1] Bundle 3, No. 127. The right margin is torn.

97   To the most honoured Lord and most
reverend Father in God, Thomas Archbishop
of Canterbury, Chancellor of England,

Hen. IV. Beseecheth your poor orator, John de Boynton, one of the Vicars of
the Collegiate Church of S. John of Beverley, and formerly one of the
servants of John de Burton, clerk, Master of the Rolls of the Chancery
of Lord Richard, the Second after the Conquest, late King of England,
whom God assoil, that whereas the said suppliant in the time of the said
late King was in the Prebend of S. Katherine in the Church aforesaid
by virtue of a collation thereof made to him by the said late King,
and he was instituted and inducted canonically therein, and continued
his possession thereof until the said Prebend was evicted against him
by the said John de Burton by process of law, one John Seggefeld
then pretending title and colour of right to the said Prebend, whereas
he had taken nothing of the fruits and profits thereof all the time that
the said suppliant occupied the same, and alleging untruly of the
said suppliant that he, in fraud and deceit of him [Seggefeld], by collusion and false covin had between the said John de Burton and the
said suppliant, had voluntarily resigned the said Prebend to the use
of the said John de Burton, and by this pretext unduly scheming
with all his might to grieve and molest and as far as in him lay to
utterly destroy the said suppliant, . . . and sued a feigned action of
trespass against him, done, as he said, in the city of York, of which
[the said suppliant] was not guilty; and he caused [the said sup-
pliant] to be arrested in his habit within the said Church, and took
him to prison, in despite of God and Holy Church . . . and hath
condemned him by inquest taken at the said city by writ of *Nisi
Prius* in the sum of 16 marks : and thereupon process was issued out
of the Common Bench and the exigent awarded against the said
suppliant, and so he will shortly be outlawed to the final destruction
and annihilation of his poor estate, if he be not provided with remedy
and succour by aid of your most sovereign and most gracious Lordship: May it please your said Lordship to consider the great wrong
and injury done to the said suppliant in this behalf, and how the said
John de Burton by good and just title had and occupied the said Prebend during his life, and to cause the said John Seggefeld to come
before you on a certain day by you to be limited, to the end that good
and reasonable accord may be made in this matter for the indemnity
of the said suppliant, in your most honourable presence or before

ou deuant autres persones a limitiers solonc vostre tres sage discrecion; Pur Dieu et en oeure de charitee.

98   [1] A tres reuerent pier en Dieux, Thomas, Archeuesque de Cantirbirs et Chaunceller d'Engleterre,

s. d. Supplie humblement vostre seruant, William de Wakefeld, qe come il, Adam de Mirfeld, Richard de Hirnyng, clerk, Johan Spenne, chapelayn, Johan de Acum, chapelayn, et William Hirnyng, fuerent seisez pur William del Wode del Wakefeld, ia morte, en diuersez terrez et tenementz en Wakefeld, Stanley et Osset en le Counte d'Euerwike en suirte [pur ent] fair sa volunte, la James de Whityngton et Cicile sa femme, Robert de Stanley de Wakefeld et Agnes sa femme, William del Shaghe de Wakefeld, Johan Sparke de Wakefeld, Johan Harwode et Thomas Megson de Wakefeld le puisne, oue plousours altrez hommez disconuz del Counte de Lancastre, oue fort mayn eux ount disseisez de lez ditz tenementz en areresment del execucion du volunte le dit William del Wode : Qe plese a vostre tres gracious seignurie grauntier au dit suppliaunt et sez compaignouns vne especiale assise apprendre deuant William Gascoigne,[2] Richard Norton,[3] Richard Gascoigne et Johan de Amyas enuers lez ditz disseisours, considerant vostre tres gracious seignurie qe le dit suppliaunt est occupiez en lez besoignez le Roy en altrez Countez ouesque les Justicez as assisez prendre en temps de generale session dez assisez tenuz en le Counte d'Euerwike ; Pur Dieux et en ouere de charite.

99   [4] A tres honure seignur et tres reuerent pier en Dieu, Thomas, l'Erceuesque de Canterbiers, Chanceller d'Engleterre,

s. d. Supplient tres humblement Johan Byngeley de Kyngeston sur Hulle et Katerine sa femme et Johan Swynflete, fitz a mesme cestuy Katerine et a Thomas Swynflete nadgairs soun primer baron, qi Dieu

[1] Bundle 3, No. 137.
[2] Perhaps the William Gascoigne who became Chief Justice of the King's Bench. He was appointed to that office Nov. 15, 1400.
[3] Appointed Chief Justice of the Common Pleas June 26, 1413.
[4] Bundle 3, No. 128.

other persons to be appointed according to your most wise discretion ;
For God and in way of charity.

98   To the most reverend Father in God,
Thomas, Archbishop of Canterbury, and
Chancellor of England,

s. d. Humbly beseecheth your servant William de Wakefield, that whereas
he, Adam de Mirfield, Richard de Hirnyng, clerk, John Spenne,
chaplain, John de Acum, chaplain, and William Hirnyng were seised
for William del Wood of Wakefield (now dead) in divers lands and
tenements in Wakefield, Stanley and Ossett in the County of York in
surety [trust] to do his will thereof, James de Whitington and Cicely
his wife, Robert de Stanley of Wakefield and Agnes his wife, William
del Shaw of Wakefield, John Sparke of Wakefield, John Harewood,
and Thomas Megson the younger of Wakefield, with many other
unknown men of the County of Lancaster, with the strong hand have
disseised them of the said tenements, to the delay of the execution of
the will of the said William del Wood : May it please your most
gracious Lordship to grant the said suppliant and his fellows a special
assize to be taken before William Gascoigne, Richard Norton, Richard
Gascoigne and John de Amyas, against the said disseisors, considering your most gracious Lordship that at the time of the General
Session of Assize holden in the County of York, the said suppliant is
engaged on the King's business in other Counties with the Justices of
Assize ; For God and in way of charity.[5]

99   To the most honoured Lord and most
reverend Father in God, Thomas, Arch
bishop of Canterbury, Chancellor of England,

s. d. Most humbly beseech John Byngeley of Kingston on Hull, and
Katherine, his wife, and John Swynflete, son of the same Katherine
and of Thomas Swynflete, her first husband, whom God assoil, that

[5] Nothing seems to turn on the fact that the plaintiffs were trustees. The plaintiff Wakefield was apparently employed in some legal capacity which prevented his being present at the Yorkshire Assizes, though it is difficult to see why his co-feoffees could not have appeared in the case. Compare Case 94.

assoille, qe come la dite Katerine quant ele fuist sole apres la mort le dit Thomas par soun escript enfeoffa vn Robert Sturmy de Coldon sur pleine et entier affience qeux el auoit en sa persone et sa foialte, de deux mees et xxxs. d'annuel rent oue les appurtenances en la dite ville de Kyngeston sur Hulle pur ent faire et disposer solonc l'entent et volente de l'auantdite Katerine; et puis apres, al procurement et par abettement de Symond Grymesby, plee fuist moeue el Court de Roy par brief de fourme donne parentre vn William del Kerre, ia mort, et l'auantdit Robert des mees et rent suisditz; et sur ceo processe fuist fait et continue iesques a tant qe la parol ent fuist adiourne deuant lors Mair et Baillifs de la dite ville de Kyngeston, a y estre pledez et terminez en la Court du dite ville de Kyngeston, solonc les libertees de mesme la ville; l'auantdit Symond par subtile ymaginacion et fraude, purposant d'auoir a soun oeps propre les mees et rent suisditz, par son maueis conseil et exitacion et auxi pur soun don[nes] et bealx promesses, fist le dit Robert comparer parsonelment en la dite Court de Kyngeston sur Hulle et la desauower vn William Waghen soun attourne combien q'il fuist pardeuant entre . . . .[1] et fuist prist a respoundre, parount le dit William del Kerre y recouera les mees et rent suisditz enuers le dit Robert par soun defaute, luy esteant illeoqes present en court, par maintenance du dit Symond et couenant et couyn entre luy et le dit William del Kerre pardeuant faite d'auoir les ditz mees et rente apres ycelle recouere ev ; luy quel William del Kerre en parfournant mesmes les couenant et couyn enfeoffa le dit Symond des mees et rente suisditz tost apres la dite recouere ; et issint le dit Symond par soun maintenance auoit et tenoit mesmes les mees et rent a son oeps propre encontre la fourme des estatutz en tiel cas purueuz, en contempt de nostre seignur le Roy, et tres grand damage et greuance les ditz Johan Byngeley et Katerine, et desheritance de mesme eeluy Katerine et le dit Johan Swynflete et de lour heirs a toutz iours: Plese a vostre tres gracious seignurie grauntier brief direct al dit Symond luy commandant sur certeine peine de venir deuant le Conseil nostre dit seignur le Roy lendemayn del Purificacion nostre dame proschein anenir, a estre y examine de la matiere suisdite et de respoundre a ycelle, et de faire outre et receyure ceo qe par le dit Conseille serra agarde celle partie ; Considerantz, tres gracious

---

[1] Illegible owing to damp

whereas the said Katherine, when she was sole after the death of the said Thomas, by her writing enfeoffed one Robert Sturmy of Coldon, upon the full and entire trust which she had in his person and faithfulness, of two messuages and 30s. annnal rent with the appurtences in the said town of Kingston on Hull, to do and dispose thereof according to the intent and wish of the said Katherine ; and afterwards, by the procurement and abetment of Simon Grimsby, a plea was moved in the King's Court by a writ of *formedon* between one William del Kerre, now dead, and the aforesaid Robert [Sturmy], concerning the messuages and rent aforesaid ; and thereupon process was made and continued, until at last the hearing thereof was adjourned before the then Mayor and Bailiffs of the said town of Kingston, there to be pleaded and ended in the Court of the said town of Kingston, according to the liberties of the said town ; the aforesaid Simon [Grimsby] by subtle scheming and fraud, purposing to have the said messuages and rent to his own use, by his evil counsel and incitement, and also by his gifts and fair promises, procured the said Robert to appear personally in the said court of Kingston on Hull, and there to disavow one William Waghen, his attorney, although he was present in [court ?] and was ready to answer, whereby the said William del Kerre by the maintenance of the said Simon, recovered the said messuages and rent against the said Robert by his default, he being there present in court, and by covenant and covin between him and the said William del Kerre formerly made [that he should] have the said messuages and rent after the recovery was obtained ; which William del Kerre in performing the same covenant and covin enfeoffed the said Simon of the said messuages and rent soon after the said recovery ; and so the said Simon by his maintenance had and held the said messuages and rent to his own use, against the form of the statutes in such case provided,[2] in contempt of our Lord the King, and to the very great damage and grievance of the said John Byngeley and Katherine, and to the disinheritance of the same Katherine and of the said John Swynflete and their heirs for ever : May it please your most gracious Lordship to grant a writ directed to the said Simon, commanding him under a certain pain to come before the Council of our said Lord the King on the morrow of the Purification of our Lady next to come, there to be examined as to the matter aforesaid, and to answer to it, and further to do and receive what shall be awarded by the said Council in this behalf ; Considering, most gracious Lord, that the

---

[2] Probably the various statutes against maintenance.

seignur, qe les ditz suppliantz sount sanz recoueree s'ils n'eient vostre tres gracious seignurie et eide touchant les choses suisditz.

100   [1] A tres reuerent piere en Dieu, Thomas, Archeuesque de Caunterbirs et Chauncheler d'Engleterre,

s. d.   Supplie humblement vostre pouere tenant Johane, nadgairs la femme Esteune Wyte de Cranebroke, qe come le dit Esteune poy deuant sa mort enfeffa de toutz sez terrez et tenementz en Cranebroke oue lez apportenantz vn Thomas Whyte et Thomas Bery de Wy vnqore en pleine vie et Johan Asselyn et William Whyte ore mortz, declarant a eux par sa darreine volonte qe la dite suppliante auereit toutz lez profitz de lez ditz terres et tenementz durant la nounage de Katerine file parentre la dite suppliante et Esteune engendre et droit heir a luy, ensemblement oue la noerture du dite Katerine ; par vertue de quele volonte la dite suppliante auoit la garde du dite Katerine et lez profitz de lez ditz terrez et tenementz de la mort du dit Esteune tanque en la feste de la Natiuite Seint Johan darrein passe, qe le dit Thomas Whyte torcionousement prist la dite Katerine hors de la possession du dite suppliante, et la vnqore detient ensemble oue les profitz dez ditz terrez et tenementz a son oeps demesne, encountre la volunte suisdite : Please a vostre tres graciouse seignurie de faire venir deuant vous le dit Esteune [2] [sic] et luy examiner de la verite de la matier suisdite, et sur ceo luy comande a restorer la dite suppliante de la garde suisdite ensemblement oue lez profitz dez ditz terrez et tenementz par luy en le mesne temps priz ; Pur Dieu et en oeure de charite.

F. *PETITION ADDRESSED TO JOHN DE SCARLE,*
1399–1401.[3]

101   [4] A tres honure et tres gracious seignur, le Chaunceller d'Engleterre,

1400   Supplie vostre pouere clerc, Johan Bremore, qe come nadgairs l'esglise de Chesterton [5] el diocise de Nicol esteant voide et appartenant . . .

---

[1] Bundle 3, No. 136.
[2] A mistake for Thomas, *i.e.* Thomas Whyte. Stephen was dead.
[3] Appointed *cir.* Sept. 5, 1399 ; his successor appointed March 9, 1401. See Foss.
[4] Bundle 3, No. 125. The right margin of this document is much damaged.
[5] Near Stilton, co. Hunts.

said suppliants are without recovery if they have not your most gracious lordship and aid touching the things aforesaid.[6]

100 To the most reverend Father in God, Thomas, Archbishop of Canterbury, and Chancellor of England,

s. d. Humbly beseecheth your poor tenant, Joan, late wife of Stephen White of Cranbrook,[7] that whereas the said Stephen shortly before his death enfeoffed one Thomas White and Thomas Bery of Wye[7] (who are still alive), and John Asselyn and William White (now dead), of all his lands and tenements in Cranbrook with the appurtenances, declaring to them by his last will that the said suppliant should have all the profits of the said lands and tenements during the nonage of Katherine, his daughter, begotten between the said suppliant and Stephen, and his right heir, together with the guardianship of the said Katherine ; by virtue of which will the said suppliant had the wardship of the said Katherine and the profits of the said lands and tenements from the death of the said Stephen until the feast of the Nativity of S. John last past, when the said Thomas White wrongfully took the said Katherine out of the possession of the said suppliant, and still detaineth her, together with the profits of the said lands and tenements to his own use, contrary to the said will : May it please your most gracious Lordship to cause the said Thomas to come before you, and to examine him as to the truth of the said matter, and thereupon to order him to restore to the said suppliant the wardship aforesaid, together with the profits of the said lands and tenements taken by him in the meantime ; For God and in way of charity.[8]

F. PETITION ADDRESSED TO JOHN DE SCARLE, 1399–1401.

101 To the most honoured and most gracious Lord, the Chancellor of England,

1400 Beseecheth your poor clerk, John Bremore, that whereas of late the church of Chesterton in the diocese of Lincoln being void and belong-

---

[6] A purely equity matter. The defendant trustee is charged with conniving at a fraudulent recovery.

[7] Kent.

[8] Another case of breach of trust.

le dit nadgairs Roy presenta le dit Johan a mesme l'esglise, qi a ycelle esglise par vertue du dit presentement canonykment fuist admys et institut et induct en ycelle, sicome par les . . . appiert, et continua sa possession en mesme l'esglise par longe temps ; la Lowys Byford, clerc, al abettement et mayntenance de Johan Trynge, Rectour de Assherugge,[1] et frere Robert [Farneburgh, Henry][2] Clerc de Bleche-don, et plusours autres, par vertue d'une prouision a dit Lowys faite de mesme l'esglise encountre lez estatutz de prouisours[3] et autres estatutz ent faitz accepta mesme l'esglise . . . de ses biens et chateux illoeqes a la value de L liures ; Et puis nient contresteant qe le dit Johan Bremore pursua diuerses briefs sur mesmes l'estatutz faitz enuers le dit Lowys .   iure deuaunt monsire Wauter Clopton, alors Chief Justice du dit nadgairs Roy, q'il iammes ne pursueroit le dit Johan Bremore encountre les leys et estatutz du Roy et . . . certeins persones furent liez et obligez en la Chauncellerie du dit nadgairs Roy en vne reconissance de C marcs qe le dit Lowys ne treieroit ne pursueroit le dit Johan Bremore . . . ne deinz le Roialme encountre les leys et estatutz auauntditz ; le dit Lowys par mayntenance et abettement suisditz et al coustage du dit Rectour ad pursue et vnqore pursue   processes enuers le dit Johan Bremore en la dite Courte de Rome en escomengeant le Prynce de Gales, Duc de Lancastre, Erceuesqes, Euesqes et toutes autres estates du Roialme   . en cas q'ils [ne ?] facent execucion de les bulles et processes de la prouision auantdite, mayntenaunt apres q'ils ent serront ou ascun de eux serra requys par le dit Lowys ou par ascun autre en son . . . Rectour ad fait publier en *Oxenford* et aillours et eux ad fait pender sur le huisses de l'esglises illoeqes ; Et outre ceo le dit Lowys fist arester le dit Johan Bremore esteant   . . Floreyns en queux il est condempnez enuers le dit Lowys en mesme la Courte a cause qe le dit Johan Bremore pursua le dit Lowys par les briefs du Roy solonc les . . . le dit Rectour ad commaunde toutz ses tenauntz et villeyns parochiens au dite esglise q'ils apportent lour dismes a lour hostelx demesne, et q'ils ne paient les rentes et autres dues   . toute ceo q'ils purront forfaire enuers le dit Rectour, qi est seignur illoeqes ; et auxi le dit Rectour fist apporter a son hostel toutz les dismes duez au dite esglise de sa demayne terre illoeqes : Plese . . . hautes et horribles contemptz et mesfaitz faitz a nostre seignur le Roy et a sa corone encountre les

---

[1] In the parish of Pilston, co. Bucks. Edmund, Earl of Cornwall, son of Richard, King of the Romans, founded here a college for a rector and twenty brethren or canons, called ' Bonhommes,' in 1283. See Tanner. See indorsement.

ing [to Richard, late King of England], the said late King presented
the said John to the same church, who was canonically admitted,
instituted and inducted thereto by virtue of the said presentation, as
by the . . . appeareth, and he continued his possession of the same
church for a long time; and Lewis Byford, clerk, by the abetment
and maintenance of John Tring, Rector of Ashridge, and Brother
Robert Farneburgh, Henry Clerk of Blechedon, and many others, took
the said church by virtue of a provision of the said church made to
the said Lewis contrary to the Statute of Provisors and other statutes
made in that behalf . . . of his goods and chattels there to the value
of £50 ; And afterwards, notwithstanding that the said John Bremore
sued divers writs on the same statutes against the said Lewis, and that
[the said Lewis?] swore before Sir Walter Clopton, then Chief Justice
of the said late King, that he would never sue the said John Bremore
contrary to the laws and statutes of the King . . . and that certain persons were bound and obliged in the Chancery of the said late King in a
recognisance of 100 marks that the said Lewis would not draw nor
sue the said John Bremore [at the court of Rome] or within the realm
contrary to the laws and statutes aforesaid ; [nevertheless] the said Lewis
by the maintenance and abetment aforesaid, and at the cost of the said
Rector, hath sued and still doth sue . . . processes against the said John
Bremore in the said court of Rome for the excommunication of the Prince
of Wales, Duke of Lancaster, Archbishops, Bishops, and all other estates
of the realm . . . in case they do not [?] make execution of the bulls
and processes of the said provision now after they or any of them shall
be requested by the said Lewis or any other in his [behalf ; and the
said] Rector hath caused them to be published in Oxford and elsewhere and hath caused them to be hung on the church doors there ;
And moreover the said Lewis caused the said John Bremore to be
arrested . . . florins in which he is condemned to the said Lewis in the
same Court [of Rome] because the said John Bremore sued the said
Lewis by the King's writs according to [the said statutes ? ; And] the
said Rector hath commanded all his tenants and villeins, parishioners of
the said church, to carry their tithes to their own houses and not to pay
the rents and other dues [upon pain of losing] all that they could forfeit
to the said Rector, who is the lord there ; And also the said Rector
caused to be brought to his house all the tithes due to the said church
from his demesne land there : May it please [your most gracious Lordship to consider the] high and horrible contempts and offences done to

---

[1] 25 Edw. III. st. 6 ; 38 Edw. III. st. 2,cc. 1_4 ; 13 Ric. II. st. 1, cap. 1 ; 13 Ric. II.
st. 2, cc. 2 and 3.

estatutz et leys de son Roialme, et les graundes parils queux purront
auenir as plusours   . et as autres honurables persones de Roialme
par ycelles processes et escomengement, si bastiue remedie ne soit
mys en celle partie; et les damages et iniuries qe le dit Johan Bremore
     Courte nostre dit seignur le Roy en la cas suisdite, de faire venir
deuaunt vous en la Chauncellerie ou deuaunt le Counseil les ditz Rectour, Robert et Henry et Phelip Morgan, Clerc, Johan Bastard [et
Johan Blewe],[1] procuratours, counseillours et fautours as ditz Rectour
et Lowys en celle partie, a vn certein iour par vous a lymyter a respoundre a nostre dit seignur le Roy sur les contemptz et mesfaitz
suisditz et a dit Johan Bremore . . . a luy faitz en la fourme
auauntdite; eux enchargeant sur vne graunde peyne par vous a
lymyter d'amesner ouesque eux toutz les bulles, sentences et processes
esteantz en lour garde touchantz la dite . . . sufficiante seurete de
cesser de tieux maintenances et iniuries, et de restorer le dit Johan
Bremore a ses dismes et reuenues, duez a sa esglise auauntdite; Pur
Dieu et en oeuere de charitee.

Indorsed.   Memorandum quod decimo die Septembris anno regni
Regis Henrici quarti post conquestum primo[2] Henricus Grene de
Wygorn' et Johannes Assheford, vicarius ecclesie de Poywyke coram
ipso domino Rege in Cancellaria sua personaliter constituti manuceperunt pro Johanne Bremore infrascripto quod ipse Johanni Trynge,
Rectori de Assherugge, et Fratri Roberto Farneburgh, Confratri eiusdem Rectoris, et Henrico Clerk, Philippo Morgan, Johanni Bastard et
Johanni Blewe infrascriptis de custibus et expensis suis rationabilibus
in hac parte satisfaciet in casu quo idem Johannes Bremore contenta
in hac billa versus prefatos Rectorem, Robertum, Henricum, Philip-
pum, Johannem Bastard et Johannem Blewe probare non poterit.

G. *PETITIONS ADDRESSED TO THOMAS BEAUFORT,*
1410–1412.[3]

102   [4]A tres honure et tres gracious seignur,
             Thomas Beaufort, Chaunceller et Admiralle
             d'Engleterre,

s.d.   Supplient tres humblement les Baillifs et Comunaltee, tenantes et
1410   liges a nostre tres redoute seignur le Roi deins les ville et seignurie
to
1412   [1] See indorsement.   [2] 1400.
           [3] Appointed Jan. 31, 1410; his successor appointed Jan. 5, 1412.
           [4] Bundle 3, No. 138.

our Lord the King and his crown, contrary to the statutes and laws of his realm, and the great perils which may happen to many . . . and to other honourable persons of the realm by these processes and excommunications, if speedy remedy be not made in that behalf, and the damages and injuries which the said John Bremore . . . the Court of our said Lord the King in the case aforesaid, to cause the said Rector, Robert, and Henry, Philip Morgan, clerk, John Bastard and John Blewe, the procurers, counsellors and abettors of the said Rector and Lewis in this behalf, to come before you in the Chancery, or before the Council,[5] at a certain day by you to be limited, to answer our Lord the King for the contempts and offences aforesaid and to the said John Bremore [for the wrongs] done to him in form aforesaid, charging them, under a great pain by you to be limited, to bring with them all the bulls, sentences and processes in their keeping touching the said [church ? and to find] sufficient surety to cease from such maintenance and injuries, and to restore the said John Bremore to his tithes and revenues, due to his church aforesaid ; For God and in way of charity.

Indorsed.   Be it remembered that on the 10th day of September in the 1st year of the reign of King Henry the Fourth after the Conquest, Henry Grene of Worcester and John Ashford, Vicar of the church of Powick, personally appeared before the King in his Chancery and undertook on behalf of the within written John Bremore that he would satisfy the within written John Tring, Rector of Ashridge, Brother Robert Farnburgh, co-brother of the said Rector,[6] Henry Clerk, Philip Morgan, John Bastard, and John Blewe, as to their reasonable costs and expenses in this behalf, in case the said John Bremore shall not be able to prove the contents of this bill against the said Rector, Robert, Henry, Philip, John Bastard, and John Blewe.[7]

G. *PETITIONS ADDRESSED TO THOMAS BEAUFORT,* 1410-1412.

102

To the most honoured and gracious Lord, Thomas Beaufort, Chancellor and Admiral of England,

s. d. Most humbly beseech the Bailiffs and Commonalty, tenants and
1410 lieges of our most redoubted Lord the King within the town and
to
1412

[5] The alternative is very instructive. See Cases 79 and 130.

[6] That is, Brother of the College.

[7] The rarity among our printed records of any proceedings against papal provisors will be a sufficient excuse for the publication of this fragmentary petition. No. 120 is a similar case.

de Retford en le Clay,[1] et lour compleynont de Rauf Puncherdon de ceo
qe mesme le Rauf, le Samady proschein apres le fest de Seint Hiller,
l'an du regne nostre dit seignur le Roy oeptisme,[2] vient oue force et
armes et encountre la pees nostre dit seignur le Roy deins la dite ville,
et illoeqes la maison d'un Johan Spanyelle, tenant a nostre dit seignur
le Roy en mesme la ville, forciblement entra, et le dit Johan la eins
esteant a soun maungier ouesque soun espee bata, naufra et malement
treta entaunt q'il estoit en [d]espoir de sa vie.

Item les ditz suppliants lour compleynont vnqore de mesme le
Rauf et Thrustane soun frere de ceo qe mesmes les Rauf et Thrustane,
le Marsdy en le secunde semaygne de quaresme, l'an nostre dit seignur
le Roi disme,[3] giseront en agaite en le haute chemyne nostre seignur
le Roy ioust Hedon Crosse, et la encountrerent vn Robert de Beyghton,
tenant a nostre dit seignur le Roy, et en luy assaut firent come ceux
qi feurent en purpos de luy auoir occys ou murdres, et ensy voudroient
auoir fait si noun qe par [la grace] de Dieux le dit Robert apparceust
ou Dame Katerine Hercy estoit sur soun veduyte celle partie et fuist
a sa presence pur socour, et ensy fuist rescoues et deliuerez hors de
lour mayns.

Item les ditz suppliantz vnqore de reschief lour compleynont du
dit Rauf, le Marsdy proschein deuant le fest de Nowelle darrein passe,
par mayntenance et supportacione de William Wastenesse de Hedon
soun maistre encountre vn Johan Cleypole, tenant a nostre dit seignur
le Roy et vn des Baillifs de mesme la ville de Retford, en la haute
chemyne nostre dit seignur le Roy, deins le champe de Hedon suisdit
sur soun chiual, et dilloeqes mesme le Johan, ouesque soun arc et
setes, par force et maistre enchacea hors de la dit chemyne droit en
le Pounfold de Hedon, et la eins le dit Johan emprisona et detient sur
soun chiual par tout le iour tanque il auoit troue seurte de fere fyn et
raunseoun ouesque le dit William a lour volunte, extorcenousement et
par expressement encountre ley et reasoun.

Item vnqore les ditz suppliantz soy compleignont des auantditz
William Wastenesse, Rauf Puncherdon et Thurston soun frere de ce
q'ils mesmes William, Rauf et Thurston et autres de lour assent et
coueigne sy durement manassent les ditz suppliantz de iour en autre
de vie et de membre q'ils noisent passer lour ville ne trauailler en
l'office q'ils ount affaire al oeps nostre dit seignur le Roy, n'entour
lour besoignez demesne par dout d'estre tuez ou murdrez par les ditz

---

[1] In the North Clay division of Bassetlaw Wapentake, co. Notts; now generally
known as East Retford.

lordship of Retford in the Clay, and complain of Ralph Puncherdon, of this, that the same Ralph, on the Saturday after the feast of S. Hilary in the 8th year of our said Lord the King,[2] did come, with force and arms and against the peace of our said Lord the King, into the said town, and there did forcibly enter the house of one John Spaniel, a tenant of our Lord the King in the same town, and there with his sword did beat the said John, who was within at his meat, and did wound and ill-treat him, so that he despaired of his life.

Also the said suppliants complain again of the said Ralph and of Thurstan his brother of this, that the same Ralph and Thurstan, on the Tuesday in the second week of Lent in the 10th year of our said Lord the King,[3] did lie in wait on the high road of our Lord the King near Headon Cross,[4] and there they did encounter one Robert de Beyghton, a tenant of our Lord the King, and did assault him as if they were purposed to have killed or murdered him, and so they would have done if it had not been that by the grace of God the said Robert perceived where Dame Katherine Hercy stood on her watch-tower[5] in that part, and he fled to her presence for help, and so was rescued and delivered out of their hands.

Also the said suppliants again and anew complain of the said Ralph, that on the Tuesday before Christmas last past, by the maintenance and support of William Wastnesse of Headon, his master, did encounter one John Cleypole, a tenant of our Lord the King and one of his Bailiffs of the same town of Retford, in the high road of our said Lord the King, in the field of Headon aforesaid, on his horse, and thence did chase the said John, with bow and arrows, by force and mastery, out of the said road right into the pinfold of Headon, and therein did imprison the said John, and did detain him on his horse for the whole of the day until he had found surety to make fine and ransom with the said William [Wastnesse] at his pleasure, wrongfully and expressly against law and reason.

Also the said suppliants again complain of the said William Wastnesse, Ralph Puncherdon and Thurstan his brother of this, that the said William, Ralph and Thurstan, and others of their assent and covin, have so seriously menaced the said suppliants from day to day of life and limb that they dare not pass their town nor work in the office that they have to do to the use of our said Lord the King, nor about their own business, for fear of being killed or murdered by the

---

[2] Jan. 13, 1407; a Thursday.
[3] 1409; Ash Wednesday fell on Feb. 20.
[4] Near Retford.
[5] Translation doubtful. The word

veduyte I take to be an early form of *vedette*, but can find no authority for it; at any rate it makes sense.

malefesours et autres de lour assent et affinitee, sy non q'altre remedie
soit fait. Sur quoy pleise a vostre tres gracious seignurie de grauntier
seueralx briefs directz as ditz Raufe, Thurstane et William, d'estre
deuant vous en la Chauncellerie pur respondre sibien a nostre seignur
le Roy come as ditz suppliantz de toutz les matiers compris deins ycest
bille et as autres matiers queux serront surmys a eux par les ditz
suppliantz, et se en le quinzisme de *P*asque proschein venant, sur
certein peyn a limiter par vostre tres sage discrecion et mys en mesmes
les briefs ; Pur Dieu et en oeure de charite.

  Plegii de prosequendo :
      Nicholaus Wyston de Retford,
      Stephanus Sadeler de Retford.

103   [1] A tres honurable et tres noble seignur, le
      Chaunceller et Admiralle d'Engleterre,

s. d. Supplie humblement Jacob Keuse, Marchaunt de Brugges en Flaun-
1410 drez, qe come le dit suppliaunt, deins cestez presentes trieues pris et
to pendauntz parentre le tres excellent seignur le Roy d'Engletere et
1412 iceux de Flaundrez,[2] venoit deins iceste Roialme pur le fait de soun
marchaundise, quidaunt d'auoir passe en ces parties suisditz saufement
et seurement saunz auoir recieux ascune damage ou desease par
[nulles] persones ; et sur ceo, apres la fait de soun marchaundie
acomplie, seu [sic] ordeigna de passer en lez parties de Flaundrez
suisdit ; Et sicome le dit suppliaunt fuist alaunt en sa viage vers la
ville de Deuorre, sur la mountaigne dehors Roucestre, le ix^e iour de
Januer darrein passe, la vient vn Lowis Robesart de Henault, Esquier
de moun tres redoute seignur le prince,[3] et par graunde sotilte disoit
a dit suppliaunt q'il vendreit en graund haste de comparer deuant le
suisdit excellent seignur le Roy pur certeins causes et lui d'estre
monstrez ; Sur quoi le dit suppliaunt affiaunt en lez . de dit
Lowys sen retorna ouesque lui, quidaunt d'auoir compare deuant le
dit excellent seignur le Roy come le dit Lowys lui auoit enfourme ;
Et fuist ensi qe qaunt le dit suppliaunt auoit passe ouesque le dit
Lowis par graund espace de chemyn, le mesme suppliaunt requira le
dit Lowis de lui amener deuant la gracious presence le suisdit puissaunt

---

[1] Bundle 3, No. 139. Decayed and
illegible in places. .
 [2] A truce for a year had been made in
1407, which was prolonged for three years
from June 15, 1408. See Ramsay, *Lan
caster and York*, i. 108, 118.

said evil-doers and others of their assent and affinity, if some remedy be not made. Whereupon may it please your most gracious Lordship to grant several writs directed to the said Ralph, Thurstan and William, [commanding them] to be before you in the Chancery to answer to our Lord the King as well as to the said suppliants touching all the matters comprised in this bill and other matters which shall be alleged against them by the said suppliants, on the quindene of Easter next to come, under a certain pain to be limited by your most wise discretion and put in the said writs ; For God and in way of charity.

Pledges for the prosecution :—

Nicholas Wyston of Retford,
Stephen Sadler of Retford.

103   To the most honourable and most noble Lord, the Chancellor and Admiral of England,

s. d. Humbly beseecheth Jacob Keuse, merchant, of Bruges in Flanders,
1410   that whereas the said suppliant, during these present truces taken
to   and pending between the most excellent Lord, the King of England
1412   and them of Flanders, came within this realm in order to deal with his merchandise, expecting to have passed in these said parts safely and surely without having received any damage or harm from anybody ; and thereupon, after the dealing with his said merchandise was accomplished, he intended to pass into the parts of Flanders aforesaid ; And as the said suppliant was going on his way towards the town of Dover, on the hill outside Rochester [4] on the 9th day of January last past, there came one Lewis Robesart of Hainault, Esquire to my most redoubted Lord the Prince [of Wales], and with great subtilty told the said suppliant that he must come in great haste to appear before the said most excellent Lord the King for certain causes to be shown to him ; Whereupon the said suppliant, trusting in the [? good faith] of the said Lewis, returned with him, thinking to have appeared before the said excellent Lord the King, as the said Lewis had informed him ; And it was so, that when the said suppliant had passed with the said Lewis along a great space of the road, the said suppliant requested the said Lewis to bring him before

---

[3] K. G. ; standard-bearer to Henry V.; married Elizabeth, Baroness Bourchier *suo jure*, and was summoned to Parliament as Lord Bourchier. He died without issue 1431.

[4] This must be the celebrated Gad's Hill.

prince le Roy ; lui quel Lowys dona respounce a dit suppliaunt qe le
Roy lui auoit done en maundement de prendre le dit suppliaunt a
soun prisoner et enuoit . . . et sur ceo prist le dit suppliaunt et lui
amesna a vne ville pres de Couentre appelle Coppeston, et la mist le
dit suppliaunt al raumsome de VC nobles, et lui tenoit en graund
duresse tanque le dit suppliaunt auoit paie a dit Lowys C marcz de
la somme suisdite, et troue sufficeaunt seurte pur le remenant de
mesme somme, a graund tort et enfrayment lez trieues auantditz :
Par quoy plese a vostre tres noble et puissant seignurie graciousement considerer iceste prise et raumsomme torcenousement fait .
et sur ceo mettre vostre noble seignurie et aide a dit suppliaunt, au
fin q'il puisse auoir briefs du tres excellent seignur le Roy directz a
dit Lowys de lui faire comparer deuaut vous en la Chauncellarie.

104   [1] A tres haute et tres sage seignur monsire
Thomas Beauffort, chiualer, Chaunceller
d'Engletere,

d.
1410
to
1412
Supplie humblement vostre pouer oratour, Thomas Bonnde,[2] qe come
vn Walter Bonnde, filtz et beire a Robert Bonnde, prist a femme vn
Alice et auoit issu le dit Thomas, viuant le dit Robert, et morist ;
apres qi mort certeyns biens et chateux a dit Thomas par lez ditz
Robert et Alice furount assignes et deliuerez au dit Robert pur
gardere al oeps et profite du dit Thomas ;[3] le quile Robert fist sez
executours vn Johan Nicholle et Thomasyn sa femme et autrez, et
liuere fuist fait as ditz Johan et Thomasyn [par] le dit Robert dez
ditz biens et chateux oue tout l'encrece par le mesne temps pur
gardere, deliuerere et acompte rendre au dit Thomas ou a ascun autre
en soun noun a ascun temps qe soient requis ; les queux biens et
chateux lez ditz executours ne voillent pas deliuerer come lour
comandement fuist par le dit Robert, a graund arerisment du dit
suppliant si vostre tres gracious aide ne soit en celle partie, qar nulle
accion est au luy done par la ley sinoun vn breoffe de detenu, a quelle
breoffe ils ne voillent pas respoundere, pur ceo qe le dit suppliant n'ad
nulle especialte dez ditz biens et chateux : Please a vostre tres haute

[1] Bundle 3, No. 140.
[2] Or perhaps 'Bounde.'
[3] The text is rather obscure here.
[4] Co. Warwick.

the gracious presence of the said puissant prince the King; the which Lewis gave answer to the said suppliant that the King had given him commandment to take the said suppliant prisoner . . . . and thereupon he took the said suppliant and brought him to a town near Coventry, called Copston,[4] and there put the said suppliant to a ransom of 500 nobles, and kept him in great duress until the said suppliant had paid the said Lewis 100 marks on account of the said sum, and had found sufficient surety for the remainder thereof, to the great wrong and breach of the truces aforesaid: Wherefore may it please your most noble and puissant Lordship graciously to consider this seizure and ransom wrongfully done . . . and thereupon to give your noble Lordship and aid to the said suppliant, to the end that he may have writs of the most excellent Lord the King directed to the said Lewis to make him appear before you in the Chancery.[5]

104   To the most high and most wise Lord, Sir Thomas Beaufort, knight, Chancellor of England,

s. d.   Beseecheth humbly your poor orator, Thomas Bond, that whereas
1410   Walter Bond, son and heir to Robert Bond, took to wife one
to   Alice, and had issue the said Thomas in the lifetime of the said
1412   Robert, and then [Walter] died; and after his death certain goods and chattels of the said Thomas were assigned and delivered by the said Robert and Alice to the said Robert to keep to the use and profit of the said Thomas;[3] the which Robert[6] made one John Nicholle and Thomasyn his wife and others, his executors, and livery was made to the said John and Thomasyn by the said Robert of the said goods and chattels, with all the increase for the mesne time, to keep, deliver, and render account for [the same] to the said Thomas, or to any other in his name, at any time when they should be required [to do so]; the which goods and chattels, the said executors will not deliver as they were commanded by the said Robert, to the great detriment of the said suppliant, if your most gracious aid be not [bestowed] in this behalf, for there is no action given him by law except a writ of detinue, to which writ they will not answer, because the said suppliant hath no specialty[7] of the said goods and

---

[4] As to alien plaintiffs see p. 4, note 3.   [5] Meaning apparently no documentary
[6] Query, a mistake for Walter.   evidence.

seignurie d'enuoier pur lez ditz executours pur examiner la dite matier deuant vous, et apres le examnement fait diffeare droiturelle remedie au dit suppliant, pur Dieu et en ouere de charite.

> Les plegges de pros' :
>> Johan Russelle et
>> Esmound Morys.

---

[1] The case is rather obscure. Apparently Robert Bond had in his lifetime delivered the goods to the persons who afterwards became executors of his will, so that the fact of the defendants being executors does not appear to have any significance. The

chattels : May it please your most high Lordship to send for the said executors, and to examine [them] before you as to the said matter, and after examination made, to make rightful remedy to the said suppliant : for God and in way of charity.[1]

Pledges for the prosecution :—

John Russell and
Edmond Morris.

real reason of the application to the Chancery thus seems to be the difficulty of proceeding at common law. The defendants however were trustees.

PART II.

SELECTED PETITIONS

A. *FRENCH PETITIONS OF VARIOUS DATES.*

105   [1] Au Chaunceller nostre seignur le Roi,[2]

1364 Monstre William de Middelton, parsone del esglise de Hamme Preston, qe come la disme garbe de totes maners des bleedz cressantz dedeinz sa dite paroche de Hamme Preston a lui appartinent et de comune droit deuient appartiner, nientmeins le Dean de Wymburne Mynstre ad acroche a lui par usurpacion la disme garbe de iiij[xx] acres de waste terre de novel assart dedeinz sa dite paroche a la value de xls. par an, en desheretison de sa dite esglise; sur quey le dit William ad sui en consistoire l'Euesque de Salesbury deuers Henry Bodyn et Wauter Caperon, qi occupieront la dite disme garbe en noun du dit Dean, pur auoir restitucion de mesme la disme garbe; et pur ce qe la chapelle de Wymburne Mynstre est la fraunche chapelle nostre seignur le Roi et exempt de jurisdiction de ordinarie, mande feust prohibicion hors de la Chauncellerie au dit Euesque et son Official q'ils ne deussent rien attempter en prejudice de nostre seignur le Roi ne de sa dite fraunche chapelle; par quey le dit Official ad sursys d'aler auant en la dite cause; par quey le dite William prie a vostre tres graciouse seignurie qe vous pleise ordiner remedie, qe sa dite esglise ne soit desherite encontre comune droit.

Indorsed. Memorandum quod xxiij die Aprilis anno regni Regis Edwardi tercii tricesimo octavo tam Willelmus de Middelton infra-scriptus in propria persona sua quam Decanus de Wymbourmynstre per Johannem de Tamworth attornatum suum venerunt in Cancellaria Regis apud Westm', et de assensu eorumdem datus est eis dies in eadem Cancellaria in quindena Sancte Trinitatis proximo futura ad faciendum et recipiendum de contentis in ista peticione quod Curia domini Regis consideraverit.

[1] Ancient Petitions, No. 15074.
[2] Simon Langham, Bishop of Ely, was Chancellor.
[3] Co. Dorset, 3 m. from Wimborne.

[4] 1364.
[5] The plaintiff does not ask for any specific remedy, and does not even ask for a writ against the defendant. Still it seems

A. *FRENCH PETITIONS OF VARIOUS DATES.*

105 To the Chancellor of our Lord the King

1364 Showeth William de Middelton, parson of the church of Ham Preston,[3] that whereas the tenth sheaf of all kinds of corn growing within his said parish of Ham Preston belongs and of common right ought to belong to him, nevertheless the Dean of Wimborne Minster hath taken to himself by usurpation the tenth sheaf of fourscore acres of waste land newly assarted within his said parish, to the value of 40s. yearly, to the disinherison of his said church; whereupon the said William hath sued in the Consistory [Court] of the Bishop of Salisbury against Henry Bodyn and Walter Caperon, who have occupied the said tenth sheaf in the name of the said Dean, in order to have restitution of the same tenth sheaf; And because the chapel of Wimborne Minster is the free chapel of our Lord the King and exempt from the jurisdiction of the Ordinary, a prohibition was issued out of the Chancery to the said Bishop and his Official, that they must attempt nothing to the prejudice of our Lord the King or of his said free chapel; wherefore the said Official hath ceased to proceed in the said cause; wherefore the said William prayeth your most gracious Lordship that you will be pleased to ordain a remedy, so that his said church be not disinherited contrary to common right.

Indorsed. Be it remembered that on the 23rd day of April, 38 Edward III.,[4] as well the within written William del Middelton, in his proper person, as the Dean of Wimborne Minster, by John de Tamworth his attorney, came to the King's Chancery at Westminster, and by consent a day was given them in the said Chancery, on the quindene of Holy Trinity next to come, to do and receive what the Court of the Lord King shall consider touching the contents of this petition.[5]

clear from the indorsement that a writ, either a *sub pœna* or a *quibusdam certis de causis*, was issued and that the defen- dant appeared in pursuance of it. The indorsement also suggests that the Court intended to deal with the whole matter.

106   [1] A Chaunceler nostre seignur le Roy,

1377 Monstre Johan Walyngfford, Priour del esglise de Seint Frisewyth d'Oxenford,[2] qe come il estoit eslieu par le Couuent de mesme l'esglise d'estre Priour par licence de sire Edward, nadgairs Roy d'Engleterre, aiel nostre seignur le Roy q'ore est,[3] patron del esglise auauntdit, et conferme par l'Euesque diocesan de mesme le lieu, et en paisible possession come Priour par trois anz tanqe il fuist ouste par Johan Dodeford;[4] Sour qei le dit Johan Walyngford est venuz a ceste presente parlement de pursuire son droit a nostre seignur le Roy et a son Conseil; et le dit John Dodeford luy ad fait prendre issi q'il est en gard de viscount de Londres: Par qei vous pleise de maundere breef a viscountz de Londres d'amesner le dit Johan Walyngford deuant vous issint q'il poet pursuir sez busoignes de la matiere auauntdit; et ensement de maunder breef al dit Johan Dodeford de vener cy a ceste presente parlement d'estree present affaire discussion de la matiere auauntdit selonc droit et reson.

Indorsed. Memorandum quod predictus Johannes Dodeford audiens de prosecucione per predictum Johannem de Walyngford sic facta, xxvj die Sept' anno r. r. Ricardi nunc primo,[5] in Cancellaria Regis apud Westm', coram venerabili patre Episcopo Meneuense, Cancellario ipsius Regis,[6] personaliter comparebat, prefato Johanne de Walyngford tunc comparere non curante, et audita materia in ista peticione contenta, protestabatur prosecucionem et suggestionem predicti Johannis de Walyngford minus veras existere, allegando ipsum Johannem Dodeford, vacante Prioratu Sancte Frideswide, per Conuentum dicte domus de eorum communi assensu de licencia regia in Priorem eiusdem domus mere electum, et super hoc, adhibito regio assensu auctoritate Ordinario, rite et legitime confirmatum fuisse, et ipsum sic Priorem et pastorem dicte domus existere; per quod petiit quod partes predicte et causa illa ipsorum Ordinario dimittantur ibidem discuciende;

Ac prefatus Cancellarius comperto per rotulos et memoranda Cancellarie Regis quod dicte electio et confirmacio in forma predicta facte fuerunt et iam resident in filaciis dicte Cancellarie, perpendens causam predictam ac cognicionem eiusdem ad forum ecclesiasticum et non ad Curiam regiam nec aliam Curiam laicalem mero iure

---

[1] Ancient Petitions, No. 15215.
[2] Prior from 1362 to 1373.
[3] Richard II.
[4] John Dodeford was elected Prior in

106   To the Chancellor of our Lord the King,

1377 Showeth John Wallingford, Prior of the church of S. Frideswide at
Oxford, that whereas he was elected by the convent of the same
church to be Prior, by licence of lord Edward, late King of England,
grandfather of our Lord the King who now is, the patron of the said
church, and was confirmed by the Bishop diocesan of that place,
and was in peaceable possession as Prior for three years until he
was ousted by John Dodeford. Whereupon the said John Wallingford hath come to this present Parliament to sue for his right to
our Lord the King and his Council ; but the said John Dodeford hath
caused him to be seized, so that he is now in the custody of the
Sheriff of London : May it please you therefore to send a writ to
the Sheriffs [*sic*] of London to bring the said John Wallingford before
you so that he may pursue his business in the matter aforesaid ;
and also to send a writ to the said John Dodeford to come hither
to this present Parliament, to be present and to discuss the matter
aforesaid, according to right and reason.

Indorsed. Be it remembered that the aforesaid John Dodeford,
hearing of the suit by the said John de Wallingford so made, personally appeared in the King's Chancery at Westminster before the
venerable Father, the Bishop of S. Davids, Chancellor of the said
King, on the 26th day of September, 1 Richard II., the said John
de Wallingford not then caring to appear, and having heard the
matters contained in this petition, protested that the suit and suggestion of the said John de Wallingford was not true, alleging that
he himself, John Dodeford, on the vacancy of the Priory of S.
Frideswide, was elected Prior of that House by the common consent of
the convent of the same House and by royal licence, and that thereupon, the royal assent being shown, by the authority of the Ordinary
he was duly and lawfully confirmed and that he was thus Prior and
pastor of the said House ; wherefore he prayed that the parties and
their dispute might be dismissed to the Ordinary to be there discussed.

And the said Chancellor, finding by the rolls and memoranda of
the King's Chancery that the said election and confirmation were
made in form aforesaid and still remain on the files of the said
Chancery, and thinking that the cause aforesaid and the consideration
thereof belong of common right to the Ecclesiastical Court and not

pursuance of the king's *congé d'élire*, dated   5 1377.
Nov. 20, 1373. He filled the office until   6 Adam de Houghton, appointed June
his death in 1391. *Mon. Angl.* ii. 138.   22, 1377.

pertinere, dimisit partes a dicta Curia ac causam et materiam supra-
dictas, precipiens et iudicialiter discernens quod partes predicte
causam illam coram Ordinario suo vel aliis iudicibus ecclesiasticis
prosequantur si sibi viderint expedire.

107   [1] A Chaunceller nostre tres redoute seignur
le Roy et a son tres sage Counseil,[2]

Cir. Supplie humblement Roger Bole, pouere tenant du noble seignur le
1384 Counte de Derby,[3] qe la ou le dit Roger clama et entra en certeins
terres, tenementz, rentz et seruices en Grant Lillyngston, et Countee
d'Oxenford, heritablement a luy descenduz en la taille par voy de
remeindre, dont il ad bones chatres et euidences ; par cause de quel
claime et entree del dit Roger, entreront en sa meison propre en la
dite ville le dismenge en my quaresme, l'an sisme du regne nostre
seignur le Roi Richard,[4] vn Thomas atte Welle, Geffrey Thurbarn,
Henry Abbot, et autres plusours, oue leur couyne, oue force et armes,
par maintenance d'un Roger atte Chambre ; et la pristrent le dit suppliant, et lui mistrent en dures feres et cips, et luy lierent les mains
come laron, issint qe le sank issist ; en queles fers et cips le dit suppliant fuist teuuz tanque al feste des Palmes proschein ensuant,[5] a quel
heure par grace de Dieu et par miracle il fuist deliuerez hors des ditz
fers et cips ; Et apres le dit suppliant auoit lettres son dit seignur le
Counte a ses seneschalx directes de ent enquere la verite ; et il por-
tant memes les lettres as ditz seneschalx, vendrent les ditz Thomas,
Geffrey, Johan le fitz le dit Thomas et Johan seruant mesme celui
Thomas, par le dit maintenance, en le clos le dit Roger suppliant la
veille de Pasque l'an vij^{me} [6] a seir a Lillyngstou, et la luy baterent et
mahimerent, a tort et en contre la pees, et as damage le dit Roger
suppliant de C li. : Qe please a vostres tres noblez et graciousez
seigneuries de faire venir deuant vous les ditz mesfesours oue lour
maintenours, de respoundre si bien a nostre seignur le Roi pur la dite
maintenance et afrai de son pees, come de tortes faites al dit Roger
suppliant ; pur Dieu et en oeure de charite.

[1] Early Chancery Proceedings, Bundle
68, No. 102.
[2] Sir Michael de la Pole was Chancellor
from Mar. 13, 1383, to Oct. 23, 1386.
[3] Henry Plantagenet, afterwards Henry IV.
[4] 1383 ; Mid-Lent Sunday fell on Mar. 1.
[5] Mar. 15.
[6] 1384 ; Easter Sunday fell on April 10.
[7] This case is a good illustration of the
difficulty of distinguishing between the
Parliament, the Council and the Chancery,
as Courts of Justice. The plaintiff ad-
dresses his petition to the Chancellor, he
comes to the Parliament to sue before the
Council, and the Chancellor adjudicates.
[8] I cannot identify this place.
[9] No equitable doctrine is involved, and
the violence and maintenance of the defen-

to the royal courts nor to any lay court, dismissed the parties and the cause and matter aforesaid to the [Ecclesiastical] Court aforesaid, holding and judicially considering that the parties aforesaid may sue the cause before the Ordinary or other ecclesiastical judges if it shall seem expedient to them.[7]

107   To the Chancellor of our most redoubted Lord the King, and to his most wise Council,

Cir. 1384 Humbly beseecheth Roger Bole, a poor tenant of the noble Lord, the Earl of Derby, that whereas the said Roger claimed and entered upon certain lands, tenements, rents and services in Great Lillingston,[8] in the County of Oxford, [which were] heritably descended to him in tail by way of remainder, of which he hath good charters and evidences ; and because of this claim and entry by the said Roger, one Thomas at Well, Geoffrey Thurbarn, Henry Abbot, and many others. of their covin, with force and arms. by maintenance of one Roger at Chamber, entered into [the plaintiff's] own house in the said town on the Sunday in Mid Lent, in the 6th year of the reign of our Lord King Richard ; and there they took the said suppliant, and put him in strong irons and stocks, and bound his hands as though he had been a robber, so that the blood flowed ; in which irons and stocks the said suppliant was kept until the Palm Sunday next following, at which time by the grace of God and by a miracle he was delivered out of the said irons and stocks ; And afterwards the said suppliant had letters from his said Lord the Earl directed to his stewards to inquire of the truth of this ; and as he was bearing the same letters to the said stewards, came the said Thomas, Geoffrey, John son of the said Thomas, and John his servant, by the said maintenance, into the close of the said Roger, the suppliant, on the eve of Easter, in the 7th year, in the evening, at Lillingston, and there they beat and maimed him, wrongfully and against the peace, and to the damage of the said Roger, the suppliant, of 100*l*. : May it please your most noble and gracious Lordships to make come before you the said evil-doers with their maintainers, to answer as well to our Lord the King for the said maintenance and affray against his peace, as for the wrongs done to the said Roger the suppliant ; For God and in way of charity.[9]

dants forms the only ground for application to the Chancellor. The case is chiefly interesting from its early date, and from the fact that it is addressed to the Chancellor *and the Council.*

108   A Gardeyn de Grand Seel nostre seygnour
le Roy,

1395 6 Supplie Johan de Elnet, Archideaken de Leycestre,[2] qe come Wauter
Barnake, clerk, Official a dit Archideaken, auoit assigne vn iour de
seier et de faire ce qa son office appartenoit en l'esglise de Seint Martyn
en la ville de Leycestre, la vn Johan Belgraue par noet deuant ou bien
matyn fist metter priuement et maliciousement vn bille escript de
mayn de texte en la dite esglise pardesuz ou le dit Officiale deuoit
seier, compernant qe le dit Officiale poait bien comparoir a les iugges
qe Sussanne condempnerent, fesant iuggementz nient droitureles,
oppressant lez innocentz, et soeffrant les malueys, et auxi a vn iugge
de deable de iniquitee, et autres plusoures paroles reprouables,
et enowtre en le dit Officiale generalment fist censures de seinte
esglise de toutz ceux mettantz la dite bille en reproue, esclaundre et
villanie de la ley de seinte esglise; le dit Johan Belgrave ouertement
et pompousement defendist qe lez ditz censures furent plus auant
publies conissant q'il l'auoit fait et le bien voleit auower; par qoy les
malfesours cellis parties sount taunt esbaudez et confortez de malfaire
et sustenir lour errours, et le dit Archideaken et sez officers eschuz et
nient hardifs de faire qa lour office appartient, qe les leys, priuelegges
et libertes de seinte esglise par tiele malueys ensaumple ne purront
estre executz, mayntenutz, ne parfornez; et par qeux riotes malfaitz
y est semblaunce qe le dit Johan Belgraue et auters a luy enherdantz
ferront insurreccion dedeins brief si due remedie par la court de nostre
souerayn seignur le Roy y ne soit mys : Qe plese a dit Gardeyn grantier
vn brief directe a dit Johan Belgraue de venir sur certayn peyne
deuaut nostre dit seignur le Roy en sa Chauncelrie en la quinzeyne de
Scinte Hillare proscheyn venant a respoundre a les articles susdites et
as toutz autres articles qe alors luy serront surmyses par le dit Archideaken dependantz sur la matiere auantdite : Pur Dieu et en oeure de
charitee.

Pleg' de Pros' { Johannes de Stuycle
              { Robertus Somery

---

[1] Early Chancery Proceedings, Bundle 68, No. 63.
[2] Appointed 1392, died 1404. No Keepers of the Great Seal during that period are mentioned by Foss, except on temporary absences of Thomas de Arundel, the Chancellor in 1393, 1394, 1395, and 1396. On the first two occasions there were two Keepers, on the last two occasions one only, John de Scarle, the Master of the Rolls. As this bill only mentions one Keeper, it may therefore be dated in 1395 or 1396.

108   To the Keeper of the Great Seal of our Lord the King,

1395 G Beseecheth John de Elnet, Archdeacon of Leicester, that whereas Walter Barnake, clerk, Official of the said Archdeacon, had fixed a day to sit and do what belonged to his office in the church of S. Martin, in the town of Leicester, one John Belgrave the night before or early the same morning privily and maliciously caused to be placed in the said church, below where the said Official ought to sit, a bill written in text hand, alleging [?] that the said Official might well compare with the judges who condemned Susannah, giving unrighteous judgments, oppressing the innocent, and suffering the evil-doers, and also [comparing him] to a judge of the devil in iniquity, with many other blameworthy words, and further made censure generally on the said Official, of the Holy Church and of all those putting the said bill in reproof, to the slander and vilifying of the laws of Holy Church ; [3] the said John Belgrave openly and proudly defended that the said censures were published a long time before, knowing what he had done, and that he would fully avow it ; whereby all evil-doers in those parts are so emboldened and comforted to do evil and to sustain their errors, and the said Archdeacon and his officers are so affrighted, not daring to do what belongs to their office, that the laws, privileges and liberties of Holy Church cannot, on account of so evil an example, be executed, maintained or performed; and through these ill-done riots it is like that the said John Belgrave and others, his adherents, will make an insurrection within a short time unless due remedy be made by the Court of our sovereign Lord the King ; May it please the said Keeper to grant a writ directed to the said John Belgrave to come before our said Lord the King in his Chancery on the quindene of S. Hilary next coming, under a certain pain, to answer to the articles aforesaid and to all other articles concerning the matter aforesaid, which shall then be alleged against him by the said Archdeacon. For God and in way of charity.[4]

    Pledges for the prosecution :

John de Stukeley,
Robert Somery.

[3] Translation doubtful ; the text is very obscure.
[4] An interesting case, but not easy to classify. It is not alleged that there was any difficulty in proceeding at common law.

109   ¹ A tres reuerent piere en Dieu et tres gracious
seignur. l'Erceuesque de Canterbirs et Chaun
celler d'Engleterre,²

1407   Supplie humblement William Farendou, Chiualer, qe come Robert
to   Wynynton, qi mort est, iadys attourne general de dit William,
1409   resceu .   diuersez sommes d'or et d'argent en diuersez parcelles,
amountantz a Dxxj li. iiij s., et auxi certeinz estatutz et minimentz de
ccccl li. et pluis, et auxi . . . a dit William certeins hanappes
d'argent, dez queux plusours furent dorrez, pur lez deliuerer a la
dame de Surgers et pur auoir pris en noun . . . dame xxij li.,
les queles mesme celluy William paia pur la dite dame pur les
hanappes suisditz a Robert Thorley a qi la dite dame auoit . . .
hanappes pur la somme de xxij li. suisdit, come par lez ditz parcelles
les quelles le dit suppliaunt auera toutz iours pristez pur monstre a
vostre gracious [seignurie] . . . pleynement purra apparoir . . . ensy,
tres gracious seignur, qe nient contresteant qe le dit Robert Wynynton
vnqes ne deliuera a dite dame les ditz hanappes ne a dit suppliant ou a
ascun en soun noun lez ditz sommes ou ascunz dycellez, et qe Alice
Kelseye, executrice del testament de dit Robert Wynynton nadgairs
conusa deuaunt Richard Whityngton nadgairs Mair de Loundrez qe
lez ditz hanappes furont en sa garde et auxi fist serement deuaunt
le dit Mair q'ele monstroit a certein iour a dit William en presence de
mesme le Mair toutz lez estatutz, minimentz, papirs et escriptz de dit
Robert Wynynton touchantz le dit William esteantz en la garde de dite
Alice, douut ele ad soulement monstre vn estatut de C li. ; et ensement
qe la dite Alice de sa frank voluntee deuaunt Richard Marlowe, Alder-
manne de Loundrez, accompta ouesque le dit William de certeins
sommes, parcelles dez sommes suisditz, resceux par le dit Robert et
paiez pur le dit William ; et pur mesme l'accompte fuist troue qe la dite
Alice auoit en sez mayns d'une parcelle dez ditz sommes ensy accomptez
vij li. xviij s.; les queux vii li xviij s. ele offrest a paier a dit William, et
de luy bailler toutz sez minimentz, si le dit William voilloit a luy faire
general acquitance; nient meyns la dite Alice refuse a present toutoutre-
ment pur monstrer lez autres estatutz, minimentz, papirs et escriptz
suisditz, et de faire restitucion a dit William de les hanappes et sommes
auauntditz ou d'ascunz dycellez, a graund arerissement del poeuere
estate de dit suppliant la ou biens et chateux a la value de vj^c marcz

¹ Early Chancery Proceedings, Bundle   is torn off.
17, No. 335. The top right-hand corner   ² This bill probably belongs to Thomas

109

To the right reverend Father in God and most gracious Lord, the Archbishop of Canterbury and Chancellor of England,

1407
to
1409

Humbly beseecheth William Farendon, Knight, that whereas Robert Wynynton, who is dead, formerly general attorney of the said William, received   divers sums of gold and silver in divers parcels, amounting to £521 4s., and also certain statutes and muniments of £450 and more, and also . . . [received] from the said William certain cups of silver, of which some were gilt, to deliver them to Dame de Surgers, and also to receive in the name [of the said William from the said] Dame £22, which William had paid for the said Dame for the cups aforesaid to Robert Thorley, to whom the said Dame had [? pledged the] cups for the sum of £22 aforesaid, as by the said parcels, which the said suppliant will always have ready to show to your gracious Lordship, more fully will appear ; But so it is, most gracious Lord, that, notwithstanding, the said Robert Wynynton never delivered to the said Dame the said cups nor to the suppliant, nor to any one in his name, the said sums, nor any of them ; and that Alice Kelseye, executrix of the will of the said Robert Wynynton of late hath confessed before Richard Whittington, late Mayor of London,[3] that the said cups were in her keeping, and also made oath before the said Mayor that on a certain day she would show to the said William in the presence of the same Mayor all the statutes, muniments, papers and writings of the said Robert Wynynton respecting the said William that were in her keeping, of which she hath only shown one statute of £100 ; and also that the said Alice of her free will before Richard Marlowe, Alderman of London, accounted with the said William for certain sums, parcel of the sums aforesaid, received by the said Robert and paid for the said William ; and by the same account it was found that the said Alice had in her hands, parcel of the said sums so accounted for, £7 18s. ; which £7 18s. she offered to pay to the said William, and also to deliver to him all his muniments, if he would make her a general acquittance ; nevertheless the said Alice doth now entirely refuse to show the other statutes, muniments, papers and writings aforesaid, and to make restitution to the said William of the cups and sums aforesaid, or of any of them, to the great diminishing of the poor estate of the said suppliant, whereas goods and chattels to

de Arundel's fourth Chancellorship, from Jan. 30, 1407, to Dec. 21, 1409.

[3] Lord Mayor 1397, 1406, and 1419. The text probably relates to his second mayoralty.

et pluis queux furent a dit Robert Wynynton, et auxi lez ditz estatutz et minimentz, deuiendront a lez mayns de dite Alice apres la mort le dit Robert Wynynton, la quele Alice est couert de baron d'un Robert Kelsey : Please a vostre tres gracious seignurie d'enuoier pur lez ditz Robert Kelsey et Alice d'estre deuaunt vous en la Chauncellarie a certein iour par vous a limiter d'estre examinee par vostre tres sage discrecion de cest matier et de prendre et resceiuer ceo qe par vostre tres gracious seignurie et tres sage discrecion serra agarde en mesme la matier ; pur Dieu et en oeuere de charitee.

Plegii de prosequendo { Johannes Thomas, \
Johannes Wolffe.

Indorsed.   Infrascripta Alicia per premunicionem sibi ex precepto Cancellarii factam, coram domino Rege in Cancellaria sua comparuit, examinataque predicta Alicia ibidem super contentis in billa infrascripta, ipsa, de aliquibus in eadem billa contentis preterquam de quodam statuto centum librarum et ceteris aliis scriptis que ipsa, vt asseruit, Drugoni Barantyn, Maiori Ciuitatis London', Willelmo Farendon infranominato detulit deliberanda, minime cognouit ; auditaque per dictum Cancellarium examinacione predicte Alicie in hac parte, idem Cancellarius eidem Alice precepit quod si ipsa plura munimenta ipsum Willelmum tangencia inuenire posset, quod tunc munimenta illa eidem Willelmo liberaret ; et super hoc fuit predicta Alicia de eadem Curia per predictum Cancellarium dimissa.

110   [1] A tres reuerent piere en Dieu et soun tres gracious seignur, le Chaunceller d'Engleterre,

robably Supplient humblement William Bardolf, chiualer, Johan Moigne, Henry V. chiualer, et Robert Dreu, qe come ils furent seisez en lour demesne come de fee de le manoir de Brugge [2] deinz l'isle de Wight en la Counte de Suth[t] puis le darrain passage de nostre tres soueraigne seignur le Roy en Normandie [3] et long temps deuaunt, tanque ore tarde q'ils furent forciblement encountre la ley disseisez de le dit manoir par Johan Taillour de Wodyngton en la dit Isle, Johan Rise l'eisne, William Burgham, Wauter Leche, et plusours auters disconuz : Qe pleace a vostre tres gracious seignurie de grauntier as ditz suppliantz seueralx

[1] Bayley's transcripts, vol. i. No. 10. \
Perhaps Brook \
[3] Perhaps for the campaign of 1417. \
[4] Drue Barentyne was Lord Mayor in

1398 and 1408. \
[5] The plaint seems merely one of account, and was apparently brought before the Chancellor, partly because there was no

the value of 600 marks and more, which belonged to the said Robert Wynynton, and also the said statutes and muniments, have come to the hands of the said Alice after the death of the said Robert Wynynton; which Alice is [now] the wife of one Robert Kelsey: May it please your most gracious Lordship to send for the said Robert Kelsey and Alice, to be before you in the Chancery on a certain day by you to be limited, to be examined by your most wise discretion touching this matter, and to take and receive that which by your most gracious Lordship and most wise discretion shall be awarded in the same matter: For God and in way of charity.

Pledges to prosecute
                    John Thomas,
                    John Wolf.

Indorsed. The within written Alice, by a monition made to her on the Chancellor's precept, appeared before the King in his Chancery, and being examined there on the contents of the within written bill, she by no means confessed anything in the bill contained except a certain statute for £100 and certain other writings which she, as she asserts, handed to Drogo Barantyn,[4] Mayor of the City of London, to be delivered to the within named Walter Farendon; and the examination of the said Alice in this behalf having been heard by the Chancellor, the said Chancellor ordered the said Alice that if she could find any more muniments touching the said William, that then she should deliver them to him; and thereupon the said Alice was dismissed by the Chancellor from that Court.[5]

110   To the right reverend Father in God and his most gracious Lord, the Chancellor of England,

'robably   Humbly beseecheth William Bardolf, knight, John Moigne, knight,
Ienry V. and Robert Drew, that whereas they were seised in their demesne as of fee of the manor of Brugge, in the Isle of Wight, in the County of Southampton, after the last passage of our most sovereign Lord the King into Normandy, and a long time before, until now of late they were forcibly and contrary to law disseised of the said manor by John Tailor of Wodyngton, in the said Isle, John Rise the elder, William Burgham, Walter Leech, and many others unknown: May it please your most gracious Lordship to grant to your said suppliants several

privity between the parties, but principally   practice for the defendant to file a written
in order to have *discovery* on oath. The \ answer.
judgment shows that it was not yet the

briefes a 'estre directz a lez ditz Johan Taillour, Johan Rise, William
Burgham et Wauter pur estre deuaunt vous en la Chauncellarie nostre
seignur le Roy a certein iour par vous a estre en celle partie a limite
sur certein peyne a respondre illeosques de la disseisin et tortes
auauntditz : Pur Dieu et en oeuere de charite. Considerantz, tres
gracious seignur, qe lez ditz suppliantz ne purront auoir auter remedie
par la comune ley en l'absence nostre seignur le Roy.

Plegii de prosequendo $\begin{cases} \text{Drugo Bardolf} \\ \text{Thomas Passeware} \end{cases}$

111   ¹ A mon tres reuerent Pier en Dieu et tres
            gracious Seignur, l'Euesque de Wynchestre,
            Chanceller d'Engleterre,²

1413   Ceo vous monstre vostre humble servitour, Thomas Okore, Esquyer,
or   qe come il estoiet enfesant son office south son meistre, Monsire Johan
1414   Daubrygecourt ³ en veilant pur le saufe gard des prisoners esteantz
deins le Toure de Loundres le neopt de Seint Katerine la virgine ⁴
darrein passe, vne Richard Wrothe, Citizen et parmyter de Loundres,
del secte et couyne de Johan Olde Castele, Bachiler, Sire de Cobham,
enuoiast lendemayn ensuant sa femme al dit Toure d'auoir enparle
ouesque certeins prisoners la detenuz pur mesme la secte des certeins
maters et causes les ditz Sire de Cobham et auters de lour secte pur
accomplire lour malueys purpos et entent entouchauntz les ditz
Richard et sa femme, fermement affermantz et disantz qe le jugement
renduz et donez enuers le dit Sire de Cobham estoiet tout outrement
encountre la deuine ley et qe le dit Sire est le fort Bachiler de Dieux,
fauxement foriugez par les Ministres d'anticrist et ses membres : Qe
plese a vostre honurable seignurie et tres sage discrecion qe le dit
Richard soit commys en garde ; Considerant, tres gracious seignur, q'il
est vne de les pluys grantz susteignours del malueys secte suisdite, et
q'il estoiet vne de ceux q'estoient assentuz a son eschape, et en ceo cace
mettre tiel remedie come mielx semble a vostre discrecion, pur eschuer
les bautz inconvenientz q'ent purrient aueigner, qe Dieux defend :
pur Dieuz et en oeure de charite.

----

¹ Early Chancery Proceedings, Bundle 6, No. 37.

² Henry Beaufort ; appointed Mar. 21, 1413; his successor appointed July 23 1417.

³ Appointed Constable of the Tower 1413–1414 ; *Rot. Pat.* 1 Henry V., pt. 3, m. 12.   ⁴ Nov. 25.

⁵ Anything preventing or hindering an action at common law was considered a suffi-

writs to be directed to the said ,ohn Tailor, John Rise, William Burgham and Walter [Leech], [commanding them] to be before you in the Chancery of our Lord the King, on a certain day to be by you limited in this behalf, under a certain pain, to answer then for the disseisin and wrong aforesaid : For God and in way of charity. Considering, most gracious Lord, that the said suppliants can have no other remedy at common law in the absence of our Lord the King.[5]

Pledges for the prosecution :

Drugo Bardolf and
Thomas Passeware.

111 To my right reverend Father in God, and most gracious Lord, the Bishop of Winchester, Chancellor of England,

1413 or 1414

Showeth to you your humble servant, Thomas Okore, esquire, that whereas he was doing his office under his master, Sir John Dabridgcourt, in looking after the safeguard of the prisoners within the Tower of London on the night of S. Katherine the Virgin last past, one Richard Wrothe, citizen and tailor of London, one of the sect and following of John Oldcastle, knight, Lord de Cobham, sent his wife on the morrow following to the said Tower to have speech with certain prisoners there detained for [being of] the same sect, touching certain matters and affairs of the said Lord de Cobham and others of their sect, to accomplish their evil purpose and intent touching the said Richard and his wife, strongly affirming and saying that the judgment rendered and given against the said Lord de Cobham was altogether contrary to divine law, and that the said Lord was the strongest knight[6] of God and falsely forjudged by the ministers of Antichrist and his members : May it please your most honourable Lordship and most wise discretion that the said Richard may be committed to ward, considering, most gracious Lord, that he is one of the greatest sustainers of the evil sect aforesaid, and that he was one of those who were privy to his escape ;[7] and in this case to ordain such remedy as shall seem best to your discretion in order to avoid the grave inconveniences which might happen, which God forbid. For God and in way of charity.[8]

cient reason for applying to the Chancellor.

[6] See p. 50, note 2. The judgment referred to was given Sept. 25, 1413. See Dict. Nat. Biog.

[7] Lord Cobham's escape from the Tower was before Oct. 10, 1413 ; the exact day seems to be uncertain. See Dict. Nat. Biog.

[8] This seems addressed to the Chancellor in his administrative rather than his judicial capacity

[1] A tres reuerent pier en Dieu, l'Euesque de Wyncestre, Chaunceller d'Angleterre,[2]

1415
to
1417
Supplient tres humblement voz poures seruitours si vous plest, Johan Craven et Simond Irby, qe come l'ou ils pristrent certeins prisonners al bataill de Achyngcourt,[3] est ainsi q'un William Bukton, escuier, a force et a tort ad tolu les ditz prisonners des ditz suppliantz et countre lour gree et assent les ad raunsones et deliueres sanz satisfaction ent fait au Roy de ceo que a luy ent appartient, a grand damage et preiudice del droit de mesme nostre tres souuerain seignur le Roy et a outre anientisement des poures estates des ditz suppliantz s'ils n'aient vostre tres socourable aide et seignurie a present ; Et come auxi les ditz suppliantz ount entenduz qe certeine quantitee d'argent amontant environ la somme de CC marcz parcelle del raunson des ditz prisonners est vnqore es maynes d'une Maude Salvayn, femme al Tresorer de Caleys : Please a vostre tres reuerent paternitee en Dieux, graunter as ditz suppliantz brief direct al dit Tresorer de Caleys ly fiermement chargeant et enioygnant qe la dite somme estant es maynes de sa dite femme soit gardee et a nully deliuree iusqes atant qe soit triee par droite et leye a quy appartiendra, et qe nostre dit seignur le Roy ait de ceo sa dehutee, et outree de vostre tres abundant grace faire venir deuaunt vostre tres graciouse presence le dit William Bukton a vous declarer les nouns des ditz prisonners · pur Dieux et en oeure de charitee.[4]

[5] A tres reuerent pier en Dieu, l'Euesque de Wynchestre, Chanceller d'Engleterre,[6]

1413
to
1417
Se pleynt Thomas de Bridsal,[7] tenaunt a nostre seignur le Roy, de Thomas Seyntquyntyn, Esquyer, del Countee d'Euerwyke, qe par l'ou vn Johan Bigge de Fridaythorpe deuaunt ces heures auoit a garder

[1] Early Chancery Proceedings, Bundle 6, No. 76.
[2] See p. 109, note 2.
[3] The battle of Agincourt was fought Oct. 25, 1415.
[4] The remedy here sought is an injunc- tion in the nature of a restraining order. It must be borne in mind that the Treasurer of Calais was a Crown official, and that no doubt he could be restrained from parting with the money without an injunction, strictly so called. Still, inasmuch as he

112

To the right reverend Father in God, the Bishop of Winchester, Chancellor of England,

1415
to
1417

Most humbly beseech your poor servants, if you please, John Craven and Simon Irby, that whereas they took certain prisoners at the battle of Agincourt, so it is that one William Buckton, esquire, hath by force and wrongfully taken the said prisoners from the said suppliants, and against their will and assent hath ransomed them and delivered them up without any satisfaction made thereof to the King of that which belongeth to him, to the great damage and prejudice of the right of the same our most sovereign Lord the King, and to the utter undoing of the poor estates of the said suppliants if they have not your most helpful aid and Lordship now; And whereas also the said suppliants have heard that a certain quantity of money, amounting to nearly the sum of 200 marks, part of the ransom of the said prisoners, is yet in the hands of one Maude Salvayn, the wife of the Treasurer of Calais : May it please your right reverend Paternity in God to grant to the said suppliants a writ directed to the said Treasurer of Calais him firmly charging and enjoining that the said sum, so being in the hands of his said wife, may be kept, and delivered to no one, until it be tried by right and law to whom it belongeth ; and that our said Lord the King may have thereof his duty ; and further of your most abundant grace to cause to come before your most gracious presence the said William Buckton to declare to you the names of the said prisoners. For God and in way of charity.

113

To the right reverend Father in God, the Bishop of Winchester, Chancellor of England,

1413
to
1417

Complaineth Thomas de Bridsall, tenant to our Lord the King, of Thomas Saintquyntyn, esquire, of the County of York, that whereas one John Bigge of Fridaythorp before this time had to keep 307

was not officially under the Chancellor, we may reasonably assume that the order here asked for was an *injunction*, and such as might have been made against any non-official person. The plaintiffs only ask for *discovery* at first. Having obtained the

names, they could file another bill.
⁵ Early Chancery Proceedings, Bundle 6, No. 77.
⁶ See p. 109, note 2.
⁷ See two former bills of h's, cases 36 and 91.

treis centz et sept herbitz, deux chiualx, treis vaches, sis porkes, fur-
ment, orge, pises, aueignes, et plusours auters biens al value de cent
liures, queux furent a dit suppliant a·Fridaythorpe, le dit Thomas
Seyntquyntyn le dit Johan esclaundera q'il fuist son vileyn, l'ou en
veritee il fuist franke ; par cause de quelle esclaundre, come comune
parlaunce y fuist, il morust illeoqes le Demaygne proschein apres la fest
del Conuercion de Seynt Paule, l'an du regne nostre seignur le Roy
H., pier nostre seignur le Roy qu'ore. est, treszisme,[1] le dit Thomas
Seyntquyntyn les biens et chateux suisditz illeosqes le Marsdy adonqes
proschein ensuant prist et amesna a tort et force et armes encountre
la pees nostre dit seignur le Roy le pier, as damages del dit Thomas
de Bridsall de deux centz liures ; d'ouut il prie remedie pur Dieu et
en oeuere de charitee.

Plegii de prosequendo ⎰ Willelmus de Misterton de London,
                       ⎱ Ricardus Reedde de Com' Norff'.

114   [2] A tres reuerent pier en Dieu, l'Euesque de
             Wynchestre et Chaunceller d'Engleterre,[3]

1413   Supplie humblement vostre pouere oratour Johan Badewelle de
to   Boxstede en le Counte de Suff', Esquier, qe come nadgairs pur et
1417   a cause de certeins matiers et couenauntz queux estoient mouez et
       pendauntz parentre Elizabeth, Dame de Clopton, ore tarde femme
       au Monsire Waulter Clopton, Chiualer, qe Dieu assoile, et William
       Clopton, Esquier, d'une parte, et Thomas Badewelle, Esquier, pier du
       dit suppliant, et mesme le suppliant d'autre parte, lez auauntditz
       partiez estoient obligez, chescune partie al autre, par lour obligacions
       en la somme de C li. sur ceste condicion, qe le dit William Clopton
       enfeofferoit le dit Johan Badewelle et Elizabeth sa femme en certeinz
       terrez et tenementz, et auxi qe le dit Thomas Badewelle enfeofferoit le
       dit William Clopton, Johan de Rokewode, Johan Badewelle et autres
       dez autres terres et tenemeniz gisauntz en la ville de Stanton, et
       auxi qe le dit Thomas Badewelle enfeoffaroit Johan de Rokewode,
       Johan Sprotte, William Rokewode et Johan Badewelle en vn Manoir
       nomme Boxstede Halle en le Countee suisdit ; lez quels condicions le

[1] Jan. 25, 13 Henry IV., 1412 ; a Monday.   [4] No special reason appears for applying
[2] Early Chancery Proceedings, Bundle   to the Chancellor.
6, No. 156.   [5] Sir Walter Clopton of Hadleigh and,
[3] See p. 109, note 2.   Wickhambrook, co. Suffolk. His will was

sheep, 2 horses, 3 cows, 6 pigs, wheat, barley, peas, oats, and many
other goods to the value of £100, which belonged to the said suppliant
at Fridaythorp, the said Thomas Saintquyntyn slandered the said John
[Bigge] that he was his villein, whereas in truth he is free ; and he
died there because of that slander, as the common parlance was, on
the Sunday after the feast of the Conversion of S. Paul, in the 13th
year of the reign of our Lord King Henry [IV], the father of our Lord
the King who now is ; and the said Thomas Saintquyntyn seized and
took away the goods and chattels aforesaid there on the Tuesday next
following, wrongfully and with force and arms, against the peace of
our said Lord the King the father, and to the damages of the said
Thomas de Bridsall of £200; of which he prayeth remedy for God
and in way of charity.[4]

Pledges to prosecute :

William de Misterton of London.

Richard Reede of the County of Norfolk.

114 To the right reverend Father in God, the Bishop of Winchester and Chancellor of England,

1413
to
1417

Humbly beseecheth your poor orator, John Badwell of Boxstead, in
the County of Suffolk, esquire, that whereas of late for and because of
certain matters and covenants which were moved and pending between
Elizabeth, Dame de Clopton, late wife [i.e. widow] of Sir Walter Clopton,
knight, whom God assoil,[5] and William Clopton, esquire,[6] of the one
part, and Thomas Badwell, esquire, the father of the said suppliant, and
the said suppliant, of the other part, the aforesaid parties were bound,
each party to the other, by their obligations [bonds], in the sum of
£100, on condition that the said William Clopton should enfeoff the said
John Badwell, and Elizabeth his wife,[7] in certain lands and tenements,
and also that the said Thomas Badwell should enfeoff the said William
Clopton, John de Rookwood, John Badwell, and others, of other lands
and tenements, lying in the town of Stanton ; And also that the said
Thomas Badwell should enfeoff John de Rookwood, John Sprotte,
William Rookwood and John Badwell, of a manor called Boxstead
Hall in the County aforesaid ; which conditions the said Thomas

dated May 5, and proved May 28, 1413.
See *Suffolk Manorial Families*, by J. J.
Muskett, i. 137, 142.
 [6] Son of Sir Thomas Clopton of Kent-

well; he was one of the executors of Sir
Walter's will.
 [7] She was daughter and co-heiress of Sir
Walter.

dit Thomas Badewelle ad accomple et parfourne de sa partie, et a lez
enfeoffamentz quelx lez ditz Elizabeth Clopton, William Clopton eux
ount agreez et consentuz, et la dite Elizabeth Clopton sur ceo au dit
Thomas ad fait vne acquitaunce : Et le quel William Clopton lez ditz
condicions ne le dit feoffement as Johan Badewelle et Elizabeth sa
femme n'ad pas fait ne parfourne soloncque ceo q'ils fuerount accordez,
mez le dit William Clopton ad pursue le dit Johan Badewelle par vne
obligacion forge et contrefait, le ou le dit Johan Badewelle a luy soule
vnqes fuist oblige sinoun au dit Elizabeth Clopton ; et a luy al final
destruccion et anenttisment du dit suppliant as toutz iours s'il en cest
cas ne soit par my vostre tres haut et tres graciouse seignurie [1] remedie :
Que please a vostre tres reuerent paternite et tres graciouse seignurie
de considerer lez premissez et qe le dit William Clopton est graunde
meintenur dez querelx, et sur ceo de grauntier vn brief directe au dit
William Clopton luy enchargeant sur vn certein peyne d'estre deuaunt
vous en la Chauncellarie a vn certein iour par vous allimiter pur estre
examine dez lez matiers suisditz, Et sur sa examinacion luy ensy
iustifier qe le dit suppliant poet auoir due remedie de sez ditz
greuauncez par vostre tres haut et tresage discrecion : pur Dieu et en
oeure de charitee. Consideraunt, tres graciouse Seignur, qe coment
le dit suppliant voudroit suer enuers le dit William Clopton par la
comune ley il ne ueindra iammez a son purpose a cause de graunde
meintenaunce de dit William en celle partie.

115   [2] A tres reuerent, tres noble et tres graciouse
             seignur et pier en Dieu, l'Euesque de
             Wyncestre et Chanceller d'Engleterre,[3]

1413   Monstre tres humblement Johan de Masham, vostre seruitour, et soy
to   greuousment compleint de Thomas Sabarn, Johan Newman, Richard
1417   Webbe, Johan Litelcok, Thomas Terry, Johan Bonser, Johan Snell,
       Thomas Hayward, Johan Lorymer, Johan Lark, William Fox, Johan
       Hale, de Edelmeton en le Countee de Middelsex, et de plousours autres,
       qe come l'ou l'auauntdit suppliaunt auoit de graunt mon tres noble
       seignur de Bemond,[4] qe Dieu assoille, vn manoir en Edelmeton
       suisdite assis ouesque terres, prees, pastures, et autres sez commoditees
       et appurtenauntz, pur le dit manoir discretement gouerner al oeps et
       profit du dit mon tres noble seignur et de ses heirs, et le quel monsire

[1] A word erased here.   See p. 109, note 2.
[2] Early Chancery Proceedings, Bundle   [4] Probably John, Lord Beaumont, who
6, No. 194.   died 1413.

Badwell hath fulfilled and performed on his side, to which enfeoff-
ments the said Elizabeth Clopton [and] William Clopton have
agreed and consented, and the said Elizabeth Clopton hath thereupon
made an acquittance to the said Thomas; The said William Clopton
hath not made and performed the said conditions nor the said feoffment to John Badwell and Elizabeth his wife, according as they were
agreed upon, but the said William Clopton hath sued the said John
Badwell upon a forged and counterfeit obligation [bond], whereas the
said John Badwell was never bound to him alone but [jointly] with
the said Elizabeth Clopton; To the final destruction and undoing
of the said suppliant for ever, if he be not aided in this case by your
most high and gracious Lordship's remedy : May it please your most
reverend Paternity and most gracious Lordship to consider the
premises, and that the said William Clopton is a great maintainer of
quarrels, and thereupon to grant a writ directed to the said William
Clopton charging him under a certain pain to be before you in the
Chancery on a certain day by you to be limited, to be examined
touching the matters aforesaid, and on his examination to so justify
himself that the said suppliant may have due remedy of his said
grievances by your most high and wise discretion : For God and in
way of charity. Considering, most gracious Lord, that howsoever
the said suppliant would sue against the said William Clopton at
common law, he can never come to his purpose, because of the great
maintenance of the said William in those parts.[5]

115   To the most reverend, most noble and most
gracious Lord and Father in God, the Bishop
of Winchester, Chancellor of England,

1413
to
1417
Showeth most humbly John de Masham, your servitor, and grievously
complaineth of Thomas Sabarn, John Newman, Richard Webbe,
John Littelcok, Thomas Terry, John Bonser, John Snell, Thomas
Hayward, John Lorymer, John Lark, William Fox, John Hale of
Edmonton in the County of Middlesex, and of many others, that
whereas the aforesaid suppliant had by grant of my most noble
lord of Beaumont, whom God assoil, a manor situated in Edmonton
aforesaid, with lands, meadows, pastures, and other commodities and
appurtenances, in order to manage the said manor discreetly to the use
and profit of the said most noble Lord and his heirs, and which Lord de

[5] The action would be one of covenant;   applying to the Chancellor.
the last paragraph supplies the reason for

de Bemond est a Dieu comaundez, come tres gracious seignur n'est pas a vous disconuz, et son fitz et heir est garde a nostre tres redoute seignur le Roy,[1] et la garde du quel a vous, tres gracious seignur, par nostre seignur le Roy est assigne, la les auauntditz Thomas, Johan, Richard, Johan, Thomas, Johan, Johan, Thomas, Johan, Johan, William et Johan, et autres malfaisours entour le noumbre de vj[xx], le disme iour de Juyn darrein passee et par autres diuerses temps, se leuerount et viendrerount oue force et armez et encountre le peas nostre seignur le Roy et rumperount suis diuerses pastures, closez et seueralx, et en eux entrerount, et eux fisrent comunes et vnqore fount; et auxi voudroient auoir batuz et tuez l'auauntdit suppliaunt si luy purroient auoir trouez, sibien en graund preiudice et disheriteson de monsire de Bemond, vostre garde, come graund damage du dit suppliaunt, et le pluis a cause des voz biens et chatelx, tres gracious seignur, la lessez, et anientisment del estat du mesme le suppliant, si ne soit remedie et socouree par vostre tres graciouse eide le pluis hastiuement : Si plese a vostre tres reuerent, tres noble et tres graciouse seignurie d'ordeigner remedie pur le contempt et trespas auauntditz faitz et qe les auauntditz trespas et contempt soient si discretement iustifiez, ensi qe tielx trespasse et contempt ore faitz ne soient disheriteson a monsire de Bemond, ore heir et garde, et a ses heirs en temps auenir ; pur Dieu et en oeuere de charitee.

116

[2] A tres reuerent piere en Dieu et son tres gracious seignur, l'Euesque de Wyncestre, Chaunceller d'Engleterre,[3]

1413 to 1417 Supplie humblement vostre pouere Chapellein, Johan Harleston, clerke, fitz et heir a William Harleston, qe come iatarde apres la morte de dit William le dit Johan sur son aler vers Jerusalem, Cristiane miere de dit Johan alors espouse a vn Johan Caltoft, bailla a dite Cristian en priuite parentre mesme celuy Cristian et le dit Johan, a garder tanque a sa reuenue, vne cofre oue certeins euidences et munimentez touchantz l'enheritance de dit Johan et les lettres de ses ordres ensemblement ouesque xl li. de monoie de dit Johan, toutz ensemble contenuz en la dite cofre, et ceo par la graunde affiance q'il auoit en sa dite miere sur toutz autres ; et esteant le dit Johan

<hr/>

[1] He was four years old at his father's death.

[2] Early Chancery Proceedings, Bundle 6, No. 245.

[3] See p. 109, note 2.

[4] It is not alleged that the plaintiff could

Beaumont is dead, as is not unknown to you, most gracious Lord, and his son and heir is in ward to our most redoubted Lord the King, and his wardship is assigned by our Lord the King to you, most gracious Lord, nevertheless the aforesaid Thomas, John, Richard, John, Thomas, John, John, Thomas, John, John, William and John, and other evil-doers to the number of sixscore, on the 10th day of June last past, and at divers other times, did levy themselves, and come with force and arms and against the peace of our Lord the King, and did break up divers pastures, closes, and severalties, and enter therein, and turn them into common, and still so make them; and also they would have beaten and killed the aforesaid suppliant if they could have found him, to the great prejudice and disinherison of my Lord de Beaumont, your ward, as well as to the great damage of the said suppliant, and the more so because of your goods and chattels, most gracious Lord, there left, and to the destruction of the estate of the same suppliant, if he be not remedied and succoured by your most gracious and most speedy aid : May it please your most reverend, most noble, and most gracious Lordship to ordain a remedy for the contempt and trespass done as aforesaid, and that the aforesaid trespass and contempt may be so discreetly rectified that such trespass and contempt now done may not be to the disinherison of my Lord de Beaumont, now heir and ward, nor to his heirs in time to come : For God and in way of charity.[4]

116   **To the right reverend Father in God, and his most gracious lord, the Bishop of Winchester, Chancellor of England,**

1418 to 1417   Humbly beseecheth your poor chaplain, John Harleston, clerk, son and heir of William Harleston, that whereas lately after the death of the said William, the said John, on his setting out for Jerusalem, delivered to Christiana his mother (who was then married to one John Caltoft), privately between themselves, a coffer with certain evidences and muniments concerning the inheritance of the said John and the letters of his orders, together with £40 of his money, all contained in the said coffer, to be kept until his return ; and this through the great trust that he had in his said mother above all others ; and while the said John Harleston was abroad, the said Christiana died ;

not proceed at common law, so that the wardship seems to be the only reason for applying to the Chancellor, except that the   Chancellor himself was interested as guardian of the ward.

Harleston de pardela, la dite Cristian moruist; et combien qe la dite
cofre oue toutz les choses auauntditz contenuz en ycelle deuiendront
as mains de dit Johan Caltoft; et qe le dit Johan Harleston souent
ad requis le dit Johan Caltoft de luy faire restitucion de dit cofre oue
toutz les biens et choses auauntditz; nientmains mesme celuy Johan
Caltoft, pur ceo q'il ne fuist priue ne partie al liuere de dit cofre a sa
dite femme come desuis est dit, en quel cas accion n'est mye
maintenable deuers le dit Johan Caltoft par la comune ley, ascun
restitucion a dit Johan Harleston de dit cofre ou d'ascuns des choses
et biens auauntditz vnqore faire ne voet, a grief damage de dit Johan
Harleston et sa final disheriteson et destruccion s'il ne soit socurrez
par vostre graciouse seignurie la ou comune ley luy faute en ceo cas :
Please a vostre graciouse paternite par consideracion des choses suisditz graunter brief direct a dit Johan Caltoft de comparer deuaunt
vous en la Chauncellarie a certein jour par vous a limiter et luy
examiner de la verite de toutz les choses auauntditz, et sur ceo
ordeigner qe le dit Johan Caltoft soit iusticies [*sic*] come la cas requiert :
pur Dieu et en oeure de charite.

117   [1] A tres reuerent et tres gracious pier en
              Dieu, l'Euesque de Duresme et Chauncellier
              d'Engleterre,[2]

1417   Supplie humblement vostre continuel oratour, Thomas Messynden le
to   puisne, qe come Thomas Messynden soun pier enfeoffa Richard
1424   Pierson, parsone de l'esglise de Hatcleue, Johan West, parsone de
          l'esglise de Bradcley, Johan Barneby de Barton le puisne et Johan See
          de Lytylcotes, en certeins terres et tenementz en la ville de Helyng en
          le Countee de Nicol al value de diz liures par an, sur condicion qe lez
          ditz enfeoffes enfeoffoirent le dit suppliant en lez terres et tenementz
          auantditz al temps q'il viendra al age de xviij anz; et ore le dit
          suppliant est del age de xviij anz et pluis, et il ad require lez ditz
          enfeoffes souentfoitz pur luy enfeoffer es ditz terres et tenementz
          solom la volunte et condicion de soun dit pier; et ils refusent outre-
          ment, et diont q'ils voillent tenir lez ditz terres et tenementz a lour
          oeps demesne : Qe please a vostre tres graciouse seignurie de grauntier
          certeins briefs pur enuoier pur lez ditz enfeoffes sur certeins peynes

[1] Early Chancery Proceedings, Bundle   [2] Thomas Langley; appointed July 23,
5, No. 11.   1417; his successor appointed July 6, 1424.

and although the said coffer, with all the said things contained therein, came to the hands of the said John Caltoft, and the said John Harleston hath often requested the said John Caltoft to make restitution to him of the coffer, with all the goods and things aforesaid; nevertheless the said John Caltoft hitherto will not make any restitution to the said John Harleston of the said coffer nor of any of the things and goods aforesaid, because he was not privy nor party to the delivery of the said coffer to his said wife, as above is said, in which case no action is maintainable against the said John Caltoft at common law, to the grievous damage of the said John Harleston and his final disinherison and destruction, if he be not succoured by your most gracious Lordship where the common law fails him in this case: May it please your most gracious Paternity, on consideration of the matters aforesaid, to grant a writ directed to the said John Caltoft to appear before you in the Chancery on a certain day, by you to be limited, and to examine him as to the truth of all the matters aforesaid, and thereupon to order that the said John Caltoft may be made to do justice as the case requires: For God and in way of charity.[3]

117   To the most reverend and most gracious Father in God, the Bishop of Durham, Chancellor of England,

1417 to 1424   Humbly beseecheth your continual orator, Thomas Messynden the younger, that whereas Thomas Messynden his father enfeoffed Richard Pierson, parson of the church of Hatcliffe,[4] John West, parson of the church of Bradley,[5] John Barneby of Barton the younger, and John See of Little Coates,[5] in certain lands and tenements in the town of Healing[5] in the County of Lincoln, to the value of £10 a year, on condition that the said feoffees should enfeoff the said suppliant in the lands and tenements aforesaid when he should come to the age of 18 years; and now the said suppliant is of the age of 18 years and more, and he hath many times requested the said feoffees to enfeoff him in the said lands and tenements according to the wish and condition of his said father; and they do utterly refuse, and say that they will hold the said lands and tenements to their own use: May it please your most gracious Lordship to grant certain writs to send for

[3] The reason for applying to the Chancellor is sufficiently set out in the bill. The action of detinue is useless, because there is no 'privy' between the parties.
[4] Query; near Grimsby, co. Linc.
[5] Near Grimsby, co. Linc.

par vous a limitez, pur respondre deuaunt vous en la Chauncellarie
et pur y declarer pur qoy ils ne voillent enfeoffer le dit suppliant
solom la volunte et condicion auauntditz; pur Dieu et en oeure de
charite. Considerant, tres gracious seignur, qe le dit suppliant ne
purra auoir ascune recouere al comune ley.

118   [1] Au tres reuerent pere en Dieu et tres
gracious seignur, l'Euesque de Duresme,
Chanceller d'Engleterre,[2]

1417
to
1424
Supplie tres humblement Johan Williamson de Walteham, qe come
vn Robert Teryngton son aiel fuist seisi en son demesne come de fee
de troys mees, iiij toftes, viij boues de terre et dimy et xx acres de
pree oue les appurtenances en Teuelby et Est Rasyn et mesmes les
tenementz dona a Henry de Radford, chiualer, William Beale, parson
de l'esglise de Ireby, Robert de Hatclif, Hugh Clerk, Chapellain,
Richard filtz John filtz Richard de Teuelby, Chapellein, et Thomas de
Wolriby, a auer et tener a eux et a lour heires a toutz iours, a tiel
entent pur parfourner la darrain volunte du dit Robert, et puis
declara sa voluntee, qe si Johan son filz fuist en vie apres sa mort,
qadonqes les ditz feffez duissent doner mesmes les tenementz au dit
Johan et a les beires de son corps engendrez, et qe si le dit Johan
deniast sauns heir de son corps engendre, qadonqes mesmes les feffes
duissent doner mesmes les tenementz a Ade file du dit Robert de
Teryngton a auer et tener a lui et a les heires de son corps engendrez;
et murust; et puis les ditz William et Robert par lour fait relesseront
as ditz Henry, Hugh, Richard et Thomas et a lour heires tout le
droit q'ils auoient en mesmes les tenementz a tiel entent pur parforner
la volunte susdite; puis quel temps le dit Henry murust; et puis les
ditz Richard et Hugh par lour fait relesseront au dit Thomas Wolriby
et a ses heires tout le droit q'ils auoient en mesmes les tenementz al
entent pur parfourner mesme la voluntee. Et puis Thomas Wolriby
auoit issu Henry et murust; quele Henry auoit issu William et murust;
apres qi mort William entra et de mesmes les tenementz enfeffa Iden
Cook, Piers Day, William Medowe, Henry Beale, William de Wathe,

[1] Early Chancery Proceedings, Bundle
5, No. 14.   [2] See p. 114, note 2.
[3] A purely equity matter. As to feoffees

the said feoffees on certain pains by you to be limited, to answer before you in the Chancery, and to declare wherefore they will not enfeoff the said suppliant according to the wish and condition aforesaid ; for God and in way of charity ; considering, most gracious Lord, that the said suppliant can have no recovery at common law.[3]

118

To the right reverend Father in God and most gracious lord, the Bishop of Durham, Chancellor of England,

1417
to
1424

Most humbly beseecheth John Williamson of Waltham,[4] that whereas one Robert Teryngton, his grandfather, was seised in his demesne as of fee of three messuages, four tofts, eight and a half bovates of land and 20 acres of meadow, with the appurtenances in Tevilby[5] and East Rasen,[6] and gave the same tenements to Henry de Radford, knight, William Beale, parson of the church of Irby,[4] Robert de Hatcliffe, Hugh Clerk, chaplain, Richard son of John son of Richard de Tevilby, chaplain, and Thomas de Wolriby, to have and to hold to them and their heirs for ever, to the intent to perform the last will of the said Robert [Teryngton] ; and afterwards he declared his will [to be] that, if John, his son, was living after his death, then the said feoffees should give the same tenements to the said John and the heirs of his body begotten, and if the said John should die without an heir of his body begotten, that then the same feoffees should give the same tenements to Ada, daughter of the said Robert de Teryngton, to have and to hold to her and the heirs of her body begotten ; and [the said Robert] died. And afterwards, the said William [Beale] and Robert [de Hatcliffe] by their deed released to the said Henry [de Radford], Hugh [Clerk], Richard [de Tevilby] and Thomas [de Wolriby], and their heirs, all the right that they [William Beale and Robert de Hatcliffe] had in the same tenements, to the intent to perform the aforesaid will ; after which time, the said Henry [de Radford] died ; and afterwards, the said Richard [de Tevilby] and Hugh [Clerk] by their deed released to the said Thomas Wolriby and his heirs all the right that they had in the same tenements, to the intent to perform the same will. And afterwards, Thomas Wolriby had issue Henry, and died ; which Henry had issue William, and died. After whose death, William entered, and enfeoffed Iden Cook, Peter Day, William Meadow, Henry Beale, William de

to uses see p. 49, note 3.
[4] Co. Linc.

[5] Now generally called Tealby ; co. Linc.
[6] Now Market Rasen ; co. Linc.

et Johan Russell, a tiel entent et purpos pur parfourner mesme la voluntee. Et ensi est qe le dit Johan filz Robert est mort sans heire de son corps, et la dite Ade est mort, par qy les ditz Henry Beale, William de Wathe et Johan Russell, de ce qe a eux atteint de les tenementz susditz solonc l'entent del dit voluntee, ount enfeffez le dit suppliant, filz et heir la dite Ade, a auer et tener a lui et a les heires de son corps engendrez, et les ditz Iden, Piers et William Medowe ne voillent mye en nulle manere le dit suppliant de ce qe a eux atteint enfeffer, ne nul estate ent a lui faire, sicome ils sount tenuz par force du volunte susdite, a graunde damage et desheriteson du dit suppliant s'il ne soit aide par vostre tres gracious seignurie en celle partie. Plese a vostre gracious seignurie de considerer qe le dit suppliant ne poet mye auer remedie par la commune ley, et sur ce enuoier pur les ditz Iden, Piers et William d'estre deuant le Roy nostre tres souerain seignur en sa Chancellarie a certein jour, sur certein peine par vous a limiter, pur illoqes respondre et estre examinez des matiers susditz, et sur ce de les arter et compeller d'enfeffer le dit suppliant de ce qe a eux atteint de les ditz tenementz en accomplisment del volunte auantdite.   Pur Dieu et en oeure de charite.

Plegii de prosequendo
{
Robertus Frende de Com' Lincoln', clericus ;
Patricius Langdale de Com' Lincoln', Gentilman.
}

119   [1] A son tres honure et tres gracious seignur, l'Euesque de Duresme, Chanceller d'Engleterre,[2]

1417 to 1424   Monstre et se pleint William de Flete, qi cy est en propre persone, de Roger Lynster, vn des Clercs escriuantz en la Chancellarie nostre seignur le Roy, de ce qe le dit Roger fraudulousement et deceyuablement ad deceu le dit William et pur ce qe par la ou le dit William le xij iour de Feuerer l'an du regne du Roy H. quart, nadgairs Roy d'Engletcrre, vij[me],[3] en la paroche de Seint Sepulcre hors Neugate en les suburbes de Londres en la garde de Faryngdon extra, retenust le dit Roger d'estre du conseil du dit William sibien en la purchace des manoirs de More et Asshelees [4] ouec les appur-

[1] Early Chancery Proceedings, Bundle 5, No. 84.   [2] See p. 114, note 2.   [3] 1406.   [4] I cannot identify these places.

Wathe and John Russell, in the same tenements, to the intent and purpose to perform the same will. And so it is, that the said John son of Robert [Teryngton] is dead, without heir of his body, and the said Ada is dead, by reason whereof the said Henry Beale, William de Wathe and John Russell, as far as concerns them, have enfeoffed the said suppliant, son and heir of the said Ada, in the tenements aforesaid, according to the intent of the said will, to have and to hold to him and the heirs of his body begotten ; but the said Iden [Cook], Peter [Day] and William Meadow will not in any wise enfeoff the said suppliant of that which concerns them,[5] nor make any estate therein to him, as they are bound [to do] by force of the aforesaid will, to the great damage and disinherison of the said suppliant, if he be not aided by your most gracious Lordship in this behalf : May it please your most gracious Lordship to consider that the said suppliant can have no remedy at common law, and thereupon to send for the said Iden, Peter and William, to be before the King, our most sovereign Lord, in his Chancery at a certain day and under a certain pain, by you to be limited, there to answer and be examined touching the matters aforesaid, and thereupon to oblige and compel them to enfeoff the said suppliant of that which concerns them in the said tenements, in fulfilment of the aforesaid will. For God and in way of charity.[6]

Pledges to prosecute :

> Robert Frende of the County of Lincoln, clerk.
> Patrick Langdale of the County of Lincoln, gentleman.

119 ## To his most honoured and most gracious Lord, the Bishop of Durham, Chancellor of England,

1417 to 1424

Showeth and complaineth William de Flete, who is here in his proper person,[7] of Roger Lynster, one of the Writing Clerks in the Chancery of our Lord the King, that the said Roger hath fraudulently and deceitfully deceived the said William, because whereas the said William on the 12th day of February in the 7th year of the reign of King Henry IV., late King of England,[3] in the parish of S. Sepulchre without Newgate, in the suburbs of London, in Ward of Farringdon Without, retained the said Roger to be of counsel with the said William (in the purchase of the manors of More and Ashleys, with the appur-

---

[5] A moiety of the legal estate was in them. feoffees to uses see p. 49, note 3.
[6] A similar case to the last one. As to   [7] See p. 37, note 5.

tenances en Countee de Hertford par le dit William de Thomas
Wybesnade et Katerine sa femme adonques bargainez, come pur la
deffens des ditz manoirs enuers vn Johan Impey et Johane sa femme
et touz autres claymantz aucune title en icelles manoirs, et enuers vn
Johan atte More de Rykmersworth, pur xiij souldz iiij d. et vne bourse
pris xx d., les queux xiij s. iiij d. et le dit bourse le dit William dona au
dit Roger en les paroche et suburbes susdites le dit xij iour de Feuerer
l'an vij⁰ susdite par les susdites causes, et apres le dite retenue ensi
fate, le dit Roger ymaginant fraudulousement deceiuer le dit William,
mesme le Roger conoissant q'il tenoit des ditz Thomas et Katerine
come de droit de la dite Katerine de lour manoir de Asshelees susdit
vn mees, clx acres de terre ouec les appurtenances en la dite ville de
Rykmersworth par homage et foialtee et par seut a la court a la dite
manoir de Asshelees de trois semaignes en trois semaignes et par les
seruices de vij s. par an paiables annuelement a la feste de Seint
Michel, le dit xij iour de Feuerer l'an vij⁰ susdite en les paroche et
garde susdites, conseilla le dit William qe mesme celui Roger serroit
enfeffez ouec le dit William et ouec diuerses autres en les manoirs
susdites, a auoir a eux et as heirs du dit William, en sachant et conoissant le susdit Roger alors et illoeques par le susdit feffement le dit
William serroit excludez des rent et seruices susditz ; Et ce le dit
William alors outrement ignorant ; Et sur ce le dit William aiant
affiance en le conseil du dit Roger, fist le dit Roger par les ditz Thomas
et Katerine estre enfeffez ouec mesme celui William et pluseurs autres
en les ditz manoirs a l'oeps du dit William, a auoir a eux et as heirs du
dit William, par la cause de quel feffement les ditz rentz et seruices
sont exteintz, paront le dit William est deceu et endamagez a tort et a
ses damages de C. li dont il prie de remede.

120   ¹ A tres reuerent pier en Dieu, l'Euesque de
           Duresme, Chaunceller d'Engleterre,²

1417 Suppliount humblement Johan Sparowe et Thomas Codyngton, naid-
to   gairs viscountz de la cite de Nicol, qe come vn Johan Ouresby, clerk, par
1424   noun de Johan Ouresby de Nicol, clerk, deuaunt les Justices de la pees

¹ Early Chancery Proceedings, Bundle   ² See p. 114, note 2.
5, No. 146.   ³ *Fraud* and *deceit* are here the grounds

tenances, in the County of Hertford, by the said William from Thomas Wybesnade and Katherine his wife, then agreed upon, as well as for the defence of the said manors against one John Impey and Joan his wife, and against all others claiming any title to those Manors, and against one John at More of Rickmansworth), for 13s. 4d. and a purse price 20d., which 13s. 4d. and the purse the said William gave to the said Roger in the parish and suburbs aforesaid on the said 12th day of February in the said 7th year, for the causes aforesaid; And after the said retainer so made, the said Roger, scheming fraudulently to deceive the said William, (knowing that he [Roger] held of the said Thomas [Wybesnade] and Katherine his wife, as of the right of the said Katherine, of their manor of Ashleys aforesaid a messuage and 160 acres of land with the appurtenances in the said town of Rickmansworth, by homage and fealty and by suit at the court of the said manor of Ashleys from three weeks to three weeks, and by the services of 7s. a year, payable annually at Michaelmas), on the said 12th day of February, in the said 7th year, in the parish and Ward aforesaid, did advise the said William that he, the said Roger, should be enfeoffed, together with the said William and divers others, in the manors aforesaid, to have to them and to the heirs of the said William; the said Roger then and there knowing and being aware that the said William would by the aforesaid feoffment be excluded from the rents and services aforesaid, of which the said William was then entirely ignorant; And thereupon the said William, having trust in the counsel of the said Roger, caused the said Roger to be enfeoffed together with the said William and many others, in the said manors by the said Thomas and Katherine, to the use of the said William, to have to them and to the heirs of the said William; By reason of which feoffment, the said rents and services are extinguished; whereby the said William is deceived and damaged wrongfully, and to his damages of £100: Of which he prayeth remedy.[3]

120   To the most reverend Father in God, the Bishop of Durham, Chancellor of England,

1417 to 1424   Humbly beseech John Sparrow and Thomas Codyngton, late Sheriffs of the City of Lincoln, that whereas one John Ouresby, clerk, by the name of John Ouresby of Lincoln, clerk, was indicted before the

for applying to the Chancellor. There seems to be also a suggestion that the clerk of the Chancery, acting as counsel, was specially under the Chancellor's supervision.

du mesme la cite de diuerses felonies en la dit cite fuist enditez, par cause du quelle enditement les ditz suppliants, adonqes esteants viscountz de mesme dit cite, certeins biens et chateux du dit Johan Ouresby en noun de nostre seignur le Roy deins la dit cite esteantz seiserount par encheson qe l'auaunt dit Johan Ouresby soy retr[ait] hors de la dit cite par cause de la felonie suisdit, les queux Justices de la pees sur les enditements suisditz encountre mesme dit Johan Ouresby solome la cours de la comune ley firent proces, cele proces deuaunt eux ent continue tanque le dit Johan Ouresby estoit mys en exigent, par caus de quelle les ditz biens et chateux remainerent es mains des ditz suppliantz come biens forfaites a Roy par caus suisdit; Pur cause de quelle seiser et retiner des ditz biens, l'auauntdit Johan Ouresby esteant es parties pardela ore tarde ad sue vn citacion en la Court de Rome encountre les ditz suppliantz et eux par vn Richard Ouresby, procuratour du dit Johan Ouresby, et vn Johan Clyfton, clerk, procuratour et notery a mesme Johan Ouresby, par force de la citacion suisdit ad fait somoner d'apparoir en la Court de Rome deuaunt l'Appostoille le cinqantisme iour apres la citacion a eux ensy fait, a graunt vexacion et aneintisment des ditz suppliantz et encountre la fourme des statutz en tielx cases purueus: Please a vostre treseint paternite et gracious seignurie de grauntier as ditz suppliantz briefs desouth peins par vous a limiters sueeralment directes as ditz Richard et Johan Clyfton, eux chargeant d'estre deuaunt vous en la Chauncellarie a vn certein iour, pur y estre examinez de la matier suisdit, et fair et resceiver cea qe la Court agardera en cest partie; pur Dieu et en eour de charite.

Plegii de prosequendo {Robertus Walssh,
Ricardus Duffeld.

121   [1] A tres reuerent piere en Dieu et son tres gracious seignur, l'Euesque de Duresme, Chaunceller d'Engleterre,

1420 to 1422 Supplie tres humblement William Burton seruant Maistre Robert Burton, clerk, vn de voz Chapellayns, et soy greuousement compleynt de Lodewyke Gryville de Countee d'Oxenford, qe come vn Robert

[1] Early Chancery Proceedings Bundle 5, No. 175.   [2] See p. 114, note 2.

Justices of the Peace of the said City for divers felonies in the said City ; and on account of that indictment, the said suppliants (being then Sheriffs of the same City) seized certain goods and chattels of the said John Ouresby, being within the said City, in the name of our Lord the King, by reason that the aforesaid John Ouresby withdrew from the said City because of the felony aforesaid ; the which Justices of the Peace upon the said indictments against the said John Ouresby made process according to the course of the common law, which process was continued before them until the said John Ouresby was put in exigent ; by reason whereof the said goods and chattels remained in the hands of the said suppliants as goods forfeited to the King for the cause aforesaid ; and on account of this seizing and retaining of the said goods, the aforesaid John Ouresby, being abroad, hath now of late sued a citation in the Court of Rome against the said suppliants, and by one Richard Ouresby, procurator of the said John Ouresby, and by one John Clifton, clerk, procurator and notary to the same John Ouresby, by force of the citation aforesaid, hath caused them to be summoned to appear in the Court of Rome before the Pope on the fifteenth day after the citation so made to them, to the great vexation and detriment of the said suppliants and contrary to the form of the Statutes in such cases provided :[3] May it please your most holy Paternity and most gracious Lordship to grant to the said suppliants writs, under pains to be limited by you, severally directed to the said Richard and John Clifton, charging them to be before you in the Chancery at a certain day, to be there examined as to the matter aforesaid, and to do and receive what the Court shall award in this behalf ; For God and in way of charity.[4]

Pledges for the prosecution :

Robert Walsh,
Richard Duffield.

121   To the right reverend Father in God, and his most gracious Lord, the Bishop of Durham, Chancellor of England,

1420 to 1422   Beseecheth most humbly William Burton, servant to Master Robert Burton, clerk, one of your chaplains, and grievously complaineth of Ludovic Greville, of the County of Oxford, that whereas one Robert

[3] The Statutes of Provisors ; see p. 96, note 3.   [4] Compare this with case No. 101, under the same statutes.

Archer, nadgairs de Wyncestre, marchaunt, par assent et abbectement du dit Lodewyke, vn Alice Wodeloke, file et heir aparant Pernelle femme le dite suppliant, mesme la file del age de vij aunz esteant, a Colyngbourne deinz le Countee de Wiltes' en la garde d'un Richard Santon[1] par le dite suppliant commys trouez, le marsdy procheyn deuant le fest del Ascension nostre Seignur, l'an du regne nostre souerayn seignur le Roy q'or'est oetisme,[2] forciblement et encountre la pees mesme nostre seignur le Roy rauysa, et d'illeoqes al meason du dit Lodewyke a Drayton deinz le Countee d'Oxenford amenast; le quele Lodewyke mesme la Alice vnqore detient atort et encountre ley, reson et bone conscience et encountre la voluntee le dite suppliant, et ne voet la dite Alice deliuerer al dite suppliant s'il ne ferreit fyn ouesque le dite Lodewyke par xl marcz et relesser par son escript a dite Robert tout le dette qe le dite Robert doit a mesme le suppliant, atort et as damages le dite suppliant de C marcz et tres graund arrerisment de son pouere estate s'il ne soit par vous tres gracious seignur eidez en cest partie : Please a vostre tres graciouse seignurie considerer cest mater et sur ceo ordeigner en ycelle mater qe le dite suppliant eit restitucion del dite Alice come ley et conscience demandent oue lour damages en celle partie; pur Dieu et en eouere de charitee.

At the foot. Consideratum quod filia fuit in custodia sua tempore quo predictus Willelmus fuit secum in domo sua, et quod ipse eandem filiam saluo custodiret nisi ipsa extra custodiam suam furata foret.[3]

Indorsed. Dies datus est ei vsque ad octabas Sancti Michaelis proximo futuri sub pena quadraginta librarum.

122   [4] A tres sage et tres graciouse seignur, le Chaunceler d'Engleterre,

1422
to
1426
Supplie tres humblement vostre poeuere oratrice, la Prioresse de Noneyns de Thetford,[5] qe come vn Thomas Empole entour xxvj ans passez enfeffa Nicholas Wychyngham et autres ore mortz en le manoir de Westhale en le Counte de Suff', quel fust de value de x li. par an, al entent de parfourner sa darrein volunte, quel fuist q'il enmortizereit le dit manoir as Noneyns de dit lieu ou le vendre a lour

---

[1] Or Sauton.
[2] Henry V., 1420. Ascension Day fell on May 16.
[3] This seems to be a note added perhaps by one of the Clerks of the Chancery. Its meaning is not very clear.
[4] Early Chancery Proceedings, Bundle 68, No. 134.

Archer, late of Winchester, merchant, with the assent and abetment of the said Ludovic, did, on the Tuesday next before the feast of the Ascension of our Lord in the 8th year of the reign of our sovereign Lord the present King, forcibly and against the peace of the same our Lord the King, ravish one Alice Wodeloke, daughter and heir apparent of Parnell, the wife of the said suppliant, the same daughter being of the age of 7 years, and being found at Collingburn in the County of Wiltshire, in the ward of one Richard Santon, [to whom she was] committed by the said suppliant, and thence brought her to the house of the said Ludovic at Drayton, in the County of Oxford ; and the said Ludovic still detaineth the same Alice, wrongfully, and against law, right and good conscience, and against the will of the said suppliant ; and will not deliver the said Alice to the said suppliant unless he will make fine with the said Ludovic for 40 marks and [also] release by his writing to the said Robert [Archer] all the debt which the said Robert oweth the same suppliant; [and this] wrongfully and to the damage of the said suppliant of 100 marks, and to the great detriment of his poor estate if he be not aided by you, most gracious Lord, in this behalf: May it please your most gracious Lordship to consider this matter, and thereupon to ordain that the said suppliant may have restitution of the said Alice, as law and conscience demand, with their damages in this behalf: For God and in way of charity.

At the foot. It is considered that while the said William [Burton] was with her in his house the daughter was in his wardship, and that he should safely keep the said daughter, unless she should be stolen from his custody.

Indorsed. A day is given him [the defendant] on the octave of Michaelmas next, under a penalty of £40.[6]

122   To the most wise and most gracious Lord, the Chancellor of England,

1422
1 to 26
4
Most humbly beseecheth your poor oratrix, the Prioress of the Nuns of Thetford, that whereas one Thomas Empole about 26 years past enfeoffed Nicholas Wychyngham and others now dead of the manor of Westhall, in the County of Suffolk, which was of the value of £10 by the year, to the intent to perform his last will, which was that he would grant the said manor to the Nuns of the said place in mortmain,

---

[5] Benedictine nuns ; see Tanner, Blome-field's *Norfolk*, Martin's *Thetford*.

[6] No reason appears why this matter should be brought before the Chancellor. It is doubtful whether the plaintiff had any right of action at common law, since he was not the girl's father; he appears, however, to have been her guardian in right of his wife ; the wife was not dead apparently.

oeps et profyt; ly quel Nicholas le ad garde en sa mayn et pris lez
profitz a soun oeps demesne, tanque ore tarde q'il le ad vendu pur
ix^{xx} marcz, lez qeux, oue lez issues et profitz en le dit mesne temps,
il retient a luy mesmes, et ent rien ne paie as ditz suppliauntz : Qe
please a vostre tres graciouse seignurie d'enuoier vn brief sub pena au
dit Nicholas q'il soit en propre persone deuaunt vous al oeptas de Seint
Trinite de respoundre a ceo qe luy serra surmys en la matier suisdit,
et ceo pur Dieu et en oeuere de charitee.

Indorsed. xv° die Maii .anno predicto [1] apud Westm' concessum
est quod dirigatur breve Nicholao Wychyngham infrascripto de essendo
coram Consilio Regis in xv^a Trinitatis proximo, reponsurus hiis que ei
tunc obicientur, et ad faciendum ulterius, etc., sub pena C li.; presentibus Dominis Duce Exon',[2] Archiepiscopo Cant', Winton' et Wygorn' Episcopis, Comite Warr', Fits Hugh, Cromewell', Tiptoft, Cancellario et Thesaurario.

At the foot of the bill. xv^a Trinitatis coram nobis et Consilio.

B. *FRENCH PETITIONS—UNDATED.*

123   [3] A le Chaunceller d'Engleterre,

s.d. Supplie humblement Johan Horsmonger qe come vn Johan Pecham
enfeffa Reynald Pympe et Walter Judde entre autres en certeins
terres et tenementz en la Countee de Kent sur certeins condicions,
entre queux il est contenuz qe la volente du dit Johan Pecham fuist
qe qaunt les ditz terres furent venduz celluy qi fuist prochein del sang
du dit Johan Pecham, au quel le heritage des terres et tenementz de-
scenderoit, auroit xl *li.* pur releuer son estat ; les quelles terres et tenementz sount ore venduz par les ditz feffez pur VC marcz, la quel some
le dit Reynald ad en sa propre garde ; Et [com]bien qe le dit suppliant come cousyn [4] et heir au dit Johan Pecham, c'est assauoir, fitz

---

[1] No year has been mentioned.
[2] Thomas Beaufort, son of John of Gaunt,
created Duke of Exeter 1416, died 1426.
He does not appear to have sat frequently
on the Council until after the death of Henry
V., but from that time until his death his
attendances were very numerous. See

Nicolas, *Proc. and Ord.*, vol. iii. *passim.*
This bill is probably, therefore, between
1422 and 1426.
[3] Early Chancery Proceedings, Bundle
68, No. 3.
[4] Cousin does not imply the exact rela-
tionship with which we associate the word ;

or sell it for their use and profit; the which Nicholas hath kept it in his own hands and hath taken the profits to his own use, until now of late that he hath sold it for ninescore marks, which, together with the issues and profits for the meantime, he retaineth for himself, and hath paid nothing thereof to the said suppliants : May it please your most gracious Lordship to send a writ of *sub pena* to the said Nicholas that he be in his proper person before you on the octave of Holy Trinity to answer to what shall be submitted against him in the matter aforesaid, and this for God and in the way of charity.

Indorsed. May 15th, in the year aforesaid, at Westminster, it is granted that a writ be directed to the within-written Nicholas Wychyngham, [commanding him] to be before the King's Council on the quindene of Trinity next, to answer to those things which shall then be objected against him, and further to do, &c., under a penalty of £100.

Present : the Lords, the Duke of Exeter, the Archbishop of Canterbury, the Bishops of Winchester and Worcester, the Earl of Warwick, [Lords] Fitz Hugh, Cromwell and Tiptoft, the Chancellor and the Treasurer.

At the foot of the bill. The quindene of Trinity before us and the Council.[5]

B. *FRENCH PETITIONS—UNDATED.*

123 To the Chancellor of England,

s.d. Humbly beseecheth John Horsmonger that whereas one John Pecham enfeoffed Reginald Pympe and Walter Judde, amongst others, in certain lands and tenements in the County of Kent, upon certain conditions, amongst which it was contained that the wish of the said John Pecham was that when the said lands were sold he who should be the nearest of blood to the said John Pecham, to whom the heritage of the lands and tenements should descend, should have £40 to relieve his estate; which lands and tenements have now been sold by the said feoffees for 500 marks, which sum the said Reginald has in his keeping; And although the said suppliant, as kinsman and heir to the said John Pecham, that is to say, son of Thomas Horsmonger, son of

it means simply kinsman, *consanguineus.*

[5] The case is similar to several of the previous ones concerning feoffees to uses; see page 49, note 3. The interesting part is the indorsement, where the defendant is summoned before the Council, notwithstanding that the bill is addressed to the Chancellor, and asks that the defendant may appear before him.

Thomas Horsmonger, fitz Thomas Horsmonger, fitz Anneys, iadys femme a Geffrey Horsmonger, soer a Thomas Pecham, piere au dit Johan Pecham, le dit suppliant ad souent foitz requis le dit Reynald de luy paier et deliuerer les ditz xl *li*. solonque la volente du dit Johan Pecham ; nientmains il ne voet paier a luy nulle denier de ces, a graund damage du dit suppliant : Et soit il, tres reuerent [seignur], qe le dit suppliant ne purra auoir remedie celle partie par la ley de Seinte Esglise ne par la comune ley de la terre : Please a vostre tres gracious seignurie, al honeur de Dieu et en accompt de droiture, grauntier briefs de faire venir deuaunt vous les ditz Walter et Raynald en la Chauncellarie du Roy, q'est court de Conscience,[1] pur respoundre ent illoesqes come reson et conscience demandent, ou autrement le dit suppliant est et serra saunz remedie, qe Dieu defende.

Plegii de prosequendo {Johannes Richelot de Kyngeston, Willelmus Halle de Com' Surr'.

124   [2] A son tres graceouse seignur, le Chaunceller d'Engleterre,

s.d. Supplie humblement Johan Shorter, Taillour, qe come le dit Johan de malice et grande enmyte est arestez et enprisonez deinz la citee de Londres et ne poet auoir notice del cause de son emprisonement, Sur quoy plese a vostre tres graceouse seignurie pur granter vn brief pur auoir le dit suppliant deuaunt vous en la Chauncellarie oue la cause de son emprisonement :[3] Pur Dieu et en eouere de charitee.

125   [4] A le Chaunceller d'Engleterre,

s.d. Supplie treshumblement Johan de la Rue, factour et attorne de Johan de la Mote, Mayr d'Estaples en Pycardie, et Henry de Mount Henry, burgeys de mesme la vyle, qe come les ditz burgeyses firent charger en vne nief de Brytaigne, dount estoit possessour Juon Lescaut, xxxix toneux de vyn de Nantes et xx milliers[5] de feer, et auters merchan- dises, de les amesner au dit ville d'Estaples ; et sicome mesme la nief fuist segland en le mier deuers la dite ville d'Estaples ouesque les

---

[1] It is much to be regretted that the document containing this interesting expression is not dated. The earliest quotation given in the *N. E. D.* is 1603.

[2] Early Chancery Proceedings, Bundle 68, No. 4.

[3] The writ of *corpus cum causa*.

[4] Early Chancery Proceedings, Bundle 68, No. 22.

[5] I cannot find this word anywhere. It

Thomas Horsmonger, son of Agnes, late wife of Geoffrey Horsmonger and sister to Thomas Pecham, father of the said John Pecham, hath oftentimes requested the said Reginald to pay and deliver the said £40 to him, according to the wish of the said John Pecham; nevertheless he will not pay him a penny of it, to the great damage of the said suppliant: And so it is, most reverend [Lord], that the said suppliant cannot have any remedy in this behalf by the law of Holy Church,[6] nor by the common law of the land : May it please your most gracious Lordship, in honour of God and on account of righteousness, to grant writs to cause the said Walter and Reginald to come before you in the King's Chancery, which is the Court of Conscience, there to answer thereto as reason and conscience demand, otherwise the said suppliant is and will be without remedy, which God forfend.

Pledges for the prosecution { John Richelot of Kingston.
William Hall of Surrey.

124   To his most gracious Lord, the Chancellor of England,

s.d. Humbly beseecheth John Shorter, tailor, that whereas the said John of malice and great enmity hath been arrested and imprisoned within the City of London, and cannot obtain notice of the cause of his imprisonment : Whereupon may it please your most gracious Lordship to grant a writ to have the said suppliant before you in the Chancery, together with the cause of his imprisonment : For God and in way of charity.

125   To the Chancellor of England,

s.d. Humbly beseecheth John de la Rue, factor[7] and attorney of John de la Mote, Mayor of Etaples in Picardy, and Henry de Mount Henry, Burgess of the same town, that whereas the said Burgesses loaded in a ship of Brittany, the owner of which was Juan Lescaut, 39 tuns of Nantes wine, and 10 tons [?] of iron, and other merchandise, to bring them to Etaples ; and as the said ship was sailing on the sea towards the said town of Etaples with the merchandise aforesaid, there came upon the

appears to mean a 'thousand-weight,'
equivalent to ten hundredweight, or half a
ton. The total shipment of iron would
thus be ten tons.

[6] Not being a testamentary matter.
[7] Factor as the equivalent of 'agent' is
still used in Scotland.

merchandises suisditz, survenoit mesme la nief vn Bartilmewe Foult, maistre d'un graunt holke d'armee d'Almaigne, ouesque ses compaignons, et pristrent la dite nief, et ycelle ouesque les merchandises suisditz ount amesnuz en le Royaume d'Engleterre, et illoesqes ount venduz beucope des ditz merchandises, c'est assauoir, a Johan Benet de Apuldre en le Counte de Kent, quatre millers de fer, et a Johan Wynchelse de Apuldre en mesme le Counte, ferrour, viij millers de fer, et a Andrew Helewyn, parson de Promell,[1] quatre millers de fer, et a William Sales de Ledys en dite Countee, mariner, deux millers de feer, a graunde damage des ditz Johan de la Mote et Henry s'ils ne soient par vous, gracious seignur, a leur biens restorez : Que plese a vostre tres noble grace de considerer les premises, et sur ceo de grauntier briefs adressez as ditz Johan Benet, Johan Wynchelse, Andrewe et William d'estre deuaunt vous au certein iour par vous a limiter et sur certein peine, a monstrer pur quoy les ditz biens et merchandises ne deyuant estre restores a les merchantz suisditz.

126

s.d. [2] Please a vous tres gracious et tres reuerent seignur de remembrer de certeinz debates queux sount pendauntez deuaunt vous parentre Nicholas Carreu et Robert Thresk, clerk, touchauntz certeinz terrez, et de examiner par vostre tres sage discrecion Richard Wakehurst, Johan Fecher et Waulter Vrre d'un feoffement de mesme la terre fait a tres haut seignur Thomas, Count d'Aroundelle, qi Dieu assoille,[3] par le dit Robert, c'est assauoir, si le dit Thomas fuist soul seisi de mesme la terre ou ioynt ouesque vn Johan Fitz Piers et le dit Richard ou noun ; et auxi pur examiner Rauf Codyngton, esquier, et Johan Roo, clerk, quel temps Johan Lungeley, citezein de Loundres, enfeoffa le dit Johan Roo en lez terres auauntditz : et ceo pur Dieu et en eouere de charite.

127

[4] A tres reuerent piere en Dieu, Chaunceller d'Englitere,

s.d. Supplie humblement vostre pouer oratour William Monye de Wodedallyng en le Counte de Norff', qe par la vn Simon Aylward de mesme

---

[1] I cannot identify this place.
[2] Early Chancery Proceedings, Bundle 68, No. 26.
[3] He died Oct. 13, 1415.

[4] Early Chancery Proceedings, Bundle 68, No. 39.
[5] As to these cases of foreign merchants see p. 4, note 3. It seems rather hard on

said ship one Bartholomew Foult, master of a great armed hulk from Germany, with his companions, and took the said ship, and they have brought it and the said merchandise to the kingdom of England, and there have sold much of the merchandise, that is to wit, to John Bennet of Appledore in the County of Kent, 2 tons [?] of iron, and to John Winchelsea of Appledore in the same County, smith, 4 tons of iron, and to Andrew Helewyn, parson of Promell, 2 tons [?] of iron, and to William Sales of Leeds in the said County, mariner, 1 ton [?] of iron, to the great damage of the said John de la Mote and Henry, if they be not restored to their goods by you, gracious Lord : May it please your most noble grace to consider the premises, and thereupon to grant writs addressed to the said John Bennet, John Winchelsea, Andrew and William, [commanding them] to be before you on a certain day by you to be limited, and under a certain pain, to show wherefore the said goods and merchandise should not be restored to the aforesaid merchants.[5]

126

s.d. May it please you, most gracious and reverend Lord, to remember certain disputes which are pending before you between Nicholas Carrew and Robert Thresk, clerk, touching certain lands, and to examine by your most wise discretion Richard Wakehurst, John Fecher and Walter Urre as to a feoffment of the same land made to the most high lord, Thomas, Earl of Arundel, whom God assoil, by the said Robert, that is to say, whether the said Thomas was seised of the said land solely, or jointly with John FitzPiers and the said Richard [Wakehurst], or not ; and also to examine Ralph Codington, Esquire, and John Roo, clerk, as to when John Longley, Citizen of London, enfeoffed the said John Roo in the lands aforesaid : and this for God and in way of charity.[6]

127   To the most reverend Father in God, the Chancellor of England,

s.d. Humbly beseecheth your poor orator, William Monye of Wood Dalling in the County of Norfolk, that whereas one Simon Aylward

---

the defendants, who, for anything that appears to the contrary, were innocent purchasers for value.

[*] This appears to be supplementary to some other proceedings.

la ville fuist ɛeisi de certeinz terrez et tenementz in mesme la ville
de Wodedallyng, et de mesmez lez terrez et tenementz enfeffa Richard
Hendrys et Thomas Trey a l'entent de parformer sa darrein volunte ;
le quel Simon in son list murant fist sa darrein volunte qe Thomas
Aylward son f[iltz] aueroit lez ditez terrez et tenementz a luy et a
sez heirez a toutz iours ; le quel Thomas Aylward par assent dez
ditez feffez vendist lez ditz terrez et tenementz al dit Suppliaunt
pur certein summe a paier a certeinz iours parentre eux acordez ; et
lez feffes sur mesme la contract ₐ greer de faire estat en fee de
mesmez lez terrez et tenementz al dit Suppliaunt quant ils furent ent
par luy requis ; Et nient obstant qe le dit Suppliaunt ad paie graunt
partie del dit summe as ditz iours et prist est de trouer sufficeaunt
suerte de paier le remenaunt as iours parentre eux limitez, lez ditz
feffeez de faire estat dez ditz terrez et tenementz al dit Suppliaunt tut
outrement refusont, nient obstant qe le dit Suppliaunt eux souent ad
requis de ceo faire : Please a vostre tres gracious seignurie de considerer
lez premissez et qe le dit Suppliaunt n'ad ent remedie al comune lay,
et de graunter seuerals briefs sur certein peine directe as ditz Richard
et Thomas Treye de comparer deuaunt vous a certein iour, et d'estre
examinez sur ycestez ; et sur celle examinacion de faire droit estre
fait al dit Suppliaunt, pur Dieu et en ouer de charite.

128   ¹ A tres gracious seignur, le Chaunceller,
d'Engletere,

s.d. Supplie humblement vostre pouere oratour, Rauf Fryday, qe come le
brace dextere du dit suppliant par certe [?] de certeines maufaisours, qi
gesoient en gait de luy tuer, fuist debruse, le quel brace bien et duement curer et sauuer vn Johan West de Leycestre a Wykyngston ² enprist ;
le quel Johan son cure entour le dit brace si noun duement de malice
et couyn des enemyes du dit suppliant fesoit, qe le dit brace corupt et
incurable deuient, en perpetuel destruccion du dit suppliant : Qe please
a vostre tres graciouse seignurie de graunter an dit suppliant vn brief
direct a dit Johan West d'apperer deuaunt vous en la Chauncellarie en
le oeptas del Purificacion Nostre Dame, sur peyne de quarant liueres,
d'estre examine par lez surgeans nostre seignur le Roy et pur autres

¹ Early Chancery Proceedings, Bundle   ² Probably   Great   Wigston,   near,
68, No. 44.   Leicester.

of the same town was seised of certain lands and tenements in the same town of Wood Dalling, and of the same lands and tenements enfeoffed Richard Hendrys and Thomas Trey to the intent to perform his last will; which Simon dying in his bed made his last will that Thomas Aylward his son should have the said lands and tenements to him and his heirs for ever; which Thomas Aylward with the assent of the said feoffees sold the said lands and tenements to the said suppliant, for a certain sum to be paid at certain days agreed between them; and the feoffees on the same contract agreed to make an estate in fee of the same lands and tenements to the said suppliant when they were required by him [to do so]; and notwithstanding that the said suppliant hath paid a great part of the said sum on the said days, and is ready to find sufficient surety to pay the remainder on the days limited between them, the said feoffees altogether refuse to make an estate of the said lands and tenements to the said suppliant, notwithstanding that the said suppliant hath often requested them to do so: May it please your most gracious Lordship to consider the premises, and that the said suppliant hath no remedy at common law, and to grant several writs under a certain pain directed to the said Richard Hendrys and Thomas Trey, [commanding them] to appear before you on a certain day, and to be examined on these matters, and on their examination to cause right to be done to the said suppliant, for God and in way of charity.[3]

128   To the most gracious lord, the Chancellor of England,

s.d. Humbly beseecheth your poor orator, Ralph Fryday, that whereas the suppliant's right arm was broken through certain evil-doers, who lay in wait to kill him, which arm, one John West of Leicester undertook at Wigston well and duly to cure and save; which John set about his cure of the said arm so improperly, through the malice and covin of the enemies of the said suppliant, that the arm mortified and became incurable, to the perpetual destruction of the said suppliant: May it please your most gracious Lordship to grant the said suppliant a writ directed to the said John West, [commanding him] to appear before you in the Chancery on the octave of the Purification of our Lady under pain of £40 to be examined by the surgeons of our Lord the

[3] An interesting case, combining *specific performance* and the obligations of feoffees to uses.

sufficiantz surgeans de ycelle cure nient duement fait, et de respoigner au dit suppliant du ycest graunde iniurie come droit et reson demaundont, pur Dieu et en oeuere de charite. Considerant, tres gracious seignur, qe le dit suppliant ne poet auoir du execucion de ley ne remedie de ycest maufait issint fait par colour de cure, s'il ne soit aide par ycest voy, par cause de graunde mayntenance encountre le dit suppliant en ycest partie.

129   [1] A Chaunceller nostre seignur le Roy,

s.d. Monstre Johan Lowaryn, qe come vn Gaillard Prouost fuist condempne enuers le dit Johan par iugement en vne certein somme pur certeinz vinz, come le dit Johan ad monstre en la Court mon seignur l'admiral, le quel iugement fuist fait en la ville de Burdeux; et fuist oblige le dit Gaillard de paier bien et loialment ceo qe fuist aiugge, sanz vener a l'encontre par voie d'appelle, ne en nulle autre manere; et a ceo est oblige par bonez cartez et instrumentez faitz en la dite ville de Bur- deux, qe sont a present en la dite Court d'admiral; et non obstant tout ceo, le dit Gaylard ad tant pursui par mauueys et friuolez sug- gestions q'il ad vn proteccion de Roy nostre seignur pur delaier le dit pouere homme et lui destrure pur toutz iours mes s'il n'eit vostre gracious eaide : Sur quoy please a vostre gracious seignurie qe la dite proteccion soit desalowe et repelle, pur Dieu et en oeure de charyte, et qe le dit Johan puisse auoir vn brief direct a mon seignur l'admiral et a ses lieu tenantz pur aler auaunt en la dite plee non obstant la dite proteccion par fraude et male engyn come piert pleinement en la dit Court d'admiral ensi purchase.

130   [2] A Chaunceller nostre seignur le Roi,

s.d. Supplie Isabelle, qi fuist la femme Thomas Burgh del Counte de Cornewaille, qe come la dite Isabelle est seisi del Manoir de Treuanek en le Counte auauntdit, a quel Manoir ele ad plousours tenaunts et diuers officers et auxint diuers auers meyneouerauntz en mesme le Manoir; de quel Manoir la dite Isabelle ad este tut temps pesiblement seisi et ces baillifs illeoqes fesauntz lour officez et auxint ces auersz pesiblement meyneouerauntz en mesme le Manoir, tounqe ore q'un

[1] Early Chancery Proceedings, Bundle 68, No. 62.
[2] Early Chancery Proceedings, Bundle 68, No. 98.
[3] An action of *assumpsit* lay at common law in such cases; see a curious example,

King, and by other sufficient surgeons, as to that cure not duly performed, and also to answer to the said suppliant for this great injury, as right and reason demand, for God and in way of charity. Considering, most gracious Lord, that the said suppliant cannot have execution nor any remedy at [common] law for this misdeed so done by colour of the cure, if he be not aided in this way, because of the great maintenance against the said suppliant in those parts.[3]

129   To the Chancellor of our Lord the King,

s.d. Showeth John Lowaryn, that whereas one Gaillard Provost was condemned towards the said John, by judgment, in a certain sum due for certain wines, as the said John hath shown in the Court of my Lord Admiral, which judgment was given in the town of Bordeaux; and the said Gaillard was bound well and lawfully to pay what was adjudged, without challenging the judgment by way of appeal, or in any other manner; and so to do was bound by good charters and instruments made in the said town of Bordeaux, which [charters] are at present in the said Admiral's Court; and notwithstanding all that, the said Gaillard hath striven, by evil and frivolous suggestions that he hath a protection from the King, our Lord, to delay the said poor man and to destroy him for ever, if he do not have your gracious aid: Whereupon may it please your gracious Lordship that the said protection be disallowed and repealed, for God and in way of charity, and that the said John may have a writ directed to my Lord Admiral and to his lieutenants to go on with the said plea notwithstanding the said protection, so purchased by fraud and ill design, as appeareth fully in the said Admiral's Court.[4]

130   To the Chancellor of our Lord the King,

s.d. Beseecheth Isabel, who was the wife of Thomas Burgh of the County of Cornwall, that whereas the said Isabel is seised of the manor of Trevanek in the County aforesaid, in which manor she hath many tenants and divers officers, and also divers beasts working in the said manor; of which manor the said Isabel hath been always peaceably seised, and her bailiffs there doing their offices, and also her beasts peaceably working in the same manor, until now of late when one Roger

in 1433, *Yorks Arch. Soc.*, Record Series, xvii., 78.

[4] The application to the Chancellor in this case seems to be in his administrative rather than in his judicial capacity.

Rogger Trewenard del Counte auauntdit vient de iour en aultre oue
force et armez extorcionousement oue diuersz gentz retenuz oue luy
en manere de guerre et a lez tenauntz et baillifs la dite Isabelle del
Manoir auauntdit fait grauntz oppressiounsz, c'est assauoir, en euxz
bataunt, naufraunt et malement tretaunt, et aultrez diuersez ledez
oue graunt force ; et ensement ad prist en le manere auauntdit de lez
auersz la dite Isabelle xxx boefz, xx vachez et bouettez et aultrez
diuersez auersz a graunt nombre ; et oue force et armez lez auersz
auauntditz ad fet amener as fortez Lewys et lez vnquore detient oue
forte mayn, issi qe la dite Isabelle ne poet en nule manere de son
Manoir auauntdit nul profit prendre, ne ou cez auers sa tere gayner
par cause des grauntz extorcionz l'auauntdit Rogger, ne auoir nul
seruaunt ou homme chiuachaunt en le haut chemyn nostre seignur le
Roi sour ascun cheual la dite Isabelle qe le dit Rogger ne voet prendre
oue cez gentz oue forte mayn et detener : Qe plese a vostre tres noble
et tres gracious seignurie de graunter a l'auauntdite Isabelle vn brief
hors del Chauncellerie nostre seignur le Roi direct a le dit Rogger luy
comaundaunt sour graunt peyne et forfaitour enuers nostre dit seignur
le Roi d'estre a vn certein iour deuaunt vous en la dite Chauncellerie
ou deuaunt la Counsail nostre dit seignur le Roi a respoundre de
ces grauntz extorciounsz et oppressiounz auauntditz, ou d'ordiner a
l'auauntdite Isabelle remedie en ceo cas ; et ceo pur Dieu et en eouere
de charite. Consideraunt, tres gracious seignur, qe l'auauntdit Rogger
est si graunt mesfesour et barettour en son pais qe la dite Isabelle ne
poet enuers luy par la comune [ley] nul remedie auoir.

131

s.d. [1] Plese a Chanceller nostre seignur le Roy granter seuerals briefs de
faire venir deuant le Conseil nostre dit seignur le Roy (en la Chancellerie)[2] ou q'il soit le xxiij iour de Feuerer proschein auenir, William
Rookwode, Nichol Segraue, Johan Ewell et Henry Stompe, a re-
sponder a nostre dit seignur le Roy de ce qe lour serra surmys par le
dit Conseil, sur certeine peine par vous a limiter ; les queux William,
Nichol, Johan et Henry, le Maresdy proschein deuant le fest de Seiut
Lucie[3] darrein passe, viendrent oue grande nombre des gentz armez
et archers, encontre le pees nostre seignur le Roy, a Neylond,[4] et
illeoqes grant affraie et manaces firent as tenantz de la dite ville,

---

[1] Early Chancery Proceedings, Bundle 68, No. 103.   [2] Interlined.   [3] Dec. 13.   [4] Nayland in Suffolk.

Trewenard of the County aforesaid cometh from day to day with force and arms, tortiously, with divers persons retained with him, in warlike manner, and maketh great oppressions on the tenants and bailiffs of the said Isabel in the manor aforesaid, that is to say, beating, wounding and ill-treating them, and other divers injuries, with great force ; and he hath also taken in manner aforesaid of the beasts of the said Isabel 30 oxen, 20 cows and bullocks, and divers other beasts to a great number ; and hath with force and arms caused the beasts aforesaid to be brought to Fort Lewis [?], and there by force he still keepeth them, so that the said Isabel cannot in any way make any profit of her manor aforesaid, nor till her land with her beasts, because of the great extortions of the aforesaid Roger, nor have any servant or man riding on the King's highway on any horse of the said Isabel's, but the said Roger would take it with the strong hand through his people, and detain it May it please your most noble and most gracious Lordship to grant th said Isabel a writ out of the Chancery of our Lord the King, directed to the said Roger, commanding him, under great pain and forfeiture to our Lord the King, to be before you on a certain day in the said Chancery, or before the Council of our said Lord the King, to answer[1] for these great extortions and oppressions aforesaid, or else to ordain a remedy for the said Isabel in this case; and this for God and in way of charity. Considering, most gracious Lord, that the aforesaid Roger is so great an evil-doer and barrator in his country that the said Isabel can have no remedy against him at common [law].[5]

131

s.d. May it please the Chancellor of our Lord the King to grant several writs to make come before the Council of our said Lord the King [in the Chancery], wherever he [the King] shall be, on the 23rd day of February next to come, William Rookwood, Nicholas Segrave, John Ewell and Henry Stompe, to answer to our said Lord the King touching that which shall then be submitted [against them] by the said Council, under a certain pain by you to be limited ; which William, Nicholas, John and Henry, on the Tuesday next before the feast of S. Lucy last past, came with a great number of armed people and archers, against the peace of our Lord the King, at Nayland, and there made a great affray and menaces against the tenants of the

[1] Note the alternative as in cases 79. and 101 ; before the Chancellor *or* before the Council.

manasantz d'arder toute la dite ville et de tuer les tenantz suisditz, et
vn de les tenantz de monsire Esteuen le Scrope,[1] seignur de mesme la
ville, illeoqes pristerent et emprisonerent et hors de la dite ville amesneront; et tiels assautes a mesme le temps firent qe le greindre partie
de les tenantz suisditz n'oseront attendre en lour propres mesons mes
feueront as procheins boys pur dout de lour mort; et pur les queux
auantdites manaces, les officers du dit monsire Esteuen n'oseront,
ne vnquore n'osent, aler ne chiuacher en pays pur faire lour seruices
et lour busoignes necessairs; dont sibien le dit monsire Esteuen
come les tenantz suisditz priont remede come la ley demande.

132   [2] A lour tres gracious seignur, Chanceller
             nostre seignur le Roy,

s.d. Supplient touz les parochiens de Gryngham iuxte Kyrketon in
Lyndesey,[3] qi sont tenantz a nostre tres redoute seignur le Roy, qe
come debate est moeue entre Robert Conyng, parson de la moitee de
l'esglise de la dite ville de Gryngham, et les ditz parochiens, touchant vne ymage qe le dit Robert ad fait mettre en vn lieu deinz lour
dite esglise a graunt nusance des ditz parochiens, issint q'ils ne purront bien veier la leuacion ne diuine seruice fait en la dite esglise; et
par cause q'ils lour veullent ent pleindre, il ad fait denuncier pur ex-
comengez touz les ditz parochiens qi luy vorroient contredire ou des-
tourber de sa volente ceste partie; et par tant q'ils ont purchacez vne
inhibicion de la dite denunciacion de lour Archidekne, le dit Robert
ad sommonez les ditz parochiens d'estre deuant l'Euesque de Nicole
deinz vn brief iour ore auenir de lour ent treher en plee et diseaser
deuant luy en qanque il puisse de sa malice; Et aussint par la ou
touz les ditz tenantz ont vsez du temps dont memorie ne courte de
soner vne campane au certeins temps en l'an de faire touz les ditz
tenantz assembler pur le rent le Roy coiller, et soun seruice et autres
choses touchant la gouernaile de la dite ville de Gryngham faire, come
soloit estre d'ancien temps, le dit Robert lour manace qe si ascun de
eux tiel chose face, ou ascun de eux pursue encontre luy en ascun
lieu pur les ditz greuances redresser, q'ils ne serront si hardyz de
demurur en lour measons illeoqes; et plusours autres tortz et gre-

---

[1] Probably the second baron of Masham,
who died in 1406.
[2] Early Chancery Proceedings, Bundle
68, No. 133.   [3] Lincolnshire.

[4] The violence and power of the defendants is the reason for applying to the
Chancellor. The interlineation is interesting; it suggests that the practice of

said town, threatening to burn all the said town and to kill the tenants
aforesaid, and there they seized one of the tenants of Sir Stephen le
Scrope, lord of the same town, and imprisoned him, and brought him
out of the said town ; and they made such assaults at that time that
the greater part of the tenants aforesaid did not dare to stay in their
own houses, but fled to the neighbouring woods for fear of death ;
and because of these aforesaid threats, the officers of the said Sir
Stephen did not dare, and yet do not dare, to go nor to ride in that
country to do their duties and their necessary business ; of which
matters as well the said Sir Stephen, as the tenants aforesaid, pray
remedy as the law demands.[4]

132   To their most gracious Lord, the Chancellor
             of our Lord the King,

s.d.   Beseech all the parishioners of Grayingham, near Kirton in Lindsey,
who are tenants of our most redoubted Lord the King, that whereas
dissension hath arisen between Robert Conyng, Parson of the moiety
of the church of the said town of Grayingham, and the said parishioners, touching an image which the said Robert hath caused to be put
in a place within their said church to the great annoyance of the said
parishioners, so that they cannot well see the elevation [of the Host]
nor the divine service done in the said church ; and because they
wished to complain thereof, he hath caused to be denounced as excommunicate all the said parishioners who would thwart or disturb
him of his will in this matter ; and forasmuch as they have purchased an inhibition of the said denunciation from their Archdeacon,
the said Robert hath summoned the said parishioners to be before the
Bishop of Lincoln within a short time now to come, to draw them in
a plea thereof and to annoy them before him [the Bishop] as much as he
can of his malice ; And also that whereas all the said tenants from a
time immemorial have used to ring a bell at certain times of the year
to cause all the said tenants to assemble in order to collect the King's
rent and to do his service and other things touching the governance
of the said town of Grayingham, as was wont to be of ancient time,
the said Robert threateneth them that if any of them do such a thing,
or if any of them sue against him in any place for the redressing of
the said grievances, that they should not be so bold as to dwell in
their houses there ; and many other wrongs and grievances hath he

summoning the defendant to appear in the   form. The Council did sometimes sit in
Chancery was not yet the usual common   the Chancery ; see Cases 6, 9, and 41.

uances lour ad fait et face de iour en autre, sanz cause resonable,
nient eiant consideracion q'ils sont tenants a nostre dit seignur le Rȯy
come dit est, ou ascun charge depar le Roy a luy fait ; Issint q'ils
n'osent illeoqes outre demurer et ensi perdra mesme nostre seignur le
Roy ses rentz de sa dite ville si remede ne soit mys celle partie.

133

s.d. [1] Plese a son tres honore et tres gracious seignur le Chaunceller d'Engleterre de grauntere brief de faire venire deuant vos et le Counseille
nostre tres redoute seignur le Roi, Walter Crauford del Counte de Buk',
a responde a (Margarete mier) [2] Johan Hampton de grauntez tortes et
damagez quex ad fait a vostre dit suppliant ; entendant, tres gracious
seignur, qe le dit Walter est si grant en ycelle pays qe nul poit auoir
droit ne reson de luy : en coure de charite.

At the foot. Idem Johannes iurauit quod querela sua est vera, et
concessit satisfacere prefato Waltero pro expensis suis veniendo coram
Consilio Regis ex causa predicta in casu quo dictam querelam suam esse
veram ibidem probare non poterit.

134   [3] A la Chaunceler nostre seignur le Roi,

s.d.   Prie Thomas de Euerwyke, qe come il soet ouerrir par la sience de
Alconemie et faire argent en plate, et ad fait en presence de bones
gentz de Londres, et l'argent assaie par les orfeures de meisme la
Citee, et troue bon, la est venu vn Thomas Crop de Londres, Espicer,
et se fist priue au dit Thomas de Euerwyke en tant qe il lui fist porter
a sa meson ses instrumenz et son elixere, et lui fist ouerir en sa meson
deuant lui ; et qant le dit Thomas Crop feust aparceu de la sience,
voillant auoir le dit Thomas de Euerwyke en daunger, par collusion
entre lui et autres de la Citee, enprisona le dit Thomas de Euerwyke
en la meson le dit Thomas Corp [*sic*] en Londres, et illoesqes il fist
faire vne obligacion de C mars de en rendre compt au dit Thomas
Crop, et puis une autre obligacion de atant de meisme la forme ; Et

---

[1] Early Chancery Proceedings, Bundle
68, No. 161.   [2] Interlined.
[3] Ancient Petitions, No. 14806.
[4] It is difficult to see why the plaintiffs
should appeal to the Chancellor. Great

stress seems to be laid on the fact that
they are tenants of the King, but that hardly
explains it.
[5] Probably an early case, as the defendant
is to come before the Council.

done them, and doeth from day to day, without reasonable cause, not having consideration that they are tenants of our said Lord the King, as is afore said, nor any charge made to him on behalf of the King; so that they dare not any more dwell there, and so our said Lord the King will lose his rents of his said town, if remedy be not done in this behalf.[4]

133 May it please his most honoured and most gracious Lord, the Chancellor of England,

s.d. To grant a writ to make to come before you and the Council of our most redoubted Lord, the King, Walter Crawford of the County of Buckingham, to answer to (Margaret, mother of) John Hampton, touching great wrongs and damages which he hath done to your said suppliant; understanding, most gracious Lord, that the said Walter is so great in that country that no one can have right or reason against him: in way of charity.

At the foot. The same John hath sworn that his complaint is true, and he hath granted to satisfy the said Walter for his expenses of coming before the Council of the King for the cause aforesaid in case he shall not be able to prove his said complaint to be true.[5]

134 To the Chancellor of our Lord the King,

s.d. Prayeth Thomas de York, that whereas he knoweth how to work by the science of alchemy and to make silver in plate, and hath done so in the presence of worthy folk of London, and the silver hath been assayed by the goldsmiths of the same City, and found good, there came one Thomas Crop of London, grocer, and made himself known to the said Thomas de York, so much so that he got him to carry his instruments and his elixir to his [Crop's] house, and got him to work in his house before him; and when the said Thomas Crop perceived the science thereof, wishing to have the said Thomas de York in danger,[6] he, by collusion between himself and others of the City, imprisoned the said Thomas de York in the house of the said Thomas Crop in London, and there made him sign a bond in 100 marks to the said Thomas Crop, as on an account rendered [?], and afterwards

---

[6] ' To have a person in one's danger ' was to have him in one's power or dependence. Shakespeare, *Merchant of Venice,* iv. 1 : ' You stand within his danger.' ' *Estre en* *dangier de quelqu'un* = etre sous sa puissance, à sa merci.' (Scheler, *Dict. d'étymol. franç.*).

issi par vertue de celes obligacions si ad le dit Thomas Corp [sic] fait prendre le dit Thomas de Euerwyke et lui enprisoner en Neugate, et lui detient son elixer et ses autres instrumenz et autres biens et chateux a la mountance de xl li. ; dont le dit Thomas de Euerwyke prie pur Dieu qe il pleise ordeiner pur sa deliuirrance, et faire venir le dit Thomas Corp oue le elixer et les instrumentz auant diz, issint q'il puisse deuant eux ouerrir et prouer sa sienee ou autres queux il plerra au Roi assigner, et qe les faux obligacions puissont estre dampnetz.

Indorsed.   Coram Rege et Magno Consilio.

Soient assignez le Meir de Londres, Sire Robert de Skarthburgh et Sire William Scot, ou deux de eux de sere a Seint Martyn, et d'enquer sur choses conteignnes en la dite peticion la verite, et doer [sic ? oyer] et terminer le trespas, et de faire outre ce qe atteint a la ley, et si le dit Thomas de Euerwyke treue bone et suffisant suerte de suer sa besoigne diligeantment, et de remouer le dit Thomas de Euerwyke a la prison en cas q'il ne perra prouer sa entencion, eit bref as mesmes les Justices de lui lesser a mainprise par la suerte auantdite.[1]

---

[1] As to commissions of *oyer* and *terminer*, see p. 29, note 1.

another bond for the like sum and in the same form; and thus, by virtue of these bonds, the said Thomas Crop hath caused the said Thomas de York to be arrested and imprisoned in Newgate, and detaineth his elixir and his other instruments and other goods and chattels, to the value of £40; whereof the said Thomas de York prayeth for God's sake that [the Chancellor] will be pleased to order his deliverance and to make the said Thomas Crop come with the elixir and the instruments aforesaid, so that he [the plaintiff] may work and prove his science before them [? the Council] or any others whom it may please the King to assign, and that the false bonds may be cancelled.

Indorsed.   Before the King and the Great Council.

Let the Mayor of London, Sir Robert de Scarborough and Sir William Scot, or two of them, be assigned to sit at S. Martin's [?], and inquire as to the truth of the things contained in the said petition, and [hear ?] and terminate the trespass, and further to do what the law demands; and, if the said Thomas de York shall find good and sufficient surety to sue this matter diligently, and to remove the said Thomas de York [back] to prison in case he cannot prove his contention, let him have a writ to the same Justices to let him to bail on the surety aforesaid.

135   To the full hye, excellent and gracious Prince, the Duc of Gloucetre, Protectour of Englande,[2]

Early
Ien. VI.   Byseketh mekely your pouere bedwoman and Widowe, Maude Annors, graciously consider that throgh the vertu of your full gracious lettres the Rector of Assherige seced and left his maintenaunce agaynes your forseid widowe, Wherfore god quyte you in heuen euerlastyngly; & thervpon she entred in her land by a writ of the statute of Northampton, and enfeoffed on Adam Alford for trust and socour in the forseid land, the whiche Adam wolde compelle your forseid widowe to gif hym the same lande for xl s. for euermore, ther it is worth xx li. clere, and halt her oute ther of : Wherfore like it to your gracious lordship to graunt your forseid bedwoman that she may haue of the Chaunceller of Englond a writ that is called *sub pena* direct to the forseid Adam, to be byfore the forseid Chaunceller the Trinite terme next comyng, to answere to the cause aforseid; for godesake and in the waye of Charite.[3]

136   [4] To his gracious lord and fader in God, the Bishop of Bathe, Chaunceller of Englond,[5]

1432
to
1443   Mekely bysechith yo[r] Chapelleyn and contynuell oratour, William Brigge, parson of the chirche of Weueton in the shire of Norff',[6] that where as William Brigge his fader was seised in his demene as

---

[1] Ancient Petitions, No. 15346.
[2] Humphrey, Duke of Gloucester, son of Henry IV. He was made Protector on the death of Henry V.
[3] I cannot explain why the plaintiff should apply to the Protector instead of to the Chancellor. The case is not very clear, but it seems that the defendant was using his position as trustee to compel the plaintiff

to release her equitable right for an inadequate price.
[4] Early Chancery Proceedings, Bundle 11, No. 111.
[5] John Stafford; appointed Chancellor May 4, 1432; consecrated Archbishop of Canterbury May 15, 1443.
[6] Wiveton, near the coast, on the river Glaven. See Blomefield's *Norfolk*, v. 970.

in fee of a place called Letheryngsete[7] and of other [property] called
Clokwode in Cleye,[8] Godwyns in Eggefeld,[9] and of a place called
Caleys Halle in Gestweyth,[10] with the app^rtenaunce in the shire of
Norff', and so seysed therof [enfeoffed] Thomas Astley and John
Bacon, esquiers, with othir, To have to hem and to ther heirs and
[assigns] to parfourme his wille; and the seid William the fader
aftirward made his wille, writen and ensealed under the seall of his
armes, and ordeyned that his seyd feffees shulde [give] the seid londes
and tenementes with appurtenaunce to one Thomas his sone and
[? heir] and to your seid bisecher, to have to hem and to the heires
of ther two bodyes laufully begotten, and for defaute of suche heyres
the seid londes and tenementes with the appurtenaunce shulde
remayne to Elyzabeth the elder and Elizabeth the yonger, doughters to
the said William the fader,[11] [their]heirs and ther assignes, as it apperith
in the seyd wille; the which feffees yaf the maner called Caleis Halle
in Gestweith, parcel ofthe londes and tenementes aboveseyd, with the
appurtenaunce to the seid Thomas, and to your said bisecher the re-
maynder . . . to the seid wille; after the which yifte the seid Thomas
hath continually occupyed soule and taken alle the hole profitz contrarie
to lawe, conscience, and the wille of the seid William the fadyr, and
wille not suffre yor seid bisecher to occupy . . . to take, and thus your
seid bisecher may nought aprowe his part of the seid londes because
ther is no particion made ther offe, for the which particion to be made
ther is non accyon atte common lawe, and thus particion ther offe
may [not be had, save through your] gracious cyde; and where that
the seid feffees shude make the astat, accordyng to the seide wille, of
the remenaunt of the seid londes and teuementes, the seid Thomas
Brigge seith and affermith that the said Feffees shulde make the
accordyng to the wordes of the wille, the wich astat he wolde ha made in
othir forme than the wille makith mencyon, and thus he lettyth the wille
of the fadyr of the seid Thomas and your seid suppliaunt; where
your seid suppliaunt was atte request and special preyer of the seid
Thomas Brigge bounde be obligacion to on Richard Pykard in x li. for
suerte of viij marc' to the foreseid Richard Pykard and John, be the
same Thomas aght,[12] the wich [sum the plaintiff] hath content and payd
to the forseid Richard Pykard, the which viij marc' the seid Thomas
Brigge refusyth to paye ayen to your seyd suppliaunt ayens conscience;

---

[7] Letheringsett, near Wiveton, also on
the Glaven.
[8] Cley-next-the-sea, near Wiveton.
[9] Edgefield, near Melton Constable.
[10] Guestwick, near Melton Constable.

See Blomefield's *Norfolk*, iv. 387.
[11] It is not very uncommon to find two
brothers or two sisters of the same christian
name.
[12] Owed.

Wherefore please hit your gracious lordeship to consider these premisses and [to grant a writ] directe to the seid Thomas upon a certeyn peyn to apper afore you in the chauncerie at a day by you limitted, and thanne [and] there to make particion of the seid londes and tenementes, or ells to fynde suerte sufficiaunt to suffre your bisecher reasona[ble] . . . him; and that in the honour of God and in the wey of charite.[1]

137　　　　　　[2] To the right reverent and worthi lord holy fader, Chaunceler of Englond,[3]

1441　Besecheth mekely yo[r] humble servaunt William Lomnour, executour of the testament of Margarete Butvyleyn, that where as Water Brett of Gyssyng, late bailly of the seid Margarete of hir Maner of Gyssyng in the Shire of Norff',[4] had gederid and resceyvid of the revenus of the seid maner x li., of whiche the seid bailly so beyng possessid bargayned with Johan Bernevyle, Fissherman, of Disse, late of Reidon in the seid shire, to bye of hym a mees-place with certein londe in Reidon in the same shire, to have to the seid Water and to his heires, and paied hym in honde in parte of paiement of the somme accorded bytwene hem the forseid x li. resceyved of the revenus of the maner aboveseid; and afterwarde the seid bailly was utlawed at a straunge man is suyte, and so died byfore any estat made to hym of the seid mees and londe accordyng to the bargayne forseid, and with out any paiement of the x li. forseid, or any peny therof, made to the forseid Margarete in hir live or to your forseid besecher after hir dethe; and now it is so that alle the goodes and catelle of the forseid Water were eschetid and seised into the Kynge's hondez by cause of the utlagare above seid, and so your seid besecher destitute of alle maner [of] remedie at the comune lawe, to his gret hurt and hyndryng of execucion of the wille of the forseid Margarete if hit be not holpyn by your gracious socour: Please hit to your good and gracious Lordship to considre these premisses and how the forseid Johan hath bothe the mees and londe aboveseid and the foreseid x li. paied in part of paiement therfor, and ther upon to graunt a writ directe to the same Johan Bernevile commaundyng hym to apere byfore yow in the

---

[1] Spence says that the Court of Chancery assumed jurisdiction in matters of partition some time in or about the reign of Elizabeth; Equit. Jur. i. 654. This case proves it to be much earlier.

[2] Early Chancery Proceedings, Bundle 9, No. 179.
[3] John Stafford, Bishop of Bath and Wells. See p. 129, note 5.
[4] Near Diss.

Chauncery at the utas [5] of the Purificacion next comyng upon a peyne after yo[r] noble discrecion to be lymytid, there to be examyned of thes premisses, and do and resceive as feith and good concience requirith in this mater; for the love of God and in wey of charite.

[A memorandum is indorsed to the effect that on November 18, 20 Henry VI. (1441), Thomas Prikfeld of London, gentleman, and Thomas Skot of London, gentleman, became mainpernors for the plaintiff. Usual form.]

138   [6] To the reverent fader in God, my lorde the
               Bisshop of Bathe, Chauncellor of Englond,[7]

1441   Besechith humbly your pouer bedeman and bedewomen, John Rous, Elizabeth his wif, and Athelyn that was the wif of William Sakevyle, sisters and heirs to William Pertsoille, that where the said William Pertsoille was seised of the maner of Pertsoille with th'appurtenaunce in the towne of Ryseley [8] in the counte of Bedford, in his demesne as in fee, and [being so] seised enfeoffed therof John FitzGeffrey and Richard Parker, and other that nowe been dede, to hem and her heires for evermore, on trust to th'entente to refeoffe him or his beires when he or they required hem.   And before eny refeoffement made, the seid William Pertsoille died withoute issu.   And your said besechers, as sisters and heirs to the said William, required the said John Fitz Geffrey and Richard Parker to refeoffe hem accordyng to th'entent of the first feoffement, and they refused hit to do, and said playnly they wolde not do it; to perpetuelle disheritison of your said besechers. Please it yo[r] gracious lordeship to consider the premisses and to graunte your said bisechers a writte directe to the said John FitzGeffrey to appere afore you in the Chauncerie at the XV[m] of Seint Hillare there to be examyned of the articles abovesaid, as faith, reason and conscience requireth : At the reverence of God and in way of charitee.

Be it remembred that at the XV[am] of Seint Hillare the yere of the reigne of Kyng Henry the vj[to] after the conquest xix[the],[9] John Fitz Geffrey, esquier, appered in the Chauncerie by vertu of a writte sued ayens him by John Rous, Elizabeth his wif and Athelyn, sum tyme the wif of William Sakevyle, sisters and heirs to William Pertsoyle, supposyng by their bille that the said William Pertsoyle was seised in the manoir of Pertsoile with th'appurtenaunce in the towne

---

[5] The octave.   9, Nos. 312, 313.   [7] See p. 129, note 5.
[6] Early Chancery Proccedings, Bundle   [8] Risley, near Kimbolton.   [9] 1441.

of Ryseley in the shire of Bedford, in his demesne as in fec, and therof enfeoffed the said John FitzGeffrey and Richard Parker, and other nowe dede, to hem and to her beires for evermore, uppon trust to refeoffe hym or his heirs whan they were therto required. To the whiche bille the said John FitzGeffrey answrith and seyth, the said William Pertsoile enfeoffed him and othir of the forsaid maner to have and holde to hem and to her heirs for evermore, upon trust, and to his use and profitte ; by force of which feoffement they contynued her estate alle the lif of the said William Pertsoile, savyng of a feld called Lowesdenfeld and a wode adjunyng therto, of the which by the wille and request of the said William Pertsoil in his lif the said John FitzGeffrey made estate to John his eldest the bastard son and . . . by his .   And the said William Pertsoille died aboute the feste of the Annunciacion of oure Lady the xvij[the] yere of the reigne of oure soverain lord the Kyng that nowe is ; [1] aftir whose decesse, alle the cofeoffees of the said John FitzGeffrey were dede ; and the said John FitzGeffrey seith that there was never wille declared to him uppon the said feffement what he shuld do with the said maner by the said William Portsoile in his lif ; And after the decesse of the said William Pertsoile, the said John Rous, Elizabeth his wif, and Athelyn, at divers tymes required him to enfeoffe theyme of the said maner as susters and heirs to the said William Pertsoile, and he wolde not for as muche as he wolde [know whether ?] William Pertsoile had made eny wille of the said maner ; And aftirward the said John Rous and his wif and Athelyn sued a writte *sub pena* ayenst the said John FitzGeffrey, and delyvered it to hym.   After which livere the said John Rous and his wif and Athelyn entred in the said maner claymyng as susters and heirs to the said William Pertsoile, in whose possession the said John Fitz Geffrey relessed alle the right that he had in the said maner the morwe after Seint Kateryn's day last passed, for as muche as at that tyme ther was no wille declared to him made by the said William Pertsoile of the said maner.   Howe be hit that Symond Roucer, oon of his cofeoffees, was of counsaille and styward of the landes of the said William Pertsoile alle his lif daies and duelled in the same towne that the said John FitzGeffrey duellith yn nowe and duelled at that tyme, and thus the said John FitzGeffrey semeth he hath done alle that conscience and lawe requireth him.

Super quo in crastino Purificacionis beate Marie venit in Cancellaria domini Regis Willelmus Sakevile, filius et heres Atheline Hoo nomine ejusdem Atheline, ac Johannis Rous et Elizabethe uxoris ejus

---

[1] March 25, 1439.

et petiit tunc ibidem dictum scriptum relaxacionis tunc in custodia Johannis Enderby existens liberari, per quod preceptum fuit eidem Johanni Enderby per Curiam predictam quod scriptum illud in eandem curiam liberaret, qui quidem Johannes Enderby scriptum predictum in Curiam predictam liberavit, postmodumque scriptum predictum prefato Willelmo ad usum predictorum Atheline, Johannis Rous et Elizabethe per Curiam predictam liberatum fuit custodiendum.[2]

139   [3] To the moste reuerent fader in God, the Archebushop of Caunterbury, Chaunceller of Englond,[4]

1443   Besecheth mekely youre pore bedeman, John Bushop, that where he
to   late was in his house at Hamell of the Rice [5] in the Counte of Suth' the
1450   xij day of Marche laste passed in godis pees and the kinge's, ther came John Wayte, Richard Neuport and John Neuport with xiij [?] other persones in theire company, arayed in maner of werre, and in full ryoutis wyse in forcible maner there and thenne entred the house of youre seid besecher aboute myddenygth, and him lyinge in his bedde toke, seesed and emprisoned, and his purse with xxvs. of money therin and the keyes of his cofres fro him toke, and the same cofres openyd, and xxviij[?]li. of his money, ij standinge cuppes of siluer gilte, vij flatte peces of siluer, ij masers, vj girdels and a baselard harneysed with siluer of the godes and catalles of William Poleyn, of the value of xl li. ther beinge in the kepinge of youre seid besecher, and v peces of kercies [6] and the stuffe of household of youre seid besecher, to the value of xxx li., ther founde, toke and bere away, and him fro thens the same nigth to Sydingworth ledde, and in horrible streyt prison kepte bi the space of ij dayes; and fro thens him caried to a place called Spereshotis Place [7] in the same shire [?], and him there in full streite grevous prison in stokkes kepte stille bi the space of v dayes; and other fulle grete wronges to him dud ayenste the pees of the kinge oure souereigne lord to tbe . . . destruccion of the body of youre seid besecher, whiche is not of power to sue his remedye bi the commune

[2] An early instance of a written answer; it does not appear that the defendant made any personal appearance. The judgment leaves it doubtful if the defendant was considered to be in default or not.
[3] Early Chancery Proceedings, Bundle 16, No. 438.
[4] Probably John Stafford; appointed Mar. 4, 1432, then Bishop of Bath and Wells; consecrated Archbishop of Canterbury May 15, 1443; resigned the Chancellorship Jan. 31, 1450.
[5] Hamble en le Rice, near Southampton.
[6] Kerseys; coarse woollen cloth.
[7] Near Winchester.

lawe, and importable loste of his godes, but yf more soner remédye be hadde for him in this behalfe : Plese it youre gracious lordshippe to graunte seueralle writtes to be directe to the seid John Wayte, Richard Neuport and John Neuport, commaundinge theim to appere afore you at a certein day by you to be lemyt, to be examined of these premisses, and to doo and receyue that gode feyth and consciens wille in this behalfe, and that they more ouer by youre discrecion be compelled to fynde sufficiaunt surete to kepe the kynge's pees ayenst youre seid besecher and ayenst alle the kinge's liege peple ; at the reuerens of god and in the wey of charite.[1]

Pleggii de prosequendo $\begin{cases} \text{Willelmus Poleyn,} \\ \text{Johannes Grene.} \end{cases}$

[2] This is the answere of John Wayte to a bille putte ayenst hym by John Bysship before the Kyng in his Chauncerie.

The seid John Wayte saith by protestacion that the said John Bysship is his villayn regardant to his Maner of Lee in the Counte of Suth[t], and he and his auncestres, all tho whos estate John Wayte hath in the same Maner, haue been seised of the said John Bysship and of his auncestres as villeyns regardantz to the said Maner fro the tyme that no mynde is ; and savyng to the said John Wayte and his heires alle maner auauntage to seise and clayme the same John Bysship and his heires and theire blode, alle theire landes and tenementez, godes and catallis, and alle maner other avauntage and obieccions of bondage of and ayenst the said John Bysshop and his blode here after, by protestacion that the said John Wayte is nat gilty of no mater conteyned in the said bille, lyke as by the same bille hit is supposed, for plee saith in asmuche as alle the maters of compleynt conteyned in the seid bille bene maters determinable by the commyn lawe of this lande in other Courtes of oure souereyn lord the kyng and nat in this Curte, asketh iugement and praieth to be dismyssed owte of this Courte after the fourme of the statute.[3]

---

[1] The poverty of the plaintiff, and his consequent inability to sue at common law, seems to be the only reason for applying to the Chancellor.

[2] Bundle 16, No. 437.

[3] The written defence soon crystallises into a common form. Allowing for differences of language and spelling, this answer might have been put in several centuries later.

⁴ This is the Replicacion of John Busshop vuto the aunswere of John Wayte.

The seid John Busshop seith that he is a free man borne and of free condicion, and not honde man of the seid John Wayte, and that alle the auncestres of the same John Busshop fro the time that no mynde is haue ben free men and of fre condicion, borne with in the parisshe off Corffe in the Counte of Dors' and not with in the maner of Lee in the Counte of Suthampt', as bi diuers true inquisicions hereof taken byfore certein Commissioners bi vertu of the kinge's Commission to theim directe hit pleinely epperith ; ⁵ whiche Commissions and Inquisicions remayneth in this place of record ; and he seith more ouer that the seid John Wayte wrongefully bi grete force hathe taken fro him his godes and catalles and him greuously enprisoned in the maner and fourme declared in his bille, and him putte to suche coste, loste of his gode, lette of his laboure and besines, and other grete troubles and vexacions, that he is so pore and brought to so grete misere that he is not of power to sue ayenst the seid John Wayte for remedie of the seid wronges bi course of the commune lawe of this lande ; Wherefor, in asmoche as he withseieth not the matier conteigned in the seid bille of complainte of the seid John Busshop, he praieth that the seid John Wayte may be compelled bi the rule and discrecion of this Courte to restore him of his seid godes and to yeue him sufficient dammages and amendis for the seid trespas to him done.

140   To the right noble and full gracious lord the Erle of Salesbury, Chaunceler of Englond,⁷

1454 Mekely beseketh [sic] youre humble Oratour, William Middilton, Squier, that where Maister William Ascogh, late Bysshop of Salesbury,⁸ of his malice and sotill ymaginacion to gete goode of youre said suppliaunt, daiely sterred the Kyng oure soueraigne lord to amove his goode grace and fauour from yoᵣ said suppliaunt, in somuche that he shuld haue be putte oute of oure said soueraigne lorde's house, and

---

⁴ Bundle 16, No. 436.
⁵ The question seems to have been in dispute before.
⁶ Early Chancery Proceedings, Bundle 24, No. 220.

⁷ Richard Neville ; appointed April 2, 1454 ; his successor appointed March 7, 1455.
⁸ Appointed 1438 ; murdered at Edington, Wilts, June 29, 1450.

kowde neuer haue knowelegge for what cause ; and therupon yor said suppliaunt sued and made grete instaunce to the said late Bisshop to be his goode lord, and the same late Bisshop said withoute he wold deliuere him xx marc he shuld be putte oute of oure said soueraigne lorde's house ; and so youre said suppliaunt, for drede and to please the said late Bisshop, toke him xx marc, to the grete hurte of youre said suppliaunt ; And howe be it that he hath often tymes required oon Sir John Depden, preest, executour of the testament and last will of the said late Bisshop, to make restitucion of the said xx marc according to his last will, the which will was that if he had vnduely offended eny man or iniustly receyued the goodes of eny persone, that his executours shuld duely satisfie theym therfore as right wold, yet the said John Depden it vtterly refuseth, contrary to the will of the said late Bisshop : that it please yor gracious lordship the premissez considered, and that yor said suppliaunt can haue remedye neither at the spirituell lawe ne commune law, to graunte vnto youre said suppliaunt a writte *sub pena* directe to the said John Depden, to do him appere afore you in the Chauncerie at a certain day vnder a certain payne by your lordschip to be limitted, to be compelled to doo there as faith and conscience requiren in this behalue ; and shall pray hertly to god for you.[1]

[Memorandum of mainprise dated June 2, 32 Henry VI., 1454, John Middilton, knight, and John Maners, esquire, being the mainpernors.]

141   [2] To the right reuerent and worshipfull Fader in God, the Archiebisshop of Caunterbury, Chaunceller of Inglond,[3]

1453 Besecheth mekely Robert Bodenham, that where as he borowed late of John Halle of Salesbury lxxx li., for the whech the seyd John, thorgh [through] sotyll promys, caused the saide Robert of trust, the fyrst day of May the xxxiij yere of the Raynyng of oure Soueraygne lorde the kynge that nowe ys,[4] to enfeffe the saide John in the manere of Shipton Berenger yn Suth' Shyre,[5] to haue and holde hit to the saide John, hys heyr and assign, vnder condicion that yif the saide Robert,

---

[1] A very curious case ; the attempt to recover the money under the clause of the Bishop's will seems most ingenious. It is a pity the judgment has not been preserved.
[2] Early Chancery Proceedings, Bundle

25, No. 131.
[3] Thomas Bourchier ; appointed March 7, 1455 ; his successor appointed Oct. 11, 1456.   [4] Henry VI. ; 1455.
[5] Shipton-Bellinger, near Andover.

hys beires or executoures paye or dyd paye to the saide John or to his assignes C li. at the feste of seynt John the Baptiste that shall be in the yere of oure lorde M. CCCC. lxj, that thenne the saide feffement sholde be voide, as by a dede endented therof made pleynly appereth, so that the said John purposeth therby to resceue and haue the issues and profites of the said manere vnto the saide day of payment, which will extende to the some of lxxxv markes, and also C li. by way of vsury for the lone of the said lxxx li., or elles the saide maner to be lost and forfeted to hym. Moreouer the saide John, ymagynynge more desceyte to distrue the said Robert, caused hym by sotelte to be bounde to the saide Robert in CCC li. by an obligacion of the Statuyt Marchant of Salesbury bereing date the ij day of the saide moneth of Maye; which the saide Robert delyuered to on John Gardner to kepe it tyll suffisant endentures in deffesaunce there of were made by men lerned bytwene the saide Robert and John that the said condicion shulde be perfourmed . And not withstanding that the saide endentures buth not yet made and that the saide obligacion remayneth with the saide John Gardner, and the saide John Halle hath sued execucion vppon the saide statute of the saide CCC li., by vertue wherof he hath take the saide Robert and put hym into streyte pryson at Salesbury; so that the saide John purposeth to have CCCCL li. and more of the saide Robert for the lenynge [6] of lxxx li., ayeynes ryght and conscience, in fynall distruccion of the saide Robert; Wherof he may haue no remedy by the Comyn Lawe. Please it youre gracious lordship to sende for the saide John by a writte *sub pena* for to appere byfore yow at a certeygne daye, to answere to the premisses, and thervppon ye to execute Justice as good feyth and consciens requyreth : for the love of god and in the werk of Charyte.

[A memorandum of mainprise is written at the foot, dated January 22, 34 Henry VI. [7]; Robert Bodenham of Ebbesborn in the county of Wilts, junior, gentleman, and William Cole of the same place, yeoman, were the mainpernors.]

[The answer [8] is much decayed and faded in places. The defendant admits the debt of £80 and the feoffment of the manor. He complains that the plaintiff had since entered upon the manor, ' and woode and vndirwoode growyng apon the same Maner solde, kytte and caryyd awaye,' and had assaulted the defendant's servants and tenants; also that he the defendant had to pay an annuity of five marks charged upon the said manor.]

---

[6] Loaning.   [7] 1456.   [8] Bundle 25, No. 130.

[1] This ys the replicacion of Robert Bodenham onto the aunswere of John Halle to the bylle of the said Robert.

The sayde Robert, not knawyng any thynge conteyned yn the sayde plee as hit ys pledid, saith that the sayde plee ys not suffysaunt to put hym to aunswere there to, for there ys no thynge conteyned yn the sayde bylle trauersed nor confessed and destruyed yn the sayde plee ; but for as moche as the sayde John knawlycheth by hys sayde plee that the sayde Robert borowed of hym iiij[xx] li. specyfied yn the sayde hylle, for syurte of whych the sayde Robert enfeffed hym by a dede in the Maner of Shypton Berynger, named yn the sayde hylle and a dede endentid bytwene theym, vnder certeyn condicions, and also a statut marchant of ccc li., specyfied yn the sayde bylle to be made therefor, the sayde Robert ys redy to repaye to the sayde John the sayde iiij[xx] li. with alle hys resonable costes spend therefor, as the Court wol awarde, and prayeth Jugement, and that the sayde John be ajugged to relyuere to hym the sayde dedes and statut and to refeffe hym yn the sayde Maner yn fee, and lete hym to be delyuered out of pryson, as gode fayth and consciens requyreth.

[2] This is the reioynyng of John Halle to the Replicacion of Robert Bodnam.

The seid John Halle saith that for as moche that he hath sufficiently answered to the maters comprehendid and conteyned in the bille of the seid Robert, to the whiche the sid Robert answerith not, the seid John Halle prayth his damages and that he may be demyssid out of the Court.

Indorsed on the bill. Memorandum quod decimo octavo die Februarii anno regni Regis Henrici sexti post conquestum Anglie tricesimo quarto,[3] tam materia in supplicacione infrascripta coram ipso domino Rege in Cancellaria sua per infrascriptum Robertum versus infrascriptum Johannem Halle exhibita, quam materiis in responsione, replicacione, et reiunccione in hac parte exhibitis, specificatis et in dicta Cancellaria lectis plenius et intellectis, habitisque deliberacione et auisamento in hac parte de et super premissis cum Justiciariis ipsius domini Regis de vtroque Banco, ac cum diuersis tam

---

[1] Bundle 25, No. 129.   [2] Bundle 25, No. 128.   [3] 1456.

seruientibus ad legem quam aliis de consilio pareium predictarum ibidem tunc interessentibus, per auisamentum eorundem Justiciariorum Consideratum est tunc ibidem, eo quod infrascriptus Robertus in eadem Cancellaria tunc et ibidem soluit infrascripto Johanni Halle quaterviginti libras infrascriptas per ipsum Robertum ab eodem Johanne Halle, vt infrascriptum est, mutuatas, et quod idem Johannes Halle infrascriptum Robertum a prisona qua ipse occasione recognicionis infrascripti statuti mercatorii de trescentis libris infrascriptis sub custodia vicecomitis Comitatus Wiltes' adtunc detinebatur, deliberari faceret et ipsum Robertum de execucione statuti predicti penitus exoneraret, et statutum predictum cassaret, adnichilaret, et cancellaret, et quod infrascriptus Johannes Halle refeoffaret infrascriptum Robertum de et in Manerio infrascripto cum suis pertinenciis siue relaxaret totum ius suum et clameum de et in eodem Manerio cum suis pertinenciis eidem Roberto, habendum et tenendum sibi, heredibus et assignatibus suis imperpetuum ; Ac eciam quod dictus Johannes Halle factum aut cartam feoffamenti per quod prefatus Robertus dictum Johannem Halle de et in Manerio predicto cum pertinenciis vt inferius specificatur feoffauit, ac eciam omnia alia cartas et munimenta que predictus Johannes Halle habuit ex liberacione et tradicione predicti Roberti premissis concernentibus eidem Roberto reliberaret.[4]

[*Translation.*—Be it remembered that on the 18th day of February, 34 Henry VI., 1456, the matters contained in the within-written supplication exhibited before the King in his Chancery by the within-written Robert (Bodenham) against the within-written John Hall, as well as the matters in the answer, the replication and the rejoinder exhibited and specified in that behalf, having been fully read and understood in the said Chancery, and deliberation and advice in that behalf of and concerning the premises had with the King's Justices of both Benches, and with divers others, as well Serjeants-at-law as others, then and there appearing as counsel for the parties aforesaid. It was then and there considered, by the advice of the same Justices that, since the within-written Robert (Bodenham) had then and there in the said Chancery paid to the within-written John Hall the said 80*l.* borrowed, as within written, by the said Robert from the said John Hall, the said John Hall should cause the within-written Robert to be delivered from prison in which he was then detained in the custody of the

[4] The pleadings and judgment are unusually full for so early a date. As to the question of mortgages, see Spence, i. 602. The earliest case he mentions is 9 Edw. IV. 1469-70. Here the mortgagee was apparently allowed to receive the rents and profits by way of interest. Taking the plaintiff's figures as correct, this was at the rate of about 70 per cent.

Sheriff of Wiltshire on account of the confession of the within-written
statute merchant for the within-written 300*l*., and should fully discharge
the said Robert from the execution of the said statute, and that the said
statute should be quashed, annulled and cancelled, and that the within-
written John Hall should re-enfeoff the within-written Robert of and in
the within-written manor with its appurtenances, or should release all
his right and claim of and in the same manor with its appurtenances to
the same Robert, to have and to hold to him, his heirs and assigns, for
ever ; and also that the said John Hall should deliver up to the said
Robert the deed or charter of feoffment by which the said Robert enfeoffed the said John Hall of and in the said manor with its appurtenances, as within specified, and also all other charters and muniments
concerning the premisses, which the said John Hall hath of the gift and
delivery of the aforesaid Robert.]

1456   **142**

[1] Besechith you ful mekely your trewe seruaunt and contynuel oratour,
William Cokayn, that for asmoch as of late tyme communicacion of a
mariage was had and riceved bitwene your seyd suppliant, one that
one partie, and Amy, the doughter of Thomas Hurst, otherwyse named
Thomas Barbour, of Asshwell in the Counte of Hertford,[2] one that
other partie, and accorde made of the said mariage bitwene the said
[parties] in the presence of John Enderby, Squyer, Thomas Boulasse,
Thomas Crake, Henry Crosse of Biggliswade, and other, in maner
and fourme as here sueth ; First, that your seyd suppliant shuld take
to wyfe the seyd Amy, and immediatly after th'espouselx bytwene
theym halowed, he shuld and ordeigne that of such londys and tenements as he was seised of in the toun of Kinebauton in the shire of
Huntyngdon[3] a sufficient and laufull estate of the seyd loudes and
tenementes to the yerly value of xl s. and above, shuld be made to
yo[r] seyd suppliaunt and the seyd Amy ioyntly, to haue and to hold to
theym and to theyr heyrs of their bothe bodyes lauffully commyng ;
For the which mariage and ioynture the seyd Thomas Hurst, fadre to
the seyd Amy, shuld make a sufficient and laufull estat of a mesuage
with appurtenaunces in the seyd toun of Asshwell to the yerly value of
xx s. and in xxx acres of land in Stepulmordon[4] to the yerly value
of xxv s., above all reprises, to haue and to hold the seyd mesuage and
xxx acres with their appurtenaunces to your seyd suppliant and Amy

---

[1] Early Chancery Proceedings, Bundle
25, No. 111. Thomas Bourchier, Archbishop of Canterbury, was Chancellor. See
p. 137, note 3.
[2] Near Royston.   [3] Kimbolton.
[4] Co. Cambridge, near Royston.

and to the heyrs of theyr bothe bodyes laufully commyng. And howe be it that yor seyd suppliant hath well and truly performed almaner thynges abouesayd touchyng his partie, and ofte tymes hath requyred the seyd Thomas Hurst to perfourme the premysses touchyng his partie, and that to doo he hath refused and yet refuseth ageyns all right and conscience : Please your highnesse the premysses tenderly to considre, and for asmoch as the seyd Thomas Hurst is visited with suche sikenes that he may not travayle, to graunt a writ of *dedimus potestatem* direct to John Leek clerk, William Seintgeorge, knyght, and William Hasilden, Squyer, that they and euery of them may ioyntly and seuerally haue power to examyn the seyd Thomas Hurst and all other persones which shall seme to theyr discrecions most necessarie to be examyned in the premysses and suche as shall be found by that examynacion to certefye the kynge's highnesse in his high Court of the Chauncerye : and yor sayd supplyant shal pray god for you.

[A writ of *dedimus potestatem*,[5] dated May 8, 34 Henry (VI.),[6] and addressed to John Leek and Walter Tayllard, is annexed, directing them to examine witnesses in the matter and to return the result into the Chancery without delay. Their certificate,[7] a lengthy document in bad condition, is also preserved.]

Indorsed on the bill. Memorandum quod quintodecimo die Februarii, anno regni Regis Henrici sexti post conquestum Anglie tricesimo sexto,[8] ista peticione coram dicto domino Rege in Cancellaria sua ac examinacionibus in hac parte captis in eadem Cancellaria lectis auditis et plenius intellectis, visum est Curie Cancellarie predicte materiam in peticione predicta specificatam fore veram et iustam, ac pro eo quod Amia, in peticione illa specificata, mortua existit, exitu de corpore suo et corpore infrascripti Willelmi legitime procreato adhunc superstite, Consideratum existit in eadem Cancellaria quod infrascriptus Thomas Hurst sufficientem statum de vno mesuagio et triginta acris terre cum pertinenciis in Asshewell et Stepulmordon in peticione predicta specificatis faceret predicto Willelmo et heredibus de corpore suo et corpore prefate Amie legitime procreatis, iuxta vim, formam, et effectum peticionis predicte.[9]

[*Translation.*—Be it remembered that on the 15th day of February,

---

[5] No. 110.
[6] 1456.
[7] No. 112.   [8] 1458.
[9] *Specific performance* of the agreement is what is asked for and decreed. The commission sent by the writ of *dedimus potestatem* is not in the nature of the com-

missions formerly referred to (p. 29, note 1). The commissioners had only power to take the defendant's answer, to examine witnesses, and to report. The practice of taking the defendant's answer by commission continued for a long period. See Spence, i. 372.

36 Henry VI., 1458, this petition (exhibited) before the King in his Chancery and the examinations (of witnesses) taken in this behalf being read, heard and fully understood in the said Chancery, it seemed to the Court of the Chancery aforesaid, that the matter specified in the aforesaid petition was true and just, and since Amy, in the petition mentioned, is dead, leaving issue of her body and of the body of the within-written William lawfully begotten still surviving. It was considered in the same Chancery that the within-written Thomas Hurst should make a sufficient· estate of a messuage and 30 acres of land with the appurtenances in Ashwell and Steeple Morden, in the aforesaid petition mentioned, to the aforesaid William and the heirs of his body and of the body of the aforesaid Amy lawfully begotten, according to the tenor, form, and effect of the aforesaid petition.]

143   [1] To the reuerent fadir in God and right gracious lorde Erchebisshop of Caunterbury, Chaunceler of Engeland, [2]

1456   Mekely besechen your pover and contynuelle Oratours, Robert Bale and Agneys his wyf, doughter and heire to John Haunsard, Brother to Thomas Haunsard, late of London, Vyntner, grevously compleynyng ageynst oon Nicholas Marchall, Irmonger of London, pretendyng hym to be executor of the seide Thomas, That where the same Thomas for mariage to be hadde betwyxte the seid Robert and Agneys graunted to geue theyme of his propre goodys an C li. in money, And over that the seide Thomas and oon Sir Henry Haunsard, Brother to the same Thomas, agreed to pay for all expensis and costis as well of arraymentis of your seide Besechers as of all other thyngis to be doon atte seide Mariage; And where as the seide Thomas and Sir Henry of grete trust were enfeffed be William Haunsard, Fysshemonger, brother to the seide John Haunsard, vnto the vse of the same John and his heyres of dyvers landys and messes atte Seynte George Barre in Suthewerk in the countee of Surrey, The seid Thomas and Sir Henry solde parcelle of the seide landys and meses after the deceas of the seide John and afore the seide mariage vnto oon Herberd Brews, Smyth, and delyuered to him the euidences thereof; For the sale of which londys the seide Thomas resceyved 1 marc vnto the vse of the seide Agneys. And where ´as oon Thomas Oswaldkirke, somtyme

[1] Early Chancery Proceedings, Bundle 25 No. 109. No. 108 is a copy.
[2] See p. 137, note 3.

person of Seynte Andrewe in Holbone, was seised of certein londys and tenementis in the parishe of Seynte Mary Magdaleyn in Suthwerk in his demesne as of Fee and, thereof seised, enfeffed theryn oon Agneys Haunsard, widowe, and the seide Thomas Haunsard, John Haunsard, Sir Henry Haunsard and also Thomas Badby and Thomas Welford, Fysshemongers, to the vse of the same John and his heyres, whiche Agneys Haunsard, widowe, John Haunsard, Sir Henry Haunsard, Thomas Badby and Thomas Welford deied soo seised, And the seide Thomas Haunsard helde hym in the same landys and tenementis be survivor vuto the day of his deth, and resceyued of the issues of the landys and tenementis after the deccas of the seide John Haunsard ix marc yerely duryng xvj yere, whiche ys an Cxliiij marc; And at his deceas he lefte the same tenementis feble and ruinous . And where as the seide John Haunsard, Fader, and Eleyn his wyf, moder to the seide Agneys your Besecher, delyuered at theire deceas of grete trust to the seide Thomas Haunsard an C marc in money & dyvers Jewelx & stuff of houshold to the value of xl li. &c., to the vse of the seide Agneys youre Besecher and of oon Johan her sustre, their doughters, beyng than wᵗyn age of vij yere, evenly to be devyded & departed betwyxte them at suche tyme as they were of full age & maried, & yf that outher of hem deceassed afore she were of full age & maryed that other of hem to haue all when she were maryed . And where as the seide Agneys Haunsard, widowe, delyuered to the seid Thomas Haunsard at her last dayes iiijᵛˣ li. to the vse of the seide Agneys & Johan, doughters of the seide John Haunsard, her son, than dede, to be devided evenly betwyxte them when they come tq full age & were maryed, And yf outher of hem deceassed afore that tyme the other of hem to haue the hooll somme when she were maryed ; Whiche Johan at her age of xij yere & vnmaryed deied, Soo that after the deceas of the seide Johan all somme of money and Jewelx & stuff of houshold forseide holly belanged of right & after consciens to your seide Besechers. Whereof & for the costis doon atte seide mariage the seide Thomas Haunsard hath paide to your seide Besechers in his lyf C marc in partye of payment, that ys to wite, the iij day after the seide mariage l marc for the arraymentis, costis & expensis doon atte seide mariage, & after the deceas of the seide Sʳ Henry, his brother, other l marc, in presence of the seide Nicholas Marchall ; and as to the residue, that ys to wite, CCCxlij li. xɪɪj s. ɪɪɪj d., and the seide Jewelx & goodys to the value of xl li., &c., the seide Thomas Haunsard kepte & hadde vnto the day of his deceas, & neuer made thereof to your seide Besecher any delyuere [delivery]. And for as moche as the seide Thomas Haunsard was aged & contynued many yeres feble [& euermore seide

T

that he wold leve your seide Besechers all their seide dutees & goodys,
& moche more by cause he]¹ hadde noo moo kynrede lyvyng than oonly
the seide Agneys your Suppliaunte, & her issue, Therfor, of grete
tendrenes & speciall love & trust, your seide Besechers lefte the seide
CCCxlij li. xiij s. iiij d., Residue, & the seide Jewelx & stuff of houshold,
to be allwey with the seide Thomas & in his kepyng wᵗout specialte or
wrytyng.   And, gracious lord, atte suche tyme as the seide Thomas
Haunsard was gretely enfebled & sykenes grewe vpon hym toward
dethe, the seide Nicholas Marchall, knowyng well that the seide Robert,
your Besecher, badde grete labour & attendaunce in dyvers wise for
the seide Thomas, and also that the same Thomas badde the seide Robert
& his wyf in grete favour & also speciall trust & lov to theym & grete
goodys of theirs in kepyng, aduertised & laboured than to the seide
Thomas Haunsard, & be vndewe meanys estraunged from hym your
seide Besechers, to th'entent to hurte & defraude them of their seide
dutees & goodys, and that the same Nicholas myght haue all the rule
hymself att his will of the goodys of the seide Thomas Haunsard after
his deceas ; Be the which labour the seide Nicholas, & oon John Childe
that nowe ys dede, beyng of covyne to giders [together] & either of hem
endetted to the seide Thomas Haunsard, that ys to wite, the seide
Nicholas in CCl marc & the same John Childe in xxxvj li., pretended
after the deceas of the same Thomas to be his executours by colour of
a feyned & pretended Testament that in the name of the seide Thomas
they [caused to] make & to be ensealed in his seide feblenes at suche
tyme as he vnderstode not well what he seide nor dedde, Wherof the
legatis passe not the somme of xxxiij li., and he was worth bettre [by
estimacion]² than Mˡ Mˡ Mˡ li., toke vpon them, after the deceas of the
seide Thomas Haunsard, the admynistracion of all his goodis ; And be
this mean the same Nicholas came to the possession of thoo goodys,
your seide Besechers in the lyf of the same Thomas Haunsard nor
after his deceas of the seide CCCxlij li. xiij s. iiij d. Residue, nor of
the seide Jewelx & goodys, nor of any parte therof, yit satesfied nor
paide, ageynst all right feithe & good consciens, & to right bevy
ensample & grete perill to the soule of the seide Thomas, wᵗout your
gracious remedy : Wherfor please hit your gracious lordeship the premysses tenderly to considre, and for as moche as your seide Besechers
by cours of the comen lawe may haue noon recover ageynst the seide
Nicholas of the seide residue, Jewelx & stuff of houshold, to graunte
a writte *subpena* to be directed to the same Nicholas Marchall,
comaundyng hym to appere afore the kyng our Soverayne lorde in his

---

¹ No. 108 only.   ² No 108 only.

Chauncery at a certeyne day & vpon a certeyne peyne be your lordeship to be limet, there to answer to the premysses, and that your seide
Besechers may be satesfied & paide of the seide CCCxlij li. xiijs. iiijd.,
and of the seide Jewelx & stuff of houshold or xl li. for them, as good
feith & consciens requyren . Atte reuerence of god & in dede of
charitee.

Plegii de prosequendo : Willelmus Prowd de London',
Peyntour [?],
Johannes More de London', Grocer.

[8] This is the answere of Nicholl Marchall to
the bylle of Robert Bale and of Agnes his
wyff, putte agayn hym in this court of
Chauncerie.

The seid Nicholl, making protestacion that he knowith not any of the
materes conteyned in the seid bille to be trewe, for his ansuere seith
that the mater conteyned in the seid bille is insufficient [to put] hym
to ansuere therto, wherfor he prayyth to be dismyssed therof oute of
this courte, and that he [may] haue his resonabill costis and damages
of the seid Robert and Agnes for his wrongefull vexacion susteyned
aboute the same, accordyng to the forme of the statut in suech cases
purveied, &c.

Nevirthelesse for the more pleyn and trewe declaracion of the
materes conteynyd in the seid bille, the seid Nicholl [etc.].[4]

[5] This ys the replicacion of Robert Bale and
Agneys his wyf vuto the answer of Nicholas
Marchall ageynst their bill, &c.

First where the seide Nicholl seith that the matier contened in the seide
bill is insufficient to putte hym to answer, Therto the seide Robert &
Agneys seyen that the seide matier ys sufficient to putte hym to answer
after the lawe of consciens, whiche ys lawe executory in this courte for
defaute of remedy by cours of the common lawe.

And where the seide Nicholl hath surmytted in his seide answer by
wey of declaracion that it ys in noowise trewe that the seide Thomas

[3] Bundle 25, No. 107.
[4] A large piece of this document is torn
off. The answer seems to have dealt with
the allegations of the Bill *seriatim*. The

main points may be gathered from the
replication.
[5] Bundle 25, No. 106.

Haunsard graunted to gef vnto the seide Robert & Agneys the hole C li. in mariage, &c., Therto seyen the seide Robert & Agneys that the forseide Thomas Haunsard graunted to gyf vnto theym the hole C li. in mariage, lyke as ys surmytted in their seide bill; and as to the C marc whiche the seide Robert resceyved of the seide Thomas Haunsard at two tymes, the seide Robert & Agneys seyen that the seide Thomas delyuered vnto the seide Robert 1 marc parcell of the same C marc for the costis & charges doon by the seide Robert at the seide mariage accordyng to his promyse & graunte, & the residue of the seide C marc was resceyved in the hous of the seide Nicholl in manere & fourme as he hath supposed in partie of payment of the seide C li., lyke as ys surmytted in their seide bill; and as for the seide mariage, the saide Thomas Haunsard sent for the seide Robert to come afore the Maistre of Seynte Thomas of Acres [1] & hym w'yn the place of Seynte Thomas there for to fynysshe & eide the seide mariage, & there by th'assent of the same Thomas the seide mariage was concludit, &c., as the seide Maistre can reporte.

And where the seide Nicholl seith that the seide Thomas aggreed hym not to pay for the costis & expensis to be doon at the seide mariage, &c., as he supposeth verely & as ferforth as ever he badde knowlege, Therto seith the seide Robert & Agneys that the seide Thomas & S[r] Henry agreed to pay for all the seide costis & expensis, lyke as the seide Robert & Agneys have surmytted in their seide bill, & accordyng to the same agrement the seide Thomas delyuered vnto the seide Robert 1 marc for the costis & expensis aforeseide, lyke as ys above reherced, &c.

And where the seide Nicholl seith that he knoweth not in any wise the seide Thomas Haunsard & S[r] Henry to haue been enfeffed in the seide meses & landys at Seynt George Barre in Suthwerk vnto the vse of the seide John Haunsard & his heyres, ne that the seide Thomas resceyved the seide 1 marc for the sale thereof to the vse of the seide Agneys, The seide Robert & Agneys, for as moche as the seide Nicholas w'seieth not but that the forseide Thomas was enfeffed of the seide meses & landys to the vse of the seide John & of his heyres, whoes heire the seide Agneys ys, & also that the seide Thomas resceyved the seide 1 marc for the sale therof, lyke as the same Robert & Agneys haue surmytted in their seide bill, they pray that this courte will awarde the seide Nicholas, to pay & content theym the seide 1 marc.

And where the seide Nicholas seith, as he supposeth & as ferforth as

---

[1] S. Thomas's Hospital was on the north side of Cheapside, in the parish of S. Mary Colechurch.

he ever badde any informacion or knowlege, ' that the seide Agneys Haunsard & her seide cofeoffes were enfeoffed of the seide londys & tenementis in the parisshe of Seynte Mary Magdaleyn to the vse of the seide Agneys Haunsard & of her heyres, & not to the vse of the seide John & his heyres, & also that he supposeth that the seide Thomas was sone & heyre vnto the seide Agneys Haunsard, The seide Robert & Agneys, for as moche as this matier allegged by the seide Nicholas ys no sufficient answer vnto the matier surmytted by the seide Robert & Agneys in their seide bill, they pray that the seide Nicholl may be compelled by awarde of this courte to satesfie the seide Robert & Agneys of the seide somme of Cxliiij marc by the seide Thomas resceyved in fourme aboveseide.

And where the seide Nicholl seith that hit may in noo wise be supposed to be trewe that the seide John Haunsard, fader, & Eleyn his wyf, modyr to the seide Agneys, wyf of the seide Robert, delyuered the seide C marc & stuff of houshold in manere & fourme as ys surmytted in the bill of the seide Robert & Agneys, &c., The seide Robert & Agneys, for as moche as the seide Nicholl w'seieth not the lyuere of the seide C marc & stuff of houshold to be made to the vse & in the fourme as ys reherced in their seide bill, pray that the seide Nicholl may be compelled by awarde of this Courte to satesfie them of the seide C marc & of the seide stuff of houshold or of xl li. for the same stuff.

And where the seide Nicholl seith that hit ys not trewe as he supposeth & as ferforth as ever he hadde any informacion or knowlege that the seide Agneys Haunsard, widowe, delyuered to the seide Thomas Haunsard iiij^{xx} li. to the vse, as ys surmytted in the bill, of the seide Robert & Agneys, &c., The seide Robert and Agneys, for as moche as the seide Nicholl w'seieth not the deliuere of the seide iiij^{xx} li. to be made to the forseide Thomas Haunsard to the vse of the seide Agneys, wyf of the seide Robert, after the maner & fourme as ys surmitted in their seide bill, they pray that the seide Nicholas be compelled by awarde of this courte to satesfie theym of the seide iiij^{xx} li.

[2] This is the reioynyng of Nicholl Marshall vuto the replicacion of Robert Bale & Agnes his wiffe.

The seid Nicholl seith that the frist article of the seid Replicacion is plenly answered by the seid Answer of the seid Nicholl.

[2] Bundle 25, No. 105.

And as to tbe ij^{de} article and the prymes of the iij^{de} article conteygnyd in the seid replicacion of the seid Robert & Agnes, The seid Nicholl seith that thai be sufficiently answerd & declaryd in the playn and true declaracion of the seid Nicholl in his seid answer thereof specifide & declaryd . And as for the conclusion of the same article, the seid Nicholl seith that he knowith not what the seid Robert & Agnes callen the conclusion of a mariage, But he seith that the same Robert & Agnes were fully concludyd & aggred and by wey of matrimony lawfully affied,[1] so that nether of theym myght duryng their lyves by eny maner of meane in other wise be maried, and that vtterly ayeinst the will or wittyng of the seid Thomas Haunserd.

And as to the iiijth, the vjth, the vijth articlez conteignyd in the seid replicacion, the seid Nicholl seith that his declaracion in his seid answer as touchyng the materz conteignyd in the same articlez is verray god and true ; And forthermor he seith that he hath made sufficient declaracion in his seid answer to be dismissyd oute of this Courte, and no thyng hath withseid concernyng eny mater of the seid articlez [or in] eny other wherfore that hym oght by lawe or ryght by the award and compulsion of this Courte to pay, satisfie or deliuere vnto the seid Robert and Agnes that thei by their seid bill, in maner & forme afore declaryd, haue desyryd.

And as to the vth article conteignyd in the replicacion of the seid Robert and Agnes, The seid Nicholl seith that the mater therof by hym alleggyd in his seid answer by wey of declaracion is sufficient to discharge hym as in this Courte ayeinst the seid Robert & Agnes of all that that thei ayeinst the seid Nicholl in that behalfe desyren.

All which maters the seid Nicholl is redy to prove and auerr as this Court will award.

Wherefore and for as mych as the seid Robert & Agnes haue not withseid diuersez and grete materes of substaunce alleggyd by the seid Nicholl, the seid Nicholl prayith to be dismissyd oute of this Courte, and to be restoryd to his reasonable costys and dammagez in maner & fourme as he in his seid answer hath desyryd.

Indorsed on bill; No. 109 *only.* Memorandum quod quintodecimo die Nouembris anno regni Regis Henrici sexti post conquestum Angliae tricesimo sexto,[2] tam materia in ista billa contenta et specificata ac responsione infrascripti Nicholai Marchall ad materiam illam, quam replicatione et reiunctione vtrarumque parcium infrascriptarum in Cancellaria predicti domini Regis apud Westm' visis, lectis, pleniusque intellectis, Habitaque matura deliberacione cum Justiciariis ipsius

---

[1] Betrothed.   [2] 1457.

domini Regis de vtroque Banco, aliisque de Consilio[3] eiusdem domini
Regis tunc ibidem presentibus, per aduisamentum eorundem Justiciariorum Consideratum est in eadem Curia quod infrascripti Robertus
et Agnes recuperent versus predictum Nicholaum centum et quater
viginti et quatuordecim marcas de bonis et catallis infrascripti Thome
Haunsard defuncti, videlicet, l marcas pro infrascriptis terris et tenementis per prefatum Thomam Haunsard venditis, situatis apud barras
Sancti Georgii in Suthwerk, in dicta billa specificatis, ac Cxliiij marcas
per prefatum Thomam Haunsard de exitibus ceterorum terrarum et
tenementorum in parochia Sanete Marie Magdalene in Suthwerk
predict' receptis, in eadem billa similiter specificatis.

[*Translation.*—Be it remembered that on the 15th day of November,
36 Henry VI., 1457, the matters contained and specified in this bill,
and the answer of the within-written Nicholas Marshall thereto, as well
as the replication and rejoinder of both the within-written parties,
having been seen, read, and fully understood in the Chancery of the
said Lord King at Westminster, and mature deliberation with the
King's justices of both Benches and others of the King's Council then
and there present having been held : It was considered in the said
court that the within-written Robert and Agnes should recover against
the said Nicholas, 194 marks of the goods and chattels of the within-
written Thomas Hansard, deceased ; to wit, 50 marks for the within-
written lands and tenements sold by the said Thomas Hansard,
situated at S. George's Bar in Southwark, and specified in the said
bill, and 144 marks received by the said Thomas Hansard of the
issues of other lands and tenements in the parish of S. Mary,
Magdalen in Southwark aforesaid, also specified in the said bill.]

144   [4] To the ryght Reuerent Lord and fader in
       God the Bysshope of Excestre, Chaunceler
       of Ynglond,[5]

1460   Besecheth lowely your poer bedemen, the Maire and Cetizins of the
to   Cite of Carlile, that wher one William Stokton and Richard Lamaton,
1465   merchauntz of Yorke, were by two obligacions iuntly bundyn to one
       John Blanerhasset, marchaunt, than Maire of the same Cite of
       Carlile, and to his successors, in lxxiij li. vj s., to the vse of the same

---

[3] It would appear from this that the
Council still sat as judges.
[4] Early Chancery Proccedings, Bundle
27, No. 390.

[5] George Neville ; appointed Chancellor
July 25, 1460 ; consecrated Archbishop of
York, June 17, 1465.

Cetizins ; And also wher John Day and John Medilton, merchauntz
of Hulle, by on oder obligacion was bundyn vnto the same John, than
Maire of the said Cite, and to his successors, in xx li. xvj s., to the
vse of the sayd Cetizins, the which thre obligacions he, vpon his
departyng of his office of Maire, delyuerd to one John Blanerhasset,
gentilman, than beyng Maire of the sayd Cite of Carlile next after
the sayd John Blanerhasset, marchaunt, to haue, keepe and sewe to
the vse of the said Cetizins ; which obligacions the said John Blanerhasset, gentilman, w'holdes, and no peny of the said somes in the
said obligacions conteigned, ne the said obligacions, ne none of
thaym, wille vnto yo' said besechers delyuer ; the which somes of
mone shold be disspended of the nessessari ordinans and abilmentes
of werre conuenyent for the kepyng and defence of the said Cite, the
which in many behalue laketh, and w'out which mone your said
besechers ar nowght of pover to by ner ordeyn : Wherfore pleas it yo'
lordchipe thies premissez tenderly to concedre, and the greete iuberte
[jeopardy] of the said Cite and the inhabitantes therin in this werre
tyeme, to graunte vnto yo' said besechers a writ to be directe vnto the
said John Blanerhasset, gentilman, to appere afor you in the Chauncery,
at certayn day and vpon certeyn payn by your lordchipe to be lemyt,
ther to answere in thies premisses, and thervpon ye to set sych rewelle
as gude fayth and conscens requyer : and yo' sayd besechers shall
euer pray for your gude estate.

145   ¹ To the right reuerent and holy fader in God
my right good and gracious lord, the Bisshop
of Excestre, Chaunceller of Englond ²

cir. Besecheth mekely and piteuously compleyneth vnto youre gracious
1464 lordship youre pouer and contynuelle bedeman, Laurence Kylwyth of
the parissh of Lanlyverey in the Counte of Cornwaile,³ tenaunt of the
right and myghty and [most] gracious lord the Erle of Warwyk and of
Salesbury,⁴ youre brother, of his lordship of Lantyan in the said
Counte of Cornewayle, That where as Herry Bothrygan, Squyer,
aboute the xiij day of August, the secunde yere of the reigne of King
Edward the fourthe,⁵ sent certeyn persones of his menyal men to the
hous of youre said besecher, where as they with force and by strength

---

¹ Early Chancery Proceedings, Bundle ³ Lanlivery, near Lostwithiel.
28, No. 338. ⁴ Richard Neville, the ' King-Maker.'
² See p. 150, note 5. ⁵ 1462.

and ageynst his wille, toke and led hym from his said bous vnto the place of the said Herry, And atte his comyng thider the same Herry came to youre said besecher and claymed of hym bondage, saying that the same youre besecher was his bondman and desired hym to make fyne and raunson and to agree w^t hym therfore; whervpon yor besecher answered hym and saide that he wolde neuer agree w^t hym for none such thyng, and how he was never no bondman, nor none of his kyn, as ferforth as he euer myght knowe, and that he wolde be reported by god and the cuntrey and by all his neyburs; And whan the said Herry conceyued that youre said besecher wolde not agree to his entent vnrightwis and vnlawfull desire, made youre said besecher to be fettered in irons and greuously emprisoned hym in his place, like as thof he had be the [King's?] aduersarie and his prisoner, during the space of a moneth and more; and after that the said Herry come to youre said besecher, so beyng in prison and in duresse, and asked hym howe he wolde be ruled, and whether he was [well] avised or not; whervpon yor said besecher answered hym and saide that he wolde neuer graunte to his askyng, insomuch as he kuewe hymself clere in that behalf; And than, accordyng to the desire of the said Herry Bothrygan, youre saide besecher fonde suirte his fader in lawe, and other sufficient persones, that were bounde to the said Herry by theire obligacion in the somme of xx li. stirlinges, w^t a condicion that yor said besecher w^{t}yn a certeyn day after shulde brynge w^t hym sufficient persones of the forsaid parissh of Lanlyverey to recorde that yor said besecher was no bondman, nor none of his progenytours; And w^{t}yn vj dayes after that the said obligacion was so made and deliuered yor said besecher had knowleche that the said Herry purposed hym to haue goon to London and there to haue ahiden vnto the tyme that the day that was lymyted to yor besecher to haue brought his recorde had be expired and past, to th'entent to haue made yor said besecher and his frendes to haue forfeted and lost the said somme of xx li. in which they stonde bounde to the said Herry, youre said besecher w^t diligence assembled togider . . . . persones of the said parissh of Lanlyverey and theraboute to the nombre of xl persones, gentilmen and other, auncient and of the eldest men of that cuntrey, and brought them to the place of the said Herry there to haue clered yor besecher before the said Herry of the bondage that he claymed of hym; And whan the same Herry had knowlech and saw the grete recorde that he brought, the said Herry and his men come oute of his place w^t bowes and arrowes, and there violently, w^{t}oute any cause, sodeynly shot at youre besecher and at such persones as came with hym, and sore bette and wowndid them, and toke away from them their horses and harneis, and drove them home ageyn; And so after that youre said besecher abode still in pease at home in his occupacion and no thing [happened] to hym by the space of xij moneth and half a yere after, till now late before Whitsontide last past [1] that the said Herry Bothrigan, not seasing his evill wille and malicious disposicion ageynst youre besecher, sent certeyn of his men ageyn vnto the hous of youre said besecher, and ther toke the same youre besecher, and brought hym ageyn vnto the place of the said Herry, and there kept hym as a prisoner; And whan yo[r] besecher had be so kept prisoner in his place the space of iij wekes and more, he besought the said Herry to lete hym haue knowleche wherfore he w[t]helde hym so prisoner in his place; and the said Herry answered hym and saide that or he passed from hym he shulde agre w[t] hym as well for the lordship [?] that he claymed of hym as for a trespas doon to his tenant, which the said Herry surmyseth that youre besecher shulde bete ; whervpon the same yo[r] besecher, vnderstanding the eville wille and malicious disposicion of the said Herry, and in eschewing of the gretter hurt and inconueniences that myght therby growe to yo[r] saide besecher and by the wrongfull surmyses [of the saide Herry] [2] yo[r] said besecher, vnknowyng to the same Herry,

departed from his place and came to the Cite of London, so that he for drede of the said Herry dare not in no wyse go home ageyn to his hous vn[to his occu]pacion, to his grete and importable hurt and to his [grievous damage], w[t]oute yo[r] gracious lordship to hym be shewed in this behalve : The premysses piteuously considered, Please it youre good and gracious [lordship] to commaunde the said Herry Bothrygan, vpon a certayn payne and on a certayn day by youre lordship to be lymyted, to appere before you, and vpon due examynacion of the premissis to [command] and ordeyne that the said Herry Bothrygan suffre youre saide besecher to kepe his hous and [that he] may lyve in goddes pease and the kynges, as right and good conscience requiren : For the loue of god and in way of charyte; And youre said besecher shall hertly pray to god for you.[3]

---

[1] This must be 1464.
[2] Query ; a hole in the document.
[3] Compare this with the other villeinage cases, Nos. 113, 139, and 146.

146   [4] To the Ryght Reuerent Fadyr in God, my Ryght good and graciouse lord, the Archebisshop of Yorke, Chaunceler of Englond,[5]

1465
to
1467 [Beseecheth][6] your lordship your trew bedeman, Robert Richard, That where oon Herry, the Pryour of the Monastary of Ely,[7] cleymed your seid bedeman to be his villayn in the Ryght of the monastary [appendant to their manor of] Sutton, whereof the seid Pryour is seysed as in the Ryght of the seid monastary, for the which his tytle and clayme in the Ryght of the seid hous the seid Pryour, by th'assent of the [convent of the same], fully aggreed and condessended w[t] your seid besecher and his Fryendys that if hit were so that your seid besecher and his Fryndys wold pay the seid Priour, as to the behofe of the seid [beseecher, the sum of x li.], oon Thomas Lamport to be suerte for payment of the same to the seid Pryour, that the seid Priour by th'assent of the Couent of the seid Monastary were aggreed to seale to your seid besecher [a manumission, freeing the said beseecher and his] heires for evermore, they to be quite of the seid villenage, yevyng full power to the seid Thomas to levy and Resseyue of your seid besecher in theyr name the seid x li., And also delyuered the [said manumission unto] the seid Thomas sauely to kepe to the behofe of your seid besecher; And at suche tyme as he, the seid Thomas, were satisfied and payd in godes or in syluyr to the seid summe of x li., than the seid [manumission was unto] your seid besecher truly to be delyuerd; where now the seid Thomas hath leuyed the seid summe of x li., and more by the summe of v marc, of the godes of your seid besecher had, taken, and prysed [to the use?] of the seid Thomas; aftyr which tyme, by cause that your seid besecher departed out of the seruice of the seid Thomas for lak of resonable sustenaunce, aswille of clothyng to alle partyes of his body as otherwyse, [and entered the service of one (?)] William Fylddyng, Squyer, of grete malyce and ongodly delyng, ayenst alle trouth and gode consience, the seid Thomas the same manumission delyuerd to the seid Priour, which seid manumission [the said Prior yet keepeth (?)], and the same Robert hath requyred the seid Priour to delyuer the seid manumission, which he vtterly denyeth and yet refuseth, to the vtter vndoyng of your seid besecher:

[4] Early Chancery Proceedings, Bundle 20, No. 134.
[5] George Neville; consecrated Archbishop of York, 1465, being then Chancellor;
resigned June 8, 1467.
[6] The left margin of this document is mutilated.
[7] Henry Peterborough, Prior, 1462-1478.

Please your gode lordship, the premisses considered and that [your said beseecher is] w'oute remedy at the Comyn lawe, to graunt a wrytt *sub pena* dyrect to the seid Priour, him comaundyng to apere by fore your lordship in the Chauncery in the quindecym of Pasch [next ensuing], to answere to the mater aboueseid and therin to be ruled as gode fayth and consciens requyreth . And he shall pray to god for the preseruacion of your noble astate.[1]

Plegii de prosequendo { Willelmus Fildyng de Ely in Com Cantebr', armiger, Willelmus Alherd de eadem, yoman.

147   [2] To the right reverent fader in God and my good and gracious lord, the bysshop of Bathe and Welles, Chaunceller of Englond,[3]

1471 Besechith youre gode lordship your humble oratours, William Revelle and Maude his wyff, Robert Blount and Ele his wyff, the which Maude and Ele bene cosyns and heyres to one Alice Flemyng, late discessed, that is to say, dowghters to Nicholas Stanlake, sone of Elizabethe Stanlak, dowghter to Johan Thorpe, Fader of Johan Thorpe, Fader to the seid Alice Flemyng, that where Edward Gower, esquier, with other were and bene enfeffed in and of the maner of Thorpe [4] with the appurtenaunce in the counte of Suthrey, in and of the maner of Henton Pippard with their appurtenaunce in the counte of Wilteshire, and of the maner of Shawe [5] with appurtenaunce in the Counte of Berk', by the seid Alice to the use and behoffe of the seid Alice and here heires ; and after the dethe of the seid Alice, youre seid besechers in the right of their seid wyffes, cosyns and heyres to the seid Alice, oftyn tymes havyn required the said Edward to make estate to the said Maude and Ele, accordyng to right and good consciens, The seid Edward that to do utterly refused, and yet dothe, contrarie to all good conscience ; of which wrong and injure youre seid suppliantes havyne no remedie by the comyne lawe : Pleasith hit your god lordship thez premissez to considere, and to graunt to your seid suppliauntes a wret of *sub pena* to be adressed to the seid Edward Gower to apere before you in the Chauncery, at a certen day uppon a payne by your lordship lamytt,

---

[1] Compare this case with Nos. 113, 139, and 145.
[2] Bayley's *Transcripts*, vol. 26, p. 7.
[3] Robert Stillington ; appointed June 20 1467, resigned 1473.
[4] Near Chertsey.   [5] Near Newbury.

their to be ruled in the premisses as Feith and good conciens requyryn; and your besechers shall pray to God for the conservacion of your said lordship.

Plegii { Willelmus Edmond de London, yoman,
Johannes Swepston de Ryslcy, yoman.

This is the answer of Edward Gower, esquier, to the bille of William Revelle and Maude his wyf and Robert Blounte and Ele his wyf, cosynes and heirs to one Alice Flemmyng.

Where it is supposed by the seid bille that the seid Edward with other were and beene enfeoffed in and of the manere of Thorpe with the appurtenauncez in the counte of Surr', in and of the manere of Henton Pyppard with the appurtenaunce in the counte of Wiltes', and of the manere of Shawe with the appurtenauncez in the counte of Berkshyre, by the seid Alice to the behof of the seid Alice and hyr heyrs, as more at the large is conteyned in the seid bille, hereto the seid Edward seith by protestacion that the seid bille, ne the matere conteyned in the same, is not sufficiaunte to pute him to answere; bot for answere he seith as to the seid manerez of Thorpe and Shawe, that he with other was infeoffed thairof by the seid Alice, which Alice declared to the said Edward and to the other cofeffes that thei shulde thaireof perfourme the wille of Johan Thorpe, hir fader, and to pay hyr dettis, and never othre wille or entent thaireof declaryd to theim; which the seid Edward is and at alle tymes hath beene redy to perfourme and to doo forthermore as this courte wille reule hym thairin. And as unto the seid manere of Henton Pyppard with the appurtenaunce, the seid Edward seith that he bought the same manere of the seid Alice for a certeyn somme of monay betwyx theim accordit, the which he welle and treuly content and payd to the seid Alice, and thaire uppon the seid Alice made astate thaireof to the seid Edward and other, to hafe and hold to theim and to the herz of the seid Edward and to his use and his herz, and not to the use of the said Alice and hyr heirs as is supposed by the seid bille . Alle which materez he is redy to prof as this Court wille reulle hym, and prayeth to be dismyssed with his costez and his damagez for his wrongfulle vexacion.

This is the replicacion of William Revelle and Maude his wyf and of Robert Blount and Ele his wyf to the answere of Edward Gower, esquier, to their bille.

Where as the seid Edward seith that Alice Flemyng enfeoffed hym and othir of the seid Manors of Thorpe and Shawe, and declared hir wille to the seid Edward and to the othir cofeoffez that they shuld therof perfourme the wille of Johan Thorp her Fader, and to paye her dettis, and never othir wille or intent therof declared to the seid feoffeez, as more pleynly is conteynyd in the seid bille,[1] hereunto the seid William Revelle, Maude his wyf, Robert Blount and Ele his wyf, seyn by protestacion that the answere of the seid Edward is not sufficiant, but for a replicacion seyn that the seid Johan Thorpe enfeoffed William Lowdelowe and othir of alle the seid londez of verry trust, and made his last wille that if the seid Alice Flemyng, his doughter, and othir her sosters, died without heire of their body lawfully begotyn, that then alle his londez, excapt londez tailed, shuld be solde by his seid feoffeez. The whiche matterz is conteyned in the bille of the seid William, Maud, Robert and Ele bene sufficiently entailled, as it shalbe pleynly shewed and proved by the grace of God . Withoute that that the seid Alice declared to the seid Edward and his cofeoffeez that they shuld perfourme the wille of Johan Thorpe, Fader to the seid Alice, and paye her dettis . And for the maner of Henton Pippard, the seid William, Maude, Robert and Ele seyn, that the seid Alice Flemyng enfeoffed the seid Edward Gower and his seid cofeoffeez to hir behoffe and of hir heirez, in the maner and fourme as is supposid by the bille of the seid William, Maude, Robert and Ele; without that that the seid Edward bought the seid maner of Henton Pippard or paied any money for the seid maner of Henton aforeseid.   Alle the whiche maters they bene redy to prove as this court wille rule thaym, and pray that the seid Edward make theym astate as right and conscience requiren.

Indorsed on the bill.   Coram domino Rege in Cancellaria sua die Sabbati proximo futuro.

Memorandum quod duodecimo die Februarii anno regni regis Edwardi quarti undecimo,[2] ista peticione per infrascriptos Willelmum Revelle et Matildam uxorem ejus et Robertum Blount et Eliam uxorem ejus, consanguineos et heredes Alicie Flemmyng, versus Edwardum Gower, armigerum, coram nobis in Cancellaria nostra, anno regni

---

[1] Query, answer.   [2] 1472.

nostri decimo exhibita, ac responsione et replicacione inter partes predictas factis et habitis inde in eadem Cancellaria lectis, auditis, et matura deliberacione intellectis per venerabilem patrem Episcopum Bathoniensem et Wellensem, Cancellarium nostrum, ac per Curiam Cancellarie, Consideratum et adjudicatum existit, pro eo quod prefatus Edwardus coram nobis in eadem Cancellaria sufficienter probavit quod ipse perquisivit et [emit] infrascriptum manerium de Hynton Pippard ad [sic] superscripta Alicia Thorp [sic] sibi, heredibus et assignatis suis imperpetuum, et pro eodem manerio dicte Alicie fuit per prefatum Edwardum satisfactum, ideo consideratum et adjudicatum est per prefatum Cancellarium ac per consideracionem Curie predicte quod idem Edwardus habeat, continuat, teneat, gaudeat et possideat predictum manerium de Hynton Pippard cum pertinenciis, sibi, heredibus et assignatis suis imperpetuum, juxta consideracionem et judicium . . quod idem Edwardus dimitteretur de Curia predicta. Et super hoc dimissus est de Curia, quietus sine die.

[*Translation.*—Be it remembered that on the 12th day of February, 11 Edward IV, 1472, this petition, exhibited before us in our Chancery in the 10th year of our reign by the within-written William Revelle and Maude his wife and Robert Blount and Ele his wife, cousins and heirs of Alice Fleming, against Edward Gower, esquire, and the answer and replication made and had thereto between the parties aforesaid having been read, heard and understood with mature deliberation in the said Chancery by the venerable father, the Bishop of Bath and Wells, our Chancellor, and by the Court of Chancery : It was considered and adjudged that, inasmuch as the said Edward hath sufficiently proved before us in the Chancery, that he purchased and bought the within-written manor of Hinton Pippard from the above-written Alice Thorpe [Fleming], to hold to himself, his heirs and assigns for ever, and satisfaction for the same manor was made by the aforesaid Edward to the said Alice, Therefore it was considered and adjudged by the aforesaid Chancellor and by the consideration of the Court aforesaid that the same Edward may have, continue, hold, enjoy, and possess the said manor of Hinton Pippard with the appurtenances, to himself, his heirs and assigns, for ever, according to the consideration and judgment aforesaid ; and that the same Edward be dismissed out of the Court aforesaid. And thereupon he is dismissed out of Court, quit and without day.] [1]

---

[1] An interesting set of pleadings. The judgment appears to have been given by the Chancellor alone, unless the phrase '*per consideracionem curie*' means that others sat with him.

GLOSSARY.

bachelor (pp. 50, 109), used by itself in the sense of 'knight'; not, apparently, 'a young knight,' as given in N. E. D.

chevesance (p. 88). This word has a variety of meanings, including both 'borrowing,' and 'lending.' See N. E. D.

enfant denys (p. 42), see note 4, p. 42. The expression seems to be merely a translation of the English word 'Child,' when used as a kind of title. It does not appear that the word 'enfant' was used in a similar way by the French; at least no examples of such use are given by Littré or Godefroy.

guerpier (p. 5), to abandon; modern Fr. *déguerpir*.

harang, blanc et sore (p. 28), white and red herring, the one being salted and the other smoked or dried; old Fr. *sorer*, to dry in the smoke; Cotgrave.

juvencle (p. 24), from *juvenculus*, a diminutive of *juvencus*, a bullock or steer.

lodesman (p. 4), not the pilot, apparently the steersman; from 'lode,' a way or course.

millier (p. 121). Query, a thousand-weight ten hundred-weight.

pirwykes (p. 30), thumbscrews; mistranslated 'hand-cuffs' in the text. See Cowell's *Interpreter*, s. v. Pyrewinkes, and Jamieson's *Scottish Dict.*, s. v. Pilliewinkes.

plates (p. 19), apparently used with the meaning of 'plate-armour.'

terre naitif (p. 79), probably equivalent to the *terra nativa* or *terra nativorum* frequently mentioned in manorial rolls.

tin-toll (p. 50), probably the same as 'tin-penny,' a tribute paid for the liberty of digging in tin mines. See Cowell.

valet (p. 60), apparently an officer of the Court employed in serving writs.

veduyte (p. 98). Query, from the Italian *veduta*, a form of *vedetta*, a watch-tower. See Canal, *Dict. Ital. e Franc.* Florio gives *veduta* = *vista* = view.

INDEX OF PERSONS AND PLACES.

N.B.—The numbers refer to the Cases, except where otherwise specified

INDEX OF SUBJECTS.

N.B.—The numbers refer to the Cases, except where otherwise specified

N.B.—The numbers refer to the Cases, except where otherwise specified

Contempt, 22, 52, 58, 69, 101, 108, 111
  of writ, 58, 82
Contract, rescission of, 56, p. xxxv
Corn, forcibly cutting, 49
  destroying, 16
Coroner, 19
Corpus cum causa, *see* Writ
Corrody, dispute as to, 39
Costs, p. xxv
  claimed, 2, 13
  plaintiff promises to pay, 133
  sureties for, *see* Mainpernors
Council, judgment by, 34, 95, 122, p. xv
  jurisdiction of, p. xvi
  list of sitting, 34, 55, 122
  defendant to come before, 7, 9, 16, 55
  bill addressed to Chancellor and, 19, 107
  order by, 55, 65
  King and, 106
  King and Great, 134
  writ to appear before, asked, 21, 46, 79, 99, 101, 130, 131
                          ordered, 55, 122
  sitting with Chancellor, 143
  Clerk of, 47
  gradual separation of Chancery from, p. xviii
  and see Appearance
Counsel, retained, 22, 119
  heard on both sides, 141
  dare not sue, 24
  fee to, 119
  Chancellor's jurisdiction over, 119
  fraudulent advice by, 119
  attorney acting as, 84
  Clerk of Chancery acting as, 22, 119
  bills signed by, p. xxviii
County, prize taken within body of, 96
Court, constitution of, 141
  defendant present in, 33
  plaintiff present in, 119, p. xxiv
Custom to ring bell, 132
Customs of port, 12

Damages claimed, 1, 13, 19, 38, 40, 49, 50, 51, 53, 60, 91, 92, 96, 107, 113, 119, 121, 139
  by replication but not by bill, 189
Day given, *see* Appearance
Dead, prayers for, 40, 44
Debt, imprisonment for, 8, 14, 53, 75, 134, 141

Debt, contracted abroad, 55, 95, 129
  wrongful detention of, 33, 53
  false action for, 38
  judgment, in Admiral's Court abroad, 129
Debtor, improper release of, 14, 53, 75
Deceit, 2
Decree, p. xxviii; *and see* Judgment
Dedimus potestatem, *see* Writ
Deeds seized, 39, 63, 94
  ordered to be given up, 141
Defendant, not guilty, 10
  avoids arrest, 93
  present in Court, 33, 47
  power and violence of, *see* Common Law
  no remedy in absence of, 73
  appears in person, 95, 106
  examined by Chancellor, 95, 109
  sworn, 95, p. xxvii
  writ to, to do justice to plaintiff, 96
  to bring documents into Court, 101
  appears by attorney, 105
  arrest of, asked for, 22, 61, 82, 93, 111, p. xxvi
  asks to be dismissed to Common Law, 139
  asks for damages, 141, 143, 147
Delivery of documents asked for, 88
Detinue, 63, 89, p. xli
  will not lie at common law without specialty, 104; or privity, 116
Discovery, p. 1, n. 3; 89, 109, 112, p. xxxii
Dismissal of bill, *see* Bill
Disseisin, 26, 65, 74, 90, 98, 110
Divine service, clerk dare not perform, 68
Divorce, 18
Documents ordered to be brought into Court, 138
  detained by executor, 109
Dower, 24, p. xxxii
Duress, 134, 145, p. xxxii

Ecclesiastical Court, bill dismissed to, 106
  libel on judges of, 108
  no remedy in, 123, 140
Ejectment, 67, 81; *and see* Forcible entry *and* Ouster
Elegit, 70
Elixir for making silver, 134
English subject abroad, 95

𝔖𝔢𝔩𝔡𝔢𝔫 𝔖𝔬𝔠𝔦𝔢𝔱𝔶.

FOUNDED 1887.

To Encourage the Study and Advance the Knowledge of the History of Englis

---

Patrons:

HER MAJESTY THE QUEEN.
HIS ROYAL HIGHNESS THE PRINCE OF WALES.
HIS ROYAL HIGHNESS THE DUKE OF YORK.
HIS EXCELLENCY THE HON. T. F. BAYARD, United States Ambassador.

President:

The Right Honourable Lord Herschell.

Vice=Presidents:

The Right Hon. Lord Justice Lindley.   The Hon. Mr. Justice Romer.

Council:

The Hon. Mr. Justice Bruce.	Mr. H. C. Maxwell Lyte, C.B.	Mr. S. R. Scargill-Bird
Mr. A. M. Channell, Q.C.	Mr. A. Stuart Moore.	The Hon. Mr. Justice St
Sir H. W. Elphinstone, Bart.	Mr. R. Pennington.	Mr. J. Westlake, Q.C.
Mr. M. Ingle Joyce.	Sir F. Pollock, Bart.	His Honour Judge M White.
Mr. B. G. Lake.	Mr. W. C. Renshaw, Q.C.	The Hon. Mr. Justice W

Literary Director: Professor F. W. Maitland (Downing College, Cambridge).

Auditors: Mr. J. W. Clark, Mr. Hubert Hall.

Honorary Secretary: Mr. B. Fossett Lock (11 New Square, Lincoln's Inn, London).

Honorary Treasurer: Mr. Francis K. Munton (95A Queen Victoria Street, London)

ANNUAL SUBSCRIPTION .   .   . ONE GUINEA.*

Persons becoming Members may subscribe for all or any of the preceding years
Society's existence, and in that case will be entitled to a copy of the publications issued f
year for which they may subscribe.

Non-members can obtain the Society's publications from

Mr. B. Quaritch, 15 Piccadilly, London, W.

The volumes already published are

I., for 1887. SELECT PLEAS OF THE CROWN. Vol. I., A.D. 1200–1225. Edited, from th
Rolls preserved in H.M. Public Record Office, by F. W. MAITLAND, Downing Professor of the Law
of England, Cambridge. With Facsimile. Crown 4to. Price to non-members, 28*s.*

A selection from the earliest records of English criminal justice. These criminal cases throw muc
light on the manners and customs of the people ; they illustrate the working of the ordeals of fire an
water, and show how a substitute was gradually found in trial by jury. They are mostly cases of felon
care has been taken to collect whatever throws light on the procedure of the Local Courts, th
system of frankpledge, the organisation of counties and boroughs for judicial purposes, &c., &c.

II., for 1888. SELECT PLEAS IN MANORIAL AND OTHER SEIGNORIAL COURTS. Vo
I., Henry III. and Edward I. Edited, from the earliest Rolls extant, by Professor F. W. MAITLAN
Crown 4to. Price to non-members, 28*s.*

A selection from the oldest manorial records. These embrace the whole legal life and much
the social life of a mediæval village ; including land held on villain tenure, services, rights of commo
personal actions for debt and trespass, leet and criminal jurisdiction, misdemeanours, the system of loc
police and frankpledge, trading communities, and the law merchant as administered at a great fai
The selections are from the rolls of the manors of the Abbey of Bec in 13 counties, of the honour
he Abbot of Ramsay in seven counties, his fair of S. Ives, and his manors in Huntingdon, and of othe
anors in Berks and Wilts.

II., for 1889. SELECT CIVIL PLEAS. Vol. I., A.D. 1200–1203. Edited, from the Plea Roll
reserved in H.M. Public Record Office, by W. PALEY BAILDON, F.S.A., of Lincoln's Inn, Barrister
t-law. Crown 4to. Price to non-members, 28*s.*

A selection from the earliest records of civil litigation. These consist largely of actions relating t
and, either directly, as in the various assises, writs of right and of entry, actions for dower, &c. ; o
ndirectly, as for feudal services, tolls, franchises, rivers, &c. Others do not concern land. The extract
llustrate the gradual evolution of the different forms of action, both real and personal.

IV., for 1890. THE COURT BARON : PRECEDENTS OF PLEADING IN MANORIAL AND OTHE
LOCAL COURTS. Edited, from MSS. of the 14th and 15th Centuries, by Professor F. W. MAITLAN
nd W. PALEY BAILDON. Crown 4to. Price to non-members, 28*s.*

This volume contains four treatises on the business of Manorial and other Local Courts, wit
recedents ; and throws light on the procedure and pleading. To these are added some ver
nteresting extracts from the rolls of the Court of the Bishop of Ely at Littleport in the Fen
principally during the reign of Edward II.).

V., for 1891. THE LEET JURISDICTION IN THE CITY OF NORWICH. Edited, from th
Leet Rolls of the 13th and 14th Centuries in the possession of the Corporation, by the Rev. W
UDSON, M.A. With Map and Facsimile. Crown 4to. Price to non-members, 28*s.*

This volume deals with mediæval municipal life ; the municipal development of a chartered boroug
with leet jurisdiction, the early working of the frankpledge system ; and generally with the judicial, com
nercial, and social arrangements of one of the largest cities of the kingdom at the close of the 13t
entury.

VI., for 1892. SELECT PLEAS OF THE COURT OF ADMIRALTY. Vol I., A.D. 1390–1404 an
.D. 1527–1545. Edited by REGINALD G. MARSDEN, of the Inner Temple. Barrister-at-law. Wit
Facsimile of the ancient Seal of the Court of Admiralty. Crown 4to. Price to non-members, 28*s.*

The business of the High Court of Admiralty was very considerable during the reigns of Henr
VIII., of Elizabeth, and of the Stuarts, and played an important part in the development of commercia
aw. There is in the Records much curious information upon trade, navigation, and shipping, and th
claims of the King of England to a lordship over the surrounding seas.

Vol. VII., for 1893. THE MIRROR OF JUSTICES. Edited, from the unique MS. at Cor College, Cambridge, with a new translation, by W. J. WHITTAKER, M.A. of Trinity Col bridge, and Professor F. W. MAITLAND. Crown 4to. Price to non-members, 28s.

The old editions of this curious work of the 13th century are corrupt, and in many intelligible.

Vol. VIII., for 1894. SELECT PASSAGES FROM BRACTON AND AZO. Edited by F. W. MAITLAND. Crown 4to. Price to non-members, 28s.

This volume contains those portions of Bracton's work in which he follows Azo parallel columns with Azo's text. The use made by Bracton of the works of Bernard of Pa canonist Tancred is also illustrated.

Vol. IX., for 1895. SELECT CASES FROM THE CORONERS' ROLLS, A.D. 1265–1413. E the Rolls preserved in H.M. Public Record Office, by CHARLES GROSS, Ph.D., Assistant P History, Harvard University. Crown 4to. Price to non-members, 28s.

The functions of the coroner were more important in this period than in modern ti Volume supplies interesting information on the history of the office of coroner, on the ear ment of the jury, on the jurisdiction of the hundred and county courts, on the collective resp of neighbouring townships, on proof of Englishry, and on the first beginnings of elective repr

Vol. X., for 1896. SELECT CASES IN CHANCERY, A.D. 1364–1471. Edited, from the Roll in H.M. Public Record Office, by W. PALEY BAILDON, F.S.A. Crown 4to. Price to non-me

These valuable records, of which few have hitherto been printed, throw new light on the of the Chancery with the Council, and the gradual separation of the two; on the early jur the Chancery, its forms and procedure, and on the development of the principles of Eq early cases illustrate the practice in the bill, appearance, answer, discovery, injunctions, & principles upon which the Court dealt with the execution of uses or trusts, fraud, mortgages specific performance, wards, wills, &c., &c. The Court also dealt with mercantile matters at the suit of aliens.

The volumes in course of preparation are

Vol. XI., for 1897 (in the press). SELECT PLEAS of the COURT of ADMIRALTY. Vol. II., A.D. edited by REGINALD G. MARSDEN.

This will be in continuation and completion of Vol. VI., and will contain a further s interesting records and a summary of all the classes of cases dealt with by the Court during t

Vol. XII., for 1898 (ready for press). SELECT PLEAS from the RECORDS* of the COURT of Vol. I., Henry VII. and Henry VIII., edited by I. S. LEADAM.

This Court, sometimes called the "Court of Conscience," was originally a Court of Equit men's causes, but later it took cognisance of all suits that by colour of equity or suppl the Prince could be brought before it. The President of the Court was the Lord Privy Seal assisted by the Masters of Requests.

The following are among the Works contemplated for future volume

Vol. . PLACITA FORESTAE.

The Forest Plea Rolls* are very interesting and little known. They begin as early as th King John, and consist of perambulations, claims, presentments and other proceedings (suc for poaching and trespass on the Forest) before the Justices in Eyre of the Forest.

Vol. . MEMORANDA of the COURT of EXCHEQUER, A.D. 1199–1272.

The Rolls* of the King's Remembrancer and of the Lord Treasurer's Remembrancer fullest light both upon the curious and intricate system of accounting at the Royal Excl the far-reaching jurisdiction of the Court, together with its relation to the Chancery and th Common Law. They deal with matters of great constitutional importance.

* For further information on these Records, see the valuable and learned "Guide to the Principal Classes of Documents pi in the Public Record Office," by S. R. SCARGILL-BIRD, F.S.A. (London : Eyre & Spottiswoode, 1891.)

Vol.   . SELECTIONS from the PLEA ROLLS* of the JEWISH EXCHEQUER, A.D. 1244–1272.

These Rolls illustrate a department of the history of English law which is at present The Justiciarii Judæorum, who had the status of Barons of the Exchequer, exercised juri all affairs relating to the Jewish community, namely, in the accounts of the revenue, in contracts made between Jews and Christians, and in causes or questions touching their lan or their tallages, fines, and forfeitures.

Vol.   . SELECT PLEAS of the COURT of STAR CHAMBER. Henry VII. and Henry VIII.

The Records* of this Court consist of Bills, Answers, Depositions, and other proceedin are of great importance as illustrating both public and private history. None of the Orders are known to exist. In the Report of a Committee of the House of Lords made in 1719, it that "the last notice of them that could be got was that they were in a house in St. Bart Close, London."

Vol.   SELECT PLEAS in MANORIAL and other SEIGNORIAL COURTS, Vol. II.

Vol.   SELECT CIVIL PLEAS, Vol. II.

Vol.   CONVEYANCING PRECEDENTS of the THIRTEENTH CENTURY.

There are several interesting sets hitherto unprinted. The mercantile transactions are ve

---

Vol.   . The HISTORY of the REGISTER of ORIGINAL WRITS :
        The reign of Henry III.
        The reign of Edward I.
        The reign of Edward III.
        The Fifteenth Century.

* For further information on these Records, see the valuable and learned "Guide to the Principal Classes of Documents pi in the Public Record Office," by S. R. SCARGILL-BIRD, F.S.A. (London : Eyre & Spottiswoode, 1891.)

The Society has also contemplated the collection of materials for an ANGLO-FREN TIONARY, for which practical instructions have been kindly drawn up by Professor Skeat. T will be glad to receive offers of help in this collection with a view to future publication.

The Council will be grateful for any information upon the contents and custod MSS. which may be of sufficient interest to be dealt with by the Society.

All communications may be addressed to the Honorary Secretary,
    Mr. B. FOSSETT LOCK, 11 New Square, Lincoln's Inn, London, W.C.

Subscriptions should be paid, and Applications for Forms of Membership or Orders and communications as to the issue of the publications should be made to the Treasurer,
    Mr. FRANCIS K. MUNTON, 95a Queen Victoria Street, London, E.C.
  or, in the United States of America, to the Local Honorary Secretary and Treas
    Mr. RICHARD W. HALE, 10 Tremont Street, Boston, Massachusetts.

January 1897.

Selden Society.

FOUNDED 1887.

RULES.

1. The Society shall be called the Selden Society.

2. The object of the Society shall be to encourage the study and advance the knowledge of the history of English Law, especially by the publication of original documents and the reprinting or editing of works of sufficient rarity or importance.

3. Membership of the Society shall be constituted by payment of the annual subscription, or in the case of life members, of the composition. Form of application is given at the foot.

4. The annual subscription shall be £1. 1s., payable in advance on or before the 1st of January in every year. A composition of £21 shall constitute life membership from the date of the composition, and in the case of Libraries, Societies, and corporate bodies, membership for 30 years.

5. The management of the affairs and funds of the Society shall be vested in a President, two Vice-Presidents, and a Council consisting of fifteen members, in addition to the *ex officio* members. The President, the two Vice-Presidents, the Literary Director, the Secretary, and the Hon. Treasurer shall be *ex officio* members. Three shall form a quorum.

6. Until the Annual General Meeting in the year 1896 the following shall be the fifteen members of the Council:—The Hon. Mr. Justice Bruce, Mr. A. M. Channell, Q.C., Sir Howard W. Elphinstone, Bart., Mr. M. Ingle Joyce, Mr. B. G. Lake, Mr. H. C. Maxwell Lyte, Mr. A. Stuart Moore, Mr. R. Pennington, Sir F. Pollock, Bart., Mr. W. C. Renshaw, Q.C., Mr. S. R. Scargill-Bird, The Hon. Mr. Justice Stirling, Mr. J. Westlake, Q.C., His Honour Judge Meadows White, the Hon. Mr. Justice Wills, five of whom (in alphabetical order) shall retire at the Annual General Meeting in the year 1896, five (in the like order) in the year 1897, and the remaining five in the year 1898. At each subsequent Annual General Meeting the five members who have served longest without re-election shall retire. A retiring member shall be re-eligible.

7. The five vacancies in the Council shall be filled up at the Annual General Meeting in and after the year 1896 in the following manner: (*a*) Any two Members of the Society may nominate for election any other member by a writing signed by them and the nominated member, and sent

185

to the Hon. Secretary on or before the 14th of February. (*b*) Not less than fourteen days before the Annual General Meeting the Council shall nominate for election five members of the Society. (*c*) No person shall be eligible for election on the Council unless nominated under this Rule. (*d*) Any candidate may withdraw. (*e*) The names of the persons nominated shall be printed in the notice convening the Annual General Meeting. (*f*) If the persons nominated, and whose nomination shall not have been withdrawn, are not more than five, they shall at the Annual General Meeting be declared to have been elected. (*g*) If the persons nominated, and whose nomination shall not have been withdrawn, shall be more than five, an election shall take place by ballot as follows : every member of the Society present at the Meeting shall be entitled to vote by writing the names of not more than five of the candidates on a piece of paper and delivering it to the Hon. Secretary or his Deputy, at such meeting, and the five candidates who shall have a majority of votes shall be declared elected. In case of equality the Chairman of the Meeting shall have a second or casting vote.

8. The Council may fill casual vacancies happening in their number. Persons so appointed shall hold office so long as those in whose place they shall be appointed would have held office. The Council shall also have power to appoint Honorary Members of the Society.

9. The Council shall meet at least twice a year, and not less than seven days' notice of any meeting shall be sent by post to every member of the Council.

10. There shall be a Literary Director to be appointed and removable by the Council. The Council may make any arrangement for remunerating the Literary Director which they may think reasonable.

11. It shall be the duty of the Literary Director (but always subject to the control of the Council) to supervise the editing of the publications of the Society, to suggest suitable editors, and generally to advise the Council with respect to carrying the objects of the Society into effect

12. Each member shall be entitled to one copy of every work published by the Society as for any year of his membership. No person other than an Honorary Member shall receive any such work until his subscription for the year as for which the same shall be published shall have been paid.

13. The Council shall appoint an Hon. Secretary and also an Hon. Treasurer and such other Officers as they from time to time think fit, and shall from time to time define their respective duties.

14. The funds of the Society, including the vouchers or securities for any investments, shall be kept at a Bank, to be selected by the Council, to an account in the name of the Society. Such funds or investments shall only be dealt with by a cheque or other authority signed by the Treasurer and countersigned by one of the Vice-Presidents or such other person as the Council may from time to time appoint.

15. The accounts of the receipts and expenditure of the Society up to the 31st of December in each year shall be audited once a year by two Auditors, to be appointed by the Society, and the report of the Auditors, with an abstract of the accounts, shall be circulated together with the notice convening the Annual Meeting.

16. An Annual General Meeting of the Society shall be held in March 1896, and thereafter in the month of March in each year. The Council may upon their own resolution and shall on the request in writing of not less than ten members call a Special General Meeting. Seven days' notice at least, specifying the object of the meeting and the time and place at which it is to be held, shall be posted to every member resident in the United Kingdom at his last known address. No member shall vote at any General Meeting whose subscription is in arrear.

17. The Hon. Secretary shall keep a Minute Book wherein shall be entered a record of the transactions, as well at Meetings of the Council as at General Meetings of the Society.

18. These rules may upon proper notice be repealed, added to, or modified from time to time at any meeting of the Society. But such repeal, addition, or modification, if not unanimously agreed to, shall require the vote of not less than two-thirds of the members present and voting at such meeting.

March 1895.

FORM OF APPLICATION FOR MEMBERSHIP.

To Mr. FRANCIS K. MUNTON, 95A Queen Victoria Street, London, E.C., *Honorary Treasurer of the Selden Society.*

I desire to become a member of the Society, and herewith send my cheque for One Guinea, the annual subscription [*or* £21 the life contribution] dating from the commencement of the present year. [I also desire to subscribe for the preceding years , and I add one guinea for each to my cheque.]

Name...

Address..

Description...

Date...

[NOTE.—Cheques, crossed " ROBARTS & Co., a/c of the Selden Society," should be made payable to the Honorary Treasurer, from whom forms of bankers' orders for payment of subscriptions direct to the Society's banking account can be obtained.]

𝔖𝔢𝔩𝔡𝔢𝔫 𝔖𝔬𝔠𝔦𝔢𝔱𝔶.

LIST OF MEMBERS.
1896.

(Those marked with an asterisk are Life Members.)

UNITED KINGDOM.

ALSOP, J. W.	16 Bidston Road, Birkenhead.
ANSON, Sir W. R., Bart.	All Souls College, Oxford.
ATKINSON, J. T.	Selby, Yorks.
ATTLEE, Henry	10 Billiter Street, E.C.
BAILDON, W. Paley	5 Stone Buildings, Lincoln's Inn, W.C.
BIRKETT, P.	4 Lincoln's Inn Fields, W.C.
BLAKESLEY, G. H.	13 Old Square, Lincoln's Inn, W.C.
BOND, Edward, M.P.	Elm Bank, Thurlow Rd., Hampstead, N.W.
BOND, Henry	Trinity Hall, Cambridge.
BRACE, L. J. K.	c/o Lloyd's Bank, 16 St. James Street, W.
BRAITHWAITE, J. B.	3 New Square, Lincoln's Inn, W.C.
BRICE, Seward, Q.C.	5 New Court, Carey Street, W.C.
BROWNE, G. F.	151 Cannon Street, E.C.
BRUCE, The Hon. Mr. Justice	Royal Courts of Justice, W.C.
BRUNEL, I.	15 Devonshire Terrace, Hyde Park, W.
BYRNE, E. W., Q.C., M.P.	3 Stone Buildings, Lincoln's Inn, W.C.
CAMPBELL, R.	5 New Court, Carey Street, W.C.
CARPENTER, R. H.	Bank Chambers, Corn Street, Bristol.
CAVE, The Hon. Mr. Justice	Royal Courts of Justice, W.C.
CHADWICK, S. J.	Church Street, Dewsbury.
CHANNELL, A. M., Q.C.	Farrar's Building, Temple, E.C.
CHARLES, The Hon. Mr. Justice	Royal Courts of Justice, W.C.
CHITTY, The Hon. Mr. Justice	Royal Courts of Justice, W.C.
CLARK, J. W.	Board of Agriculture, St. James' Sq., S.W.
COHEN, A., Q.C.	26 Great Cumberland Place, W.
COLVILLE, H. K.	Bellaport Hall, Market Drayton.
*CONNAUGHT, H.R.H. The Duke of	Buckingham Palace, S.W.
COOK, C. A.	108 Park Street, W.
COOLIDGE, Rev. W. A. B.	Magdalen College, Oxford.
CORNISH, J. E.	16 St. Ann's Square, Manchester.
COUCH, The Right Hon. Sir R.	25 Linden Gardens, W.
COZENS-HARDY, H. H., Q.C., M.P.	7 New Square, Lincoln's Inn, W.C.
CRACKANTHORPE, M. H., Q.C.	1 New Square, Lincoln's Inn, W.C.
CRACROFT, R. W.	12 King's Bench Walk, Temple, E.C.
CREWE, W. O.	Central Bdgs., North John Street, L'pool.
CROSS, W. C. H.	13 Clare Street, Bristol.

CUNLIFFE, R.	43 Chancery Lane, W.C.
CURREY, C. H.	14 Great George Street,Westminster, S.W.
CUTLER, J.	4 New Square, Lincoln's Inn, W.C.
DANCKWERTS, W.	7 New Court, Carey Street, W.C.
DAVEY, The Right Hon. Lord	10 Queen's Gate Gardens, S.W.
DEES, R. R.	Wallsend, Newcastle-on-Tyne.
*DERBY, The Right Hon. the Earl of	Derby House, St. James's Square, S.W.
DICEY, A. V., Q.C.	The Orchard, Banbury Road, Oxford.
DONNITHORNE, Nicholas	Fareham, Hants.
ELPHINSTONE, Sir Howard W., Bart.	2 Stone Buildings, Lincoln's Inn, W.C.
ELTON, C. I., Q.C.	33 Chancery Lane, W.C.
EVANS, A. J.	Christ's College, Cambridge.
EVANS, Sir John	Nash Mills, Hemel Hempstead, Herts.
FARWELL, G., Q.C.	10 Old Square, Lincoln's Inn, W.C.
FISHER, H. A. L.	New College, Oxford.
FORD, J. Rawlinson	61 Albion Street, Leeds.
FRY, The Right Hon. Sir E.	Failand, near Bristol.
GALPIN, H. F.	4 George Street, Oxford.
*GIFFARD, Henry A., Q.C.	9 Old Square, Lincoln's Inn, W.C.
GRANTHAM, The Hon. Mr. Justice	Royal Courts of Justice, W.C.
GRAY, W. H.	Ormond House, Great Trinity Lane, E.C.
GRAY-HILL, J. E.	Liverpool.
GRUCHY, W. L. de	12 Highbury Mansions, N.
HADFIELD, G.	20 St. Ann's Square, Manchester.
HALL, Hubert	Public Record Office, Chancery Lane,W.C.
HALLIDAY, J.	5 Holland Park, W.
HARRIS, D. L.	Downing College, Cambridge.
HARRIS, W. J.	Sittingbourne, Kent.
HARRISON & SONS	59 Pall Mall.
HEALEY, C. E. H. Chadwyck, Q.C.	7 New Square, Lincoln's Inn, W.C.
*HEAP, Ralph	1 Brick Court, Temple.
HOLLAMS, J.	30 Mincing Lane, E.C.
HUDSON, Rev. W.	42 Prince of Wales Road, Norwich.
HUMPHRYS, W. J.	Hereford.
HUNTER, John	9 New Square, Lincoln's Inn, W.C.
HUTCHINS, F. L.	11 Birchin Lane, E.C.
JACKSON, C. S.	15 Old Square, Lincoln's Inn, W.C.
JELF, A. R., Q.C.	9 King's Bench Walk, Temple, E.C.
JENKYNS, Sir Henry, K.C.B.	3 Whitehall Gardens, S.W.
JEUNE, The Right Hon. Sir Francis H.	37 Wimpole Street, W.
JOYCE, M. Ingle	4 Stone Buildings, Lincoln's Inn, W.C.
KAY, The Right Hon. Lord Justice	Royal Courts of Justice, W.C.
KEKEWICH, The Hon. Mr. Justice	Royal Courts of Justice, W.C.
KENNY, Courtney S.	Downing College, Cambridge.
KEY, Thomas	9 Old Square, Lincoln's Inn, W.C.
KING, H. C.	17 Serjeants' Inn, Fleet Street, E.C.

LAKE, B. G.	10 New Square, Lincoln's Inn, W.C.
LAWRENCE, P. O., Q.C.	4 New Court, Lincoln's Inn, W.C.
LAWSON, W. N.	6 Stone Buildings, Lincoln's Inn, W.C.
LEWIS, Frank B.	11 Old Jewry Chambers, E.C.
LEWIS, His Honour Judge	Llandundid, Radnorshire.
LINDLEY, The Right Hon. Lord Justice	Royal Courts of Justice, W.C.
LINDSAY, W. A.	College of Arms, Queen Victoria Street, E.C.
LISTER, J.	Shelden Hall, near Halifax.
LOCK, B. Fossett	11 New Square, Lincoln's Inn, W.C.
LUSHINGTON, His Honour Judge Vernon	Pyports, Cobham, Surrey.
LYTE, H. C. Maxwell	Public Record Office, Chancery Lane, W.C.
MACNAGHTEN, The Right Hon. Lord	179 Queen's Gate, S.W.
MAITLAND, F. W.	Downing College, Cambridge.
MALDEN, H. E.	Kitlands, Holmwood, Surrey.
MARKHAM, Christopher	Sedgebrook, Northampton.
MARSDEN, R. G.	6 New Court, Carey Street, W.C.
MARTIN, C. Trice	Public Record Office, Chancery Lane, W.C.
MATTHEWS, J. B.	6 Sansome Place, Worcester.
MOORE, A. Stuart	6 King's Bench Walk, Temple, E.C.
MOULTON, J. Fletcher, Q.C.	11 King's Bench Walk, Temple, E.C.
MUNTON, F. K.	95A Queen Victoria Street, E.C.
NASH, E.	2 Stone Buildings, Lincoln's Inn, W.C.
NEILSON, G.	34 Granby Terrace, Glasgow.
NORTH, The Hon. Mr. Justice	Royal Courts of Justice W.C.
OXFORD, The Rt. Rev. the Lord Bishop of	Cuddesden Palace, Oxford.
PALMER, F. Danby	Great Yarmouth.
PARKER, Kenyon C. S.	13 Old Square, Lincoln's Inn, W.C.
PARKER, R. J.	9 Stone Buildings, Lincoln's Inn, W.C.
PENNINGTON, R.	64 Lincoln's Inn Fields, W.C.
POLAND, Sir H. B., Q.C.	5 Paper Buildings, Temple, E.C.
POLLOCK, The Hon. Mr. Baron	Royal Courts of Justice, W.C.
POLLOCK, Sir F., Bart.	13 Old Square, Lincoln's Inn, W.C.
POORE, Major R.	1 Carlyle Gdns., Cheyne Row, Chelsea, S.W.
PRIEST, F. J.	163 Canning Street, Liverpool.
PRIVY PURSE, The Keeper of H.M.'s	Buckingham Palace, S.W.
PROTHERO, G. W.	2 Eton Terrace, Edinburgh.
RADFORD, G. H.	40 Chancery Lane, W.C.
RAIKES, F. W.	7 King's Bench Walk, Temple, E.C.
RENSHAW, W. C., Q.C.	5 Stone Buildings, Lincoln's Inn, W.C.
RIDLEY, E.	48 Lennox Gardens, S.W.
RIGBY, The Right Hon. Lord Justice	Royal Courts of Justice, W.C.
RIGG, J. M.	9 New Square, Lincoln's Inn, W.C.
ROMER, The Hon. Mr. Justice	Royal Courts of Justice, W.C.
ROSS, Dr. J. Carne	Parsonage Nook, Whittington, Manchester.
ROYCE, Rev. David	Nether Swill Vicarage, Stow-on-the-Wold.
RUSSELL OF KILLOWEN, The Rt. Hon. Lord	Royal Courts of Justice, W.C.
RUSSELL, C. A.	2 Harcourt Buildings, Temple, E.C.
RYE, W.	16 Golden Square, W.

SALISBURY, The Rt. Hon. the Marquis of	20 Arlington Street, W.
SCARGILL-BIRD, S. R.	Public Record Office, Chancery Lane,W.C.
SEEBOHM, F.	Hitchin Bank, Hitchin.
SHADWELL, C. L.	c/o Messrs. James Parker, Oxford.
SHARP, J. E. E. S.	Public Record Office, Fetter Lane, E.C.
SLATTER, Rev. J.	Whitchurch Rectory, Reading.
STEPHENS, H. C., M.P.	Avenue House, Finchley, N.
STEVENS, T. M.	1 Garden Court, Temple, E.C.
STEVENS & HAYNES	Bell Yard, Temple Bar, W.C.
STIRLING, The Hon. Mr. Justice	Royal Courts of Justice, W.C.
STIRLING, Hugh	11 Birchin Lane, E.C.
SWEET, Charles	10 Old Square, Lincoln's Inn, W.C.
THORNELY, J. L.	5 Fenchurch Street, Liverpool.
THORNTON, C.	41 Manchester Road, Nelson, Lanc.
THRELFALL, Henry S.	12 London Street, Southport.
TURNER, G. J.	14 Old Square, Lincoln's Inn, W.C.
TURTON, R. B.	24 Old Square, Lincoln's Inn, W.C.
*WALKER, J. Douglas, Q.C.	4 Brick Court, Temple, E.C.
WALL, C. Y.	New Exchange Buildings, Durham.
WALLER, W. Chapman	Loughton, Essex.
WALLIS, J. P.	1 Harcourt Buildings, Temple, E.C.
WALTERS, W. M.	9 New Square, Lincoln's Inn, W.C.
WARRINGTON, T. R., Q.C.	6 New Court, Carey Street, W.C.
WATNEY, J.	Mercers' Hall, E.C.
WEBSTER, Sir R. E., A.G., M.P.	2 Pump Court, Temple, E.C.
*WELBY, Edward M. E.	Norton House, Norton, Sheffield.
WESTLAKE, J., Q.C.	River House, Chelsea Embankment, S.W.
WHITAKER, F.	Duchy of Lancaster Office, W.C.
WHITE, His Honour Judge Meadows	42 Sussex Gardens, W.
WHITTUCK, E. A.	77 South Audley Street, W.
WIGHTMAN, A.	Bank Chambers, George Street, Sheffield.
WILLIAMS, T. W.	Bank Chambers, Corn Street, Bristol.
WILLS, The Hon. Mr. Justice	Royal Courts of Justice, W.C.
WILLS, W.	4 Paper Buildings, Temple, E.C.
WILSON, J. C.	Shelwood House, Oxford.
WOODS, Grosvenor, Q.C.	9 Old Square, Lincoln's Inn, W.C.

SOCIETIES, LIBRARIES, &c.

BIRMINGHAM:	
CENTRAL FREE LIBRARY	Ratcliff Place.
CAMBRIDGE:	
TRINITY HALL.	
DUBLIN:	
KING'S INN.	
GLASGOW:	
FACULTY OF PROCURATORS	88 St. Vincent Street.
MITCHELL LIBRARY	21 Miller Street.
LIVERPOOL:	
FREE PUBLIC LIBRARY.	
INCORPORATED LAW SOCIETY	13 Union Court.
TATE LIBRARY	University College.

LONDON :
    GLADSTONE LIBRARY   National Lib. Club, Whitehall Place, S.W.
    GRAY'S INN.
    INCORPORATED LAW SOCIETY   Chancery Lane, W.C.
    INNER TEMPLE.
    LINCOLN'S INN.
    LONDON LIBRARY   14 St. James's Square, S.W.
    MIDDLE TEMPLE.
    PUBLIC RECORD OFFICE   c/o Eyre & Spottiswoode, Gt. New St., E.C.
    SION COLLEGE   Victoria Embankment, E.C.
    SOCIETY OF ANTIQUARIES   Burlington House, W.
    TREASURY (PARLIAMENTARY COUNSEL) c/o Eyre & Spottiswoode, Gt. New St., E.C.
MANCHESTER :
    FREE REFERENCE LIBRARY   King Street.
    MANCHESTER LAW LIBRARY   Kennedy Street.
NEWCASTLE-ON-TYNE :
    LITERARY AND PHILOSOPHICAL SOCIETY.
OXFORD :
    ALL SOULS COLLEGE.

COLONIAL AND FOREIGN.

DENMARK :
    COPENHAGEN ROYAL LIBRARY   c/o Sampson Low & Co., Fetter Lane, E.C.
DOMINION OF CANADA :
    ARMOUR, Hon. Chief Justice   Cobourg, Ontario.
    PROUDFOOT, W.   3 Queen's Park, Toronto.

    LIBRARY OF PARLIAMENT, OTTAWA   c/o E. G. Allen, 28 Henrietta St., W.C.
    UNIVERSITY OF TORONTO   c/o E. G. Allen, 28 Henrietta St., W.C.
FRANCE :
    BIBLIOTHÈQUE NATIONALE   Paris.
GERMANY :
    BERLIN ROYAL LIBRARY   c/o Asher & Co., 13 Bedford Street, W.C.
INDIA :
    NICHOLS, G. J., Cawnpore   c/o Grindlay & Co., Parliament St., S.W.
QUEENSLAND :
    * GRIFFITH, Sir W.   Brisbane.
SOUTH AFRICA :
    * FINNEMORE, Mr. Justice   Supreme Court, Pietermaritzburg, Natal.
SWITZERLAND :
    UNIVERSITÄTS-BIBLIOTHEK   Basel.
TASMANIA :
    TENISON, C. M.   Hobart.
UNITED STATES OF AMERICA :
    CALIFORNIA :
        SAN FRANCISCO LAW LIBRARY   San Francisco.
    DISTRICT OF COLUMBIA :
        * FULLER, Hon. M. W.   Washington.
        * GRAY, Hon. Horace   Washington.

CONNECTICUT:
   CONNECTICUT STATE LIBRARY   Hartford.

MARYLAND:
   THE BALTIMORE BAR LIBRARY   Baltimore.
   THE JOHNS HOPKINS UNIVERSITY Baltimore.

MASSACHUSETTS:
   * ABBOT, E. H.   50 State Street, Room 81, Bosto .
   ADAMS, Walter S. O.   Framingham.
   * AMES, Professor James B.   Law School, Cambridge.
   BEALE, J. H.   13 Chancery Street, Cambridge.
   BIGELOW, Professor M. M.   409 Washington Street, Boston.
   * COXE, Brinton   c/o Mr. Schoenhof, 144 Tremont St., Bstn
   GRAY, Professor J. C.   50 State Street, Room 44, Boston.
   HALE, Richard W.   10 Tremont Street, Boston.
   HILL, A. D.   19 Marlborough Street, Boston.
   HOLMES, Hon. C. W., Jun.   Boston.
   HUDSON, J. E.   125 Milk Street, Boston.
   KEENER, Professor W. A.   Cambridge
   KENNISON, T. D.
   LEVERITT, George V.   53 Devonshire Street, Boston.
   SHATTUCK, George O.   35 Court Street, Boston.
   SIMPSON, Alexander, Jr.
   THAYER, Professor James B.   Law School, Cambridge.
   WARREN & BRANDERS   220 Devonshire Street, Boston.
   BOSTON UNIVERSITY   Boston.
   BOSTON PUBLIC LIBRARY
   BOSTON ATHENÆUM   } c/o Kegan Paul & Co., Paternoster House,
   HARVARD COLLEGE LIBRARY   Charing Cross Road, W.C.
   HARVARD LAW SCHOOL   Cambridge.
   SOCIAL LAW LIBRARY   Boston.

MINNESOTA:
   YOUNG, Hon. G. B.   Gilfillan Block, St. Paul.
   THE MINNEAPOLIS BAR ASSOC.   Minneapolis.

NEW JERSEY:
   COLLEGE OF NEW JERSEY   New Jersey.

NEW YORK:
   BACON, Theodore   Rochester.
   BRAINERD, C.   111 Broadway, New York City.
   CUSHING & Co.
   DIVEN, George M.   212 E. Water Street, Elmira.
   GULICK, J. C.   132 Nassau Street, New York City.
   HAND, Billings L.   224 State Street, Albany.
   LOEWY, Benno   206 Broadway, New York City.
   MILBURN, J. G., Buffalo   c/o B. F. Stevens, 4 Trafalgar Square, W.C.
   STARBUCK, Henry P.   Columbia College, New York City.
   STRONG, C. E.   36 Wall Street, New York City.
   ASTOR LIBRARY   c/o B. F. Stevens, 4 Trafalgar Square, W.C.
   CORNELL UNIVERSITY LIBRARY c/o E. G. Allen, 28 Henrietta Street, W.C.
   LONG ISLAND HISTORICAL SOC.   c/o B. F. Stevens, 4 Trafalgar Square, W.C.
   NEW YORK BAR ASSOCIATION   New York City.

Ohio:
    Cincinnati Law Library   c/o W. A. Anderson & Co., 22 Main Street, Cincinnati.
    Law School, Cincinnati College Cincinnati.

Pennsylvania:
    Bispham, G. T.   402 Walnut Street, Philadelphia.
    *Gest, John M.   400 Chestnut Street, Philadelphia.
    Law Assoc. of Philadelphia   Philadelphia.
    Library Co. of Philadelphia   c/o E. G. Allen, 28 Henrietta St., W.C.

Vermont:
    Taft, The Hon. R. S.   Willeston.

Washington:
    Shepard, Charles J.   Bailey Building, Seattle.

LOCAL SECRETARIES AND CORRESPONDENTS.

UNITED STATES OF AMERICA:
    LOCAL SECRETARY AND TREASURER:
    RICHARD W. HALE   10 Tremont Street, Boston, Massachusetts.

    CORRESPONDENTS:
Illinois:
    JOHN HENRY WIGMORE   710 Masonic Temple, Chicago.

Michigan:
    THOMAS SPENCER JEROME   44 Newberry Buildings, Detroit.

Minnesota:
    HENRY B. WENZELL   601 New York Life Building, St. Paul.

DOMINION OF CANADA:
    LOCAL SECRETARY:
    W. McGREGOR YOUNG   The Law School, Osgoode Hall, Toronto.

PRINTED BY
SPOTTISWOODE AND CO., NEW-STREET SQUARE
LONDON